OUTLINES

OF THE

LAW OF AGENCY

BY

FLOYD R. MECHEM

LATE PROFESSOR OF LAW IN THE UNIVERSITY OF CHICAGO;
AUTHOR OF MECHEM ON AGENCY AND OTHER TREATISES;
REPORTER ON AGENCY FOR THE AMERICAN LAW INSTITUTE

FOURTH EDITION

BY

PHILIP MECHEM

PROFESSOR OF LAW, UNIVERSITY OF PENNSYLVANIA

CHICAGO
CALLAGHAN & COMPANY
1952

PREFACE TO THE FOURTH EDITION

In preparing the fourth edition the reviser has attempted to adhere strictly to the purpose of the earlier editions, namely to provide a brief and compact outline of the subject. The temptation to increase the size of the book has been resisted. The text, however, has been largely rewritten. Only in portions of two chapters has the original text been in substance retained; in those instances, of course, the notes have been restudied and brought down to date. In rewriting the text the basic purpose has been to develop individual topics more thoroughly and with some scope for discussion of principle, even at the obviously necessary expense of decreasing the number treated. The hope has been thus to provide the student or attorney with a rather careful study of the more active subjects of litigation in the law of Agency. This shift in approach involves no criticism of the earlier editions (whose wide use over many years amply attests their excellence) but merely reflects the reviser's view of what is needed at the present time; it is a satisfaction to him to be sure that the author of the original editions would have been the first to approve—in fact to urge—that the reviser feel quite free to pursue such a course.

In general a conservative view of the scope and limits of the subject has been retained. Without denying the importance of labor legislation, unemployment compensation, and other instances of social legislation, the reviser feels that they have a different focus than, and are allied to, rather than part of, the law of Agency. Accordingly no attempt is made to treat them. The inclusion of some brief discussion of workmen's compensation, an apparent exception, is due to the reviser's feeling that the subject is an inevitable pendant to the law of respondeat superior.

The reviser's obligations are too numerous and too obvious to list. It is impossible, however, not to mention the name of Warren A. Seavey, whose writings on the subject are of first importance to any worker in the field. Thanks should also be

iii

given to Alfred F. Conard and Elvin R. Latty, whose recent casebooks have proved most stimulating and from whom the reviser has derived many ideas, usually impossible to acknowledge specifically.

PHILIP MECHEM

Chicago, July 1, 1952

TABLE OF CONTENTS

v

TABLE OF CONTENTS

REFERENCES ARE TO SECTIONS

CHAPTER III

PRINCIPAL AND AGENT: REAL AUTHORITY

1. *Power and Authority Compared*

2. *Analysis of Real Authority*

3. *Types of Real Authority:* (a) *Express Authority*

4. *Types of Real Authority:* (b) *Incidental Authority*

5. *Types of Real Authority:* (c) *The Wife's Authority*

6. *Types of Real Authority:* (d) *Implied Authority*

TABLE OF CONTENTS

CHAPTER IV

FURTHER OF REAL AUTHORITY: INSTANCES

1. *Authority of a Salesman*

2. *Authority to Manage a Business*

3. *Authority to Collect*

4. *Authority to Warrant (Herein of Special and General Agents)*

5. *Authority of Attorneys at Law*

6. *Authority to Delegate*

CHAPTER V

PRINCIPAL AND AGENT: APPARENT AUTHORITY AND AGENCY POWERS

TABLE OF CONTENTS

REFERENCES ARE TO SECTIONS

CHAPTER VI

PRINCIPAL AND AGENT: THE AGENT'S MISREPRESENTATIONS

1. *History of the Doctrine*

2. *The Principal's Liability Where the Agent Had Power or Authority to Make the Representation*

3. *The Principal's Liability Where the Agent Had No Power or Authority to Make the Representation*

CHAPTER VII

PRINCIPAL AND AGENT: THE PARTLY DISCLOSED AND UNDISCLOSED PRINCIPAL

1. *Rationale of Undisclosed Principal*

ix

TABLE OF CONTENTS

2. *Nature of Undisclosed Principal's Liability*
(Herein of Election)

3. *The Undisclosed Principal May Not Enforce the Contract Where the Effect Is to Prejudice the Third Party*

4. *Special Problems: Apparent Authority*

5. *Special Problems: Setoff*

CHAPTER VIII

RATIFICATION: RATIONALE AND VOLUNTARY RATIFICATION

TABLE OF CONTENTS

CHAPTER IX

FURTHER OF RATIFICATION: INVOLUNTARY RATIFICATION, RATIFICATION AGAINST UNWILLING THIRD PARTIES, AND RATIFICATION AS AFFECTING THE AGENT

TABLE OF CONTENTS

CHAPTER XI

PRINCIPAL AND AGENT: PARTIES TO CONTRACTS MADE BY AN AGENT AND AGENT'S LIABILITY TO THIRD PARTIES

1. *The Normal Liability of Parties to a Contract Made by an Agent*

2. *Types of Written Contracts and the Liability of Parties Thereto*

3. *Liability of the Unauthorized Agent*

TABLE OF CONTENTS

CHAPTER XII

THE MASTER'S TORT LIABILITY: RATIONALE

CHAPTER XIII

THE MASTER'S TORT LIABILITY: COURSE OF EMPLOYMENT

TABLE OF CONTENTS

REFERENCES ARE TO SECTIONS

CHAPTER XIV

THE MASTER'S TORT LIABILITY: SERVANT OR NOT?

TABLE OF CONTENTS

6. *The Borrowed Servant Problem*

CHAPTER XV

DANGEROUS ACTIVITIES AND INSTRUMENTALITIES: EXTENSIONS OF VICARIOUS LIABILITY

1. *Dangerous Instrumentalities*

2. *Special Doctrines Applicable to Motor Cars*

3. *Disappearing Immunity of the Employer of an Independent Contractor*

CHAPTER XVI

THE DUTIES AND LIABILITIES OF THE AGENT TO THE PRINCIPAL

CHAPTER XVII

THE DUTIES AND LIABILITIES OF THE PRINCIPAL TO THE AGENT

I. THE PAYMENT OF COMPENSATION

1. *Interpretation of the Contract and Rights on Termination*

2. *Special Problems:* (a) *Contracts for "Permanent" or "Life" Employment*

(b) *Brokers' Commissions*

TABLE OF CONTENTS

II. REIMBURSEMENT AND INDEMNITY OF AGENT

III. PROTECTION FROM PHYSICAL INJURY

1. Common-law Rules

2. Statutory Modification of Common-law Rules

3. Workmen's Compensation

TABLE OF CONTENTS

xxii

TABLE OF CASES

TABLE OF CASES

1

CHAPTER I

INTRODUCTION

§ 1. Meaning of the word. It not infrequently happens that in discovering the ideas which lie behind a given word, a consideration of its etymology will be helpful. That is especially true in the present case. The word agent or agency, from *ago, agere, agens, agentis,* denotes an actor, a doer, a force or power that accomplishes things. Observation will show that the word has a wide range of use. Thus the chemist speaks of chemical agents, and the physician of therapeutic agents, the moralist declares that this or that institution or organization is an agency for good or evil; we say that man is a free moral agent. In a recent editorial the writer referred to party allegiance as the "great agency" for securing majority rule, and to a political party as a "responsible agent" of government. This agent or agency may at times be a physical or material thing; at others it may be intangible and immaterial. It may be used for a person or against him. When physical or material, it may be a person, an animal or a tool. In the sense in which it is used in the present subject it denotes usually one human being who is used by another as a means of accomplishing some purpose of the latter.

§ 2. Agency primarily a commercial subject. The law of Agency is primarily to be considered as one of the two basic constituents of the general law of Business Organizations. It is true that fundamental agency rules may and do operate in noncommercial settings. The father may make his son his servant to drive the father's car or his agent to buy gasoline for the car and have it charged to the father's account at the filling station. However, except in a few situations (e. g., the application of agency or quasi-agency doctrines to bailors of motor cars) the operation of agency principles in a noncommercial context is insignificant, both in bulk and importance.

1

§ 3. Natural division of the law of Business Organizations.
It is apparent on a little thought that very little business in the
modern world is done by individuals carrying on alone without
others to help them. The small boy bootblack on the street
or the village grocer may be an instance, and the doctor
practicing without nurse or receptionist another, but such
instances are rare. Typically the work of the world is done by
(1) a business unit which owns and controls the business, and
(2) a group of persons who in one way or another perform
services for the unit. This suggests the natural division of the
law of Business Organizations.

§ 4. Same: Internal law of the business unit. First, there
is law of the business unit, if, as is increasingly common, it
it not an individual. It may be a corporation or a partnership
or a stock company or a business trust. In such cases there is
bound to be a body of law governing its organization, operation and dissolution, i. e., the law of the internal government
of the unit. The most extensive and conspicuous illustration
of this is the great body of law dealing with the internal
government of corporations.

**§ 5. Same: External law of the business unit: The law of
Agency.** Second, there is the law governing the relations of
the business unit with those who perform services for it, and
the law governing the obligations and rights of the unit to
third persons arising from the activities of those who perform
services for it. This is the law of Agency.

§ 6. The law of Agency: Illustrations. Consider the Eureka
Laundry Company. Its manager contracts for the purchase
of 100 gallons of X liquid soap, hires Y, the plumber, to fix
a leaking tank and orders a full page advertisement in the
Sunday edition of the Z newspaper. Miss P, an operative,
catches her hand in the wringer, or carelessly drops boiling
water on Miss Q, another operative. Mike, who drives the
Eureka delivery truck, goes out of his way to pay a visit to
his old mother and, returning from the visit, runs into Mr. P

because he is using both hands to light his pipe. Miss Jones, the cute cashier, shortchanges one customer and extends a special rate to another who is tall and dark and handsome.

§ 7. ——— These raise questions, familiar questions, of agency, because they ask how far the business unit is affected by the conduct (usually misconduct) of those who are performing services for it. And it should be observed that the questions are the same whatever the nature of the business unit. Whether Eureka Laundry is simply the name under which Mr. Smith carries on business, or whether it is a partnership or a corporation is irrelevant. The law of Partnership is no more involved if it is a partnership than the laws of physiology and psychology are if the Laundry Company is just Mr. Smith's alter ego. One branch of law deals with the nature of the constituent and his (or, usually, its) internal problems; ours assumes a constituent, and asks how he (or it) is affected by the conduct of his employees who are constantly injuring themselves and the public, and just as commonly selling for $75 the horse on which the constituent set a minimum price of $100, and warranting it to be a lineal descendant of Man O' War to boot.

§ 8. **Exclusions: (A) Labor Law.** Is Labor Law part of the law of Agency? Quite possibly, as a matter of logic, but according to the categories which lawyers and law teachers have framed, it is not. It is too big and too autonomous; it deals with workers as a group or class rather than primarily as individuals. It might comparably be asked: Are Bills and Notes part of the law of Contracts?

§ 9. **Same: (B) Unemployment compensation.** Is unemployment compensation part of Agency? Agency might be said to deal with employment; certainly unemployment is an aspect of employment. However, again, it has not been common to treat such legislation as a part of Agency. It is social legislation affecting employees as a group and not primarily having to do either with their relations to their employer or

3

affecting his relations with third parties. It seems more appropriate to treat it as an independent subject or, conceivably, as
part of a group of similar instances of social legislation.

§ 10. Why Workmen's Compensation is included. Is Workmen's Compensation similarly to be excluded? A number of
elementary treatises and casebooks on the subject do so
exclude it, but a brief treatment is included here because in
the writer's opinion it is an integral part of the subject. No
treatment of Agency could be complete without discussion of
the principal's liability to his agents for injuries received in
his service and this subject, once exclusively a common-law
subject, is now largely governed by statutes, of which the
various state Workmen's Compensation Acts and the Federal
Employers' Liability Act are the most important. Discussion
of this legislation is a necessary complement to any discussion
of the common-law rules, if only to delimit the zone in which
they still operate.

§ 11. Distinctions. It has been customary to classify the
field of Agency in a number of ways. Recently a disposition
has been shown to doubt the usefulness and even the existence
of these distinctions. The present writer recognizes that, like
other distinctions in the law, they will not always work. In
some instances, for example, it will be futile to ask whether
a given person is a servant or an agent; it may make no difference or he may plainly be both. Nevertheless, it is believed
that if one keeps in mind that no such distinctions can always
be valid, they serve in a majority of instances a useful purpose
in analyzing and classifying the subject.

The relationships dealt with in the law of Agency are ordinarily said to be three. These are treated in the following
sections.

§ 12. (A) Principal and agent. The distinguishing characteristic of the *agent* is that he represents his principal contractually. If properly authorized he makes contracts or other
negotiations of a business nature on behalf of his principal
and by which his principal is bound. Thus a real estate agent

may be authorized to find a buyer for P's land, to make a contract to sell the same, or to convey the land. In either case, if there was authority, the transaction has the same effect as if done personally by P, and any writings involved will normally be executed by A in P's name, although with an indication that the signing was done by A. It is to be noted that the agent does not work for P physically, nor is he subject to the control of P in his physical actions. Hence P is normally not liable for torts committed by A, although A at the moment was working on P's business as, e. g., taking a prospective buyer in his car to look at P's land.

§ 13.   (B)   **Master and servant.** A servant is one who works physically for another, subject to the control of that other, who is called the master. The statement that the servant is subject to the control of the master does not mean that the master must stand by constantly and observe and supervise the work; it means merely that the relation presupposes a right on the part of the master to have the work performed in such manner as he directs and a correlative duty on the part of the servant to perform in the manner directed, expressly or by implication, by the master. The servant, as such, has no power to bind the master in contract; it is obvious, however, that a person can and in many instances will be employed in a capacity where he is simultaneously or alternately a servant and an agent. Thus the express company's truck driver is a servant in driving the truck and an agent when he receives a package and signs a bill of lading binding the company to deliver it.

§ 14.   (C)   **Employer and independent contractor.** Formerly it would not have been inapt to say that the independent contractor is included in this analysis largely by way of exclusion. He is one who performs services for the constituent, but neither as a servant nor as an agent. His function is to do a job for a price, the finished job to meet certain specifications but the manner and control of doing it to be up to the contractor. Obviously such a function includes no power to represent the principal contractually; he fails to be a servant because

of the absence of any control by the constituent. Thus, while
there is, of course, a contractual nexus between the constituent
and the contractor, creating contractual obligations of the
ordinary sort, the contractor in no way represents the constituent towards third persons and has no power to create tort or
contract obligations against him.

§ 15. **Same: Changing status.** This definition of the independent contractor is still valid in many instances. It is true
of the man who repairs your watch or your car; it is true of
the taxi driver, unless conceivably the passenger effectively
asserts and exercises control of the driving. Today, however,
there is a growing body of authority which makes the constituent liable for the torts of the contractor, particularly in
cases of work to be done on the premises of the constituent
where the nature of the work is such as to make it dangerous
to the public unless proper precautions are taken. The modern law of independent contractor is largely concerned with
the nature and extent of this exception to the basic rule that
the constituent is not liable for the torts of the contractor.

§ 16. **Types of agents.** Agents are sometimes classified by
the functions they perform with particular reference to certain familiar and standardized types of agents as attorneys,
auctioneers, factors and brokers. The characteristics of such
agents will not be set forth here but reference to them and
their functions will be made at suitable places hereafter.

§ 17. **General and special agents.** It has been customary
to make another classification of agents, namely that into general and special agents. Some modern writers criticize this
distinction. Mr. Powell, for example, has said that it is "mean-
ingless and confusing." [1] Plainly it is a difference in degree
rather than a difference in kind. However, such distinctions
are often useful if their limitations are kept in mind, and the

---

[1] Tiffany on Agency (2d Ed. by Powell) pp. 50, 51. Cf. American Law Institute, Restatement of Agency (hereinafter simply cited as "Restatement") § 3.

distinction between special and general agents seems so firmly established in the decisions that it is unlikely to be abandoned. According to the Restatement, a general agent is one "authorized to conduct a series of transactions involving a continuity of service" while a special agent is one authorized to conduct "a single transaction or a series of transactions not involving continuity of service." From this distinction a number of consequences flow, the most important of which is the vastly greater extent of the implied and apparent authority of the general agent.[2]

2 See §§ 93, 97, post.

CHAPTER II

PRINCIPAL AND AGENT: CAPACITY AND FORMALITIES

§ 18. What acts can be done by agent. Generally speaking, anything one can lawfully do personally, one may also do by agent. Where the purpose of the agency is to do something unlawful or against public policy, the consequences are substantially the same as though no agency had been involved. No rights can be created by such a transaction, and this includes rights between the purported principal and agent or arising from the purported agency; hence it is commonly said that the agency is void. A statement as to what contracts are void for illegality is beyond the scope of this book.[1]

A number of functions are commonly said not to be performable by agent, because of considerations of policy. For instance, one cannot normally vote, marry or make a will by agent (although one may, under statutes, vote or marry by proxy and grant a power *in* a will). These exceptions are infrequent and unimportant.

Two questions of rather more importance are: (a) who may be principal (or agent), and (b) what formalities, if any, are necessary to create the relation? These questions are discussed in following sections.

1. *Capacity to Be Principal or Agent*

§ 19. Who can be an agent. Generally speaking, anyone can be an agent who is *in fact* capable of performing the functions involved.[2] The agent normally binds not himself but his principal by the contracts he makes; it is therefore not essen-

---

[1] See Williston, Contracts (Rev. Ed. 1938) § 1628 et seq.; Corbin, Contracts (1951) § 1373 et seq.

[2] See Restatement, § 21.

tial that he be legally capable to contract (although his duties and liabilities to his principal might be affected by his status). Thus an infant or a lunatic may be an agent, though doubtless the court would disregard either's attempt to act if he were so young or so hopelessly devoid of reason as to be completely incapable of grasping the function he was attempting to perform.

§ 20. Who may be a principal: (A) Infants. It would seem that the proper view should be that anyone may be a principal who has the mental power to act at all, and that if he is a person of no, or limited, contractual power, his incapacity should be reflected solely in the contract made for him by his agent, which contract would stand on the same footing as if he had made it in person. Thus, in the case of an infant principal, it seems unnecessary to speak of his infancy as giving him the right to disaffirm the agency. As will be pointed out hereinafter,[3] every principal has the power to terminate the authority of his agent at any time, though it may in some instances expose him to liability for breach of contract. The infant principal has this power like any other principal, though his infancy would normally be a defense to a suit for breach of contract where the termination was in violation of agreement. Where he does not so elect to terminate the authority of his agent, the resulting contract should bind him as if he had made it himself; he then would have the same power to disaffirm the contract as any other infant. By this analysis the law of Agency would not be affected by the principal's infancy and the ordinary rules of contracts applicable to infants would be invoked.

It has to be admitted, however, that the cases have not always used this approach. The older cases, relying on English authorities, have said that the attempt of the infant to appoint an agent was void.[4] The modern cases tend to say that the appointment is voidable; precisely what this means

[3] See Chapter VIII, post.
[4] Saunderson v. Marr (1788) 1 H. Bl. 75; Lawrence v. McArter (1840) 10 Ohio 37; Waples v. Hastings (1842) 3 Harr. (Del.) 403.

is not clear, since all agencies are voidable, but the result of the cases is generally the same as would be reached under the analysis suggested in the preceding paragraph.[5]

§ 21. (B) Insane persons. The status of a person *non compos mentis* as a principal is likewise somewhat obscure, doubtless because of the confused status of the law as to contracts made directly by such a person.[6] Where there has been a judicial finding of insanity, it is commonly said that the purported appointment of an agent is void;[7] where there has been no adjudication, the status of the lunatic appears to be very much that of the infant, that is, the appointment as such is not void but the resulting contracts are subject to the same defenses that could be made if the lunatic had contracted, or attempted to, in person.[8]

§ 22. (C) Married women. Formerly married women lacked contractual capacity and it was said that a married woman's attempt to appoint an agent, or the purported contract resulting therefrom, was void. Today, statutes have generally given married women more or less complete contractual capacity and, in general, there is no longer reason to suggest limits on their power to act as principals. Where any limitations persist, the effect in terms of the wife's power to have an agent would be determinable only by a careful investigation of local authorities.

In most jurisdictions, husband and wife can be agents for each other and considerable litigation deals with the extent and nature of the authority vested in the husband or wife under various circumstances.[9]

[5] See Casey v. Kastel (1924) 237 N. Y. 305, 142 N. E. 671, 31 A. L. R. 995; King v. Cordrey (1935) 6 W. W. Harr. (36 Del.) 418, 177 Atl. 303, noted in 83 U. Pa. L. Rev. 1031; Crawford v. Firmin (1936) 144 Kan. 270, 59 P.2d 27; Restatement, § 20.

[6] See Williston, Contracts (Rev. Ed. 1938), § 249 et seq.

[7] See Carter v. Beckwith (1891) 128 N. Y. 312, 28 N. E. 582; American Trust Co. v. Boone (1897) 102 Ga. 202, 29 S. E. 182.

[8] See Restatement, § 20.

[9] See post, §§ 47–50.

2. *Formalities Essential to Establishment of the Relation*

§ 23. Is a contract necessary? Authority rests on consent rather than contract. It should be understood at the outset that while authority often results from a contract or is incorporated in one, no contract is necessary for the creation of authority of any kind. Consideration is not necessary nor need either party to the relation promise to do anything. Consent is the basis of authority. When we say that P has authorized A to represent him in a certain way, we mean that P has expressed to A his consent (and usually, but not necessarily, his desire) to A's representing him in that fashion. P says to his friend A: "If you are passing the X Drug Store today and think of it and have time, drop in and pick up a carton of cigarettes for me and charge them to me." A says: "I'll try to remember if I'm going by." It is clear that nothing in the nature of a contract has arisen. P has promised nothing but (by implication) gratitude; A has not promised to buy the cigarettes. If he fails to do so, he is not in default; if P calls A on the phone and says: "Don't bother about those cigarettes; my wife just brought in a couple of cartons," the authority is revoked but there is not liability for breach of contract.

§ 24. Ordinarily no formality required. The foregoing considerations tend to explain why there is ordinarily no formality required in the creation of an agency. It may be created by informal writing, by word of mouth or by conduct. No doubt in many instances prudence dictates that the authority be spelled out carefully and in detail in a formal written instrument, but usually there is no such legal requirement.[10]

Two exceptions need to be mentioned:

§ 25. Sealed instruments. At common law the rule was strictly enforced that authority to execute a specialty, i. e.,

[10] Laymen, law students and sometimes even judges are prone to make such statements as: "A written contract requires written

11

a sealed instrument, had to be given under seal.[11] Otherwise, it was thought, an instrument of the highest solemnity would be executed and bind the party although he had never affixed his seal thereto. A disputed question was whether an instrument of a type which would be valid without a seal but which was in fact executed under seal was valid when executed by an agent without authority under seal. The strict rule, and perhaps the better logic, held that since the instrument was in fact sealed it required sealed authority, the fact that the instrument could have been executed without a seal being irrelevant.[12] A more modern and perhaps more practical view is that sealed authority is unnecessary where the instrument could have been executed so as to have substantially the same effect, without a seal.[13]

§ 26. **Where seals abolished.** In many states the seal has either been abolished for all purposes or rendered unnecessary for many or all purposes.[14] In such states the consequence has been to render the old rule requiring authority under seal largely or completely obsolete. One curious question is suggested by a few cases, with the answer obscure. In jurisdictions where a deed conveying land no longer requires a seal, but still must be in writing and signed, may authority to execute it be given orally? Some cases appear to suggest that because of the formality and importance of the instru-

authority," or "the authority must be of as great formality as the contract." Such statements should be regarded with caution; they are normally not true. See Weisenberger v. Corcoran (1938) 275 Ky. 322, 121 S.W.2d 712.

[11] See Gordon v. Bulkeley (1826) 14 Serg. & R. (Pa.) 331; Heath v. Nutter (1862) 50 Me. 378; Cadell v. Allen (1888) 99 N. C. 542, 6 S. E. 399; Hutchinson v. Platt (1919) 119 Miss. 606, 81 So. 281; Forrest v. Hawkins (1938) 169 Va. 470, 194 S. E. 721.

[12] Wheeler v. Nevins (1852) 34 Me. 54; United Leather Co. v. Proudfit (1921) 151 Ga. 403, 107 S. E. 327, noted in 36 Yale L. J. 1176.

[13] Wagoner v. Watts (1882) 44 N. J. L. 126, aff'd (1883) 45 N. J. L. 184; Worrall v. Munn (1851) 5 N. Y. 229; Alfano v. Donnelly (1934) 285 Mass. 554, 189 N. E. 610, noted in 14 B. U. L. Rev. 701.

[14] The statutes are collected and analyzed in Williston, Contracts (Rev. Ed. 1938) § 218.

ment, the authority to execute it should be given in as formal a way as the law now provides, namely, by a signed writing. Others perhaps warrant the interpretation that, the requirement of the seal being abolished, the deed stands on the same footing as any other act and may be authorized orally.[15]

§ 27. **Statutory formalities.** The original English Statute of Frauds [16] provided, as to certain transactions, that the memorandum be signed by the party to be charged "or his agent lawfully authorized," and as to others by the party "or his agent lawfully authorized in writing." Quite logically it was held in the first case that the agent need not be authorized in writing, but simply in any manner normally lawful, e. g., orally,[17] but that in the second case the language of the statute unmistakably called for written authority. Quite a number of modern statutes, usually statutes of frauds, provide that authority to make named contracts be given in a particular way, usually by a writing signed by the principal to be charged. Other statutes provide that authority to enter into any contract required by law to be in writing can only be given by an instrument in writing, or that an agency must be created with the same formality as that prescribed for the act itself. Such statutes are mandatory and a contract executed by an agent not properly authorized will not bind the principal.[18]

§ 28. **Exceptions.** There are a number of real or apparent exceptions, applicable both in the case of sealed instruments and of statutory formalities. Thus, where an instrument is executed for the principal by a third party but in the presence and under the direction of the principal, it is commonly said not to be an act of agency. As said in a

---

[15] See Gage v. Gage (1855) 30 N. H. 420; Daniel v. Garner (1903) 71 Ark. 484, 76 S. W. 1063; Halliwill v. Weible (1918) 64 Colo. 295, 171 Pac. 372.

[16] 29 Charles II, c. 3, §§ 1, 3, 4.

[17] For a recent instance, see Texas Co. v. Aycock (1950) 190 Tenn. 16, 227 S.W.2d 41.

[18] See Simpson v. Commonwealth (1889) 89 Ky. 412, 12 S. W. 630; Seymour v. Oelrichs (1909) 156 Cal. 782, 106 Pac. 88; Lund v. Thackery (1904) 18 S. D. 113, 99

famous case: "The name being written by another hand, in the presence of the grantor and at her request, is her act. The disposing capacity, the act of mind, which are the essential and efficient ingredients of the deed, are hers, and she merely uses the hand of another, through incapacity or weakness, instead of her own, to do the physical act of making a written sign." [19] In such a case the writer is sometimes referred to as an "amanuensis" and the derived rule as the Amanuensis Rule.[20]

Again, if the instrument has been made by another but the principal delivers it, it becomes valid by acknowledgment or adoption. "The acknowledgment and delivery are acts of recognition and adoption, so distinct and emphatic they will preclude the grantor from afterward denying that the signing and sealing were also his acts. They are his by adoption." [21]

§ 29. **Filling blanks.** A number of cases deal with instruments, executed by the principal but with some term (often the name of the grantee) left blank, and given to an agent with oral authority to fill in the blank and deliver the instrument. If the instrument is under seal or one for whose execution by an agent there is a statutory requirement of written authority, it can be argued that since the instrument is inoperative with the blank unfilled, the filling of the blank was in substance the execution of it and could only be done by an agent having proper formal authority. This argument appears logical and has been adopted by many cases.[22]

N. W. 856; Georgia Peanut Co. v. Famo Products Co. (1938) 96 F.2d 440; Byrd v. Piha (1927) 165 Ga. 397, 141 S. E. 48; Leach v. Hazel (1947) 398 Ill. 33, 74 N.E.2d 797; Schweitzer v. Evans (1949) 360 Pa. 552, 63 A.2d 39.

[19] Gardner v. Gardner (1850) 5 Cush. (Mass.) 483.

[20] For other illustrations, see Reed v. Cedar Rapids (1908) 138 Iowa 366, 116 N. W. 140; Pierce v. Dekle (1911) 61 Fla. 390, 54 So.

389; Selma Sav. Bank v. Webster County Bank (1918) 182 Ky. 604, 206 S. W. 870, 2 A. L. R. 1136; Mondragon v. Mondragon (1923) 113 Tex. 404, 257 S. W. 215; Guthrie v. Gaskins (1930) 171 Ga. 303, 155 S. E. 185; Normand v. Brawley (1933) 63 F.2d 446.

[21] Clough v. Clough (1882) 73 Me. 487.

[22] See Lafferty v. Lafferty (1896) 42 W. Va. 783, 26 S. E. 262; Calhoun v. Drass (1935) 319 Pa.

Other cases, and perhaps increasingly, have taken the convenient view that the instrument has already been executed and that the filling of the blank merely perfects what was hitherto imperfect.[23] Where the matter filled in can be called "immaterial," e. g., the date of the instrument, no doubt any court will regard the instrument as valid.[24]

§ 30. **Consequences of lack of formal authority.** Where authority of the proper dignity is wanting, the normal consequence is to make the instrument unenforceable against the principal. It is nominally also unenforceable against the third party but the principal's power of ratification will

449, 179 Atl. 568; Edmonson v. Waterston (1938) 342 Mo. 1082, 119 S.W.2d 318; Durbin v. Bennett (1939) 31 F. Supp. 24, noted in 18 Tex. L. Rev. 498. "When the instrument is a sealed instrument, when signed by the party, the filling in of the blanks afterwards by another is not, strictly speaking, the execution of a sealed instrument. That has already been done by the party himself. The third party does not make it a specialty by his act. It was one before. The filling up merely perfects an imperfect sealed deed or bond." Inhabitants of South Berwick v. Huntress (1865) 53 Me. 89, 96.

[23] See Lund v. Thackery (1904) 18 S. D. 113, 99 N. W. 856; Harris v. Barlow (1919) 180 Cal. 142, 179 Pac. 682; Williams v. Courton (1926) 172 Ark. 129, 287 S. W. 745; Bretta v. Meltzer (1932) 280 Mass. 573, 182 N. E. 827, noted in 21 Ill. B. J. (No. 4) 37.

[24] See Vose v. Dolan (1871) 108 Mass. 155. It is also possible that the principal may be treated as having estopped himself from denying the agent's authority to

fill the blanks. In Phelps v. Sullivan (1885) 140 Mass. 36, 2 N. E. 121, Morton, C. J., said: "When a grantor signs and seals a deed, leaving unfilled blanks, and gives it to an agent with authority to fill the blanks and deliver it, if the agent fills the blanks as authorized, and delivers it to an innocent grantee without knowledge, we think the grantee is estopped to deny that the deed as delivered was his deed. Otherwise, he may by his voluntary act enable his agent to commit a fraud upon an innocent party. Whether, if the agent violates the instructions in filling the blanks, the grantor would not in like manner be bound, we do not discuss, as it is not involved in this case. To hold that such deeds are invalid, because the authority to fill the blanks is not under seal, would tend to unsettle titles, and would be mischievous in its results. Few deeds are written by the grantors. Most are written by scriveners, and a grantee to whom a deed is delivered has no means of determining whether the body of the

normally enable the principal to correct the [25] difficulty and enforce the contract against the third party. It should also be noticed that in some instances it may not be wholly nugatory as against the principal. Thus if the agent, on written but not sealed authority, has executed a sealed deed in the principal's name, the deed will be inoperative as a conveyance but may serve as a binding memorandum of a contract to convey the land which will permit a court of equity to force the principal to convey by a proper deed.[26]

deed was written before or after the signature was affixed. It would be very dangerous to allow titles to be defeated by parol proof that a deed, without suspicion on its face, duly signed and sealed by the grantor, which he authorized to be delivered, was in fact written in some part after he executed it, by an agent having only oral authority. We think a person taking such a deed in good faith has the right to rely upon it; and that the grantor cannot be permitted to aver that it is not his deed." See also Macurda v. Fuller (1916) 225 Mass. 341, 114 N. E. 366; Guthrie v. Field (1911) 85 Kan. 58, 116 Pac. 217.

[25] See Chapter VII, post.

[26] See Hytken v. Bianca (1939) 186 Miss. 323, 186 So. 624, where defendant claimed under a lease executed by an agent under a power of attorney. It was claimed that the lease was invalid because the power of attorney had not been acknowledged as required by statute but the court refused to decide the correctness of that contention because the lease "if void as such, constitutes in equity a contract to make a lease, and is admissible in evidence in support of the appellants' claim to continue in possession of the property. . . . In Lobdell et al. v. Mason, supra [71 Miss. 937, 15 So. 44], decided before this amendment to the statute was made [requiring an agent executing a contract within the Statute of Frauds to be authorized in writing] this Court held that a lease for more than a year made for his principal by an attorney in fact under verbal authority so to do was void as a lease but valid in equity as a contract to make a lease. The only change in this decision wrought by the addition of the words 'in writing' to the statute is that the agent's authority must now be in writing. It follows that if the lease here under consideration is void as such, as to which we express no opinion, it is valid in equity as a contract to make a lease, the agent's appointment being in writing." Accord, Blacknall v. Parish (1860) 6 Jones Eq. (N. C.) 70.

CHAPTER III

PRINCIPAL AND AGENT: REAL AUTHORITY

§ 31. Relation of formalities to types of authority. The formalities discussed in the preceding chapter, as it there appears, are required only in a limited group of transactions. It should further be pointed out here that where applicable at all, they are pertinent only to what is commonly, if redundantly, called *real* or *actual* authority.[1] There can properly be no such thing as "apparent authority" to execute a sealed instrument. If P, in a jurisdiction where deeds still require seals, says to T: "You may safely take a deed executed by A since I have given him sealed authority to execute it," and T in reliance thereon takes a deed executed by A, and it then turns out that P had *not* given A sealed authority, it would seem clear that P is, as against T, estopped to deny that A had proper authority. The deed, however, is still not valid as a deed because it lacks the legal requirement that a deed to be valid must be sealed either by the grantor or by an agent who has sealed authority from the named grantor.[2]

§ 32. —— If the rule were otherwise the law could readily be evaded by P's statement that it had been complied with.

[1] It is easy to point out the "authority" means precisely that, and that the adjectives "real" or "actual" add nothing. However, redundancy may be vivid and descriptive. More people will react quickly and accurately if you speak of "real and imitation pearls" than if you say simply "pearls and imitation pearls."

[2] "As to defendant's contention that the lease had been ratified, and plaintiffs were estopped by the acts of their predecessors in title from questioning the term named, we said, concerning a somewhat like contention . . . 'It would be vain for the statute to declare that the agent should be originally constituted in writing, if courts of law should hold that a subsequent parol recognition of the acts of the agent, not constituted originally in writing, would satisfy the law.'" Mott v. Kaldes (1927) 288 Pa. 264, 135 Atl. 764;

Comparable might be the case of a purported marriage by agreement in a jurisdiction not recognizing common-law marriages. The man's representation to the woman that such a marriage was perfectly valid, and her reliance thereon, would not make her his wife nor entitle her to a widow's share on his death, whatever other rights his misrepresentation might give her. In the case of the deed, however, just as in the analogous case discussed in the preceding section, equities would be created which would in most instances enable the third party to secure a valid deed.

1. *Power and Authority Compared*

§ 33. Power and authority compared. Any discussion of authority must be prefaced with a discussion of "power." *Power* is a difficult word to define because, in the last analysis, it means simply and exactly "power." [3] It is the fact that one is able to achieve a given legal result. Most commonly the use of the word denotes an isolation of the proposition from any consideration of how, or of why, or of ought or ought not. Absent the possibility of specific performance, a contracting party has the power to break the contract, although the world regards it as wrong and the law imposes penalties. One has a power to commit a trespass, although the exercise of the power is a legal wrong to the possessor. A thief has the power to pass to a bona fide purchaser good title to the stolen money.

§ 34. —— In the principal and agent context "power" normally indicates the fact that the agent *can* bind the principal, irrespective of how or why, and likewise irrespective of whether he was supposed to, or should have, or should not. The proposition is simple—the agent bound the principal; ergo, he had power to do it.

cf. **Alabama** G. S. R. Co. v. South & N. A. R. Co. (1887) 84 Ala. 570, 3 So. 286; Fleming v. Dolfin (1931) 214 Cal. 269, 4 P.2d 776, 78 A. L. R. 585, noted in 20 Calif. L. Rev. 663; Corporation of America v. Harris (1935) 5 Cal.App.2d 452, 43 P.2d 307; Dalton v. Shelton (1937) 267 Ky. 40, 101 S.W.2d 208.

[3] Restatement, § 6, evades this difficulty ingeniously by saying that a power is an ability.

When we talk of authority, we are assuming power, and discussing the oughtness and lawfulness of it. The principal was bound (the agent had power to bind him)' because—the agent had actual authority or apparent authority (or conceivably some other form of authority or even something not accurately defined in terms of authority at all).[4]

2. *Analysis of Real Authority*

§ 35. **Nature of real authority.** Real authority is simply the fact presupposed in the ordinary concept of agency, namely that a person called a principal has manifested to another person, called an agent, his willingness that the agent act on his behalf in some specified way in some specified transaction. It is thus defined by the Restatement.[5] "Authority is the power of the agent to affect the legal relations of the principal by acts done in accordance with the principal's manifestations of consent to him."

It would seem that so simple and fundamental a concept would neither require nor permit any very elaborate analysis. On the contrary there is often grave difficulty on two points: (a) What precisely is the nature and extent of the "actual" authority he has, and (b) is it so completely clear after all that what he has—the power he has—is *precisely* actual authority?

§ 36. **Example: The authority of a salesman.** Consider the case of the salesman. In the first place, if he is one of many, it is quite possible that he may have been hired and sent out without any very clear and explicit understanding between him and his employer as to precisely what he is supposed to do. If so, and the problem becomes acute, there are several very choice indicia or data to which reference may be made. What do salesmen of this type usually do? What do the other salesmen of this type employed by this particular principal usually do? What—if there has been time for a history to develop—has *this* salesman done, with the apparent approba-

---

[4] See the discussion of "agency powers" in the following chapter.   [5] Restatement, § 7.

19

tion of his employer? This data bears on actual authority as
showing what the employer *probably* intended the salesman
to do. Since the employer didn't bother to be specific, we are
thus forced to fall back on probabilities.

§ 37. **Further considerations.** At this point the question
might occur to the reader: What of these probabilities as they
appear to the person who deals with the salesman? He deals
commonly with salesmen; he knows their usual routines and
powers. Is it up to him at his peril to find out if this particular one has unusual powers or limitations on his powers,
or may he safely deal with him as any other salesman?

§ 38. **Apparent authority: Does it differ from real authority?** These questions are not only most reasonable, they
are also highly pertinent and significant. Two points suggest
themselves: (1) It must necessarily be true that appearances
and usages are important and that, at least to the extent that
the principal has caused or allowed his agent to assume a
certain role, he must be bound by the things the agent does
that are appropriate to the role. Otherwise, no one could
afford to deal with an agent. Where the principal is thus
bound by something done by the agent, although something
he was not supposed to do, we say that the agent had "apparent" authority. This subject is treated in the following
chapter. (2) It would seem that nothing could be more anti-
thetical than the apparent and the real—yet in such a case
as that of the salesman it seems that whether you consider
his real or his apparent authority, in either case the ultimate
source is the same: what salesmen usually do. That is, if it is
doubtful what authority the principal really gave the salesman, as because the evidence is conflicting or because, what
is more likely, the evidence is skimpy or it clearly appears
that the matter was never gone into thoroughly between principal and agent, the only reasonable assumption is that both
parties intended the salesman to have the authority such salesmen usually have. And the criterion will be the same if the
question is: what authority did the salesman, to a reasonable
merchant used to dealing with such salesmen, appear to have?

Postponing further reference to apparent authority, a number of typical aspects of real authority will now be set forth. It is hoped that the foregoing discussion suggests that the topic is not as simple as the definition might imply, and why it is thought appropriate to develop the analysis in some detail.

§ 39. **Types of real authority.** In the cases and in the texts a number of adjectives will be found, designed to distinguish different types of real authority or perhaps, more accurately, the manner or source from which the authority is derived. Thus it is common to speak of "implied" authority, of "express" authority and of "incidental" authority.

3. *Types of Real Authority:* (a) *Express Authority*

§ 40. **Express authority.** Express authority requires little definition. As the name suggests, it means that it can be proved that the principal in express and explicit language made clear to the agent his willingness or desire that the act in question be done.

§ 41. **Same: Written instruments.** Where express authority is created by a formal written instrument, as a power of attorney, the problems presented will normally be problems of construction. Few rules of construction can be stated, the cases being too diverse on their facts to permit of such, but a few basic considerations can be stated. Thus caution must be used in construing language of apparently broad scope, in two regards. First, broad language is usually limited in its application by the nature and incidents of the transaction for which the power was given. Thus, where a farmer about to leave the state temporarily gives an agent power "to sign my name in the general transaction of my business, giving and granting unto my said attorney full power and authority to do and perform all and every act or thing whatever, requisite and necessary to be done in the general transaction of my business . . ." it was held this did not authorize the agent to sign principal's name to a note given in settlement of his alleged liability on a penal bond, given in a matter having no

21

connection with his farming business.[6] Second (although this may be merely another aspect of the same basic proposition), very clear and explicit language must be found in the instrument to warrant the conclusion that the agent is authorized to exercise the power for his own benefit. So in Reckitt v. Barnett, Pembroke & Slater, Ltd.,[7] where P wrote his bankers that he wished the power "to cover the drawing of cheques upon you by [the agent] without restriction" this was held not to authorize the agent to pay for a Rolls Royce car, bought for his own use, by a check drawn on the principal's account.[8]

§ 42. **Same: Parol evidence.** Although cases in the Agency field are not numerous, it is clear that a power of attorney is subject to the same canon of evidence as any other integrated writing, namely, that it is not to be added to or contradicted by parol evidence. Thus a written authority to sell machinery, prescribing that the agent in selling an article should not accept in payment more than two notes, did not permit oral evidence that the principal told the agent he might accept three notes if he thought it wise; accordingly in an accounting between principal and agent, the latter was not allowed credit for a third note taken in payment for a machine. This rule is subject to the same limitations and exceptions applicable in other fields. Thus, if the instrument is ambiguous, evidence to explain its meaning is admissible. And only contemporary or prior parol understandings are excluded by the rule; there is no prohibition against showing that the authority was modi-

[6] Brantly v. Southern Life Ins. Co. (1875) 53 Ala. 554.

[7] [1929] A. C. 176, noted in 17 Calif. L. Rev. 258, 3 Camb. L. J. 445, 42 Harv. L. Rev. 270, 77 U. Pa. L. Rev. 271, 45 L. Q. Rev. 6 and 38 Yale L. J. 254.

[8] See also Brown v. Laird (1930) 134 Ore. 150, 291 Pac. 352, 73 A. L. R. 877; Luikart v. Boland (1933) 45 Wyo. 461, 21 P.2d 542; Dillard v. Gill (1936) 231 Ala. 662, 166 So. 430; Von Wedel v.

McGrath (1950) 180 F.2d 716. In the last cited case, Goodrich, Circ. J., concurring, said: "I go along with the result because I think it is supported by authority and the subject is not one on which to try to start a revolution. But it seems to me that the whole thing is incongruous. A man has said, in effect, that he gives another the power to do everything for him. Then he enumerates certain specific things which the other may do,

fied by a subsequent parol agreement (so long as the latter
is one which can validly be made by parol).[9]

4. Types of Real Authority: (b) Incidental Authority

§ 43. Incidental authority. This term seems usefully and
properly used to describe the consequences of a simple and
obvious proposition, namely, that it is not necessary, in the
giving of any kind of express authority to spell out every
detail; hence the giving of authority to do a particular act
or occupy a particular status will be taken as conferring authority to do the things normally incident to the act or status.
Thus a power of attorney authorizing the agent, among other
things, to convey the principal's lands in a distant state was
taken to include authority to give warranty deeds, it being
customary to give warranties in the state where the lands
were situate.[10] So an agent authorized to sell and convey land
has incidental authority to receive the purchase price.[11] Authority to manage a business normally includes authority to
hire and discharge employees, buy and sell stock in trade and

carefully saying, however, that he
does not mean to alter the general
power by stating specific powers.
Then he ends up by saying that he
means his language to be as broad
as he stated it. Yet the rule seems
to be that he is held to mean something much less than indicated by
the language he used. Perhaps the
law cannot quite say that white is
black. But in this instance it certainly can make white look a
pretty dark grey."

[9] See generally Hartford Fire
Ins. Co. v. Wilcox (1870) 57 Ill.
180; Plano Mfg. Co. v. Eich (Iowa,
1904) 97 N. W. 1106; Brown v.
Laird (1930) 134 Ore. 150, 291 Pac.
352, 73 A. L. R. 877.

[10] LeRoy v. Beard (1850) 8 How.
451, 12 L. Ed. 1151. Contra, Nixon

v. Hyserott (1809) 5 Johns. (N.
Y.) 58; cf. Schultz v. Griffin (1890)
121 N. Y. 294, 24 N. E. 480. As to
whether authority to make a contract of sale would include authority to bind the principal to give a
warranty deed, see Jasper v. Wilson (1908) 14 N. M. 482, 94 Pac.
951; Georgacopulos v. Hruby
(1925) 316 Ill. 439, 147 N. E. 376.

[11] Peck v. Harriott (1820) 6
Serg. & R. (Pa.) 146. In Mac-
Donald v. Gough (1950) 326 Mass.
93, 93 N.E.2d 260, noted in 49 Mich.
L. Rev. 755, it is held that a power
of attorney to X to "negotiate and
settle" a putative widow's claims
against an estate "must be held to
include authority to procure the
execution of such written instruments as would ordinarily be re-

the like, but not authority to borrow money or give negotiable paper.[12]

§ 44. Authority by necessity.

In a certain number of cases, mostly falling into a rather narrow category factually, it has been said that authority may be created by or arise out of necessity. Thus in a recent New Jersey case [13] defendant's bus became disabled in the middle of a bitter February night and the driver, after attempting unsuccessfully to get help from a superior, finally managed to secure a bus and driver from another party; the passengers were transferred to this bus and were injured when it went off the road through the negligence of the driver. It was held that in the emergency defendant's driver had authority to secure another bus and employ another servant for defendant, thus making defendant liable for the [temporary] driver's negligence. The court spoke of the authority as "implied" from the unforeseen contingency, referring to Sec. 79 of the Restatement where it is said that it is *inferred* that an agent has such authority.[14]

§ 45. Railroad accidents.

The most common application of this doctrine has been in the case of railway accidents, where an employee, passenger, or, in some instances even a trespasser, has been injured and needed immediate medical care. Most courts have been inclined to hold that the highest ranking agent on the scene is authorized within certain limits to summon medical aid on behalf of the company; the

quired to have the settlement recorded in definite and final 'form.''

12 See Jenkins S. S. Co. v. Preston (1911) 196 Fed. 609; Merritt v. Huber (1908) 137 Iowa 135, 114 N. W. 627; Exchange Bank v. Thrower (1903) 118 Ga. 433, 45 S. E. 316; American Nat. Bank of Sapulpa v. Bartlett (1930) 40 F.2d 21; Coover v. Davis (1941) 112 Mont. 605, 121 P.2d 985.

13 Sibley v. Transit Co. (1949)

2 N. J. 458, 66 A.2d 864.

14 See also De Pasquale v. Societa de M. S. Maria (1934) 54 R. I. 399, 173 Atl. 623; G. H. Mumm Champagne v. Eastern Wine Corp. (1943) 52 F. Supp. 167, aff'd (1944) 142 F.2d 499, certiorari denied (1944) 323 U. S. 715, 65 S. Ct. 41, 89 L. Ed. 575; Carlson v. Hannah (1951) 6 N. J. 202, 78 A.2d 83.

limits commonly set are that the employee must be unable to
get in touch with some higher official and that the authority
is to employ aid only for the period until the matter is taken
over by some higher official having clear authority to decide
what further steps, if any, the company should take in the
premises.[15] A few cases have applied the doctrine to non-
railway accidents such as injuries caused by factory machinery
or automobiles.[16] In a Wisconsin case the court refused to
apply the doctrine where defendant's son, driving defendant's
car with defendant's permission but for his own pleasure,
struck a pedestrian and thereupon took him to the hospital
and summoned a doctor on defendant's behalf.[17] It is believed
that most, if not all, of the cases, involve action in an emergency by someone already a servant or agent in some capacity,
of the defendant.

§ 46. **Analysis.** There is some disagreement as to the
proper analysis of these cases, but to the present writer
it seems simplest as well as most accurate to treat them as
special instances of the "incidental" authority discussed in
the previous section. That is, it seems fair to think that it is
an incident of every job to look after the principal's interest
in an emergency, with the amount and nature of the looking-
after depending on the nature and extent of the emergency,
the availability of superior officers and the like. If the driver
in the Sibley case had said to some superior: "What shall I do
if my bus breaks down some cold night?" the answer might
well have been: "Get in touch with the nearest office, and if
you can't, or they can't help you, try to locate another bus to
get your passengers home before they freeze to death."

[15] See Vandalia Ry. Co. v. Bryan
(1915) 60 Ind. App. 223, 110 N. E.
218, noted in 16 Col. L. Rev. 262
and 29 Harv. L. Rev. 547, and cases
cited therein.

[16] See Jones v. Pennsylvania
Coal & Coke Corp. (1917) 255 Pa.
339, 99 Atl. 1008; Barnes v. Blue
Plate Foods (La. App., 1936) 167
So. 219. Cf. Sheehan v. Elliott
Mfg. Co. (1929) 83 N. H. 542, 145
Atl. 139, 71 A. L. R. 633, noted in
78 U. Pa. L. Rev. 101.

[17] Habhegger v. King (1912)
149 Wis. 1, 135 N. W. 166.

5. *Types of Real Authority:* (c) *The Wife's Authority*

§ 47. The wife's authority. There is some confusion in the
books as to the status of the wife as the husband's agent, and
statements can be found that she is his agent "by necessity"
or "as a matter of law." [18] It is believed that clarification can
readily be attained here by segregating three unquestioned
and quite distinct propositions.

§ 48. Same: (1). No agency whatever, in the proper sense
of the term, arises merely from marriage. The wife is no more
the husband's agent after the marriage than she was before
(and doubtless no less, if she was his agent before).

§ 49. Same: (2). By the law of marriage (which obviously
cannot be gone into in detail here) the husband is obliged to
support his wife. One form which this obligation takes is the
husband's liability (within certain limits) for necessaries pur-
chased by his wife on his credit. It is in this situation that it
is sometimes said that the wife has "authority" to act as her
husband's agent, created by necessity or operation of law. No
doubt the consequences of this rule of marriage law *look like*
the consequences of an agency: the wife has bought on the
husband's credit and charged him thereby. All of the basic
incidents of a genuine agency are lacking, however. The husband has not consented to be represented by the wife; he can
neither limit her "authority" nor terminate it. The wife's
charging the goods is simply the act which puts into effect the
liability already existing as a matter of law, and determines
that it shall take one form rather than another. It is believed
that it is not only inaccurate and unnecessary, but positively
misleading to speak of "agency" in this connection.

§ 50. Same: (3). It is immediately apparent that from the
fact of a normal, going marriage, various forms of real agency
will usually result. The husband will probably expect the wife

[18] For an interesting instance of confusion in this area, see Jordan   Marsh v. Hedtler (1921) 238 Mass. 43, 130 N. E. 78.

to order the household supplies; she will be authorized, expressly or tacitly, to charge them to the husband. In many homes her authority, as manager of the home, will be much broader. Thus, depending naturally on the circumstances and habits of the particular family, a very considerable zone of authority will be created. It may well involve apparent as well as real authority. Thus, if the wife has bought widely in the establishments of the community, on the husband's credit, and this is well known in the community and permitted by the husband (whether or not he likes it or, indeed, ever has expressly authorized it) it will be impossible for him either to disclaim responsibility entirely or to limit his wife's power to bind him by instructions and limitations not made known to the merchants. It is constantly to be emphasized that this form of authority, while very real, does not arise from the marriage per se but is simply an illustration of the way in which authority, real and apparent, will naturally arise from the circumstances of a particular context.[19]

6. *Types of Real Authority:* (d) *Implied Authority*

§ 51. **Different uses of "implied authority."** The cases teem with references to "implied" authority. Unfortunately, the usefulness of the term is virtually nullified by the fact that it is used in different senses, sometimes in the same case, so that it cannot be said to have any accepted and precise meaning. It is perhaps for this reason that the term is not used in the Restatement.[20] At least four different uses can be distinguished:

[19] See generally Evans v. Crawford County Farmers' Mut. Fire Ins. Co. (1906) 130 Wis. 189, 109 N. W. 952; Jackson v. Lang (1946) 74 Ga. App. 247, 39 S.E.2d 418; Engle v. Farrell (1946) 75 Cal.App.2d 612, 171 P.2d 588; Leach v. Hazel (1947) 398 Ill. 33, 74 N.E.2d 797; Smedley v. Sweeten (1950) 11 N. J. Super. 39, 77 A.2d 489; Saks & Co. v. Bennett (1951) 12 N. J. Super. 316, 79 A.2d 479.

[20] There is no such heading in the extensive index. Under "Authority" appears "Implied authority, definition" with a reference to Sec. 8d, which deals generally with apparent authority. Comment "d" distinguishes apparent authority from inferred authority "which indicates authorization created otherwise than by express language." No mention of implied authority is made but the implica-

§ **52.** **(1) Meaning apparent authority.** The term is often used as synonymous with, or as describing some versions of apparent authority. I. e., the principal's conduct indicates that the agent has authority though in fact he hasn't. This is probably the least common and certainly the least accurate and useful of any.[21]

§ **53.** **(2) Meaning incidental authority.** Sometimes the phrase is used as if it were synonymous with what has been described above as incidental authority. Thus in Stevens v. Frost [22] it is said: "An employee has implied authority such as is usual, customary and necessary." This is not a surprising or illogical use ("by authorizing him to give a deed he by implication authorized him to give a warranty deed, since such is the usual practice"), but it is believed not to be the most useful or desirable one.

§ **54.** **(3) As analogous to contract implied in fact.** A contract implied in fact is like any other contract in legal effect; it differs from an express contract only in that the promise is expressed, wholly or in part, by conduct rather than by words. Thus the party who enters a barber chair, rubs his hand over his beard, and nods when the barber picks up a razor, has contracted for a shave which he will have to pay for, although nothing has been said by either party.[23] Similarly a principal may, by conduct alone or mixed words and conduct, express to his agent his willingness or desire that the agent exercise certain authority. The authority thus created is as "real" as if it had been created by the formal language of a power of attorney under seal. The most common instance of this type of authority is found in cases where the agent has repeatedly exercised some power not expressly given

tion may be that implied and inferred authority are the same.

[21] See Campbell v. John Deere Plow Co. (1946) 197 Okla. 403, 172 P.2d 319, where the phrase seems to be used interchangeably, in this sense and in the one discussed in § 54, post.

[22] (1943) 140 Me. 1, 32 A.2d 164.

[23] See Restatement, Contracts, § 5.

him and the principal, with knowledge of the same, has, by making no objection, tacitly sanctioned the continuation of the practice. Thus, in the leading case of Dobbs v. Zink,[24] an agent authorized to make loans for his principal and to collect interest but not (originally) to collect principal, repeatedly collected principal and remitted it to his principal who received it without objection. At the agent's death it was found that he had also collected principal which he had not accounted for and it was attempted, as against the borrower to treat this principal as unpaid, on the ground that the agent had no authority to collect it, but it was held that by receiving the other items of principal, without objection, implied authority to collect principal in general had been given. Agency can be proved, the court said, "by showing either a contract of agency or circumstances to prove implied agency by a course of dealing on the part of the agent in a particular capacity, and recognition of his acts by the principal."

§ 55. —— It is believed that the term "implied authority" is most usefully and properly used in this sense.[25] It conforms

[24] (1927) 290 Pa. 243, 138 Atl. 758.

[25] "Implied authority of an agent is actual authority evidenced by conduct, that is, the conduct of the principal has been such as to justify the jury in finding that the agent had actual authority to do what he did. This may be proved by evidence of acquiescence with knowledge of 'the agent's acts, and such knowledge and acquiescence may be shown by evidence of the agent's course of dealing for so long a time that knowledge and acquiescence may be presumed." Moore v. Switzer (1925) 78 Colo. 63, 239 Pac. 874, noted in 10 Minn. L. Rev. 162.

"If a party by his words or conduct, reasonably interpreted, has caused one, assuming to act as agent for such party in the making of a contract, to believe that such one had the necessary authority to make the contract, such party will be bound by the contract, regardless of whether any words or conduct of such party caused the other party to the contract to believe that the one so assuming to act had authority to make the contract. . . . In such instances the terms 'implied authority' or 'actual implied authority' are often used to describe or label what is so treated as the equivalent [sic] of authority." Miller v. Wick Bldg. Co. (1950) 154 Ohio St. 93, 93 N.E.2d 467.

"Implied authority, it is submitted, is actual authority which, not

to contract usage, as well as to the natural antithesis expressed
by the words "express" and "implied." No word but "implied"
can be thought of that readily describes the sort of authority
meant here, whereas "incidental," "apparent," and the like are
quite adequate to express other shades of meaning. It must
be admitted that no great body of authority expressly supports this use of the word "implied," and many of the cases
which may support it could also be construed as supporting
the use discussed in the following paragraph.

§ 56.   (4) As real authority proved by circumstantial evidence.   In many cases the use of the term "implied authority" seems to describe, not the nature and source of the authority, but simply the manner of its proof. Thus in Dobbs v.
Zink, supra,[26] the court said: "Although express proof of
agency was wanting in this case, we are of opinion the evidence was sufficient to submit to the jury on the question of
implied agency. Evidence of a course of dealing between
parties to a transaction is competent to show their intention
and the fact that a person has acted as agent for another in
previous transactions is evidence tending to prove agency to
act in a similar transaction. . . . Implied agency is actual
agency and the difference between it and express agency is
mainly one of method of proof." On this analysis of implied
agency it is quite possible that the principal expressly told
the agent to collect principal if he saw fit; the word "implied"
simply means that we have no proof of express authorization
but think the appearances warrant a finding that in some way
the agent was authorized to collect principal.

being expressed, must be inferred
from the conduct of the principal."
Note, 1 U. Chi. L. Rev. 337, 338.
     See Haluptzok v. Great Northern
Ry. Co. (1893) 55 Minn. 446, 57 N.
W. 144; First Nat. Bank v. Ridpath
(1896) 47 Neb. 96, 66 N. W. 37;
Ragatz v. Diener (1934) 218 Iowa
703, 253 N. W. 824; Schlick v. Berg
(1939) 205 Minn. 465, 286 N. W.
356; Standard Oil Co. v. Lyons
(1942) 130 F.2d 965; Campbell v.
John Deere Plow Co. (1946) 197
Okla. 403, 172 P.2d 319; Horner v.
Holt (1948) 187 Va. 715, 47 S.E.2d
365.
     [26] Note 24.

Similarly, in Stevens v. Frost, supra,[27] the court said: "Implied authority is actual authority circumstantially proven from the facts and circumstances attending the transaction in question and includes such incidental authority as is necessary, usual and proper as a means of effectuating the purpose of the employment, and this is so whether the agency is general or special."

§ 57. Schlick v. Berg. The case of Schlick v. Berg [28] is instructive as to this dualism of meaning where implied authority is concerned. Plaintiff was injured by the negligence of a workman engaged in making certain repairs on a store. The material for the repair job was furnished by the Dorenkamper Lumber Company and it was paid for the lumber. The contract was made with Dorenkamper's son, Carl, and he made the contract, supervised the job and, it is said, received the profits, although on what basis does not appear. Suit was brought and recovery allowed on the theory that Carl was his father's agent in making the contract. The court gave a very lucid analysis of implied authority along the lines suggested in subdivision (3) of this section. "[Actual authority] . . . can of course be shown by express agreement between principal and agent. But it can also be inferred from the course of dealing between the two. All authority must be traced to the principal. But it may be found in his adoption of, or acquiescence in, similar acts done on other occasions by the assumed agent. It then becomes what is conveniently but inaccurately [query: why?] called implied authority. In result it is actual or express authority, its expression being by the conduct rather than by the words of the principal. Only the evidence of it is found in implication by conduct."

§ 58. —— It is interesting to observe that in the actual case the evidence treated by the court as decisive had to do with a similar contract with another party made *after* the injury

[27] Note 22. And see Boillin-Harrison Co. v. Lewis & Co. (1945) 182 Tenn. 342, 187 S.W.2d 17.

[28] (1939) 205 Minn. 465, 286 N. W. 356.

which was the subject of the suit. It appeared (1) that Carl signed the contract expressly on behalf of the lumber company, and (2) that when the customer heard of the accident and expressed some doubt as to just whom he was dealing with, Dorenkamper told him not to be alarmed, saying: "We stand back of this contract. My son does that work for me all the time like this." This is certainly suggestive evidence—but it is hardly evidence that the father gave authority to the son by conduct rather than by words.

§ 59. —— It may be thought that the foregoing analysis of implied authority is too meticulous to serve any practical purpose. The writer believes not, however. On the contrary it seems to him to illustrate something which manifests itself in every field of agency and needs to be reckoned with in any attempt to make a realistic appraisal of the judicial process in the agency field. That is the tendency, underneath the conventional analytical divisions of authority and the like, to decide cases on a basis which is rather different from the ostensible one. The real basis is usually either an appearance or a generalized and conventionalized deduction drawn from some readily observable and unchallenged fact.

Consider the case of the Dorenkampers, father and son. It is established beyond substantial doubt that in a number of instances the son has made contracts purportedly on behalf of his father; there is no evidence that the father has ever objected to this or tried to prevent its happening again.

§ 60. —— We may look at this from three conceivable standpoints:

(1) The standpoint of the other contracting party. He knows that Carl has been purporting to represent his father; he has not heard of the father's attempting to prevent it. Hence he reasonably assumes that Carl is authorized. If the jury agrees that it was a reasonable assumption, they will protect the third party's reliance on it. In other words, the facts will establish apparent authority. (It should be noted that in the actual case this analysis was not available to plain-

tiff since she was not a contracting party but the victim of a tort.)

(2) Carl's standpoint. Carl said to himself: "I guess the Old Man is willing to have me act as his agent." In other words the father's conduct, viz., his failure to object, made it look to Carl as though he was authorized. Hence there was implied authority in the sense of the phrase as set forth in subsection (3) of Sec. 32, supra.

(3) The court's standpoint. The court says to itself: "I guess the boy must be authorized. He's been doing this, and his father doesn't seem to have objected. Of course the father denies it now—but naturally he would." That is, it looks, not to the public, not to the son—but to the court that the boy must have had authority. If so, it is of no great importance *how* he was originally authorized.

7. *A Realistic Analysis of Authority*

§ 61. The essentially unitary nature of authority. It thus appears that three analytically very different types of authority may all be found simply by looking at the same admitted facts from three slightly different points of view. This suggests two things: (a) The analytical classifications of types of authority while useful, and indeed essential to any thorough knowledge of the subject, are not to be taken at their face value nor to be thought of as necessarily the bases of the decision of the court in a particular case. (b) If the preceding generalization is sound it becomes important to ask whether it is possible to any extent to categorize the bases on which decisions are actually made. One such basis is suggested by the Schlick case: namely *appearance*. The principal has created or permitted an appearance; what he really authorized or expected cannot be ascertained but the appearance is readily susceptible of interpretation; therefore let him be judged on the basis of the appearance he has created.

This is the factual basis for many findings of authority. P appears to have authorized A. It may appear that way to A, or to the public or to the court—and the adjective applied to the authority is likely to be different in each instance—but the real basis is one and the same appearance.

§ 62. ——— A second fundamental basis is generalization, from transaction or occupation. It is common to find statements in the books that a travelling salesman has such and such authority, and that authority to "sell" land empowers the broker to do this but not that. Plainly one who employs a travelling salesman may give him such authority as he likes and one who employs a real estate broker may instruct him in an almost infinite number of ways. The statements mentioned above must mean simply that such is the normal way in which travelling salesmen do business and the normal way in which land is sold; hence one employed in such a capacity or for such a transaction will be presumed to have the normal authority unless the contrary is clearly shown. Thus, since as already pointed out, it is often so difficult to find out what authority was really given, the cases tend to be decided in terms of a generalization based upon what is normal in the transaction or occupation at hand.

§ 63. **Same: Rationalization.** It is inevitable that this be so. The judicial process must go on; agency cases have to be decided. In many cases it is peculiarly difficult to find out what the parties really intended; it is not uncommon to find that they apparently never really reached any agreement even between themselves as to what they intended. Some objective standard, readily applied, is called for. It will usually be difficult neither to establish the externals of the course of conduct between the parties nor the usages of a given calling or transaction. Furthermore, such a process is not likely to be unfair to the principal. The very fact that we are basing our finding on *normal* behavior in such a setting renders it statistically likely that the normal pattern was being followed in the particular instance. If not, the normal pattern is not likely to be harmful even to a principal who did not intend to abide by it. Finally, if the principal is harmed, it can fairly be said that a person dealing in a context where there is a familiar and normal pattern should be very sure to prevent misunderstanding if for any reason he does not wish to abide by the normal pattern.

In the following chapter a few familiar and common instances of authority deduced from an occupation or transaction will be discussed.

CHAPTER IV

FURTHER OF REAL AUTHORITY: INSTANCES

1. *Authority of a Salesman*

§ 64. Salesmen. It is of course impossible to put all salesmen into one category. Nevertheless the great bulk of cases
coming before courts deal with one type of salesman, namely
the so-called "travelling salesman" who travels about attempting to sell his firm's goods to dealers. Normally, and for
obvious reasons, he does not carry goods with him to sell
and deliver. (There are of course exceptions; vide the famous
Fuller Brush man.) He will very likely have samples of his
wares; these he is not authorized to sell.[1] And he is not authorized to contract to sell his principal's goods; his function
is to solicit orders for goods which are then sent to the principal for acceptance [2] (which normally occurs as a matter of
course). It is said that usually he has authority to fix the price
and terms, within reasonable limits, but it is likely that the
literature and forms with which the salesman is supplied will
set forth the credit terms and perhaps the price.[3]

§ 65. —— Plainly such a salesman has no authority to
receive the price, either when he takes the order or, as is possibly more likely to happen, after it has been filled, as, for
example, when the salesman comes around to solicit further
orders.[4] However, if the salesman is of a type who does have

[1] Cleveland Knitting Mills Co. v.
Shaff (1914) 160 App. Div. 107,
145 N. Y. S. 109; Ann., 57 A. L. R.
396.
[2] Ammons v. Wilson & Co. (1936)
176 Miss. 645, 170 So. 227; Wrenn
v. Ehrlich (1937) 59 R. I. 87, 194
Atl. 534; Dayton Bread Co. v. Montana Flour Mills Co. (1942) 126
F.2d 257; State of Delaware v.
Massachusetts Bonding & Insurance Co. (1943) 49 F. Supp. 467.
[3] Restatement, § 54.
[4] Fairbanks Morse & Co. v. Dale
& Co. (1935) 172 Miss. 271, 159
So. 859; Velvet Ridge School Dist.

possession of goods for sale, as a clerk in a store or the man who sells and delivers a vacuum cleaner or parts therefor, he will normally and naturally have authority to receive the price.[5] He must receive it in cash,[6] however; he is not authorized to make a trade or to sell the goods in payment of his own debt.[7] The fact that the clerk in the store has authority to receive payment for goods just sold by him does not mean that he necessarily has general authority to receive payment;[8] if the customer who bought shoes on credit a week before comes in and wishes to pay for them it is doubtful that the clerk who sold them has authority to receive the payment; the cashier or bookkeeper should be sought out. Likewise possession for another purpose will not suffice. Thus, where a salesman had possession of tires but not for the purpose of sale and delivery, his sale and delivery of them did not authorize him to collect payment.[9]

§ 66. Real estate transactions. Agency transactions involving the sale of land are very markedly categorized. The typical mandate is authority to "sell" P's land. This is interpreted as authorizing the agent simply to find and produce a person ready, willing and able to buy P's land on the terms named by P.[10] The agent is not authorized to contract for the sale of the land, much less to convey it. Doubtless the agent has prepared a contract, but it is the principal who signs it, if he

No. 91 v. Bank of Searcy (1940) 200 Ark. 85, 137 S.W.2d 907; Anns., 8 A. L. R. 214, 105 A. L. R. 720.

[5] Oleson v. Albers (1936) 130 Neb. 823, 266 N. W. 632. But see Pasco County Peach Ass'n v. J. F. Solley & Co. (1945) 146 F.2d 880.

[6] Zazzaro v. Universal Motors (1938) 124 Conn. 105, 197 Atl. 884; Saulsbury Oil Co. v. Phillips Petroleum Co. (1944) 142 F.2d 27, 39, cert. den. (1944) 323 U. S. 727, 65 S. Ct. 62, 89 L. Ed. 584.

[7] Globe Securities Co. v. Gardner Motor Co. (1935) 337 Mo. 177, 85

S.W.2d 561; Monroe Milk Station Inc. v. Sur-Wa Stores (La. App., 1936) 167 So. 771.

[8] Hirshfield v. Waldron (1884) 54 Mich. 649, 20 N. W. 628.

[9] Boice-Perrine Co. v. Kelley (1923) 243 Mass. 327, 137 N. E. 731.

[10] See Yadwin v. Arnold (1920) 94 N. J L. 500, 110 Atl. 903; Brown v. Hogan (1921) 138 Md. 257, 113 Atl. 756; Payne v. Jennings (1926) 144 Va. 126, 131 S. E. 209, 48 A. L. R. 628; D. N. Toohey & Co. v. Davis (1931) 85

so elects, just as it is the principal who later executes the deed. If the principal refuses to sign, he is not in any way bound to the prospective purchaser; he is, however (as discussed in Chapter XVI, infra), bound to pay the agent the commission earned by the production of a proper purchaser.

This transaction, it will be observed, amounts in substance to an offer by P to pay A a stipulated amount for the performance of a stipulated service. It comes very close to being no agency at all. In what regard, it may be asked, is the agent authorized to represent his principal? Certainly to a very limited extent. However, the broker here probably does have a modicum of authority. For example, though to an extremely limited extent, he may bind his principal by representations as to the location and size of the land.[11] Other instances might be discovered.

The principal may of course, if he wishes, authorize the agent to contract for him to sell the land, or even to convey it. Such authority, if found, will usually be express and explicit. Occasionally, where the authority is nominally only to "sell," the instrument may contain such a plenitude of detail as to the way in which the transaction is to be handled and the terms on which it is to be made as to warrant the interpretation that it must have been intended to authorize the agent not simply to find a buyer but to contract for the sale of the property in the principal's name.[12]

Authority to contract does not normally include authority to convey.

2. *Authority to Manage a Business*

§ 67. Scope varies with the business. Authority to manage P's business is one which obviously must vary widely with the nature and extent of the business or enterprise to be managed.

N. H. 80, 153 Atl. 832; Dwiggins v. Roth (1948) — Fla. —, 37 So.2d 702.

[11] See post, § 139.

[12] See Lyon v. Pollock (1878) 99 U. S. 668, 25 L. Ed. 265; Winch v. Edmonds (1905) 34 Colo. 359, 83 Pac. 632; Hedrick v. Donovan (1911) 248 Ill. 479, 94 N. E. 144; McCartney v. Campbell (1932) 216 Cal. 715, 16 P.2d 729.

The power may be simply of the administrative sort, that is, to direct in pursuance of policies fixed by the principal, or it may be so wide in itself as to include the fixing of policy as well as the executing of it. Presumptively, in either case it will include authority to do all the things which are necessary and proper to be done in carrying on the business in the usual and accustomed way and which the principal would usually do if he were managing the affair in person. Nevertheless the power of the principal is greater than the authority of a manager. The principal may change, expand or terminate the business, while the manager would ordinarily be expected to conduct it but not to alter or terminate it. A manager given complete charge of a business requiring the usual and ordinary servants or agents, may ordinarily employ them,[13] he may buy customary and necessary supplies,[14] he may decide incidental questions necessary to be decided in order to carry on; [15] if the purpose of the business is to produce and sell the product, he may sell the product in the usual way [16] and decide upon the ordinary questions therein involved.

[13] See Jenkins S. S. Co. v. Preston (1911) 196 Fed. 609; King v. Seaboard Air Line R. Co. (1906) 140 N. C. 433, 53 S. E. 237; Blowers v. Southern Ry. Co. (1906) 74 S. C. 221, 54 S. E. 368; Merritt v. Huber (1908) 137 Iowa 135, 114 N. W. 627; Grand Pacific Hotel v. Pinkerton (1905) 217 Ill. 61, 75 N. E. 427; Davis v. Matthews (1896) 8 S. D. 300, 66 N. W. 456.

But he has no implied authority to employ for unusual purposes or on unusual or extraordinary terms. See Stephens v. John L. Roper Lumber Co. (1912) 160 N. C. 107, 75 S. E. 933; Thied Detective Service Co. v. McClure (1906) 142 Fed. 952; Schlapback v. Richmond R. Co. (1890) 35 S. C. 517, 15 S. E. 241.

[14] See Beecher v. Venn (1877) 35 Mich. 466; Louisville Coffin Co. v. Stokes (1884) 78 Ala. 372; Wallis Tobacco Co. v. Jackson (1892) 99 Ala. 460, 13 So. 120; Pacific Biscuit Co. v. Dugger (1901) 40 Ore. 302, 67 Pac. 32; Witcher v. Gibson (1900) 15 Colo. App. 163, 61 Pac. 192.

[15] See Michaud v. MacGregor (1895) 61 Minn. 198, 63 N. W. 479; Tice v. Russell (1890) 43 Minn. 66, 44 N. W. 886; Indianapolis Rolling Mill v. St. Louis, F. S. & W. Ry. Co. (1886) 120 U. S. 256, 7 S. Ct. 542, 30 L. Ed. 639; Henderson Bridge Co. v. McGrath (1889) 134 U. S. 260, 10 S. Ct. 730, 33 L. Ed. 934.

[16] See Robert E. Lee Silver Mining Co. v. Omaha & Grant

§ 68. —— But, on the other hand, authority to manage a business, to which such an authority is not shown to be a usual incident, does not imply authority to make negotiable paper,[17] or to sell the business; [18] or to borrow money unless absolutely necessary; [19] or to pledge or mortgage the principal's property; [20] or to make any contract not within the usual scope of the business.[21]

3. *Authority to Collect*

§ 69. **Collecting principal and interest.** A substantial body of authority deals with the lending of money and the collection of principal and interest on the same, when some part or parts of the transaction are handled by an agent. Authority to receive payment of principal or interest is not to be implied merely from the fact that the agent had negotiated the loan

Smelting & Refining Co. (1891) 16 Colo. 118, 26 Pac. 326.

[17] See New York Iron Mine v. First Nat. Bank (1878) 39 Mich. 644; Perkins v. Boothby (1880) 71 Me. 91; Jackson Paper Co. v. Commercial Nat. Bank (1902) 199 Ill. 151, 65 N. E. 136; Helena Nat. Bank v. Rocky Mountain Telegraph Co. (1898) 20 Mont. 379, 51 Pac. 829.

Compare Glidden Varnish Co. v. Interstate Bank (1895) 69 Fed. 912.

No authority to make accommodation notes: Gulick v. Grover (1868) 33 N. J. L. 463.

[18] See Vescelius v. Martin (1888) 11 Colo. 391, 18 Pac. 338; Dearing v. Lightfoot (1849) 16 Ala. 28.

None to transfer the business and property or the bulk of it to pay debts, Claflin v. Continental Works (1890) 85 Ga. 27, 11 S. E. 721, or to make general assignment for benefit of creditors, Gouldy v. Metcalf (1889) 75 Tex. 455, 12 S. W. 830. None to embark on a different business, Campbell v. Hastings (1874) 29 Ark. 512.

[19] See Hawtayne v. Bourne (1841) 7 M. & W. 595; Exchange Bank v. Thrower (1903) 118 Ga. 433, 45 S. E. 316; Bickford v. Menier (1887) 107 N. Y. 490, 14 N. E. 438; Consolidated Nat. Bank v. Pacific Coast S. S. Co. (1892) 95 Cal. 1, 30 Pac. 96.

[20] See Despatch Line v. Bellamy Mfg. Co. (1841) 12 N. H. 205; Edgerly v. Cover (1898) 106 Iowa 670, 77 N. W. 328; Golinsky v. Allison (1896) 114 Cal. 458, 46 Pac. 295; First Nat. Bank v. Kirkby (1901) 43 Fla. 376, 32 So. 881.

[21] See Brockway v. Mullin (1884) 46 N. J. L. 448 (manager of hotel has no authority to agree that livery supplied to guests might be charged to the hotel and that

on which the money is payable.[22] The principal may, of course, now give him actual authority to receive the payment,[23] and authority to receive payment in a given case may be inferred from the principal's knowledge of and real or apparent acquiescence in a course of conduct in prior cases.[24]

Even if no actual authority can thus be shown, an "apparent" authority may at times be established, as in the case of the loan agent. In the latter case from the fact that the securities, as for example the note or bond and mortgage, are left or put in the possession of the *agent who negotiated the loan* (even without actual authority to receive payment), an apparent authority to receive payment is said to arise which will protect

---

hotel would be responsible for safe return of horses and vehicles so supplied).

[22] Thus as has been seen, ante, a travelling salesman, or "drummer," authorized to solicit orders for goods to be sent by his principal, and who takes such an order for goods which are so supplied, has thereby no implied authority to subsequently collect payment for them. McKindly v. Dunham (1882) 55 Wis. 515, 13 N. W. 485; Janney v. Boyd (1883) 30 Minn. 319, 15 N. W. 308; Butler v. Dorman (1878) 68 Mo. 298; Simon v. Johnson (1894) 105 Ala. 344, 16 So. 884; Kornemann v. Monaghan (1871) 24 Mich. 36, and other cases there cited.

As to the broker, who does not have possession, see Lawrence Gas Co. v. Hawkeye Oil Co. (1917) 182 Iowa 179, 165 N. W. 445, 8 A. L. R. 192, Note.

As to the loan agent, see Smith v. Kidd (1877) 68 N. Y. 130; Joy v. Vance (1895) 104 Mich. 97, 67 N. W. 140; Fortune v. Stockton (1899) 182 Ill. 454, 55 N. E. 367;

Security Co. v. Graybeal (1892) 85 Iowa 543, 52 N. W. 497.

Notice of lack of authority may be given by a sufficiently prominent or conspicuous and unequivocal statement on the bill, or by letter, or by an express provision in the contract, and the like: See McKindly v. Dunham, supra; Law v. Stokes (1867) 32 N. J. L. 249; Putnam v. French (1881) 53 Vt. 402; Trainor v. Morison (1886) 78 Me. 160; Metz v. Building & Savings Ass'n (1907) 117 App. Div. 825, 102 N. Y. Supp. 980; Pioneer Mortgage Co. v. Randall (1923) 113 Kan. 62, 213 Pac. 668.

[23] Sending coupons or notes, etc., to the agent for collection is one of the most common and unequivocal methods of conferring actual authority.

[24] In a great many cases courts have held that an inference of authority to receive payment might properly be drawn from courses of dealing or conduct, although the agent did not have possession of the securities, as, for example, where the principal had repeatedly per-

a *bona fide* payer who relies upon it.[25] Not so, however, where the person paying did not know, or was not truthfully told, that the agent had the possession of the securities at the time he made the payment.[26]

The fact that the money is made payable at the office of the agent is not enough of itself to show either actual or apparent authority in him to receive the payment.[27]

Actual authority to receive payment of one of several bonds by depositing that one for collection would not of itself give

mitted, acquiesced in or encouraged the act of the agent in collecting, remitting, renewing, etc., without express instructions and without objection.

See Fowle v. Outcalt (1902) 64 Kan. 352, 67 Pac. 889; Bissell v. Dowling (1898) 117 Mich. 646, 76 N. W. 100; Harrison Nat. Bank v. Austin (1902) 65 Neb. 632, 91 N. W. 540; Johnson v. Milwaukee & Wyoming Investment Co. (1895) 46 Neb. 480, 64 N. W. 1100; Campbell v. Gowans (1909) 35 Utah 268, 100 Pac. 397; Bautz v. Adams (1907) 131 Wis. 152, 111 N. W. 69; Judith v. Dicola (1935) 317 Pa. St. 353, 176 Atl. 238; Brientnall v. Peters (1935) 317 Pa. St. 356, 176 Atl. 240; Campbell v. John Deere Plow Co. (1946) 197 Okla. 403, 172 P.2d 319, noted in 45 Mich. L. Rev. 624.

25 See Crane v. Gruenewald (1890) 120 N. Y. 274, 24 N. E. 456; Central Trust Co. v. Folsom (1901) 167 N. Y. 285, 60 N. E. 599; Doubleday v. Kress (1872) 50 N. Y. 410; Haines v. Pohlman (1874) 25 N. J. Eq. 179; Union Trust Co. v. McKeon (1904) 76 Conn. 508, 57 Atl. 109; Stiger v. Bent (1884) 111 Ill. 328; Jolly v. Huebler (1908) 132 Mo. App. 675, 112 S. W.

1013; Pioneer Mortgage Co. v. Randall (1923) 113 Kan. 62, 213 Pac. 668. And see Pampegian v. Richmond (1946) 319 Mass. 216, 65 N.E.2d 316, 163 A. L. R. 1206, noted in 32 Va. L. Rev. 1190.

In such a case, if the principal retains possession of the securities, the fact that the agent made the loan is not alone enough. Joy v. Vance, ante; Smith v. Kidd, ante; Fortune v. Stockton, ante.

26 See Crane v. Gruenewald, ante.

According to these cases possession of the securities (unless given to the agent in order that he might collect, in which case he would have actual authority) will not suffice; the payer must have been deceived by that fact into believing that the agent had an authority which in fact he did not possess. Withdrawing papers previously held (but not so as to create a continuing actual authority) destroys the appearance of authority: Bloomer v. Dau (1899) 122 Mich. 522, 81 N. W. 331.

27 See Bartel v. Brown (1899) 104 Wis. 493, 80 N. W. 801; Klindt v. Higgins (1895) 95 Iowa 529, 64 N. W. 414; Ward v. Smith (1869) 74 U. S. (7 Wall.) 447, 19 L. Ed. 207.

authority to receive payment of the others not deposited for collection.[28]

§ 70. —— Incidental acts. Authority to receive interest does not of itself justify receiving payment of the principal.[29] Authority to receive payment will not justify a sale,[30] release or compromise of the debt,[31] an extension of the time,[32] a change in the terms,[33] a receipt before maturity where this might prejudice the principal,[34] or even a partial payment within the same limitation.[35] Mere authority to demand or receive payment would not justify suits at law to collect, but an agent charged with the duty of collecting might be justified

[28] See Ward v. Smith, ante.

[29] See Doubleday v. Kress (1872) 50 N. Y. 410; Hoffmaster v. Black (1908) 78 Ohio St. 1, 81 N. E. 423; Wilson v. Campbell (1896) 110 Mich. 580, 68 N. W. 278; Burnham v. Wilson (1911) 207 Mass. 378, 93 N. E. 704; Koen v. Miller (1912) 105 Ark. 152, 150 S. W. 411.

[30] See Dingley v. McDonald (1899) 124 Cal. 682, 56 Pac. 790; Quigley v. Mexico Bank (1883) 80 Mo. 289; Moore v. Skyles (1905) 33 Mont. 135, 82 Pac. 799.

[31] See Melvin v. Lamar Ins. Co. (1875) 80 Ill. 446; Danziger v. Pittsfield Shoe Co. (1903) 204 Ill. 145, 68 N. E. 534; Eaton v. Knowles (1886) 61 Mich. 625, 28 N. W. 740. No authority to release balance on receiving part, McHany v. Schenck (1878) 88 Ill. 357, or to release one joint debtor upon receiving security from the other, Cram v. Sickel (1897) 51 Neb. 828, 71 N. W. 724.

No authority to release or waive liens, or release securities without payment of the debt: First Nat. Bank v. Farmers' Savings Bank (1922) 195 Iowa 1260, 193 N. W. 573 (superseding 187 N. W. 474); Porter v. Packers' Nat. Bank (1914) 95 Neb. 223, 145 N. W. 255.

[32] See Powell v. Henry (1892) 96 Ala. 412, 11 So. 311; Hutchings v. Munger (1869) 41 N. Y. 155; Karcher v. Gans (1900) 13 S. D. 383, 83 N. W. 431; Lawrence v. Johnson (1872) 64 Ill. 351.

[33] See Tootle v. Cook (1893) 4 Colo. App. 111, 35 Pac. 193; Halladay v. Underwood (1899) 90 Ill. App. 130.

[34] See Park v. Cross (1899) 76 Minn. 187, 78 N. W. 1107; Kansas Educational Ass'n v. McMahan (1935) 76 F.2d 957, 100 A. L. R. 384; Meier v. Geldis (1947) 148 Neb. 234, 26 N.W.2d 813.

[35] Authority to collect undoubtedly often is given under such circumstances as to show that the agent is expected to take partial payments on account if he cannot get it all; but there may also be cases in which to take part only would prejudice the principal. Compare Lowenstein v. Bresler (1895) 109 Ala. 326, 19 So. 860.

in suing.[36] Having received the money, the agent would have no implied authority to loan it, reinvest it, pay debts with it, buy goods with it, or, in general, do anything else than account for it to his principal.[37] He may properly give, upon receiving the money, such receipt or acquittance as is customary in such cases.[38]

The fact that an agent authorized to collect money afterwards misappropriates it, will not affect the payer, if he has himself acted in good faith.[39]

§ 71. —— **What may be received in payment.** An agent authorized to receive payment has no authority to receive anything but *money* in payment. He therefore may not accept goods, land, stocks, bills, drafts or promissory notes, whether of the debtor, third persons, or himself.[40] He would have no incidental authority to accept a check as *payment*, unless that were usual.[41] If he received it conditionally and got the money upon it, the money would constitute the payment.[42]

---

[36] See Joyce v. Duplessis (1860) 15 La. Ann. 242.

Foreclosure: Mere authority to receive interest or principal on a note and mortgage would not justify a foreclosure of the mortgage if not paid. Burchard v. Hull (1898) 71 Minn. 430, 74 N. W. 163; Dexter v. Morrow (1899) 76 Minn. 413, 79 N. W. 394; White v. Madigan (1899) 78 Minn. 286, 80 N. W. 1125, though a known course of conduct, i. e., a known practice of doing so, may justify it. Springfield Sav. Bank v. Kjaer (1901) 82 Minn. 180, 84 N. W. 752.

Employing counsel: If the agent were in fact authorized to begin suit, he would ordinarily have implied authority to employ counsel. Ryan v. Tudor (1884) 31 Kan. 366, 2 Pac. 797.

[37] See Haynes v. Carpenter (1900) 86 Mo. App. 30.

[38] See Dawson v. Wombles (1905) 111 Mo. App. 532, 86 S. W. 271.

[39] See Grant v. Humerick (1904) 123 Iowa 571, 94 N. W. 510.

[40] See Ward v. Smith (1868) 74 U. S. (7 Wall.) 447, 19 L. Ed. 207; Barker v. Greenwood (1837) 2 Younge & Col. 414; Dixon v. Guay (1900) 70 N. H. 161, 46 Atl. 456; Miller v. Edmonston (1846) 8 Blackf. (Ind.) 291; Cram v. Sickel (1897) 51 Neb. 828, 71 N. W. 724; cf. Shriver v. Sims (1934) 127 Neb. 374, 255 N. W. 60, 94 A. L. R. 779; Black v. Krauss (1949) 119 Ind. App. 529, 85 N.E.2d 647.

The money received must either be that "which the law declares to be a legal tender, or which is by common consent considered and treated as money and passes as such at par."

[41] See Hall v. Storrs (1858) 7 Wis. 253 (agent liable for loss

If he were authorized to receive a check in payment, and has taken one payable to the order of his principal, he would ordinarily have no implied authority to endorse the check and get the money thereon.[43] If he was authorized to take a check to his own order as a means of getting the money, he might, of course, endorse it in his own name for that purpose, and if he received the money it would be a good payment.[44]

4. *Authority to Warrant (Herein of Special and General Agents)*

§ 72. **In general.** A number of cases deal with the existence and extent of the agent's power to warrant. As has already been seen,[45] authority to convey land normally includes authority to give a warranty deed, since it would be unusual for a purchaser to be expected to take anything less. Whether an agent selling chattels has authority to

---

caused by taking check); Harlan v. Ely (1886) 68 Cal. 522, 9 Pac. 947 (same); Pape v. Westacott [1894] 1 Q. B. 272 (same).

[42] See Griffin v. Erskine (1906) 131 Iowa 444, 109 N. W. 13.

[43] See Jackson v. National Bank of McMinnville (1893) 92 Tenn. 154, 20 S. W. 802; McFadden v. Follrath (1911) 114 Minn. 85, 130 N. W. 542; Jackson Paper Mfg. Co. v. Commercial Nat. Bank (1902) 199 Ill. 151, 65 N. E. 136; Graham v. United States Sav. Institute (1870) 46 Mo. 186; Pickle v. Muse (1889) 88 Tenn. 380, 12 S. W. 919; Crahe v. Mercantile Trust & Sav. Bank (1920) 295 Ill. 375, 129 N. E. 120, 12 A. L. R. 92; Arcade Realty Co. v. Bank of Commerce (1919) 180 Cal. 318, 181 Pac. 66, 12 A. L. R. 102; Coleman v. Seattle Nat. Bank (1919) 109 Wash. 80, 186 Pac. 275, 12 A. L. R. 108 and Note.

But where an agent operating in another state, and expected to deal for cash, received a check on a local bank to the order of his principal and endorsed it and received the money, it was held that the circumstances justified the conclusion that he was authorized to do so. Chamberlin Weatherstrip Co. v. Bank of Pleasanton (1920) 107 Kan. 79, 190 Pac. 742, 12 A. L. R. 97. Compare Galbraith v. Weber (1910) 58 Wash. 132, 107 Pac. 1050.

[44] See Cohen v. O'Connor (1873). 5 Daly (N. Y.) 28, 8 Albany L. J. 189; Harbach v. Colvin (1887) 73 Iowa 638, 35 N. W. 663; Bridges v. Garrett (1870) L. R. 5 Com. Pl. 451.

[45] Ante, § 43.

warrant their quality is doubtful. Probably it would ordinarily be said that a special agent has no such authority.

In this connection it may be useful to consider the distinction between general and special agents, already adverted to.[46]

§ 73. Special agents. Various definitions have been offered and discussed, but to the writer, in the light of what has previously been said about the authority of an agent, real or apparent, usually turning on appearance or generalization, it seems that the most useful thing that can be said about a special agent is that he is one who falls outside the ambit of any useful generalization. He is a special case; it cannot be said of him that *he* usually does thus and so, or that agents of his type usually do thus and so.

Thus, in a famous New Jersey case [47] the principal, a coal and lumber merchant, being sick in bed, was approached by a third party who wished to buy a horse the principal owned. The latter sent word through one of his employees that he would sell the horse for a given amount. The sale was made, the employee warranting, on behalf of the principal, that the horse was sound. The principal was held not bound by the warranty.

§ 74. —— It is believed that the explanation of the decision is obvious. There was nothing from which either the agent or the third party could reasonably infer that a warranty was intended. The principal was not in the horse-selling business, which would have made the usages of the business relevant. This employee had not, as far as appeared, sold horses for him before; there was no practice of warranting, on which reliance could be placed. The principal said he would sell for a certain sum; that was all. The third party was relying on a very special authority and had to ascertain its limits at his peril.

Thus special authority is in the nature of something negative: it is in the absence of any justification for relying on

---

[46] Ante, § 17.
[47] Cooley v. Perrine (1879) 41   N. J. L. 322, affirmed in a brief opinion (1880) 42 N. J. L. 623.

anything but the real facts, with the burden on the third party of showing that they support his case.

§ 75. General agents. Where the agent is a general agent selling standardized goods which it is customary to warrant, it is natural to find him treated as authorized to give the customary warrant since otherwise he could hardly be expected to sell the goods. It must be customary. Thus, in a Colorado case where the agent (apparently general, though no point is made of it) of a used car dealer warranted that the cylinders of a used car were not scored, it was held that the principal was not bound since there was no evidence of express authority and it was not shown that it was customary to make such a warranty in the sale of a used car.[48] On the other hand, in Pioneer Electric Co. v. McCurdy [49] where a general agent sold an electrical plant with warranty of its quality and capacity, the case was said to fall within the general rule that "an agent with authority to sell property usually the subject of warranty, has implied power to sell with a warranty of capacity and fitness, as binding on the principal as though the agent was clothed with express authority to that effect." [50]

5. *Authority of Attorneys at Law*

§ 76. —— The attorney at law is an officer of the court in which he practices, and is, in some sense, an officer of the state. The relationship of the attorney to his client, however, is largely governed by the law of Agency and is in general

---

[48] Moore v. Switzer (1925) 78 Colo. 63, 239 Pac. 874, noted in 10 Minn. L. Rev. 162. And see Johnson v. City Co. of New York (1935) 78 F.2d 782.

[49] (1922) 151 Minn. 304, 186 N. W. 776.

[50] See also Fulwiler v. Lawrence (Tex. Civ. App., 1926) 7 S.W.2d 636; A. Leschen & Sons Rope Co. v. Case Shingle & Lumber Co. (1929) 152 Wash. 37, 276 Pac. 892;

Bagnall v. Frank Fehr Brewing Co. (1920) 203 Mo. App. 635, 221 S. W. 793; Sharlette v. Lake Placid Co. (1921) 194 App. Div. 844, 185 N. Y. S. 543; Miller v. Economy Hog & Cattle Powder Co. (1940) 228 Iowa 626, 293 N. W. 4; Boehm v. Friedman (1941) 190 Miss. 664, 1 So.2d 508; Distillers Distributing Corp. v. Sherwood (1950) 180 F.2d 800.

governed by the same rules which apply to other agencies.[51]

No formal authorization is ordinarily necessary but the attorney's authority may be shown by the same kind of evidence which would suffice in other cases. It may, for example, be inferred from conduct, and a subsequent ratification may cure the lack of precedent authorization.[52]

Moreover, when a duly admitted attorney appears for a party in a cause the law presumes that his appearance was authorized,[53] and while this presumption is not conclusive,[54] it will suffice until some showing is made to the contrary, and then the attorney may be required to produce his authority. Of course, a court may require an attorney to show the authority for his appearance on its own motion,[55] and a purported client can demand such proof in the proceeding.[56] On appeal or in a subsequent attack on the judgment, even the client has the burden of overcoming the presumption.[57] The opposing party always has the burden of showing lack of authority of the attorney.[58]

Proceedings taken in reliance upon such an appearance are, by some courts, also presumed to be valid, and only to be impeached upon a direct attack.[59] If the principal is injured by the application of this rule to proceedings really unauthorized,

[51] Clinton v. Miller (1951) — Mont. —, 226 P.2d 487.

[52] Hot Springs Coal Co. v. Miller (1939) 107 F.2d 677; Felker v. Johnson (1940) 189 Ga. 797, 7 S.E.2d 668; Donner v. Honstead (1940) 61 Idaho 669, 106 P.2d 677.

[53] Bowles v. American Brewery Inc. (1945) 146 F.2d 842; Moe v. Zitek (1947) 75 N. D. 222, 27 N.W.2d 10.

[54] Wilson v. Barry (1951) 102 Cal.App.2d 778, 228 P.2d 331.

[55] Miller v. Continental Assurance Co. (1910) 233 Mo. 91, 134 S. W. 1003.

[56] Felker v. Johnson (1940) 189 Ga. 797, 7 S.E.2d 668.

[57] Cummins v. Chandler (1939)

186 Okla. 200, 97 P.2d 765; Jackson v. Jackson (1945) 199 Ga. 716, 35 S.E.2d 258.

[58] Paradise v. Vogtlandische Maschinen-Fabrik (1938) 99 F.2d 53; Kahn v. Brunswick-Balke-Collender (Mo. App., 1941) 156 S.W.2d 40; Mullins v. LaBahn (1943) 244 Wis. 76, 11 N.W.2d 519. Compare Mitchell v. McDonald (1943) 114 Mont. 292, 136 P.2d 536. In York Harbor Village Corp. v. Libby (1928) 126 Me. 537, 140 Atl. 382, it was held that the point could not be raised by demurrer.

[59] Hirsch Bros. & Co. v. Kennington Co. (1929) 155 Miss. 242, 124 So. 344.

it is said that he has a remedy against the attorney. Other courts permit a showing to be made, even in collateral proceedings, that there was no authority.[60]

§ 77. —— Broadly speaking, an attorney has authority "to do all acts in or out of court necessary or incidental to the prosecution or management of the suit, and which affect the remedy only, and not the cause of action." [61] It is impossible, however, by any general statement to indicate the line between the acts which such an agent may and may not do. He may make admissions of fact; [62] he may adopt any mode of prosecuting the case which the law provides, as, for example, he may submit the case to arbitration,[63] or stipulate that a reference be had; [64] he may stipulate that the judgment shall be the same as in another pending action; [65] he may waive the right to appeal; [66] he may dismiss or continue the action; or release an attachment before judgment.[67] On the other hand, he may not release the cause of action [68] or release property of defendant from the lien of a judgment or execution, except in conformity to statutory provision.[69] It is well established that he may not compromise the claim.[70] Yet there is a

---

[60] The cases are collected in Ann., 88 A. L. R. 12.

[61] Hale v. Wheeler (1928) 264 Mass. 592, 163 N. E. 178; Noska v. Mills (Tex. Civ. App., 1940) 141 S.W.2d 429.

[62] Harris v. Diamond Const. Co. (1946) 184 Va. 711, 36 S.E.2d 573; Housing Authority of City of Bridgeport v. Pezenik (1951) 137 Conn. 442, 78 A.2d 546; Ann., 97 A. L. R. 374.

[63] Maroulas v. State Industrial Accident Commission (1926) 117 Ore. 406, 244 Pac. 317.

[64] Hale v. Wheeler (1928) 264 Mass. 592, 163 N. E. 178.

[65] Laird v. Dixie Motor Coach Corp. (Tex. Civ. App., 1938) 122 S.W.2d 244.

[66] Bernstein & Loubet v. Minkin (1937) 118 N. J. L. 203, 191 Atl. 733; Fowlkes v. Ingraham (1947) 81 Cal.App.2d 745, 185 P.2d 379.

[67] American Rattan & Reed Mfg. Co. v. Handel-Maatschappij Moraux & Co. (1920) 194 App. Div. 90, 185 N. Y. S. 480.

[68] See Jacob v. City of New York (1941) 119 F.2d 800, rev'd on other grounds (1942) 315 U. S. 752, 62 S. Ct. 854, 86 L. Ed. 1166.

[69] See Starling v. W. Erie Ave. Building & Loan Ass'n (1939) 333 Pa. 124, 3 A.2d 387.

[70] Ricketts v. Pennsylvania R. Co. (1946) 153 F.2d 757; Ann., 66 A. L. R. 107.

marked split in the cases on the question whether he may confess judgment against his client.[71] Those cases holding that he may are plainly inconsistent with the authority on compromises.

6. *Authority to Delegate*

§ 78. In general. It is ordinarily said that an agent has no authority to delegate, i. e., to turn over to another (known as a subagent) his authority to represent the principal. *Delegatus non potest delegare.* The reason is fairly obvious: the risks of agency are substantial and a person has a right not to be represented, save at his own election and by an agent of his own choice.[72]

On the other hand it is often useful or even necessary for the agent to be able to use an assistant or to delegate some or all of his authority to others. Nothing prevents the principal from authorizing them, expressly or in some other way.

As a practical matter, then, two questions arise about delegation: (a) what are the consequences of an authorized delegation, and (b) what less than express authorization will sanction delegation.

§ 79. Consequences of authorized delegation. A distinction needs to be taken here. It is not infrequent to find it one of the functions of an agent to employ other agents

[71] Midtown Chains Hotel Co. v. Merriman (1948) 204 Ga. 71, 48 S.E.2d 831; Renken v. Sidebotham (1950) — Mo. —, 227 S.W.2d 99; Bielby v. Allender (1951) 330 Mich. 12, 46 N.W.2d 445 (attorney has implied power to confess judgment or enter consent decree); Addressograph-Multigraph Corp. v. Cooper (1945) 60 F. Supp. 697, speaks of a presumption of authority to enter consent decree. Holding that the attorney has no implied authority: Galbraith v. Monarch Gold Dredging Co. (1938) 160 Ore. 282, 84 P.2d 1110; Early v. Burns (1940) 142 S.W.2d 260; Town of Bath v. Norman (1946) 226 N. C. 502, 39 S.E.2d 363.

[72] In Washington Trust Co. v. Bishop (1951) — R. I. —, 80 A.2d 185, where an attorney left to his secretary the making of the affidavit required by statute s a prerequisite to the issuance of an attachment, the court said: "The relation [of attorney and client] thus created is one of the utmost trust and personal confidence. Where an agency of such character

for his principal. Thus the local manager of a plant or store normally hires and fires the personnel. This does *not* involve delegation; those so hired are not subagents but simply new or additional agents of the principal, differing from others only in the manner of their appointment. It is not to be supposed, e. g., that the appointing agent is bound by their contracts: they are not his agents.

By delegation is meant that the agent is permitted to use agents of his own in performing the function he is employed to perform for his principal, delegating to them the discretion which normally he would be expected to exercise personally. These agents are known as subagents to indicate that they are the agent's agents and not the agents of the principal. Normally (though of course not necessarily) they are paid by the agent.[73] The agent is liable to the principal for any injury done him by the misbehavior of the agent's subagents.[74]

§ 80. —— Finally (and most important) the principal is bound by acts done by the subagent within the authority properly delegated to him.[75] This is not because the subagent is his agent; it is rather that he is bound by the act of his own agent who, in this instance, is (properly) doing the act through the subagent. This distinction is rather a subtle one and since in this connection it has no practical consequences,

exists, requiring as it does the exercise of special knowledge, judgment and discretion, it is generally held that the agent may not delegate the performance of his duties in the matter without express authority from the principal unless such authority is necessarily implied for the proper execution of the agency. This rule, which is so fundamental as to require no citation of authorities, does not apply if the delegated act is ministerial only. The facts in the record before us bring the case within the general rule and not the exception."

See also Lynn v. Burgoyne (Ky., 1852) 13 B. Mon. 400; Montgomery Ward & Co. v. Arbogast (1938) 53 Wyo. 275, 81 P.2d 885; Hackney v. Fairbanks, Morse & Co. (Mo. App., 1940) 143 S.W.2d 457.

[73] Bradford Co. v. Hill's Son & Co. (1922) 1 W. W. Harr. (Del.) 546, 116 Atl. 353. And cf. Gulf Refining Co. v. Brown (1938) 93 F.2d 870, 116 A. L. R. 449.

[74] See Klein v. May Stern & Co. (1941) 144 Pa. Super. 470, 19 A.2d 566.

[75] See McKinnon v. Vollmar (1889) 75 Wis. 82, 43 N. W. 800.

it is not surprising that courts often overlook it and treat (new) agents and subagents as if they were the same. The distinction exists, however, and may be of practical importance as in the case already mentioned of the agent's liability to the principal for the misconduct of the subagent.[76]

§ 81. **When delegation is permitted.** Aside from instances of express authority to delegate, the cases allowing delegation fall mostly into two groups: (1) where the acts to be done by the delegate are purely "ministerial" and (2) where the nature of the job makes it a natural assumption that the agent was expected to delegate.

§ 82. **(1) Ministerial acts.** The rule allowing the delegation of ministerial acts is scarcely more than the obverse of the rule prohibiting delegation in general. It is the skill and discretion of the agent that the principal is entitled to; if this has been exercised, it is immaterial who performs the necessary mechanical acts needed to implement the agent's decision. If the agent dictates the letter it cannot matter to the principal who types it. If the agent decides to give a deed, and supervises its preparation, it is immaterial who hands it to the grantee. The agent may even delegate to a subordinate the signing of the instrument, if he has properly decided that the instrument should be executed and what it should contain.[77] It is such mechanical acts, involving no exercise of judgment or skill, that the agent may properly delegate.[78]

§ 83. **(2) Delegation a necessary or natural incident.** If the work to be done is such that it could not be handled by one person, the assumption is inevitable that the agent was expected to employ helpers. So where a fire insurance agent

[76] See Restatement, § 5, and other sections therein cited.

[77] Kadota Fig Ass'n v. Case-Swayne (1946) 73 Cal.App.2d 815, 167 P.2d 523.

[78] See Rohrbough v. United States Express Co. (1901) 50 W. Va. 148, 40 S. E. 398; Mercantile Trust Co. v. Paulding Stave Co. (Mo. App., 1919) 210 S. W. 438; Empire Gas & Fuel Co. v. Allen (1923) 294 Fed. 617; Wright v. Providence Washington Ins. Co. (1930) 130 Kan. 438, 286 Pac. 237;

was put in charge of a territory including several populous counties, it was held that he must have been intended to use helpers because of the amount of work involved.[79]

Again, if the owner of property employs a broker to "find a buyer" for it, may the broker use his own employees, or even other brokers, on the job? Here the cases are not in complete agreement. Some have said that since discretion is involved there may be no delegation without express authorization.[80] Other, and it is believed better, cases have allowed the delegation.[81] In the latter cases it has been common to speak of the function of finding a buyer as "ministerial" but it is believed that the better explanation is that suggested in this section, namely, that under current real estate usages it is so common and so normal for the broker to have a staff or to utilize the services of other brokers that it is taken for granted that the owner expects and sanctions this unless he specifies to the contrary. Under this view the helper is a typical subagent. He has no claim against the owner; the broker collects his full fee from the owner and the rights of the sub-agent are strictly a matter of agreement between him and the broker.[82]

Federal Deposit Ins. Corp. v. Beakley (1940) 124 N. J. L. 445, 12 A.2d 700.

[79] Insurance Co. of North America v. Thornton (1001) 130 Ala. 222, 30 So. 614. And see Altermatt v. Rocky Mountain Fire Ins. Co. (1929) 85 Mont. 419, 279 Pac. 243.

[80] See Doggett v. Greene (1912) 254 Ill. 134, 98 N. E. 219; Brutinel v. Nygren (1916) 17 Ariz. 491, 154 Pac. 1042; Young v. Crumbie (1927) 5 N. J. Misc. 1051, 139 Atl. 326, aff'd memorandum decision (1928) 104 N. J. L. 669, 141 Atl. 922.

[81] Shannon v. Cobboll (1017) 67 Pa. Super. 538; Cotter v. Maguire (1929) 269 Mass. 468, 169 N. E. 433; Philbrick v. Chase (1948) 95 N. H. 82, 52 A.2d 317, 3 A.L.R.2d 526.

[82] See cases cited in preceding note.

CHAPTER V

PRINCIPAL AND AGENT: APPARENT AUTHORITY AND AGENCY POWERS

§ 84. **Rationale of apparent authority.** The basic idea underlying the concept of apparent authority is one readily grasped, yet there has been some difference of opinion as to the proper technical terminology to be employed in rationalizing the subject. Clearly one who allows another to appear to be his agent must bear any loss resulting to a third party from his dealings with the apparent agent in that capacity in reliance on his supposed authority. But, precisely how is the apparent principal's liability to be explained, and under precisely what circumstances is it to be enforced?

1. *Estoppel or Objective Contract?*

§ 85. **The estoppel theory.** It has been most common to say that the (apparent) principal is estopped to deny the authority of the (apparent) agent. Thus, in Reynell v. Lewis [1] Pollock, C. B., said ". . . agency may be created by the immediate act of the party, that is, by really giving the authority to the agent, or representing to him that he is to have it, or by constituting that relation to which the law attaches agency; or it may be created by the representation of the defendant to the plaintiff, that the party making the contract is the agent of the defendant, or that such relation

---

[1] (1846) 15 M. & W. 517, cited by the late Walter Wheeler Cook, in his article "Agency by Estoppel," 5 Col. L. Rev. 35, 38, the leading article urging the proposition that apparent authority is *not* based on estoppel. He also quotes language similar to that employed by Pollock, C. B., from the opinion of Lord Cranworth in Pole v. Leask (1863) 33 L. J. N. S., c. 155. These citations appear rather odd considering that Mr. Cook, as of 1905, was expressing the idea that the view of Pollock, C. B., and Lord Cranworth was a "new" one "which seems to be gaining acceptance."

exists as to constitute him such; and if the plaintiff really makes the contract on the faith of the defendant's representation, the defendant is bound; he is estopped from disputing the truth of it with respect to that contract; and the representation of an authority is, quoad hoc, precisely the same as a real authority given by the defendant to the supposed agent." The last clause should be noted carefully; to Pollock, C. B., the result of apparent authority is precisely the same as that of real authority.

§ 86. **Criticism of this theory.** It has lately been fashionable to criticize the view that apparent authority is based on estoppel. Two objections are made. First, if T has done nothing more than make a contract in reliance on the supposed agent's authority, there has been no change of position and hence no estoppel. Second, granting the existence of an estoppel, there is no real contract between P and T. P is estopped to deny its existence—but if P were attempting to enforce the contract against T (as distinguished from the common case where T is seeking enforcement against P), T, having done nothing to mislead P, would not be estopped from asserting A's lack of real authority (there would be no estoppel against him), the supposed contract would not be enforceable against him, and so there would be no real contract.

§ 87. —— These difficulties, it will have been observed, did not occur to Pollock, C. B., nor does it seem that they are substantial. The law of Estoppel is not like that of the Medes and Persians; it is a concept of equity and capable, like other equitable concepts, of adaptation to the particular problem. The proposition that a person who has dealt with an apparent agent, who has negotiated the terms of a contract and seen them put in final form, and who has, in reliance on the supposed contract, dismissed from his mind the possibility of making such a contract with someone else—the proposition that in such a case there has been a sufficient change of position to warrant holding the guilty party estopped to deny the validity of the contract does not seem to the present writer in the least unreasonable: nor does it seem conclusive that

55

there might not be thought to be a change of position for other purposes.[2] Why should not the law of Agency for its own purposes establish its own definitions of what is a change of position?[3]

§ 88. —— Again, where one party has unmistakably bound himself by his personal manifestations, and the other one is estopped to deny that he has bound himself, is there any necessary reason for denying that a "real" contract has been formed? Or, if it be thought that the concept of estoppel traditionally is unilateral and binds one rather than both, is it important that T is not bound? Cases are hard to find in which this has made any practical difference. In most instances P can rectify his original inability to enforce by ratifying; he cannot, by the prevailing American view,[4] only in the unlikely case where T discovers A's lack of authority and withdraws before P ratifies. If the law of ratification sets this limit to a person's ability to enforce a contract he did not authorize, there seems no very cogent reason for extending the limit in case of a person who has carelessly or intentionally misrepresented his agent's authority.

§ 89. **The objective contract theory.** Mr. Cook[5] and others[6] insist that where the agent is apparently authorized he has power to make a "real" contract to which his principal is one party. This is under, or by analogy to, the objective contract theory. The principal is bound, says Mr. Cook,[7] "be-

---

[2] E. g., to make one a bona fide purchaser. See Ringo v. McFarland (1930) 232 Ky. 622, 24 S.W.2d 265.

[3] Reo Motor Car Co. of Texas v. Barnes (Tex. Civ. App., 1928) 9 S.W.2d 374, noted in 42 Harv. L. Rev. 570, is the only case the writer has encountered in which the fact that T had contracted but had not paid or otherwise "changed his position" is used as a basis

(though, in the instant case, not the only one) for denying recovery. Quaere, does the sparsity of authority indicate that the problem seldom arises or, conceivably, that the issue is not raised?

[4] See post, § 251.

[5] See n. 1, ante.

[6] See references to Powell and Seavey, post.

[7] Op. cit., n. 1, ante, at p. 38.

cause according to all sound principles he has entered into a contract with the third party." Further, he says:[8] "If the principal has said to the third party 'This man is authorized to manifest my intention to you,' and then the agent makes an offer within this apparent authority, has not the principal on all sound principles manifested to the third party his intent to contract?"

This is plausible enough. It is certainly at least a permissible explanation of the factors involved. It does not, however, appear inevitable or quite to warrant the assumption that all other explanations of apparent authority are unsound. Much less can one agree with Mr. Powell when he says that the "theories of these two views are fundamentally different."[9] It seems quite plain, on the contrary, that they are simply superficially different expressions of the same idea.

That idea may be thus expressed: While contractual dealings are normally based on the intent of the parties—otherwise law would make no sense—yet as a matter of what is practical (and fair to the intent of the other party) the intent of a transacting party must be judged by what he says or does and not by what is hidden in his mind; if, innocently or otherwise, he has said something other than what he really intends, any resultant hardship should be on him. This idea is fundamental in our law; presumably it is fundamental in any law that purports to maintain some rapport with justice. It is unfortunate

---

[8] Ibid., at p. 43.

[9] Tiffany on Agency (2d Ed. by Powell) p. 39. Cf. Seavey, who adopts the objective contract approach but remarks that "doubtless the basis for liability is much the same as in estoppel." The Rationale of Agency, 29 Yale L. J. 859, 873, Studies in Agency (1949) 83. In his essay on Agency Powers, 1 Okla. L. Rev. 1, 6, Studies in Agency (1949) 181, 184, he says: "Estoppel is fundamentally a tort theory, based upon a misrepresentation of facts by one person to another which creates a situation in which it is desirable to prevent harm to the other by requiring the first to make good his words. It would follow, therefore, that if apparent authority is based upon this theory there is no contract between the principal and the person with whom the agent deals unless the agent is authorized, and the principal is bound if, but only if, the other has changed his position."

that it should take different and technical names in differing contexts—estoppel and objective contract—thus tending to obscure the singleness of the proposition really involved.

§ 90. The distinction relatively unimportant. To the present writer it seems unfortunate that so much time has been spent and so much heat generated over scarcely more than a difference in terminology. Few practical consequences will result from the choice of one formula rather than the other. If a preference must be expressed, the present writer tends to favor the language of estoppel. It appears that the exponents of the objective contract theory have over-simplified the matter.

After all, it is one thing for a man to say, in person, "I agree to buy your horse and pay you $500 for him," and another for him to say "My principal agrees to buy your horse, etc." Nothing is gained by pretending that the two situations are factually identical. And it would seem to be immaterial in the latter case whether the principal is bound because the agent has real authority or apparent authority; either way, it is still different from the contract made by the party in person.

To talk objective contract is to ignore this distinction; to talk estoppel is to acknowledge it and to talk the language of agency. And as a practical matter many situations, hard to force on to a Procrustean bed of objective contract, present no difficulty when treated as problems of agency. It is hard to see how you can make a "real contract" in the sense used by Mr. Cook, with a person of whose very existence you are unaware; it is not at all hard, as will be seen, to understand why the law of Agency treats such a person for many purposes as if he had made a real contract. Similar difficulties might be met in the field of ratification, and elsewhere. Our problems, it seems, are everywhere simplified and made more realistic if we everywhere keep in mind that we are engaged in examining and delimiting the bases for holding that a person has become bound, not directly and immediately, but vicariously.

Without further attempt to solve this vexed problem, we proceed to discuss typical situations involving apparent authority as well as some involving a closely-related concept, now commonly known as an agency power.

2. *Types of Apparent Authority*

§ 91.   Where the apparent agent has no real authority. Cases are relatively rare where the apparent agent is in fact not P's agent at all; nevertheless, they exist. Thus, in an Ohio case,[10] it appears that defendant ran a hotel in Cleveland—obviously a small and unpretentious place—and that on plaintiff's arrival, late at night, a man in the lobby "who appeared to be in charge" went behind the counter, registered plaintiff, and took jewels and cash from plaintiff to be put in the safe, giving him a receipt therefor, signed in defendant's name. In the morning it was discovered that the man "who appeared to be in charge" had not put the valuables in the safe but had decamped with them. Defendant claimed that the man was not her agent, and had no authority to receive valuables on her behalf and that, accordingly, she was not responsible. The court, however, held that defendant "by her voluntary act, or by her negligence, had placed someone in a position where it would appear to anyone coming in to become a guest at the hotel that he was properly in charge, and that therefore she had made herself by her conduct responsible for his acts." The agency, the court said further, "is created by estoppel."

A similar result was reached in a Missouri case [11] where an imposter in defendant's transfer office received plaintiff's trunk check, which was never heard of again.[12]

---

[10] Kanelles v. Locke (1919) 12 Ohio App. 210.

[11] Miltenberger v. Hulett (1915) 188 Mo. App. 273, 175 S. W. 111.

[12] And see Reifsnyder v. Dougherty (1930) 301 Pa. 328, 152 Atl. 98, noted in 6 Notre Dame Law. 387; Diuguid v. Bethel Church (1935) 119 Pa. Super. 493, 180 Atl. 737, noted in 34 Mich. L. Rev. 404; Sells Lumber Co. v. Carr Lumber Co. (1935) 179 S. C. 407, 184 S. E. 674; Manuel v. Calistoga Vineyard Co. (1936) 17 Cal.App.2d 377, 61 P.2d 1204; Edgecombe Bonded Warehouse Co. v. Security

§ 92.   Permitted exercise of power by a real agent.   In some instances apparent authority is based on the principal's allowing, to T's knowledge, the exercise of some power by an agent which the agent does not "really" possess. A rather extreme instance is afforded by a North Carolina case [13] where plaintiff was hired as a painter "for all the fall and part of the winter" by the chief engineer of defendant hotel, who had no actual hiring authority and was apparently not in the habit of hiring, but had in two prior instances hired plaintiff for short periods by the express authority of the manager. In reversing a nonsuit the Supreme Court held that a jury could find that the engineer had "apparent authority" to hire plaintiff.

§ 93.   The normal powers of a familiar position.   In many instances it is held that where P puts A into a position where certain powers are normally expected to be exercised, P will be bound by the exercise of those powers even if the one in question has been specifically withheld. Thus where a country club hired one to act as steward and it was customary in the community for country club stewards to buy food on the club's credit, the club was held liable for supplies furnished the steward on the club's credit, although between the club and the steward it was understood that the steward should

Nat. Bank (1939) 216 N. C. 246, 4 S.E.2d 863; Luken v. Buckeye Parking Corp. (1945) 77 Ohio App. 451, 68 N.E.2d 217; Ford v. S. Kann Sons Co. (D. C. Mun. App., 1950) 76 A.2d 358; Will Doctor Meat Co. v. Hotel Kingsway (1950) — Mo. App. —, 232 S.W.2d 821; Smith v. Wood (1950) 100 Cal.App.2d 96, 223 P.2d 103.

[13] Colyer v. Vanderbilt Hotel Co. (1939) 216 N. C. 228, 4 S.E.2d 436. Cf. White Co. v. Citizens' Bank & Trust Co. (1930) 110 Conn. 635, 149 Atl. 133; Northwestern Mutual Life Ins. Co. v. Steckel (1933) 216 Iowa 1189, 250 N. W. 476; Hansche v. A. J. Conroy, Inc.

(1936) 222 Wis. 553, 269 N. W. 309; Shuell v. London Amusement Co. (1941) 123 F.2d 302; Fidelity & Casualty Co. of N. Y. v. First Nat. Bank of Fargo (1941) 71 N. D. 415, 1 N.W.2d 401.

As to other aspects of authority to "hire and fire" see Standard Oil Co. v. Nickerson (1931) 103 Fla. 701, 138 So. 55; Herfurth v. Horine (1936) 266 Ky. 19, 98 S.W.2d 21; Alfred J. Silberstein, Inc. v. Nash (1937) 298 Mass. 170, 10 N.E.2d 65; Desrochers v. Brady (1938) 299 Mass. 269, 12 N.E.2d 861; Sater v. Cities Service Oil Co. (1940) 235 Wis. 32, 291 N. W. 355; Lynch v. R. D. Baker Const. Co. (1941)

pay for the supplies and make his remuneration in the form of the profit made (if any) on serving meals.[14] And so in a Pennsylvania case where the local manager of an auto finance corporation made an arrangement with a buyer in arrears whereby the company retook the car but agreed to return it later, on full payment, it was held that the local manager had at least apparent authority to make such an arrangement.[15] "One may gauge the agent's authority by tasks at which the principal has set him." [16] But of course there are limits to the apparent authority even of a general manager. Thus the manager of a bulk oil station who was supposed to deal only in supplies furnished by his principal, had no apparent authority to borrow oil from a neighboring dealer when he ran short.[17]

§ 94. **The appearance must come from the principal.** It is important to keep in mind that this doctrine rests on an appearance created by the principal. Agents are often ingenious and successful in creating an appearance of authority by their own acts and statements but such an appearance does not create apparent authority.[18] Thus in an Oklahoma case,[19] after the

297 Mich. 1, 296 N. W. 858; Lochner v. Silver Sales Service (1950) 232 N. C. 70, 59 S.E.2d 218.

[14] Heckel v. Cranford Golf Club (1922) 97 N. J. L. 538, 117 Atl. 607.

[15] Bush v. Atlas Automobile Finance Corp. (1937) 129 Pa. Super. 459, 195 Atl. 757. And see Western Union Telegraph Co. v. Heathcote (1907) 149 Ala. 623, 43 So. 117; Braniff v. McPherren (1936) 177 Okla. 292, 58 P.2d 871; Mulhern v. Public Auto Parks Inc. (1938) 296 Ill. App. 238, 16 N.E.2d 157, noted in 28 Ill. B. J. 90; Southern Packing Corp. v. Crumpler (1940) 175 Va. 431, 9 S.E.2d 446; Kesselman v. Goldstein (1947) 148 Neb. 452, 27 N.W.2d 692.

[16] Shahan-Taylor Co. v. Foremost Dairies (Tex. Civ. App., 1950) 233 S.W.2d 885, 890.

[17] Cue Oil Co. v. Fornea Oil Co. (1950) 208 Miss. 810, 45 So.2d 597. And see Brenard Mfg. Co. v. Sketchley Store (1919) 185 Iowa 694, 171 N. W. 18; Anheuser-Busch, Inc. v. Grovier-Starr Produce Co. (1942) 128 F.2d 146; In re Union City Milk Co. (1951) 329 Mich. 506, 46 N.W.2d 361.

[18] See Wilson v. Beardsley (1886) 20 Neb. 449, 30 N. W. 529; Burton v. Brown (1935) 219 Wis. 520, 263 N. W. 573; Dohrmann Hotel Supply Co. v. Beau Brummel, Inc. (1940) 99 Utah 188, 103 P.2d 650; In re Estate of Thornwall (1943) 233 Iowa 626, 10 N.W.2d 35; Fischer Co. v. Morrison (1951) — Conn. —, 78 A.2d 242.

[19] Home Owners' Loan Corp. v. Thornburgh (1940) 187 Okla. 699, 106 P.2d 511.

foreclosure of an H. O. L. C. mortgage, the mortgagor relied on an agreement made with an H. O. L. C. field agent by which, on certain consideration, the deficiency judgment was to be released. The mortgagor knew that ordinarily the agent had no authority to make such an agreement but that authority could be secured from regional officials; however, the agent informed him that he had called the regional office and secured the authority for this occasion. This was untrue and the court held there was no apparent authority.

This is undoubtedly a hardship on the third party and it can be fairly said that the principal made possible, or at least facilitated, the fraud by setting up the wrongdoer as its agent and sending him out to deal with mortgagors. However, the same thing could be said with varying degrees of force in all situations in which the agent is guilty of misconduct, and to regard it as a basis for liability in general would destroy the practice (and in consequence the law) of Agency since no one could risk having an agent on such terms. It remains basic to the law of Agency that the third party takes the risk of being fooled by the unauthorized misrepresentations of the agent and that the principal is only liable where he has either authorized the representations or done something from which reasonable people would draw the inference that he had authorized them.[20]

In the case just stated the court also points out an obvious limitation on the operation of apparent authority. It is not the appearance which is the basis of P's liability, but the fact that T is fooled thereby; therefore, if T knows that the agent is in fact not authorized, he cannot rely on the appearance to the contrary.[21] So, in the case stated, any argument that the

[20] As to the fraud of the agent committed within the real or apparent scope of his authority, see post, Chapter VI.

[21] See Columbia Outfitting Co. v. Freeman (1950) 36 Cal.2d 216, 223 P.2d 21; Fischer Co. v. Morrison (1951) — Conn. —, 78 A.2d 242.

The converse proposition should be noted, viz., that if A is in fact authorized, he binds P even though T suspects or is convinced that A is not authorized. Stanfill v. Bell (1940) 44 N. M. 576, 106 P.2d 540.

H. O. L. C. by sending out an agent to handle mortgages had created apparent authority to release deficiency judgments would be idle in the face of T's knowledge that there was no such authority in fact.

§ 95. **Representations, testimony and declarations.** It has just been stated that the agent cannot create authority by his own representations of authority (unless they are authorized by the principal, in which case they have the same effect as if the principal had made them in person). Two somewhat different propositions must be distinguished.

In the first place testimony by the agent as to the nature and extent of his authority is obviously and necessarily admissible. Along with the principal's own testimony it would ordinarily be the best possible evidence. Accordingly, subject to the ordinary rules of evidence, such testimony is freely admissible [22] (though the cases often suggest that principal and agent did not in fact testify).

In the second place, declarations of the agent (i. e., testimony by others of his statements outside of court) as to his authority are normally not admissible. These, if they could be treated as statements made by the principal, would normally be admissible as admissions. However, they cannot be treated as statements of the principal unless it can be shown by other and competent evidence that the agent was authorized to make them, which seldom happens.[23] To be distinguished is the question whether declarations of an admitted agent are admis-

[22] Shama v. United States (1938) 94 F.2d 1; Stern v. DeKelbaum (1943) 153 Pa. Super. 452, 34 A.2d 272; Gesmundo v. Bush (1947) 133 Conn. 607, 53 A.2d 392; Boone v. Hall (1950) 100 Cal.App.2d 738, 224 P.2d 881.

[23] See cases cited in preceding note and also Deater v. Penn Machine Co. (1933) 311 Pa. 291, 166 Atl. 846; LeBron Electrical Works v. Livingston (1936) 130 Neb. 733, 266 N. W. 589; Smith v. Pleasant (1940) 200 Ark. 1190, 139 S.W.2d 377; Sullivan v. Associated Dealers (1940) 4 Wash.2d 352, 103 P.2d 489; Brownell v. Tide Water Associated Oil Co. (1941) 121 F.2d 239; Bell v. Washam (1950) 82 Ga. App. 63, 60 S.E.2d 408; Mueller v. Seaboard Commercial Corp. (1950) 5 N. J. 28, 73 A.2d 905. And see annotation, 3 A.L.R.2d 598; Restatement, § 285.

sible, not to show authority but as bearing on the facts (e. g., the negligence of the servant) of the event in question.[24]

3. *The Problem of "Instructions"*

§ 96. Instructions, secret and otherwise. The matter of "instructions" is one of the most puzzling and troublesome to be found in the whole field of authority. In the famous case of Hatch v. Taylor [25] it is said that there is "a distinction between the authority given to an agent, which he is not only bound to pursue, in duty to his principal, but a deviation from which will render his act void . . . , and the instructions or directions which he may receive from his principal, relative to the manner in which he is to execute authority, which are matters between the principal and agent, so that a disregard of them, by the latter, although it may make him liable to the principal, will not vitiate the act, if it be done within the scope of the authority itself."

Unless the court is dealing with purely legal conclusions, i. e., is talking of power rather than authority, this assumes that there may be an act which, though done in violation of the principal's instructions, is still within the scope of the authority.

§ 97. —— Section 160 of the Restatement says that a "principal authorizing an agent to make a contract, but imposing on him limitations as to incidental terms intended not to be revealed" is liable on a contract made in violation of such limitations, if T doesn't know of them. Section 161 makes the principal of a *general* agent liable for normal incidents of an authorized contract, though the particular incidents have been forbidden. The latter section, it would seem, simply makes the doctrine of Sec. 160 applicable to a general agent, even though the limitations were not ones "intended not to be revealed."

---

[24] This is properly a topic of the law of Evidence, particularly as it relates to *res gestae* and the like, and too extensive to be treated here. See, however, Notes, 43 Harv. L. Rev. 936; 60 Harv. L. Rev. 976; 47 Col. L. Rev. 1227; 36 Geo. L. J. 648.

[25] (1840) 10 N. H. 538.

And a comment to the latter section states that it may apply in cases where there is no apparent authority.

These statements challenge inquiry. Are they true? Why are they true? Where do they apply?

It seems possible to assert certain propositions:

§ 98. Instructions do limit authority.

Except as to instructions or limitations meant to be merely suggestions and not to be mandatory—and obviously the court and the Restatement are not talking of such—it seems to be impossible to say that an act can be in violation of instructions and still within the scope of the authority. P says to A: "I authorize you to sell my horse. Do not, however, sell it for less than $250 or to any milk dealer." A proceeds to sell the horse for $200, or for $250 to a milk dealer. Plainly such a sale is not within the scope of the authority. Plainly the only proper way of defining the authority for this purpose is to say that it is the sum total of all the mandates meant to be binding: "I authorize you to sell my horse to anyone but a milk dealer for not less than $250." To make any other interpretation is to give an arbitrary and disproportionate importance to generalizations and to ignore details which taken together may indicate the real substance of the authority. It is like the stupid dogma still sometimes to be found in will construction cases to the effect that you can't cut down a fee.

Clearly then the language quoted from Hatch v. Taylor (and typical of the language of many cases) cannot mean precisely what it says. It must mean that for some reason or reasons, not stated or implicit in the quotation, the courts will hold a principal bound if the act is within the general scope of the authority although it is not within the authority in some particular regard. Or, to state it otherwise, a sale by A to a milk dealer, or for $200, may be within A's power but not within his authority.

§ 99. Secret instructions.

Where the instructions are secret ones, "intended not to be revealed" as put in the Restatement,[26]

---

[26] Restatement, § 160.

somewhat plausible reasons can be suggested why they should
not be binding on a third party ignorant of their existence.
It can be said that the case is one involving a limitation inconsistent with the authority apparently given A. "Thus if P
tells A to represent to buyers that he is P's horse-selling agent
and instructs him not to warrant, as is the custom, but also
not to disclose this want of authority, A creates in himself
a power to warrant by following the instructions. This is true
whether A is a 'general' or a 'special' agent, since the power
is created not by the agreement between P and A as to A's
authority, but by the authorized statement that he is a horse-
selling agent." [27]

In this view the case is the same as that already discussed,
i. e., that of a person having the normal powers of a familiar
position, the only difference being that in the latter case the
appearance is created by the act of P in installing A in a
position whose normal incidents are well known whereas here
it is created by the representations of A, representations, however, which P has authorized him to make.

The instance given, however, does not seem altogether a
happy one. Why should P withhold from A a normal power
and at the same time bid him not disclose the withholding?
It seems an abnormal and unrealistic hypothesis. A little more
satisfactory is the common instance given (and used as an
illustration in Restatement, § 160) of the agent authorized
to sell for not less than a specified price but forbidden to
disclose the specified minimum. If the A says: "$500 is the
least I can sell for," he will not, it is thought, be likely to get
more than $500. The instance we are concerned with is that
where A sells for less than $500; in such a case *he* will not
have disclosed the limit. We must assume that T gets in touch
with P and asks: "What is the minimum price at which A may
sell?" and that P answers: "I won't tell." We are then able
to say that since P wishes T to buy and at the same time refuses
to disclose the minimum price, he cannot equitably complain

[27] Seavey, The Rationale of
Agency, 29 Yale L. J. 859, 875,
Studies in Agency (1949) 85.

if A sells at any *reasonable* price. Quaere, however, if these assumptions are really any too realistic.

§ 100. **Rationale.** Perhaps the best explanation of the confusing language and law dealing with "instructions" (secret and otherwise) is that courts feel that one who is taking advantage of the benefits offered by agency should pay therefor by being bound where the agent has made no more than a minor deviation from the general scope of his authority. In other words, courts are applying to the law of principal and agent the same approach that, as will be seen,[28] is conventionally applied to master and servant, namely that the master is bound where the servant, while engaged in the master's business, makes a minor deviation from the strict course of employment.

§ 101. **Edison's case.** The classic exposition of this point of view is to be found in the opinion of Learned Hand, J., in the case of Kidd v. Thomas A. Edison, Inc.[29] There the Edison Company proposed to demonstrate the merits of their phonograph records by hiring singers to give concerts at which, one surmises, records of the same performance were to be played. The business was entrusted to one Fuller and he was authorized to hire singers only where some dealer or dealers would agree to pay for the demonstration. He hired the plaintiff to sing, the agreement embodying no such limitation. The court held plaintiff entitled to recover. It was said that the case could be rested on apparent authority, based on estoppel. It is doubtful, however, if apparent authority in the ordinary sense could be found, or if the court was talking in that sense. No details are given as to how Fuller proceeded in making contracts, but there is nothing to show that defendant put him in a position where he "appeared" to be anything. (As distinguished, e. g., from the drug clerk whom P puts behind a counter in his drug store, where he "appears" to be an ordinary drug store clerk, having the authority of any other drug

[28] Post, Chapter XIII, passim.
[29] (1917) 239 Fed. 405.

clerk.) The case certainly permits, and perhaps suggests, the inference that Fuller went to Miss Kidd or her agent, said: "I'm representing the Edison Company" and proceeded to sign her up. If so it is difficult to talk estoppel. Fuller created his own appearance; he was not authorized to appear as one who could hire plaintiff without limit, but just as one who could hire her subject to a very peculiar and important condition. Judge Hand quite explicitly recognizes this. "It is only a fiction to say that the principal is estopped, when he has not communicated with the third party and thus misled him."

§ 102. —— The true basis for liability Judge Hand states as follows:

"The responsibility of a master for his servant's act is not at bottom a matter of consent to the express act, or of an estoppel to deny that consent, but it is a survival from ideas of status, and the imputed responsibility congenial to earlier times, preserved now from motives of policy. While we have substituted for the archaic status a test based on consent, i. e., the general scope of the business, within that sphere the master is held by principles quite independent of his actual consent, and indeed in the face of his own instructions. . . . Hence, even in contract, there are many cases, in which the principle of estoppel is a factitious effort to impose the rationale of a later time upon archaic ideas, which, it is true, owe their survival to convenience, but to a very different from the putative convenience attributed to them.

"However it may be of contracts, all color of plausibility falls away in the case of torts, where indeed the doctrine first arose, and where it still thrives. It makes no difference that the agent may be disregarding his principal's directions, secret or otherwise, so long as he continues in that larger field measured by the general scope of the business entrusted to his care. . . .

"If a man select another to act for him with some discretion, he has by that fact vouched to some extent for his reliability. While it may not be fair to impose upon him the results of a total departure from the general subject of his confidence, the detailed execution of the mandate stands on a different footing. The very purpose of delegated authority is to avoid constant recourse by third parties to the principal, which would be a corollary of denying the agent any latitude beyond his exact instructions. Once a third person has assured himself widely of the character of the agent's mandate, the very purpose of the relation demands the possibility of the principal's being bound through the agent's minor deviations."

§ 103. —— Query, was this a *minor* deviation? Query also whether the defendant would subscribe to the concluding statement of the opinion:

"It would certainly have been quite contrary to the expectations of the defendant, if any of the prospective performers at the recitals had insisted upon verifying directly with [D] the terms of her contract. It was precisely to delegate such negotiations to a competent substitute that they chose Fuller at all."

§ 104. —— It will be noted that Hand, J., does not state whether he regarded the agency as a general or a special one. It would seem that in his analysis the distinction would be of little significance. And in spite of its adoption by the Restatement it is doubtful that the distinction will be fruitful in decided cases. Most cases will be susceptible of treatment as instances of apparent authority. Where not, the liability of the principal, if imposed, will doubtless be on the broad basis suggested by Judge Hand.[30]

---

[30] In the leading case of Butler v. Maples (1869) 9 Wall. 766, 19 L. Ed. 822, Mr. Justice Strong said: "Looking to the agreement between Bridge & Co. and Shepherd, it cannot be doubted that it created a general agency. It was a delegation of authority to buy cotton in Desha County and its vicinity, to buy generally, from whomsoever the agent, not his principals, might determine. It had in view not merely a single transaction, or a number of specified transactions, which were in the mind of the principals when the agent was appointed, but a class of purchases, a department of business. It is true that it contained guards and restrictions which were intended as regulations between the parties, but they were secret instructions

4. *Agency Powers*

§ 105. **Where only the agent knows whether his act is within his known authority.** There are a number of situations where the authority of the agent is well known or readily ascertainable but where only the agent himself may know whether what he is doing is in fact within that authority. Thus it is well known that the freight agent of a railroad has authority to issue bills of lading for goods received for shipment— and *only* for goods so received. Suppose, however, that the agent issues a bill of lading on a carload of grain not in fact received. No one but the agent would normally be in a position to know whether or not the bill represented a real or a fictitious carload of grain. If a prudent person, proposing to advance money on the strength of the bill, were to call higher officials

---

rather than limitations. They were not intended to be communicated to the parties with whom the agent should deal, and they never were communicated. It was, therefore, not error to instruct the jury as the court did, that the agency was a general one, and that the defendants were bound by the contract, if Shepherd held himself out as authorized to buy cotton, and if the plaintiff had no knowledge of the instructions respecting the mode in which the agent was required to act.

"It may be remarked here that the reasons urged by the plaintiffs in error in support of their denial of liability for the engagements made by Shepherd are that he agreed to pay forty cents per pound for the plaintiff's cotton; that he bought the cotton where it lay instead of requiring delivery on board a steamboat, or within the protection of a gunboat; and that he did not obtain a permit from the government to make the purchase. The argument is that in the first two particulars he transcended his powers, and that his authority to buy at all was conditioned upon his obtaining a permit from the government. All this, however, is immaterial, if it was within the scope of his authority that he acted. The mode of buying, the price agreed to be paid, and the antecedent qualifications required of him, were matters between him and his principals. They are not matters in regard to which one dealing with him was bound to inquire."

Cf. Harrigan v. Dodge (1914) 216 Mass. 461, 103 N. E. 919; Butler v. Marsh (1919) 66 Colo. 45, 178 Pac. 569; Mitchell v. Canadian Realty Co. (1922) 121 Me. 512, 118 Atl. 373.

of the road and ask if the bill were genuine, they could only refer him to the agent.

Again, if a local manager is authorized to buy goods on credit only up to a certain amount and a potential seller, knowing this, were to attempt to find out whether the limit had been reached, in most instances recourse to the manager would be inevitable, since such other possible alternatives as an audit of the books would be too slow for the needs of commerce.

§ 106. —— Again, let us assume (though no doubt this is not necessarily true) that an act externally within the course of authority may not be so if done by the agent not for the principal's benefit but for his own. Then let us suppose that an agent authorized to write guarantee policies writes one, but with the secret motive of supporting the credit of a doubtful concern in which he is interested rather than with the motive of doing a desirable piece of business for his principal. If we assume that such an act is unauthorized in fact, it is certainly not within the agent's apparent authority, since no one would suppose he was authorized to write policies in such a case. Again, however, it is unlikely that either P or T could promptly or readily ascertain the motive with which A is writing the policy; A is the only readily available source of information and A, naturally, is not telling.

§ 107. **No apparent authority involved.** It must be kept in mind in all these cases that there is no apparent authority. A does not appear to be authorized to issue bills of lading without grain behind them, to buy on credit in excess of the known limit, or to write insurance for his own benefit and to his principal's detriment. There is what might be called "apparent conformity." A hasty view could suggest that the difference is immaterial. On the contrary, the difference is fundamental and vital. In the case of apparent authority the principal is held for misrepresentations he is responsible for, a false appearance which he has intentionally or carelessly created. In the cases at hand, the principal has made no

71

misrepresentation—the authority itself is unquestioned—and the misrepresentation—as to the conformity of the act to the authority—is solely that of the agent. Whether he says: "I have called up my principal and he has authorized me to do this," or "The grain is received" (A's authority to issue bills of lading on grain received being unquestioned), there is simply a lie told by the agent, for which the principal is in no way responsible.

§ 108. **Should the principal be held?** Nevertheless, in each of these cases our instinct is likely to suggest that the principal should be held. The situation is too harshly loaded against the third party. As in the case of "secret" instructions he is expected to deal with the agent for the principal's benefit—but wholly at his own risk. Going to the principal and verifying the authority (something which third parties seldom do but which we always tell them they should have, when they have relied to their detriment on the representation of the agent as to what he is authorized to do or what he has done) will do the third party no good here; he is helpless.

§ 109. **The authorities.** In the first and third of these cases, the law today agrees with our instinct. In the bill of lading cases, in which the principal's nonliability was once authoritatively stated, both in England [31] and America,[32] his liability is now clearly established, at least in America, both by statute and decision.[33] The English law appears uncertain.[34]

[31] Grant v. Norway (1851) 10 C. B. 665.

[32] Baltimore & Ohio Ry. v. Wilkens (1876) 44 Md. 11; Friedlander v. Texas & P. R. Co. (1888) 130 U. S. 416, 9 S. Ct. 570, 32 L. Ed. 991; National Bank of Commerce v. Chicago, B. & N. R. (1890) 44 Minn. 224.

[33] Gleason v. Seaboard Air Line Ry. Co. (1929) 278 U. S. 349, 49 S. Ct. 161, 73 L. Ed. 415, noted in 29 Col. L. Rev. 531, 27 Mich. L. Rev. 697, 13 Minn. L. Rev. 626, 77 U. Pa. L. Rev. 689, and 38 Yale L. J. The federal statute is set forth in this case and it has sometimes been thought that the decision was based on the statute; in fact, the statute did not cover the precise situation.

Cf. Fargo Nat. Bank v. Agricultural Ins. Co. (1950) 184 F.2d 676.

[34] See Kleinwort Sons & Co. v.

In the case of the agent externally acting within his authority, but with an improper motive, a leading English case [35] establishes the principal's liability and while American authority is scarce, it would seem to favor the same view.[36]

§ 110. —— Only one clear-cut case is known to the writer involving the situation where the agent, authorized to buy goods only to a certain amount, and having already bought that amount, induces further credit by misrepresenting to T the amount already bought. This is the famous Massachusetts case of Mussey v. Beecher.[37] It was held that the principal was not bound. It was urged that on such a view no one could safely deal with the agent, but to Shaw, C. J., it seemed an adequate answer to say that no one had to deal with the agent; if one chose to do so, it was at his peril. One judge dissented cogently. It appears at least doubtful that the case would be followed today.[38]

§ 111. Rationale of the cases: The agency power. It remains to be asked how these cases are to be explained, since the agent concededly has neither real nor apparent authority. Perhaps the simplest answer is to say that the fairness (both as a matter of abstract equity and of business convenience) of holding the principal is so obvious that the law must find a way of doing it, whether or not it involves going beyond established agency concepts. In Restatement, § 140, it is said that P is bound where A was authorized, was apparently authorized or "had a power arising from the agency relationship and not depending upon authority or apparent authority." It is accordingly now common to say that P is bound in cases

Associated Automatic Machines Corp. (H. L. 1934) 151 L. T. 1, 39 Com. Cas. 189, noted in 13 Can. B. Rev. 116, 50 L. Q. Rev. 456, and 174 L. T. 484.

[35] Hambro v. Burnand [1904] 2 K. B. 10, noted in 17 Harv. L. Rev. 56, and discussed by Montrose, 50 L. Q. Rev. 224, 228.

[36] See North River Bank v. Aymar (1842) 3 Hill (N. Y.) 262; Hellmann v. Potter (1856) 6 Cal. 13; Macklin v. Macklin (1944) 315 Mass. 451, 53 N.E.2d 86.

[37] (1849) 3 Cush. 511.

[38] See Restatement, § 171.

of the sort we have been discussing because A had an "Agency Power." [39]

Other instances where this concept—or perhaps it is only a phrase—may usefully be employed have been seen and will be seen again. Thus the cases where the approach of Judge Hand in Edison's Case [40] is employed and P is held despite a breach of "instructions," although there is no real or apparent authority, may conveniently be so categorized.[41] And the doctrine of Watteau v. Fenwick, to be discussed later,[42] where we encounter that extraordinary anomaly, the apparent authority of the agent of an undisclosed principal, can be accurately labelled (if not explained) in the same fashion. And, as will quickly be seen, the cases to be discussed in the following sections need some such rationalization.

5. *The Power of a Person Having Possession or Indicia of Ownership*

§ 112. **The agent's power to deal with property in his possession.** A considerable number of cases deal with the unauthorized disposition by one accurately or roughly describable as an agent of property which he has in his possession, and in connection with which he has some authority—but not the authority he purports to exercise. Thus a factor, or other agent in possession, may pledge the goods for his own debt. Or an agent, authorized to find a buyer or to sell the property on certain conditions, may sell it without compliance with the specified terms or conditions. Or, very commonly today, a dealer holding merchandise on chattel mortgage or trust receipt, may sell it without first securing a release of the lien.

§ 113. —— These cases are difficult to analyze because of the complexity of the considerations on which they rest. While

---

[39] The classic discussion is to be found in Seavey, Agency Powers, 1 Okla. L. Rev. 3, Studies in Agency (1949) 181. The present writer's obligation to this article is obvious.

[40] Ante, n. 29.

[41] See the discussion by Mr. Seavey in the essay cited in n. 9, supra.

[42] Post, § 174.

not infrequently spoken of as involving apparent authority
they cannot very accurately be put into that category; where
the principal is bound it is probably because the agent has
a power in the sense discussed in the preceding section. There
is undoubtedly an appearance and it is undoubtedly an important factor. On the other hand the power does not arise from
the appearance as (so it is conventionally assumed) in the
case of apparent authority. And the appearance itself is likely
to be ambiguous; it may be an appearance of ownership, an
appearance of authority, or one susceptible of either interpretation. Furthermore, the extent of the inference to be drawn
from appearance varies with the context; it is more likely that
a car left with a car dealer will be thought to be for sale than
one left with a car repairer.

In addition to these difficulties arising from the appearance
modern cases are likely to be complicated by the technical
nature of the agent's interest, as where he is holding under
a chattel mortgage, a bailment lease, or a trust receipt.

§ 114. **Possession alone gives no power.** It is clear that
a bailee, as such, has no power to dispose of the chattel.[43]
(This is what is fatal to the apparent authority theory.) No
doubt a dangerous and misleading appearance is created by
every bailment. One in possession of a dollar bill, a watch,
a horse or an automobile, will naturally seem to be the owner
of it. If there is nothing to put a third party on guard the
bailee's statement that he *is* the owner is quite likely to carry
conviction, to the resulting detriment of the third party. This,
too, the bailor could readily foresee.

In such a case it can only be said that the result must be
reached by a balancing of interests. The interest of a property
owner in the right to use the property freely—which naturally
includes the right to bail it for his own or the bailee's benefit—
must be weighed and compared with the interest of the third

---

[43] See Cadwallader v. Shaw
(1928) 127 Me. 172, 142 Atl. 580,
noted in 27 Mich. L. Rev. 223;
McCabe v. Williams (Del., 1944)
45 A.2d 503. Cf. American Exchange Nat. Bank v. Winder (1929)
198 N. C. 18, 150 S. E. 489, noted
in 43 Harv. L. Rev. 1309.

party in not being deceived and thereby led to change his position. Normally the law values more highly the interest of the property owner in being able to use the property freely; it is only in rare cases such as that of the dollar bill that the contrary appraisal is made.

One way of stating the problem under discussion would be to say that that question is: What factors in addition to possession are sufficient to outweigh the owner's interest in the free use of his property?

§ 115. **Indicia of title.** Where possession is coupled with "indicia of title" a power to dispose is likely to result. A common instance is illustrated by the famous case of McNeil v. The Tenth National Bank [44] where the owner of a stock certificate endorsed it in blank and gave it to his broker to secure an advance; the broker pledged it to defendant to secure his own debt. It was held that defendant was protected. The court, after saying that the delivery of possession of a chattel plainly gave no power of disposal, proceeded: "But if the owner intrust to another, not merely the possession of the property, but also written evidence, over his own signature, of title thereto, and of an unconditional power of disposition over it, the case is vastly different. There can be no occasion for the delivery of such documents, unless it be intended that they shall be used, either at the pleasure of the depositary or under contingencies to arise. If the conditions under which this apparent right of control is to be exercised are not expressed upon the face of the instrument, but remain in confidence between the owner and the depositary, the case cannot be distinguished in principle from that of an agent who receives secret instructions qualifying or restricting an apparently absolute power."

§ 116. —— The same doctrine has been applied where an agent was allowed to take a bill of sale of personal property

[44] (1871) 46 N. Y. 325. See also   Co. (1929) 206 Cal. 334, 274 Pac.
Powers v. Pacific Diesel Engine   512, 73 A. L. R. 1398.

in the agent's name,[45] where the principal had stored hemp
put on the wharfinger's books in the agent's name,[46] where
the principal taking in a used car in trade had the seller
endorse the statutory "title" in blank and turned the latter
over to defendant's agent,[47] and where an employer in the
business of renting wagons had his servant's name painted on
one of them and turned it over to the servant who promptly
sold it to an innocent purchaser.[48]

§ 117. **Chattel turned over to a dealer in such chattels
with some power of disposition.** The most common and
troublesome case in this category is that where property—
typically an automobile in the modern instances—is turned
over to a dealer, for the purposes of its eventual sale, yet
with substantial limitations on the authority of the dealer.

Where the authority was simply to find a buyer, the earlier
cases mostly agreed that a sale by the agent would not pass
title. Thus, in a leading New York case plaintiff entrusted
a salesman with diamonds, taking a written receipt stating
that the diamonds were "on approval, to show to my customers." It was shown that in the trade this was understood
not to confer an authority to sell but simply one to find a
buyer. It was held that the salesman's sale passed no title
to a good-faith buyer. The court cited McNeil v. The Tenth
National Bank, supra, and added: "But mere possession has
never been held to confer a power to sell."[49]

[45] Nixon v. Brown (1876) 57
N. H. 34. And see J. L. McClure
Motor Co. v. McClain (1949) 34
Ala. App. 614, 42 So.2d 266.

[46] Pickering v. Busk (1812) 15
East. 38.

[47] Commercial Finance Corp. v.
Burke (1944) 173 Ore. 341, 145
P.2d 473. See also Rice Street Mo-
tors v. Smith (1950) 167 Pa. Super.
159, 74 A.2d 535; Kelley Kar Co. v.
Finkler (1951) 155 Ohio St. 541,
99 N.E.2d 665; Moss v. John A.
McCrane Motors (1951) 15 N. J.

Super. 461, 83 A.2d 542; Parker v.
First Citizens' Bank & Trust Co.
(1948) 229 N. C. 527, 50 S.E.2d
304; cf. Erwin v. Southwestern
Investment Co. (1948) 147 Tex. 260,
215 S.W.2d 330. And see Note, 42
Col. L. Rev. 154.

[48] O'Conner v. Clark (1895) 170
Pa. 318, 32 Atl. 1029.

[49] Smith v. Clews (1889) 114
N. Y. 190, 21 N. E. 190. Cf. Nelson
v. Wolf (1950) 4 N. J. 76, 71 A.2d
630.

The same court applied this in 1927 to the sale of a car by a dealer to a good-faith buyer;[50] plaintiff claimed under a chattel mortgage which provided that the mortgagee-dealer should not sell or do anything more than exhibit the car without a release from plaintiff. The court relied in part on a leading English case[51] in which again there was only authority to show, and where Wills, J., remarked "that if the plaintiff had given general authority to the jeweler to sell, any limitation imposed as to the terms on which, or the manner in which, the sale should be conducted, would have been unavailing, but that here v. .s no such case since the jeweler was not to sell the table top at all until further authority was given."

§ 118. —— This distinction was adopted by the Restatement, promulgated in 1933. Section 175 provides in substance that if a special agent is given possession of a chattel, with authority to deal with it in a particular way, the principal is bound by an [unauthorized] transaction of the same kind as that authorized, if within the usual course of business, but not by a kind different from that authorized.

This section was presumably approved in 1947 by Mr. Seavey when he reported to the Law Institute that no amendments to the Agency Restatement were necessary,[52] but in an article published in 1948[53] he remarks that the rules stated in this section "are probably too narrow in view of present trends."

§ 119. —— The impact of the automobile on the law of Agency had already begun to produce these trends at least as early as 1922. In Carter v. Rowley,[54] a California case decided in that year, it appeared that plaintiff had left his car with a used car dealer, authorizing him only to find a buyer;

---

[50] Utica Trust & Deposit Co. v. Decker (1927) 244 N. Y. 340, 155 N. E. 665, noted in 27 Col. L. Rev. 334.

[51] Biggs v. Evans [1894] 1 Q. B. 88.

[52] Restatement of the Law, 1948 Supplement, ix.

[53] Seavey, Agency Powers, 1 Okla. L. Rev. 3, 18, Studies in Agency (1949) 181, 199.

[54] (1922) 59 Cal. App. 486, 211 Pac. 267. Cf. Reed v. Linscott (1934) 87 N. H. 139, 175 Atl. 240; Berger v. Noble (1950) 81 Ga. App. 34, 57 S.E.2d 844.

a good-faith purchaser, however, was protected. "Whatever may have been the private arrangement between plaintiff and McNabb [the dealer], whatever the latter's *actual* authority may have been, plaintiff by his own voluntary act clothed McNabb with such *indicia* of authority to sell the car as usually accompanies such authority according to the custom of trade and the general understanding of businessmen."

§ 120. **The modern trend.** As suggested by Mr. Seavey, *ubi supra*, the modern trend is definitely in the direction of protecting the good-faith buyer.[55] Typically the competition is between the buyer and the finance company which has advanced to the dealer the money with which he has bought the car from the manufacturer; the finance company will have retained some kind of security interest in the car by way of chattel mortgage, trust receipt or the like.

This element of personnel is far from unimportant. The finance companies are the real enterprisers as far as the merchandising of cars is concerned. Theirs is the substantial investment and a generous share of the profit. It seems fair to put the risk on them, since they are so well able both to bear and to spread it. Otherwise the innocent purchaser, usually quite ignorant of the financing practices involved, must look to the dealer who, almost ex hypothesi, is worthless.

§ 121.   —— The courts are doubtless not unaware of these considerations; the cases, however, in terms, are likely to turn on an idea of estoppel. Thus in a case where it was established that plaintiff finance company "expected to have the dealer sell the car in the ordinary retail way and pay the mortgage

[55] See Moore v. Ellison (1927) 82 Colo. 478, 261 Pac. 461; Oleson v. Albers (1936) 130 Neb. 823, 266 N. W. 632, 105 A. L. R. 714, noted in 50 Harv. L. Rev. 126 and 16 Neb. L. Bull. 196 (with which cf. Seigal v. Wanick (Tex. Civ. App., 1948) 214 S.W.2d 883); Handy v. C. I. T. Corp. (1935) 291 Mass. 157, 197 N. E. 64, 101 A. L. R 447; Boice v. Finance & Guaranty Co. (1920) 127 Va. 563, 102 S. E. 591, 10 A. L. R. 654; Fogle v. General Credit, Inc. (1941) 122 F.2d 45, 136 A. L. R. 814; Daas v. Contract Purchase Corp. (1947) 318 Mich. 348, 28 N.W.2d 226. And see extensive note, 43 Mich. L. Rev. 605.

from the sale price; that this was the way many similar transactions had been had by the mortgagor and mortgagee for several months, covering a period of time both before and after the transaction in question; and that no objection was made by plaintiff to this course of dealing until it discovered that the dealer was bankrupt, and could not pay its obligations," it was said:

"No tags or marks were placed upon the cars to warn or notify prospective purchasers that the cars were mortgaged, the mortgagee relying solely upon its mortgage and the constructive notice with which it claimed innocent buyers were charged, if the dealer failed to account for the money received from the sales.

"By the contract and by the course of conduct of the mortgagor and mortgagee, the mortgagor was allowed to hold itself out to the public as a retail dealer in automobiles, with the· right to sell the mortgaged cars without let or hindrance; and now to permit the mortgagee to assert its mortgage against the defendant, an innocent purchaser for value and without notice, would be, under the circumstances of this case, a fraud upon such innocent party, and would permit the one who made the fraud possible to take advantage of its own wrong." [56]

§ 122. **Mortgagees and other dealers.** That these cases are largely motivated by desire to protect ordinary purchasers, not likely to seek legal advice before buying a car nor, without it, to know anything of "floor plans" or security practices, is shown by the unwillingness of courts to protect a mortgagee from the dealer or another dealer who buys from the financed dealer.[57]

[56] Hostetler v. National Acceptance Co. (1930) 36 Ohio App. 141, 172 N. E. 851.

[57] As to mortgagees, cf. Bauer v. Commercial Credit Co. (1931) 163 Wash. 210, 300 P. 1049, noted in 45 Harv. L. Rev. 375, with National Guarantee & Finance Co. v. Pfaff Motor Co. (1931) 124 Ohio 34, 176 N. E. 678, noted in 27 Ill. L. Rev. 57, and Tropical State Bank v. Sunshine Motor Co. (1939) 137 Fla. 703, 188 So. 595. And see Nash Miami Motors v. Bandel (1948) 160 Fla. 925, 37 So.2d 366.

As to dealers, see Colonial Finance Co. v. McCrate (1938) 60 Ohio App. 68, 19 N.E.2d 527. Cf.

§ 123. Statutes. The problem under discussion may be affected by a number of typical statutes, in particular factors' acts, the Uniform Conditional Sales Act, and the Uniform Trust Receipts Act. The Uniform Sales Act also contains a relevant provision [58] but it seems to do no more than summarize agency problems. Consideration of space forbids dealing with these statutes at length here; only their moot salient features can be summarized.

§ 124. Factors' acts. A number of states [59] have so-called "factors' acts." These began to be passed in the early years of the last century, based on comparable English legislation. The New York act, which is fairly typical, provides in substance: ". . . every such factor [60] or agent not having the documentary evidence of title, who shall be intrusted with the possession of any merchandise for the purpose of sale . . . shall be deemed to be the true owner thereof, so far as to give validity to any contract made by such agent with any other person for the sale or disposition . . . of such merchandise . . . [or] for any money advanced . . . by such other person on the faith thereof." [61]

These acts were passed primarily to change the common-law rule that a factor could not pledge for his own debt.[62] Some of the acts, e. g., Pennsylvania,[63] cover only such a transaction,

Associates Discount Corp. v. Fay Co. (1941) 307 Mass. 577, 30 N.E.2d 876, 132 A. L. R. 519.

[58] Section 23 (1) provides: " . . . where goods are sold by a person who is not the owner thereof, and who does not sell them under the authority or with the consent of the owner, the buyer acquires no better title to the goods than the seller had, unless the owner of the goods is by his conduct precluded from denying the seller's authority to sell."

[59] Williston, Sales (Rev. Ed. 1948) § 320, lists California, Maine, Maryland, Massachusetts, Montana, New York, North Dakota, Ohio, Pennsylvania, Rhode Island and Tennessee as having factors' acts.

[60] For various definitions of "factor" see McCarley v. Foster-Milburn Co. (1950) 93 F. Supp. 421.

[61] New York Personal Property Law, § 43.

[62] Paterson v. Tash (1742) 2 Strange 1178.

[63] Purdon's Penna. Stats. Ann., Title 6, §§ 201, 202. It may be suggestive that the annotations to these sections contain no case decided since 1883.

and it appears that it has likewise been the most common subject of litigation. In New York, e. g., many of the not very numerous cases that have arisen under the act deal with the pawning of jewelry entrusted to salesmen.[64] On the whole it appears that this legislation has not been, and is not, of very great significance in the field under discussion.[65]

§ 125. The Uniform Conditional Sales Act. Section 9 of the Uniform Conditional Sales Act, adopted in a dozen states, provides that "When goods are delivered under a conditional sale contract and the seller expressly or impliedly consents that the buyer may resell them prior to performance of the condition, the reservation of property shall be void against purchasers from the buyer for value in the ordinary course of business, and as to them the buyer shall be deemed the owner of the goods, even though the contract or a copy thereof shall be filed according to the provisions of this act."

Of this section the Commissioners' Note says: "Where the same seller attempts to reserve the property in himself and at the same time to allow a resale by a retailer in the ordinary course of business, he is doing two inconsistent things. A purchaser from a retailer in the ordinary course of business ought not to be obliged to examine the records to determine whether retailer has title or whether title has been reserved under a conditional sale contract. That the goods have been put into the retailer's stock with the consent of the wholesaler is conclusive evidence that they are there for sale and that the retailer has the title or the right to convey."

[64] See Freudenheim v. Gutter (1911) 201 N. Y. 94, 94 N. E. 640; Thompson v. Goldstone (1916) 171 App. Div. 666, 157 N. Y. S. 621; Green v. Wachs (1930) 254 N. Y. 437, 173 N. E. 575, noted in 44 Harv. L. Rev. 865, 15 Minn. L. Rev. 837 and 5 Tulane L. Rev. 670; Nelkin v. Provident Loan Society (1934) 265 N. Y. 393, 193 N. E. 245, noted in 5 Brooklyn L. Rev. 80 and 9 St. John's L. Rev. 390; Sweet & Co. v. Provident Loan Society (1939) 279 N. Y. 540, 18 N.E.2d 847, noted in 16 N. Y. U. L. Q. Rev. 162 and 496, and 13 St. John's L. Rev. 381; Zendman v. Harry Winston (1949) 196 Misc. 924, 94 N.Y.S.2d 878.

[65] See Cleveland Knitting Mills Co. v. Shaff (1914) 160 App. Div. 107, 145 N. Y. S. 109; International Trust Co. v. Webster Nat. Bank (1926) 258 Mass. 17, 154 N. E.

The act has been construed in conformity with these views.[66]

§ 126. **The Uniform Trust Receipts Act.** The financing of merchandise, particularly automobiles, through the use of a somewhat anomalous form of document known as a "trust receipt" has become very common in late years. To standardize this practice the Uniform Trust Receipts Act was promulgated in 1933 and has now been adopted in more than twenty-five states. Under Sec. 9 of this act where the trustee [i. e., retailer] has "liberty of sale" (sic) or where the "entruster" (e. g., finance company) consents to the placing of the goods in the retailer's stock of trade or allows their being put on exhibition in his salesroom, a buyer in the ordinary course of trade takes free of the entruster's security interest.[67]

330, 49 A. L. R. 267; Osgood Bradley Car Co. v. Standard Steel Motor Car Co. (1927) 259 Mass. 302, 156 N. E. 446. On factors' acts generally, see Williston, Sales (Rev. Ed. 1948) §§ 318–323.

[66] See Finance Corporation of New Jersey v. Jones (1922) 98 N. J. L. 165, 119 Atl. 171; Dransfield v. Boone-Armstrong Motor Co. (1926) 102 W. Va. 370, 135 S. E. 286; First Nat. Bank of Binghamton v. Hermann (1949) 275 App. Div. 415, 90 N.Y.S.2d 249.

[67] On trust receipts and the uniform act see Williston, Sales (Rev. Ed. 1948) §§ 338a–338c.

CHAPTER VI

PRINCIPAL AND AGENT: THE AGENT'S MISREPRESENTATIONS

§ 127. **General considerations.** The question of the consequences to the principal of misrepresentations made by his agent is a rather complicated and difficult one; this is so for a number of reasons. The law dealing with the liability of a person for his own representations is a complicated one and it is not made simpler by adding an agent to the picture. Misrepresentation savors of tort and one would normally expect the matter to be governed by the doctrines developed with reference to a master's liability for the torts of his servant;[1] in fact the law is written largely in terms of principal and agent and scope of authority. Finally, in some instances, the law of misrepresentation tends to merge almost insensibly into another difficult matter, that of ratification.

1. *History of the Doctrine*

§ 128. **The early view.** Until 1867 it was the common-law view that a principal was not liable in tort for his agent's misrepresentation unless the misrepresentation (as distinguished from the transaction in the course of which it was committed) was authorized or ratified. This view seems to have been based at least in part on the mistaken notion that the principal could not be held unless he personally were in some way at fault. Thus in the leading case of Udell v. Atherton,[2] Bramwell, B., said: "When it is considered that to

---

[1] This point of view has been urged. See Vance, Liability for the Unauthorized Torts of Agents, 4 Mich. L. Rev. 199; Ferson, Agency to Make Representations, 2 Vand. L. Rev. 1; cf. Horack, Vicarious Liability for Fraud and Deceit in Iowa, 16 Iowa L. Rev. 361.

[2] (1861) 7 H. & N. 172.

84

support this declaration the plaintiff must prove actual moral
fraud, . . . it seems manifest, according to common sense
and plain English, that the plaintiff must fail; for it is admitted that no such fraud has been committed by the defendant
himself, nor authorized by him either by previous authority
or by any ratification or adoption of it when he knew of it."
(A similar idea occasionally crops up in modern times, e. g.,
in the cases reluctant to hold a corporation for the slander of
a servant, apparently on the idea that a corporation is incapable of malice.)

§ 129. **The current view.** In 1867 the matter was put on
a sound footing by the celebrated case of Barwick v. English
Joint Stock Bank [3] where the defendant's manager, seeking
to collect a bad debt, induced the plaintiff, by misrepresentations, to make further advances to the debtor. The bank was
held liable, the court saying that a master's liability for an
agent's fraud should stand on the same footing as his liability
for any other tort and that he should be liable for every such
wrong "committed in the course of the service and for the
master's benefit."

This view (though usually not its use of Master and Servant
terminology) has found general acceptance. See, for example,
Restatement, § 257, where it is said: "A principal is subject
to liability for loss caused to another by the other's reliance
upon a deceitful representation of an agent if the representation is: (a) authorized; (b) apparently authorized; or (c)
within the power of the agent to make for the principal within
the rules stated in §§ 160–162 and 194–196."

§ 130. **Minority jurisdictions.** In a few jurisdictions—not-
ably New Jersey [4] and Pennsylvania [5]—the older view persists.[6]

[3] L. R. 2 Ex. 259.
[4] See Sewell v. Metropolitan Life
Ins. Co. (1937) 118 N. J. L. 308,
192 Atl. 575; Mesce v. Automobile
Ass'n of New Jersey (1950) 8 N.
J. Super. 130, 73 A.2d 586; note,
3 U. of Newark L. Rev. 75.

[5] See Littler v. Dunbar (1950)
365 Pa. 277, 74 A.2d 650.
[6] See also Janeczko v. Manheim-
er (1935) 77 F.2d 205; Lawrence
v. Wise (1937) 27 Ala. App. 597,
177 So. 175.

It should be kept in mind that this simply limits the principal's liability to a tort action; in those states as elsewhere the injured third party has a right to rescind, as discussed below.

2. *The Principal's Liability Where the Agent Had Power or Authority to Make the Representation*

§ 131. Where not "for the master's benefit." In the Barwick case [7] it. was stated to be essential to the principal's liability that the wrong be committed "for the master's benefit." This was a natural consequence of stating the matter in terms of a master's liability for the torts of his servants. It quickly becomes apparent, however, that the real analogy is to the principal's responsibility for the transactions of his agent. The misrepresentations are usually made in connection with a contract; the harm arises, as in any other case where the principal's liability is in question, from reliance on statements made by an agent in the course of (really or ostensibly) doing his principal's business. It is both difficult and unrealistic to distinguish between the agent's authority to make representations inducing a contract and his authority to make the contract itself.

Once it is conceded that the case is determined by contractual principles, the liability of the principal is apparent. The situation is closely analogous to that of Hambro v. Burnand, discussed in a prior section [8] where the agent doing an act externally within his authority is in fact acting for his own benefit. It is curious that when the liability of the principal was at last authoritatively determined in England,[9] as lately as 1912, only one of the judges relied on the Hambro case; the majority of the opinions are devoted to the attempt to establish that Willes, J., could not have meant what he said in the Barwick case.

---

[7] Ante, n. 3.
[8] See § 106, ante.
[9] Lloyd v. Grace, Smith & Co. [1912] A. C. 716, noted in 47 Am. L. Rev. 600, 26 Harv. L. Rev. 449, 24 Jurid. Rev. 323, and 133 L. T. 472. And see Uxbridge Permanent Bldg. Society v. Pickard [1939] 1 K. B. 266, noted in 55 L. Q. Rev. 174.

§ 132. **Same: The American authorities.** A number of recent American cases and the Restatement [10] accept the proposition that P may be liable, though A was not acting for his benefit. Thus in a leading California decision the manager of a bank which held a mortgage on a ranch owned by plaintiff, a widow inexperienced in business affairs, induced her to sell the property at a grossly inadequate price by fraudulent representations that the sale was necessary and that if the sale was not made the bank would foreclose the mortgage. The manager acted in collaboration with the purchaser and received $2500 from him for perpetrating the fraud. The bank was held liable. The court saying that the manager's position "conferred upon him potential power which he could and did use in a coercive manner in accomplishing a wrongful act under color of the office which he occupied. The result would be the same whether he kept the money for his personal use or turned it over to the bank provided the plaintiff was damaged by the fraudulent act of the bank's officer." [11]

§ 133. —— In a considerable group of cases P's clerk or delivery man deliberately overcharges customers, putting in his pocket the excess over the proper price for which he must account to P. Here again P is usually held liable.[12] It is in such cases, perhaps, that the Master and Servant analogy is superficially most persuasive but at the same time most misleading since it is questionable if a master would often be held liable for the servant's wilful tort, committed solely for his own benefit, though while serving the master.[13]

---

10 Restatement, § 262.

11 Rutherford v. Rideout Bank (1938) 11 Cal.2d 479, 89 P.2d 978, 117 A. L. R. 383. And see National City Bank v. Carter (1929) 31 F.2d 25, noted in 5 N. C. L. Rev. 349; Standard Surety & Casualty Co. v. Plantsville Nat. Bank (1946) 158 F.2d 422; Viner & Miller v. Phillips, Canby & Fuller (1949) 82 F. Supp. 692.

12 See Ripon Knitting Works v. Railway Express Agency (1932) 207 Wis. 452, 240 N. W. 840, noted in 16 Marq. L. Rev. 274 and 30 Mich. L. Rev. 1333; Grigsby v. Hagler (1938) 25 Cal.App.2d 714, 78 P.2d 444; Yoars v. New Orleans Linen Supply Co. (La. App., 1939) 185 So. 525; Gartin's Grocery v. Lucas County Co-operative Creamery Ass'n (1941) 231 Iowa 204, 1 N.W.2d 194.

13 See post, § 367.

§ 134. **The bill of lading cases.** Attention should be called
to a group of interesting cases, already discussed,[14] namely
those involving a ship master or freight agent who issues
a bill of lading for goods in fact not received, with a
view to using it, personally or through a confederate, to raise
money on. These cases have been dealt with herein as illustrat-
ing the "agency power" concept, that is, of holding a principal liable in certain cases, as a matter of policy, though the
agent had neither. real nor apparent authority. It is considered most useful·so to analyze them. It is apparent, however,
that they can readily be used as instances of the proposition
just stated, namely, that the principal may be responsible for
the fraud of the agent, committed externally in the scope of
his authority though in fact for his own benefit.[15]

§ 135. **The agent's fraud in collecting insurance.** Many fire
insurance policies contain a provision voiding the policy in
case the insured attempts to defraud the company before or
after a loss. If the insured's agent obtains the policy in the first
instance by false representations, there can be no doubt that
the policy is avoided, though the insured is personally innocent.[16] If, after loss, the insured's agent (not uncommonly a
spouse) makes misrepresentations as to the extent of the loss
in attempting to collect from the company, the case is more
difficult. The innocent insured (if limited to the true loss) is
not attempting to profit by the agent's fraud but simply to
prevent the forfeiture of his otherwise meritorious claim. The
case is no harder, however, than those mentioned above in

[14] See ante, § 105.

[15] For other cases, involving
agents in a position somewhat
analogous to that of the station
agent, see Havens v. Bank of Tar-
boro (1903) 132 N. C. 214, 43 S. E.
639; Williams v. Commercial Casualty Ins. Co. (1931) 159 S. C. 301,
156 S. E. 871; Wise v. Western
Union Telegraph Co. (1934) 6 Harr.
(Del.) 155, 172 Atl. 757, noted in
14 B. U. L. Rev. 767; Defiance
Lumber Co. v. Bank of California
(1935) 180 Wash. 533, 41 P.2d 135,
noted in 10 Wash. L. Rev. 209;
Conaway v. New York Life Ins.
Co. (1937) 171 Tenn. 290, 102
S.W.2d 66.

[16] Freedman v. Providence Washington Ins. Co. (1897) 182 Pa. 64,
37 Atl. 909.

which the principal must answer for the agent's fraud, though not committed on the principal's behalf.[17] And, as pointed out in a recent case:[18] "Any other result would tend to circumvent the public policy which calls for the enforcement of the clause. . . . All that would be necessary is a complete delegation by the insured of the responsibility for the adjustment of the loss to a third party whose acts might be disavowed at the option of the insured to escape the consequences. And in the absence of detection the gain would accrue to the insured." The majority of cases have held the insured barred.[19]

§ 136. **Where principal but not agent knows the falsity of the representation.** In the ordinary case the elements of fraud are complete in the agent; he makes the representation, knowing it to be false. The principal has not authorized the representation nor known of its making; it is irrelevant that he would or would not have known of its untruth. Occasionally a kind of converse case arises, where the agent makes a material representation honestly believing it to be true but the principal knows of its untruth.

§ 137. **Same: Cornfoot's case.** In the famous English case of Cornfoot v. Fowke[20] T, dealing with A, contracted to rent P's house. A stated to T that there was nothing objectionable about the house. In fact the adjoining house was a "brothel of the worst description" a fact which A did not know but of which P was fully aware. To an action for breach of the contract, T set up fraud and misrepresentation. A majority of the court held the plea not made out, since P made no representation and A's representation was innocent. Lord Abinger dis-

[17] See ante, § 113.
[18] Bockser v. Dorchester Mut. Fire Ins. Co. (1951) — Mass. —, 99 N.E.2d 640.
[19] Davis Scofield Co. v. Reliance Ins. Co. (1929) 109 Conn. 686, 145 Atl. 42; Jervis v. Burlington Mut. Fire Ins. Co. (1944) 113 Vt. 518, 37 A.2d 374; Bockser v. Dorchester

Mut. Fire Ins. Co. (1951) — Mass. —, 99 N.E.2d 640. Cf. Metzger v. Manchester Fire Assurance Co. (1894) 102 Mich. 334, 63 N. W. 650; Virginia Fire & Marine Ins. Co. v. Hogue (1906) 105 Va. 355, 54 S. E. 8.
[20] (1840) 6 M. & W. 358.

sented, saying that it had never occurred to him to doubt "upon principle or upon the authority of the decided cases, that the knowledge of the principal was the knowledge of the agent, and the knowledge of the agent the knowledge of the principal."

§ 138.　Same:　On principle and the authorities. It would seem that the view of the majority as to fraud is clearly sound, whatever might be held today as to the effect on a contract of innocent misrepresentation.[21] Lord Abinger's suggestion that the knowledge of the principal should be imputed to the agent seems unwarranted. The cases show [22] how doctrinaire and un-

[21] See Restatement, Contracts, § 476. And see Gibson v. Cottingham (1916) 23 B. L. R. 392, 32 D. L. R. 213, noted in 17 Col. L. Rev. 436.

[22] Note on Imputation of Agent's Knowledge. It is commonly said that the knowledge of the agent (or servant) is imputed to the principal (or master). The term is unfortunate; it smells of fiction and suggests that we are pretending that the principal knows something he really doesn't know. Likewise unfortunate are the common rationalizations of the doctrine. Thus it is usually said that the knowledge is imputed because of the unity of principal and agent or because, where it is the agent's duty to convey information to the principal, it will be presumed that he has done so. Fay v. Swicker (1950) 154 Ohio St. 341, 96 N.E.2d 196.

In fact, the great bulk of the cases where knowledge is imputed can be explained on a rather simple theory. If the servant driving the master's car, with knowledge that it has a loose wheel, gets into an accident in consequence, we do not think it necessary to impute the knowledge to the principal; we simply say that the master is liable for the servant's negligence. So if the agent selling the principal's horse and happening to know of a defect in the animal, intentionally misrepresents the facts to the purchaser, we do not feel obliged to pretend that the principal knew what the agent knew; since the agent was authorized to contract for the principal, the principal is responsible for the way the agent elected to do it. Now if the agent is buying land or negotiable paper for the principal, it seems to follow that the agent's knowledge of outstanding equities against the property will prevent the principal from being a bona fide purchaser, not because we pretend he knew what the agent knew but for the reasons decisive of the cases just stated. As said by Goodrich, J., in In re Mifflin Chemical Corp. (1941) 123 F.2d 311: "No reliance need be made on any fictional attributing of knowledge to Mifflin. The employers are responsible for

reasonable courts sometimes are in imputing the knowledge
of the agent to the principal; the converse imputation is even
more questionable. However, courts have tended to accept
Lord Abinger's proposition.[23]

On principle it would seem that the principal should be liable
for fraud (as distinguished, i. e., from innocent misrepresentation) only where he can be treated as being himself responsible
for the misrepresentation made. This would plainly be true
if he directed the agent to make it; it should also be true if he

the knowledge of the facts had by
their agents in doing the very
business for which they were employed." See also Hopkinson v.
First Nat. Bank of Provincetown
(1936) 293 Mass. 570, 200 N. E.
381; Huff v. United Van Lines
(1947) 238 Iowa 529, 28 N.W.2d
793; McHugh v. Duane (1947, D.
C. Mun. App.) 53 A.2d 282.

Where the agent got the information at an earlier time or in a different transaction it is sometimes
held that the knowledge will not be
imputed, but this seems unsound.
The question is what the transacting agent *did* know when he
transacted for his principal, not
when or how he learned it. Hopkinson v. First Nat. Bank of Provincetown, supra; Aiken Petroleum Co. v. National Petroleum
Underwriters (1945) 207 S. C. 236,
36 S.E.2d 380. The gravest problems are caused by the cases in
which the agent is acting for himself and, not infrequently, defraud-
ing his principal. Here it is often
said that there is no imputation
because under such circumstances
it is not to be presumed that the
agent would confide in the principal. More realistic it would be
to say that in many such cases

the agent was not acting within
the scope of his authority so as
to charge the principal in any way.
On the other hand it seems that the
principal should not be allowed to
retain property wrongfully acquired
by the agent, whether or not he
was acting in the course of employment. In re Brainerd Hotel
Co. (1935) 75 F.2d 481; Gordon v.
Continental Casualty Co. (1935)
319 Pa. 1238, 181 A. 574, 104 A. L.
R. 1238; Federal Deposit Ins.
Corp. v. Pendleton (1939) 29 F.
Supp. 779; Blumberg v. Taggart
(1942) 213 Minn. 39, 5 N.W.2d
388. The classic discussion of the
subject is to be found in Seavey,
Notice through an Agent, 65 U. Pa.
L. Rev. 1, Studies in Agency, 29.

[23] See Mayer v. Dean (1889) 115
N. Y. 556, 22 N. E. 261; S. Pear-
son & Son, Ltd. v. Dublin Corp.
[1907] A. C. 351; London, etc.,
Properties, Ltd. v. Berkeley P. &
I. Co. [1936] 2 All. E. L. R. 1039.
Cf. 53 L. Q. Rev. 344 and 15 Can.
B. Rev. 716. And cf. Armstrong v.
Strain (1951, K. B. D.) 95 Sol. J.
318, noted in 95 Sol. J. 588, where
Devlin, J., said: "There was no
way of combining an innocent
principal and agent so as to pro-
duce dishonesty."

intended the agent to make it or, without intending it to be made, created an unreasonable risk that it would.[24]

§ 139. **Authority to make representations.** It must be kept in mind that while the cases no longer require authority to make misrepresentations, authority to make representations in the premises is essential. The most troublesome problem here is that of the authority of a real estate broker, employed to "find a buyer," to make representations about the property. The tendency is to limit his power in this regard to a minimum. He may identify the property and state its area; [25] little or nothing more. Representations as to the plumbing,[26] the heating system,[27] the quality of the soil,[28] or the intentions of a prospective lessee [29] have been held unauthorized.[30] These limitations appear somewhat surprising until it is remembered that the broker's function is solely to find a possible buyer who will dicker with the principal and that except so far as the principal has made statements about the property, which the broker is naturally authorized to repeat, he is supposed to say in answer to the prospect's questions: "Take that up with the owner." [31]

[24] See the opinion of Lord Atkinson in S. Pearson & Son, Ltd. v. Dublin Corp. [1907] A. C. 351, 367. And see Restatement, § 256.

[25] See McKinnon v. Vollmar (1889) 75 Wis. 82, 43 N. W. 800; Lemarb v. Power (1929) 151 Wash. 273, 275 Pac. 561. Cf. Eamoe v. Big Bear Land & Water Co. (1950) 98 Cal.App.2d 370, 220 P.2d 408.

[26] See Friedman v. New York Telephone Co. (1931) 256 N. Y. 392, 176 N. E. 543. Cf. Handelman v. Arquilla (1950) 407 Ill. 552, 95 N.E.2d 910.

[27] See Smith v. Miller (1938) 225 Iowa 241, 280 N. W. 493.

[28] See Ellison v. Stockton (1919) 185 Iowa 979, 170 N. W. 435; Light

v. Chandler Improvement Co. (1928) 33 Ariz. 101, 261 Pac. 969, 57 A. L. R. 107, noted in 1 U. Chi. L. Rev. 137; Loma Vista Development Co. v. Johnson (1944) 142 Tex. 686, 180 S.W.2d 922; Peoples Nat. Bank v. Brown (1950) 37 Wash.2d 49, 221 P.2d 530. But cf. Sullivan v. Ulrich (1949) 326 Mich. 218, 40 N.W.2d 126, where the principal was held bound by the broker's misrepresentations that the house was not infested with termites.

[29] See Lemarb v. Power (1929) 151 Wash. 273, 275 Pac. 561.

[30] See annotation, 95 A. L. R. 763.

[31] See ante, § 66

Where the broker is authorized to contract or to convey, his authority to make representations is naturally greater. Since the agent is authorized to close the deal and no negotiation between T and P is anticipated, it is naturally taken for granted that the agent has authority to make ordinary representations about the nature and condition of the premises.[32]

Likewise a general agent to sell personal property will normally have considerable authority to make representations as he does to make warranties.[33]

3. The Principal's Liability Where the Agent Had No Power or Authority to Make the Representation

§ 140. Rescission where representations unauthorized. Where the representations are unauthorized, the principal cannot be held in tort. It does not follow that he is unaffected by them. It is usually held that though the representations were unauthorized, a third party who has relied on them in good faith may have rescission against the principal.[34] This is analogous to the modern rule which allows rescission for innocent misrepresentation.[35] I. e., while a person not at fault, personally or vicariously, cannot be amerced as for a tort, he can likewise not be allowed to enrich himself unjustly by retaining something secured by his own misrepresentations, however innocent, or by the innocent or guilty misrepresentations of his agent, however unauthorized.

[32] See Haskell v. Starbird (1890) 152 Mass. 117, 142 N. E. 695; Matteson v. Rice (1903) 116 Wis. 328, 92 N. W. 1109; Taylor v. Wilson (1932) 44 Ohio App. 100, 183 N. E. 541; Bishop v. Strout Realty Agency (1950) 182 F.2d 503.

[33] See Jacobson v. Skinner Packing Co. (1929) 118 Neb. 711, 226 N. W. 321; Saberton v. Greenwald (1946) 146 Ohio 414, 66 N.E.2d 224, 165 A. L. R. 599.

[34] See Speck v. Wylie (1934) 1 Cal.2d 625, 36 P.2d 618, 95 A. L. R. 760; Smith v. Miller (1938) 225 Iowa 241, 280 N. W. 493; Thrams v. Block (1938) 43 N. M. 117, 86 P.2d 938; Lindlots Realty Corp. v. Suffolk County (1938) 278 N. Y. 45, 15 N.E.2d 393, 116 A. L. R. 1401; Bailey v. Kuida (1950) 60 Ariz. 357, 213 P.2d 895.

[35] See Restatement, Contracts, § 476.

§ 141. Contractual limitation of responsibility for agent's misrepresentation. It is not uncommon for principals employing salesmen to have the final contract embodied in a printed form, embodying the warranties and representations the principal wishes to be bound by and specifically providing that it has not authorized and will not be bound by any other warranties or representations. The cases differ as to the effect of such a provision on the position of the principal where the agent nevertheless makes unauthorized representations and the purchaser relies on them.

Such provisions are valid and not against public policy, though it is usually said that a person cannot lawfully contract away the consequences of his own fraud.[36] If by fraud in the factum the agent hides from the purchaser knowledge of the existence of such a clause in the contract and the purchaser signs in ignorance of it, it is not binding on him. This will normally give the purchaser only a right of rescission, since representations made in such a context are not likely to be authorized.

If the purchaser signs, knowing of the existence of such a provision, it will normally preclude a tort action against the principal since the purchaser is put on notice that the representations were unauthorized.[37] Some cases hold that the same is true of an attempt to rescind, since the purchaser has estopped himself from claiming he was misled.[38] A majority of the cases, however, allow rescission in spite of the provision.[39]

---

[36] See Williston, Contracts (Rev. Ed. 1936) § 811.

[37] But see Herzog v. Capital Co. (1945) 27 Cal.2d 349, 164 P.2d 8, noted in 34 Calif. L. Rev. 751; Hall v. Crow (1948) 240 Iowa 81, 34 N.W.2d 195, noted in 35 Iowa L. Rev. 105.

[38] See J. I. Case Threshing Machine Co. v. Broach (1912) 137 Ga. 602, 73 S. E. 1063; J. B. Colt Co. v. Thompson (1926) 114 Okla. 61, 242 Pac. 1030; Hill & MacMillan v. Taylor (1931) 304 Pa. 18, 155 Atl. 103; Ernst Iron Works v. Duralith Corp. (1936) 270 N. Y. 165, 200 N. E. 683, noted in 11 St. John's L. Rev. 129; General Office Service Co. v. Letbetter (Tex. Civ. App., 1949) 221 S.W.2d 932.

[39] See Harnischfeger Sales Corp. v. Coats (1935) 4 Cal.2d 319, 48 P.2d 662; Angerosa v. The White Co. (1936) 248 App. Div. 425, 290 N. Y. S. 204, affirmed without opinion (1937) 275 N. Y. 524, 11

§ 142. —— This view is a little difficult to explain. It probably rests on the feeling that since the purchaser in fact has been misled the principal should not profit in consequence, though he himself has been guiltless of fraud and has in fact done all he could to protect the purchaser. A balance of hardship is involved. The principal, though not forced to pay damages, is put to the trouble and expense of a law suit and deprived of his bargain and, no doubt, in many instances, of his good will; this, it would seem, is in the opinion of courts more than outweighed by the hardship to the purchaser if he is forced to stand by the contract.

In such case it could be argued that the result might turn to some extent on the status of the purchaser. I. e., the housewife who buys Power & Light stock, relying on the salesman's oral promise that the company will buy it back on demand at par, is more in need of protection than the businessman who buys a five-ton truck in reliance on the salesman's assurance that it will really carry ten tons. No such distinction, however, is recognized in the cases, at least explicitly.

§ 143. **Possible ratification.** It should be kept in mind that where the third party is entitled to rescission for the agent's unauthorized representation, if the principal refuses to rescind voluntarily he may find his refusal treated as a ratification, making him liable in tort for the misrepresentation. This possibility is discussed, post, in the chapter on ratification.[40]

N.E.2d 325; noted in 22 Cornell L. Q. 102; 14 N. Y. U. L. Q. Rev. 416; and 11 St. John's L. Rev. 339; Robinson v. Main (1940) 227 Iowa 1195, 290 N. W. 539; Bates v. Southgate (1941) 308 Mass. 170, 31 N.E.2d 551, 133 A. L. R. 1349, noted in 21 B. U. L. Rev. 352; Utilities Engineering Institute v. Criddle (1943) 65 Idaho 201, 141 P.2d 981. And see Annotation, 133 A. L. R. 1360.

[40] See post, §§ 233-235.

CHAPTER VII

PRINCIPAL AND AGENT: THE PARTLY DISCLOSED AND UNDISCLOSED PRINCIPAL

§ 144. Distinctions. The Restatement [1] divides principals into (a) disclosed (those whose existence and identity are known to the third party), (b) partially disclosed (those whose existence but not whose identity is known to the third party), and (c) undisclosed (those whose existence and, a fortiori, whose identity, are unknown to the third party).

This terminology, doubtless both logical and useful, is relatively a novel one so far as it uses the phrase "partially disclosed principal." The term was perhaps coined by the makers of the Restatement; it is not to be found in Mechem on Agency, the earlier editions of this book, nor in Powell's edition of Tiffany; [2] it does not seem to have been employed in the earlier cases. Recent decisions, citing the Restatement, are beginning to use it and it will doubtless ultimately prevail, but the typical attitude of courts, particularly in the older cases, has been to make a two-way division, in substance lumping together the partially disclosed and the totally undisclosed, and to apply to both the name and rules of undisclosed principal.

1. *Rationale of Undisclosed Principal*

§ 145. The "anomalous" doctrine of undisclosed principal. It is settled law that, subject to some limitations and exceptions to be stated later, a contract made in fact on behalf of a principal, though his existence was unknown to T when the contract was made and T supposed he was dealing only with A, may, on the principal's coming forward or being discovered, be enforced by or against him like any other contract made by

[1] Restatement, § 4.
[2] Powell, § 90, speaks of principals being disclosed, unnamed and undisclosed.

an agent having authority on behalf of a principal. This doctrine has been much discussed and often criticized; in fact it is almost conventional to speak of it as "anomalous."

No doubt it is, at least superficially, rather extraordinary. It makes possible finding oneself under contract to a person one never heard of or, even, a person one has heard of all too much and would never willingly choose to contract with. Having contracted with Jones (or so one thought) one finds oneself asking for or giving performance to Smith. What becomes of liberty of contract? What becomes of meeting of minds when one of them is a mind you have never properly been introduced to?

Further thought makes these results a little less striking. They are, it can be discovered, little different from results reached under other names with which we are quite familiar and find not at all surprising. Indeed, it may be asserted that the law of undisclosed principal, whether anomalous or not, is almost inevitable.

§ 146. —— To begin with, the *fact* of undisclosed agency is neither surprising nor shocking. People often have quite honest reasons for not wishing their connection with a business or transaction known. Thus we are likely to find Adams doing business for Perkins, but not disclosing the connection. People who think they are doing business with Adams are, at least as far as economic facts are concerned, doing business with Perkins since to him belong the control, the profits and very commonly the equipment and stock in trade. Economic facts cannot be ignored. The law must find some way of dealing with the consequences of this rather normal and quite legitimate setup.

§ 147. —— Much can be explained in terms of trust law. Plainly legal realities compel us to say that T has contracted *at least* with Adams. Adams could not fairly be allowed to deny it, as against T, and there seems no reason why T should be allowed to deny it as against Adams. Adams is thus the legal holder of a right; unknown to T he holds it on behalf of and for the benefit of Perkins. This is a pure trust situation.

And Adams is strictly a fiduciary. On the other hand, some aspects do not fit at all into the trust concept. Thus Perkins intends to have, and presumably does have, control of the way the business is carried on. Included in this control is the right to take charge, if he chooses, of any litigation which may arise. He is effectively the real party in interest in a way that the cestui is not.

§ 148. —— Again, a contract approach would explain much. Perkins might be a third-party beneficiary. Or he might be an assignee, Adams having contracted by arrangement with Perkins and being under an enforceable obligation to him to assign his contract rights to Perkins on demand.

It is not difficult under a number of these theories to see how Perkins can have a right to enforce the contract. It is perhaps a little more difficult to explain his liability. However, the beneficiary of a trust which he has set up himself and whose operation he has a right to control would plainly be under an implied obligation to indemnify the trustee (or we may assume for this purpose that he has expressly agreed to do so); it is then merely a procedural shortcut to allow the trustee's creditor to enforce this right of the trustee directly against the beneficiary.[3]

§ 149. —— It is not intended to labor this point unduly but rather to point out that the consequences of the doctrine of undisclosed principal are not, in themselves, extraordinary or even unusual in our law. It would seem to follow that the doctrine itself cannot be so very extraordinary. A simple and fair statement would seem to be that the practice of undisclosed agency is common and not undesirable and that little difficulty is found legally in handling it by familiar principles of agency.[4]

---

[3] See Scott, Trusts (1939) § 278.

[4] For discussions of undisclosed principal, see Ames, Undisclosed Principal, 18 Yale L. J. 443; Lewis, The Liability of the Undisclosed Principal in Contract, 9 Col. L. Rev. 116; F. R. Mechem, The Liability of an Undisclosed Principal, 23 Harv. L. Rev. 513, 519; Goodhart and Hamson, Undisclosed Principals in Contract, 4 Camb. L. J. 320.

§ 150. **Undisclosed principal: His rights.** The rights of the undisclosed principal, and the method of their enforcement, differ very little from those of the disclosed principal. He sues in his own name and right; when his existence is disclosed it is in general the obligation of the third party to treat him as in all regards the principal. He may sue for breach of the contract and ordinarily, as will be seen later,[5] T may not successfully set up as a defense that he knew neither of P's existence nor his connection with the contract. (The very troublesome question of the third party's right to set off a claim he has against the agent is likewise discussed in a later section.) [6]

It is true that the agent is a party to the contract, and has a legal power to enforce it in his own name.[7] Very often it is intended that he shall, and he proceeds to do so. However, it is clear that the agent's legal power in this respect is subordinate to the principal, and that the latter has the right to prevent any attempt on the part of the agent to enforce the contract that is inconsistent with the principal's interests.[8]

2. *Nature of Undisclosed Principal's Liability (Herein of Election)*

§ 151. **Undisclosed principal: His liability.** It is likewise quite clear that the contract may be enforced against the principal, once he is discovered.[9] "From the authorities cited above, as well as from the very nature of the situation, this right of

[5] See post, § 165 et seq.

[6] See post, §§ 177–183.

[7] See Joseph v. Knox (1813) 3 Camp. 320; Gardner v. Davis (1825) 2 Car. & P. 49; Short v. Spackman (1831) 2 B. & Ad. 962; United States Telegraph Co. v. Gildersleeve (1868) 29 Md. 232; Ludwig v. Gillespie (1887) 105 N. Y. 653, 11 N. E. 835; Carter v. Southern Railway Co. (1900) 111 Ga. 38, 36 S. E. 308. And see Restatement, § 364.

[8] See Restatement, § 370.

[9] See Thomson v. Davenport (1829) 9 B. & C. 78; Darrow v. Produce Co. (1893) 57 Fed. 463; Mississippi Valley Co. v. Abeles (1908) 87 Ark. 374, 112 S. W. 894; Curran v. Holland (1903) 141 Cal. 437, 75 Pac. 46; Steele-Smith Grocery Co. v. Potthast (1899) 109 Iowa 413, 80 N. W. 517; Edwards v. Gildemeister (1899) 61 Kan. 141, 59 Pac. 259; Maxcy Mfg. Co. v. Burnham (1897) 89 Me. 538, 36 Atl. 1003; Schweyer v. Jones (1908) 152 Mich. 241, 115 N. W.

action does not depend upon the third person's knowledge, when dealing with the agent, that the latter was acting for another instead of for himself. Obviously everyone, when dealing with an agent for a wholly undisclosed principal, believes that he is dealing with the agent only, relies solely upon the agent individually, and, if credit be extended, extends that credit to no one but the agent. However, and herein lies the anomaly, the creditor has a right of action against the undisclosed principal, when discovered, even though he never learned of the existence of the latter until after the bargain was completed, if he can prove, as in every other case of agency, that the agent's acts were within the scope of authority."[10]

§ 152. **Nature of the liability.** However, the exact nature of the undisclosed principal's liability to the third party requires further analysis. Does it supersede that of the agent once the existence of the principal is discovered? Or are both principal and agent liable, jointly or jointly and severally? As will be seen,[11] it is possible for one dealing with the agent of a disclosed principal, by the form of the agreement, to have not only the principal but the agent bound by the contract. The nature of the agent's liability in such a case depends on the understanding of the parties and the form of the agreement. Rather commonly the agent is in the nature of a surety but it may also be agreed that he is to be a joint and several contractor with the principal.

It would be supposed that the position of the undisclosed principal would be of a similar nature. He might be thought to be a surety, guaranteeing performance by the agent, or he

---

974; City Trust Safe-Deposit & Surety Co. of Philadelphia v. American Brewing Co. (1903) 174 N. Y. 486, 67 N. E. 62; Harper v. Tiffin Nat. Bank (1896) 54 Ohio St. 425, 44 N. E. 97; Waddill v. Sebree (1892) 88 Va. 1012, 14 S. E. 849; Belt v. Washington Water Power Co. (1901) 24 Wash. 387, 64 Pac. 525; Union Trust Co. of Maryland v. Rodeman (1936) 220 Wis. 453, 264 N. W. 508; Marr v. Postal Union Life Ins. Co. (1940) 40 Cal.App.2d 673, 105 P.2d 649; Manchester Supply Co. v. Dearborn (1940) 90 N. H. 447, 10 A.2d 658.

[10] Woodbury, J., in Manchester Supply Co. v. Dearborn (1940) 90 N. H. 447, 10 A.2d 658.

[11] Post, § 297 et seq.

might, on being disclosed, be treated as a joint and several contractor. Either of these views would give the third party the full benefit of the principal's obligation, something to which it seems he should be entitled, if the undisclosed principal is to be treated like any other.

§ 153. **Liability is normally alternative.** In fact the liability of the undisclosed principal takes a different form. By the usual view he and the agent are liable in the alternative. One or the other, but not both, may be held. Why this should be so does not ever seem to have been satisfactorily explained. Statements that there is really only one contract do no more than beg the question. And the suggestion that T has contracted for only one liability ignores the obvious consideration that T's right to hold the undisclosed principal is never based on intent to contract for such a right.[12] The rule is surely more anomalous than that which makes the undisclosed principal liable at all. However, it has been widely followed.

[12] "Respecting election, what difference in reason does it make whether the seller ascertains the identity of the principal before he delivers the goods and extends the credit, or after delivery but before he seeks to exact payment? In the first case, we understand plaintiffs to agree that the seller must elect. In the second, the seller manifestly has passed on the credit of but a single person. If before payment, he finds out who the principal is, it is but just that he should be able to hold the agent, for the agent offered his own credit and it was accepted. It is also just that the seller should be permitted to abandon the right he had in the first instance to pursue the agent, and to hold the principal, for the contract of purchase was in reality the principal's. When, after delivery, but before seeking to exact payment, the seller learns the identity of the principal, he has an opportunity for investigating and comparing the standing of agent and principal, just as he would have had if he had known the principal before delivery. We apprehend no rule of law that warrants the conclusion that the seller must elect in the one case and not in the other. We perceive no solid reason why the law, in behalf of the seller, who in both cases has really contemplated and contracted for a single credit only, should in the one case more than the other create a contract under which the agent and principal stand as joint and several, or several, obligors." Baker, Circ. J., in Barrell v. Newby (1904) 127 Fed. 656.

§ **154. Determination of the incidence of liability: Merger.**
Accepting this postulate, it remains to be asked: how is it
determined which of the two parties the third party must
ultimately accept as his judgment debtor? Two theories operate here, one that of merger, the other that of election. The
doctrine of merger is simple: once there is a recovery on a
cause of action, the cause of action is gone; in its place there
is something else, viz., a judgment. As Baron Parke said in
King v. Hoare:[13] "Hence the legal maxim, 'Transit in rem
judicatam'; the cause of action is changed into matter of
record, which is of a higher nature, and the inferior remedy
is merged in the higher."

§ **155. Election.** The doctrine of election is likewise
quite simple. There are a number of places in the law
where a person may exercise one or the other, but not both,
of two rights. Thus a widow may take under a will or against
it, a defrauded party may rescind and have restitution, or
affirm and have damages, and a third party who has contracted
with the agent of an undisclosed principal may collect from
the agent *or* the principal. The law of election thus deals with
the question: by what act or acts does the party having the
election commit himself irrevocably to enforcing one, rather
than the other, of the two rights?[14]

§ **156. The English rule.** It is not clear whether the English
rule is based on merger or election. In Kendall v. Hamilton[15] plaintiffs had dealt with a partnership composed (as
they supposed) of Wilson and McLay. They sued them
and recovered judgment, which was not completely satisfied.
Subsequently they discovered that one Hamilton was a secret
partner, and sued him. It was held that they were barred.
Earl Cairns, L. C., said:[16] ". . . having taken this course,
they exhausted their right of action, not necessarily by reason
of any election between two courses open to them, which would

[13] (1844) 13 M. & W. 494, at 504.
[14] See A. S. Deinard & B. S.
Deinard, Election of Remedies, 6
Minn. L. Rev. 340 and 480.
[15] (1879) 4 App. Cas. 504.
[16] At p. 515.

imply that, in order to an election, the fact of both courses being open was known, but because the right of action which they pursued could not, after judgment obtained, co-exist with a right of action on the same facts against another person. If *Wilson & McLay* had been the agents, and *Hamilton* alone the undisclosed principal, the case could hardly have admitted of a doubt; and I think it makes no difference that *Wilson & McLay* were the agents and the undisclosed principals were *Wilson, McLay* and *Hamilton*."

§ 157. —— This plainly sounds in terms of merger.[17] And the case is the critical one, where judgment is had against the agent before the existence of the principal is known. (If the existence of the principal is known when the agent is sued it makes little difference, as appears in following sections, whether the result is phrased in terms of merger or election.) However, the case is not quite a square authority since, whatever the resemblance between undisclosed principal and dormant partner, the court plainly regards them as not precisely the same.[18]

[17] A Canadian case, M. Brennan & Sons v. Thompson (1915) 33 Ont. L. Rep. 465, 22 D. L. R. 375, puts the matter flatly in terms of merger: "A goes to C and buys goods ostensibly for himself. Credit is given to him. C then discovers (as he believes) that B is the real purchaser, and A only an agent for his undisclosed principal, B. C (1) may sue A, and will succeed if he proves the sale only; or (2) may sue B, when he will succeed if he prove A's agency. In either case the action is the same, for 'goods bargained and sold and delivered'; there is only one cause of action, the one contract: a contract to which C is one party and either B or A [at C's option] the other. If he take judgment against either, the contract transit in rem judicatam and is merged, gone. He cannot thereafter say that the contract is in existence. Nor can he, having taken a judgment against one, revive against the other the dead contract; it stays dead. There is indeed no objection to suing the agent and principal in separate actions; it is not the writ which merges the contract, but the judgment: and, so long as the plaintiff stops short of a judgment, he can proceed safely with the other action."

[18] The same is true of another case talking merger: Hammond v. Schofield [1891] 1 Q. B. 453.

On the other hand, in what is regarded as the leading case on the subject, Priestly v. Fernie [19] (which, incidentally, appears to be a case of partly disclosed, rather than undisclosed, principal), where the existence of the principal was known when judgment was taken against the agent, the opinion, as far as can be determined, puts the matter in terms of election. And it is so treated in Halsbury.[20]

§ 158. The American rule.

By the widely prevalent American rule the matter is treated as one of election and not one of merger. There can, of course, be an express election as in other situations where election is involved, but such instances are rare; for the most part it is the effect of litigation that is involved. The mere presentation of a claim or commencement of a suit, it is generally agreed, does not constitute a binding election.[21] The common case is that of claim reduced to judgment; this is, by the greatly prevailing rule, a binding and final election.[22] There is one exception: a person cannot fairly be said to have elected when he did not know he had a choice but supposed he had one credit to rely on and one only. Accordingly the reduction of the claim to a judgment against the agent *before the existence of the principal is known* does not bar a suit against the principal upon discovery of his existence.[23] (What the effect of the subsequent

[19] (1865) 3 H. & C. 977.

[20] Halsbury, Laws of England (1931) I, § 466.

[21] See Curtis v. Williamson (1874) L. R. 10 Q. B. 57; Cobb v. Knapp (1877) 71 N. Y. 348; Hoffman v. Anderson (1902) 112 Ky. 893, 67 S. W. 49. Cf. Barrell v. Newby (1904) 127 Fed. 656; Campbell v. Murdock (1950) 90 F. Supp. 297, noted in 49 Mich. L. Rev. 438.

[22] Priestly v. Fernie (1865) 3 H. & C. 977; Kingsley v. Davis (1870) 104 Mass. 178; Lindquist v. Dickson (1906) 98 Minn. 369, 107 N. W. 958; Georgi v. Texas Co. (1919) 225 N. Y. 410, 122 N. E. 238; Old Ben Coal Co. v. Universal Coal Co. (1929) 248 Mich. 486, 227 N. W. 794; Eckstein v. Caldwell (1938) 61 R. I. 142, 200 Atl. 434, 119 A. L. R. 1311; Walston v. R. B. Whitley & Co. (1946) 226 N. C. 537, 39 S.E.2d 375. This rule was adopted by the Restatement (see § 210) but not without reluctance; see 7 Proc. A. L. I. 256.

[23] Greenburg v. Palmieri (1904) 71 N. J. L. 83, 58 Atl. 297; Lindquist v. Dickson (1906) 98 Minn.

suit on the judgment against the agent is, is not clear.) [24]

§ 159. **Criticism.** The illogicality and unfairness of the conventional rule has by no means escaped notice. In a federal case,[25] A. N. Hand, J., dissenting, said: ". . . as I feel that the doctrine of election ought only to apply to a case where there has been both judgment and satisfaction, and that anything less than a complete satisfaction or an estoppel in pais affords no logical basis for barring a remedy against both agent and undisclosed principal, I must record my disagreement, even though it be a case of vox clamantis in deserto." Another federal judge refers to it as a "harsh doctrine, resting at most on a rather barren logic. . . ." [26] Commentators have almost universally condemned the rule.[27]

§ 160. **Minority view.** It is now provided by statute [28] in New York, which formerly followed the prevailing rule,[29] that an unsatisfied judgment against either agent or undisclosed principal "shall not be deemed an election of remedies which bars an action against the other." In a few jurisdictions the same result has been reached by decision. The best known case is Beymer v. Bonsall [30] where it is said: "Undoubtedly an agent who makes a contract in his own name without disclosing his agency is liable to the other party. The latter acts upon his credit and is not bound to yield up his right to hold

369, 107 N. W. 958; Restatement, § 210.

[24] See Restatement, § 337, Comment *a*.

[25] Johnson & Higgins v. Charles F. Garrigues Co. (1929) 30 F.2d 251.

[26] Clark, Circ. J., in Ore S. S. Corp. v. Hassel (1943) 137 F.2d 326.

[27] See Clayton, Election Between the Liability of an Agent and of His Undisclosed Principal, 3. Tex. L. Rev. 384; Holloway, Undisclosed

Principal — Election, 98 Cent. L. J. 280; Merrill, Election Between Agent and Undisclosed Principal: Shall We Follow the Restatement? 12 Neb. L. Bull. 100; Comment, 39 Calif. L. Rev. 409.

[28] N. Y. Laws 1939, Chap. 128.

[29] Georgi v. Texas Co. (1919) 225 N. Y. 410, 122 N. E. 238.

[30] (1875) 79 Pa. 298, approved in Joseph Melnick Building & Loan Ass'n v. Melnick (1949) 361 Pa. 328, 64 A.2d 773. See also Maple v. Cincinnati, H. & D. Ry. (1883)

the former personally, merely because he discloses a principal who is also liable. The principal is liable because the contract is for his benefit, and the agent is benefited by his being presumably the creditor, for there can be but one satisfaction. But it does not follow that the agent can afterwards discharge himself by putting the creditor to his election. Being already liable by his contract, he can be discharged only by satisfaction of it, by himself or another. So the principal has no right to compel the creditor to elect his action, or to discharge either himself or his agent, but can defend his agent only by making satisfaction for him."

The same view has apparently been followed in a recent federal case [31] and this may afford some basis for the hope that such a view will ultimately still prevail.

§ 161. Can T collect through A's right of exoneration? It has been suggested [32] that T might secure payment from P, even where he is barred from a direct suit against P by a prior judgment taken against A, by levying in equity on A's right of exoneration. "The relation of principal and agent carries with it without any express agreement, the obligation on the part of the principal not only to repay the agent for all illegitimate disbursements, but also to save him harmless from all authorized undertakings made by him as agent. In other words, the principal is subject to two distinct duties, the duty of reimbursement and the duty of exoneration." [33] The latter is an asset on which T might levy in equity on a proper showing, namely that he is unable to collect from A.

40 Ohio St. 313; Williamson v. O'Dwyer & Ahern Co. (1917) 127 Ark. 530, 192 S. W. 899; North Carolina Lumber Co. v. Spear Motor Co. (1926) 192 N. C. 377, 135 S. E. 115, noted (by K. C. Sears) in 22 Ill. L. Rev. 181; Pittsburgh Terminal Coal Corp. v. Bennett (1934) 73 F.2d 387.

[31] Joseph De Nunzio Fruit Co. v. Crane (1948) 79 F. Supp. 117, affirmed (1951) 188 F.2d 569, noted in 24 Ind. L. J. 446. Desirable as the result of this case is, one is obliged to doubt the soundness of the court's view that the question involves a matter of procedure and so permits a holding by the Federal Court inconsistent with settled California law.

[32] By the late Dean Ames, 18 Yale L. J. 443, 449 et seq. And see ante, § 148.

[33] Ibid., at p. 449.

This suggestion appears without doubt to be sensible. However, the writer knows of only one case [34] in which it has been applied and it seems necessary to say that it has become no part of the accepted law of undisclosed principal.[35]

§ 162. Judgment for defendant. Where T sues agent or undisclosed principal, and there is judgment for defendant, it is still possible to talk election though, of course, not merger. In a leading case, the decision was in fact based on election.[36] It seems, however, that different considerations are involved. In the case mentioned judgment in the first suit was for defendant, the undisclosed principal, though the agency was not denied. It did not appear what the basis of the jury's decision was but the court said that it must be presumed that the decision was on the merits. In such a case to allow the third party subsequently to sue the agent is to allow him to relitigate an issue already determined against him.

Had the decision, on the other hand, been based on the agent's lack of authority, suit against the agent could on no theory be precluded. There is no res judicata, since the merits have not been litigated. And there can be no election, since election supposes two rights and it is now established that there was (at most) but one.

Were the first suit against the agent, a similar rationale would be applicable. Judgment on the merits would preclude a subsequent suit against the principal. And, in the rather unlikely event of a judgment for the agent not on the merits (as, conceivably, because of the agent's minority) there would be neither election nor res judicata.[37]

§ 163. Joinder of agent and undisclosed principal. The position of the third party is a little ameliorated by the rule of some modern cases which permits joinder of the principal and

[34] Evans, Colman & Evans v. Pistorino (1923) 245 Mass. 94, 139 N. E. 848.

[35] See Mechem, Agency (2d Ed. 1914) § 1731, n. 49; Comment, 39 Yale L. J. 265, 266.

[36] Murphy v. Hutchinson (1909) 93 Miss. 643, 48 So. 178, noted in 22 Harv. L. Rev. 532.

[37] See Merrill, article cited, ante, n. 27, at 12 Neb. L. Bull. 127.

agent in one suit, with the third party required to elect after verdict against which defendant he wishes to take judgment.[38] This, of course, will not help matters if the judgment the third party elects to take proves uncollectible. It will, however, permit clearing up in one suit all questions as to the liabilities of the defendants and perhaps save an unnecessary suit where one, but not both, of the parties is bound.

3. *The Undisclosed Principal May Not Enforce the Contract Where the Effect Is to Prejudice the Third Party*

§ 164. Exceptions to power of undisclosed principal to enforce contract made on his behalf. It is commonly said in the cases that the undisclosed principal may disclose himself and enforce the contract against the third party, unless the result will be in some way to prejudice the third party. In a number of situations this may result from the nature of the contract.

[38] See Gay v. Kelley (1909) 109 Minn. 101, 123 N. W. 295; Klinger v. Modesto Fruit Co. (1930) 107 Cal. App. 97, 290 Pac. 127; State ex rel. Bronson v. Superior Court (1938) 194 Wash. 339, 77 P.2d 797; Hospelhorn v. Poe (1938) 174 Md. 242, 198 Atl. 582, 118 A. L. R. 682 (with annotation on the point). The exact time and mechanics of the election do not appear very clearly in the cases. In Klinger v. Modesto Fruit Co., supra, the court says: "The law will not require a litigant to gamble on his remedy. It would seem a wiser and better rule of procedure, where there is an issue or a doubt as to the relationship of a principal and agent, to require a motion for election to be made, and even then to hold the motion under advisement until the liability and relationship of the respective parties have been determined, and then render judgment accordingly. If both are found to be liable because of the relation of agent and undisclosed principal, then the court should direct an election to be made and enter judgment accordingly. If the demand for an election is not raised by demurrer or motion during the process [sic] of the trial by the party for whose benefit this doctrine is intended, it should be deemed to have been waived. While an election under such circumstances as this case presents may reasonably be required on motion, and when exercised should be a bar to a subsequent effort to hold the other party defendant liable, yet, in the absence of a demand or motion for such election, there appears to be no good reason why each defendant who would otherwise be obligated, should not be held liable."

Thus if P is seeking to enforce a contract to sell and convey land, T may make the objection that he had expected a deed with a warranty binding the person (i. e., the agent) with whom he dealt.[39] This could be obviated by a conveyance to the agent, and a subsequent tender of a deed from him, but the agent would not necessarily be willing or compelled to do this. If the principal gives his own deed, the agent's original contractual liability is doubtless merged in it; even if the agent joins in the deed it may be doubtful that his liability on the warranty runs with the deed. Where the contract is to sell personal property, no difficulty on this score seems to have been felt; perhaps the agent's implied warranty is thought not to be merged.[40]

Again, a contract to loan money to the agent would plainly not be enforceable by his undisclosed principal, since the credit of an unknown person cannot thus be thrust on the lender; nor would the promise to secure the loan by a mortgage on an identified piece of land cure the difficulty, since it is not to be supposed that the lender meant to rely wholly on the security.[41]

Again, the principal, when disclosed, may turn out to be one with whom T could not legally deal, or with whom he could deal only in violation of some contractual obligation. So, where the ostensible buyer was a broker but the real buyer was not, and the sale, under the local blue-sky law, was legal to a broker but not to a member of the public.[42] So, it would seem, where a dealer sells to an ostensible buyer within the dealer's contract zone, but the real buyer lives in another zone, making the sale a violation of the dealer's contract.[43]

§ 165. **Undisclosed principal personally distasteful to third party.** By far the most common claim of prejudice to the

[39] See Birmingham Matinee Club v. McCarty (1907) 152 Ala. 571, 44 So. 642; Pancoast v. Dinsmore (1909) 105 Me. 47, 75 Atl. 43. And see Sladovich v. Glaser (1922) 150 La. 918, 91 So. 297.

[40] See Hawkins v. Windhorst (1912) 87 Kan. 176, 123 Pac. 761.

[41] Shields v. Coyne (1910) 148 Iowa 313, 127 N. W. 63.

[42] Howell v. First of Boston International Corp. (1941) 309 Mass. 194, 34 N.E.2d 633.

[43] But see Morrison v. F. A. Dutton Motor Co. (1925) 251 Mass. 431, 146 N. E. 713.

third party arises from his insistence that the principal, when disclosed, is someone with whom he would not have cared to do business, had his existence and identity been known. This is at first sight a plausible claim. "A party," it was said in the well-known case of Boston Ice Co. v. Potter,[44] "has a right to select and determine with whom he will contract and cannot have another person thrust upon him without his consent."

Examination, however, shows that this doctrine cannot be asserted with such broadness and such confidence. Most commercial contracts are assignable; there is ordinarily nothing to prevent a buyer on whose "character, credit and substance" [45] the seller has relied, from turning around the next minute and reselling to one to whom the seller would never have sold. As far as undisclosed principal is concerned it is plainly not enough that the third party finds himself bound to someone he did not expect to be bound to; [46] there are really only two situations where the third party may hope successfully to complain of the identity of the now disclosed principal.

§ 166. (A) Personal contract. It is obvious—and no doubt the very obviousness of the proposition explains why there is such scanty authority—that a contract by which services are to be rendered or performance is to be given, which services or performance are personal in nature, cannot be enforced by an undisclosed principal who would substitute his own services or performance for that which the third party contracted for. Thus, although it would be hard to find a case to vouch, no one supposes that a contract to marry could be enforced by an undisclosed principal. Less fantastic, but equally unthinkable, is the proposition that a stranger could be brought forward as the principal in a contract to remove an

---

[44] (1877) 123 Mass. 28.
[45] (1848) 12 Q. B. D. 310.
[46] See Mitchell v. Locurto (1947) 79 Cal.App.2d 507, 179 P.2d 848.

And see Cole v. Hunter (1910) 61 Wash. 365, 112 Pac. 368; Hood v. Cline (1949) 35 Wash.2d 192, 212 P.2d 110.

appendix, paint a portrait, or play third base. A few decided cases can be found to illustrate this proposition.[47]

§ 167. **(B) Misrepresentations or nondisclosure as to the identity of the contracting party.** In a number of cases it has appeared that the principal knew or suspected that T would or might not wish to deal with him because of his identity, his business, the use he planned to make of the property or the like, and that the principal has sought to get around this difficulty by using an agent who expressly or tacitly represented himself either as dealing on his own behalf or on behalf of a fictitious principal or one who was just a straw man. Here T has more of a grievance than simply that he discovers he has unwittingly dealt with someone he would not have dealt with had he known the facts; he has been deliberately tricked into this position. He has been the victim of what is in some cases nothing less than fraud and in others at least sharp practice.

§ 168. **Analogies.** Here it might be said that T could always have achieved the same result by having a sale or contract made to A, on the tacit assumption that A would assign [48] or convey to T. Conceding the truth of this, it by no means follows that courts ought to assist T in doing a wrong by the undisclosed principal technique just because he might have been able to achieve the same wrong by other techniques. Further, the concession is by no means inevitable. If A has made affirmative misrepresentations or, in some situations, concealments, the resulting transaction will be voidable so that the nominal buyer, A, can neither successfully assign nor convey. Certainly the attempt to gain the end through the employment of the agent-undisclosed-principal device should be at least as vulnerable as the attempt to do it by assignment or resale. And the cases indicate that this is usually, but not always, so.

[47] See Walton v. Davis (1913) 22 Cal. App. 456, 134 Pac. 795; Said v. Butt [1920] 3 K. B. 497; Note, 44 Harv. L. Rev. 1271.

[48] See Restatement, Contracts, § 151.

. § 169. **The authorities.** In a well-known New York case, plaintiff, wishing to buy asphalt blocks from a competitor, and "suspecting" the competitor might not wish to name him a price, employed an agent who dealt in his own name. The agent made no statements, and was not asked, about a possible principal. The court, speaking through Cardozo, J., refused to set the contract aside "because of a secret belief in the mind of the undisclosed principal that the disclosure of his name would be prejudicial to the completion of the bargain." Had there been a false assertion, the court said, that the real principal had no interest in the transaction, the result might have been otherwise.[49]

§ 170. —— The result was otherwise in Winchester v. Howard,[50] where the principal sold oxen to defendant, the agent affirmatively stating that the oxen were his and had no connection with the principal. It was known to all parties that the buyer would have no dealings with the principal. The sale was rescinded for the misrepresentation.

On the other hand, in an English case,[51] where T had been in T's employ and had been discharged for misconduct, he successfully bought land from T by employing a friend who did not disclose the agency but was not asked if he was buying for anyone and made no statements on the subject. Specific performance was granted.[52]

[49] Kelly Asphalt Block Co. v. Barber Asphalt Paving Co. (1914) 211 N. Y. 68, 105 N. E. 88. Cf. Kaufmann v. Sydeman (1925) 251 Mass. 210, 146 N. E. 365, noted in 5 B. U. L. Rev. 187. And cf. Kayton v. Barnett (1889) 116 N. Y. 625, 23 N. E. 24.

[50] (1867) 97 Mass. 303.

[51] Dyster v. Randall & Sons [1926] 1 Ch. 932, noted in 75 U. Pa. L. Rev. 761.

[52] Lawrence, J., said: ". . . it is essential to bear in mind that the agreement which the plaintiff seeks to enforce is not one in which any personal qualifications possessed by Crossley formed a material ingredient, but is a simple agreement for sale of land in consideration of a lump sum to be paid on completion. It is an agreement which the defendants would have entered into with any other person. It is well settled that the benefit of such an agreement is assignable and that the assignee can enforce specific performance of it. If Crossley had entered into the agreement on his own behalf (as the

§ 171. **Specific performance.** Specific performance has been involved in a number of cases. A late Illinois case [53] refused specific performance where the existence of the agency was concealed and P ". . . obviously . . . feared" that T would refuse to deal with him. The court seems to go to the extent of saying that an undisclosed principal can never have specific performance. "In [Cowan v. Curran] [54] we held in a contract of sale of real estate one has a right to select and determine with whom he will deal and a failure to disclose an unknown, undisclosed principal is ground for denying specific performance."

Other cases, without laying down so broad a doctrine, have refused specific performance where there has been express or tacit misrepresentation as to the existence or identity of the principal.[55]

defendants believed he had) he could immediately have assigned it to the plaintiff and the defendants would have been bound to convey the plots to the plaintiff. Moreover, as Crossley had not, before signing the agreement, disclosed the fact that he was acting as agent, he was liable under it as principal and the defendants could have compelled him to complete the purchase.

"Further it is to be noted that in this case there was no direct misrepresentation such as there was in Archer v. Stone, 78 L. T. 34. Crossley was not asked by the defendants whether he was buying for the plaintiff and he made no statement to the defendants on the subject. The real question therefore is whether Crossley's silence, in the circumstances, amounted to a misrepresentation which renders the agreement unenforceable in this Court. In my judgment mere

nondisclosure as to the person actually entitled to the benefit of a contract for the sale of real estate does not amount to misrepresentation, even though the contracting party knows that, if the disclosure were made, the other party would not enter into the contract; secus., if the contract were one in which some personal consideration formed a material ingredient. . . ."

[53] Wloczewski v. Kozlowski (1946) 395 Ill. 402, 70 N.E.2d 560, discussed in 15 U. Chi. L. Rev. 107, 143.

[54] (1905) 216 Ill. 598, 75 N. E. 322.

[55] Lee Miller v. Fulmer (1904) 25 Pa. Super. 106; New York Brokerage Co. v. Wharton (1909) 143 Iowa 61, 119 N. W. 969; Siess v. Anderson (1911) 159 Mo. App. 656, 139 S. W. 1178; White Tower Management Corp. (1939) 302 Mass. 453, 19 N.E.2d 700, 121 A. L.

§ 172. The Restatement. In Sec. 304 of the Restatement, the blackletter appears to limit relief to the case where there is "misrepresentation" but the comment states that non-disclosure "may" justify rescission.

4. *Special Problems: Apparent Authority*

§ 173. The principal's liability to third parties as affected by his nondisclosure. It might be supposed, on casual thought, that the contract liability of the undisclosed principal would raise no special problems, since no questions of apparent authority could be involved and since the rules as to actual authority would be the same in the case of an undisclosed principal as in the case of any other. This may be to some extent true; however, there are a number of situations where the nondisclosure of the principal raises special problems.

§ 174. The "apparent" authority of the agent of an undisclosed principal. Can the agent of an undisclosed principal have apparent authority? In Watteau v. Fenwick,[56] the defendants bought a beerhouse but retained the prior owner as manager, no notice of the change in ownership being given and the prior owner's name remaining painted over the door. The manager was authorized to buy nothing but bottled ales and mineral water, but when he bought cigars and other things on credit the defendants were held liable. It was urged on the court that there could be no apparent authority, but Wills, J., said: ". . . once it is established that the defendant was the real principal, the ordinary doctrine as to principal and agent applies—that the principal is liable for all the acts of the agent which are within the authority usually confided to an agent of that character, notwithstanding limitations, as between the principal and the agent, put upon that authority."

§ 175. Rationale. A few cases[57] have refused to follow this view, and it has been criticized by some commentators,[58]

R. 1158. And see VanHall v. Gehrke (1947) 117 Colo. 223, 185 P.2d 1016.

[56] [1893] 1 Q. B. 346, noted in 10 Col. L. Rev. 763, 7 Harv. L. Rev. 49 and 9 L. Q. Rev. 111.

[57] In McLaughlin v. Gentles (Ont. S. C., 1919) 51 D. L. R. 383,

but there is no doubt that it represents the law in England and the prevailing view in this country.[59] With all respect to those who have dissented, it seems that the criticisms have been based on too narrow and literal an interpretation of the idea of apparent authority or, perhaps, on the unwillingness to admit that a principal can properly be held in some instances where there is neither real nor apparent authority. The reason for the principal's liability would seem to be analogous to that for holding the mortgagee of a car who allows it to be put on a dealer's floor along with other cars for sale. In neither case is there genuine apparent authority since in neither case does the third party know of the agency, let alone the identity of the principal. In either case, however, the principal has knowingly set up a situation in which there is an unreasonably great risk that a customer will change position in reliance on the apparent ownership of the dealer; so great a risk that as between the principal and the innocent third party, the prin-

it is said: "It seems to be straining the doctrine of ostensible agency or of holding out, to apply it in a case where the fact of agency and the holding out were unknown to. the person dealing with the so-called agent at the time, and to permit that person, when he discovered that his purchaser was only an agent, to recover against the principal, on the theory that he is estopped from denying that he authorized the purchase. It appears to me that the fact that there was a limitation of authority is at least as important as the fact that the purchaser was an agent." And see Hollywood Holding & Development Corp. v. Oswald (1931) 119 Cal. App. 21, 5 P.2d 963; Essex County Acceptance Corp. v. Pierce-Arrow Sales Co. of Boston (1934) 288 Mass. 270, 192 N. E. 604, 95 A. L. R. 1314; McCabe v. Williams (Del., 1944) 45 A.2d 503.

[58] The doctrine of Watteau v. Fenwick is discussed by F. R. Mechem, 23 Harv. L. Rev. 513, 599–601; by Seavey, 29 Yale L. J. 859, 879–881, Studies in Agency, 90–92; by Goodhart and Hamson, 4 Camb. L. J. 320, 336; by Montrose, 17 Can. B. Rev. 693.

[59] Hubbard v. Tenbrook (1889) 124 Pa. 291, 16 Atl. 817; Ernst v. Harrison (1904) 86 N. Y. S. 247; Brooks v. Shaw (1908) 197 Mass. 376, 84 N. E. 110 (with which cf. Essex County Acceptance Corp. v. Pierce-Arrow Sales Co. of Boston (1934) 228 Mass. 270, 192 N. E. 604, 95 A. L. R. 1314); Napa Valley Wine Co. v. Casanova (1909) 140 Wis. 289, 122 N. W. 812; Herkert-Meisel Truck Co. v. Duncan (1935) 141 Kan. 564, 42 P.2d 587, noted in 1 Mo. L. Rev. 343. And see Restatement, § 195.

cipal ought to bear it. In other words, here is another instance of the "agency power." [60]

§ 176. **Traders' acts.** To implement the policy involved with complete accuracy the principal's liability should be limited to the value of the assets of which he has made the agent the apparent owner. This limitation does not seem to have been imposed in any common-law case, but may exist under statutes found in a few southern states, commonly known as Traders' Acts.[61]

5. Special Problems: Setoff

§ 177. **In general.** Where the third party pays the agent for the principal's goods, or attempts to pay for them by setting off a debt owed him by the agent, complicated problems arise. These problems are commonly treated as if they were independent and as if there were a separate department of the law of Agency devoted to such matters. It is important to note and remember that this is not true, and that in fact such cases are simply parts of the law dealing with the undisclosed principal's liability for unauthorized acts of his agent.

Where the principal is wholly or partially disclosed there can be no question of setoff unless the principal has actually authorized it. Apparent authority is not involved since the third party will not normally or reasonably assume that the agent is authorized to pay his own debt with the principal's goods. Likewise, unless the job is one where the agent is entrusted with the possession of goods for sale, the third party will not be warranted in assuming that he is authorized to collect the price for his principal's goods. The cases are nearly

---

[60] See ante, § 111.

[61] The Mississippi statute provides: "If a person shall transact business as a trader or otherwise, with the addition of the words 'agent,' 'factor,' and 'company,' or '& Co.,' or like words, and fail to disclose the name of his principal or partner by a sign in letters easy to be read, placed conspicuously at the house where such business is transacted, or if any person shall transact business in his own name without any such addition, all the property, stock, money, and choses in action used or acquired in such

unanimous in holding that there can be no setoff where the third party knows or suspects there is a principal.[62]

§ 178. —— Where the agency is undisclosed, however, it will be natural for the third party, thinking the agent owns the goods and is selling them as his own, to assume that he can pay the agent or set off the money the agent owes him. It will still be true, however, that the agent is not authorized to accept payment or to transfer the goods in payment of his own debt. The question, then, will really be this: What are the circumstances, if any, in which it will be held that the agent has "apparent authority" or an "agency power" which will enable him to bind the principal by accepting payment or selling the goods in substance for his own debt? These circumstances seem properly to be two, namely: (x) where the principal has authorized the agent to deal in his own name, and (y) where the principal has given the agent possession of the goods.

§ 179. (x) Where the principal has authorized the agent to deal in his own name. Of this, the first comment may be: Is this not just the same as saying "where the principal is undisclosed"? But it is not; an undisclosed principal is one of whose existence the third party has no notice, not one of whose existence he is not supposed to have notice.

If the principal has in fact authorized the agent to deal in his own name, he must necessarily be treated as having by im-

business shall, as to the creditors of any such person, be liable for his debts, and be in all respects treated in favor of his creditors as his property." Miss. Code, 1930, § 3352.

See Gloria Apparel Shops v. Roberts (1936) 85 F.2d 931; Merchants' Grocery Co. v. Gulley Grocery Co. (1950) 210 Miss. 33, 48 So.2d 606; National Cash Register Co. v. Thompson (1950) 210 Miss. 37, 48 So.2d 608.

For a discussion of this and analogous legislation, see Glenn, Fraudulent Conveyances (Rev. Ed. 1940) §§ 362, 363. And see notes, 16 Va. L. Rev. 308 and 18 Miss. L. J. 417.

[62] See Miller v. Lea (1872) 35 Md. 396; Baxter v. Sherman (1898) 73 Minn. 434, 76 N. W. 211; Darling-Singer Lumber Co. v. Commonwealth (1935) 290 Mass. 488, 195 N. E. 723; Standard Brick & Tile Co. v. Posey (1937) 56 Ga. App.

plication authorized the agent to act in a way normal under the circumstances. If the agent is one to sell goods, he must naturally be expected to receive payment for them. If not, if some other arrangement has been made so that the agent is not in fact authorized to accept payment, it must still be said that the principal has made it so natural and likely that the agent *will* accept payment that he must assume such a risk. Furthermore, it is scarcely to be expected that the agent will say to T: "I am selling to you but only on the understanding that you are not to set off the money I owe you." Thus, whether it be put on the basis of implied authority or of estoppel or policy in the abstract, it is clear that the principal must assume responsibility for things which are the natural, and in some instances inevitable, consequence of the authority to deal in his own name. If, as in Watteau v. Fenwick,[63] the undisclosed principal is liable for the price of goods bought in violation of orders, it is not surprising that he is bound when the agent, selling the goods, collects the price.

§ 180. (y) **Where the principal has given the agent possession of the goods.** The most common cases involve factors and others given possession of the goods. Here the power of the agent to collect the price and the power of the third party to set off his claim against the agent would seem to be simply further illustrations of the rule already encountered that where an agent is given possession of a chattel and some authority to deal with it, he will be treated as having apparent authority (properly, an agency power) to deal with it in a manner in excess of his real authority.[64]

§ 181. **The authorities.** These distinctions are recognized in the Restatement.[65] And they find explicit recognition in some of the cases. Thus in Cooke v. Eshelby,[66] Lord Watson said: "It must be shown that he sold the goods as his own, or,

686, 193 S. E. 613; Syriani v. Gebhart (1950) — Md. —, 72 A.2d 766. Cf. Greer v. Downs Supply Co. [1927] 2 K. B. 28, noted in 13 Corn. L. Q. 426.

[63] Ante, n. 56.
[64] Ante, § 117.
[65] Restatement, § 306.
[66] (1887) 12 App. Cas. 271.

in other words, that the circumstances attending the sale were calculated to induce, and did induce, in the mind of the purchaser a reasonable belief that the agent was selling on his own account and not for an undisclosed principal; and it must also be shown that the agent was enabled to appear as the real contracting party by the conduct, or by the authority, express or implied, of the principal."

And in Bernshouse v. Abbott [67] the court adopts the statement in Chitty on Contracts that "Where a principal permits one who is not known to be an agent to sell as apparent principal, and afterwards intervenes, the buyer is entitled to be placed in the same situation at the time of the disclosure of the actual principal as if the agent had been the real contracting party; and he is entitled to the same defense against the principal, whether it be by common law or by statute, as he was entitled to at that time against the agent, the apparent principal. Accordingly, if in such a case the defendant has acquired a set-off against the agent, before the principal has interposed, the latter will be bound by the set-off . . . But this doctrine does not apply where the agent is a mere broker, and has not the possession of or is not intrusted with the *indicia* of property in the goods."

§ 182. —— It must be admitted, however, that in many cases these distinctions are not recognized, at least in terms. "It is undoubtedly the law that, where an undisclosed principal sues on a contract made by his agent in his own name with some person who had no knowledge of the agency but supposed that the agent dealt for himself, such suit is subject to any defense or set-off acquired by the third party against the agent, before he had notice of the principal's rights." [68]

It is believed that such broad statements are due to the fact that in all probability one or both of the factors mentioned above is to be found present in most of the cases. It is usually not difficult to tell whether the agent had possession of the

[67] (1883) 45 N. J. L. 531.
[68] Frazier v. Poindexter (1906) 78 Ark. 241, 95 S. W. 464, citing 2 Clark & Skyles, Agency, § 537, and Tiffany, Agency, p. 311. And see Tiffany, Agency (Ed. by Powell) § 98.

goods but it is often impossible to tell whether the nondisclosure of the principal's existence was with or without that principal's authority. Since it is usually the principal rather than
the agent who has reasons for not wishing the connection to
be known, it seems fair to assume that in most instances the
nondisclosure is in conformity to the principal's wishes.[69]

§ 183. **Crosby v. Hill.** The case of Crosby v. Hill [70] is
thought to afford an instructive illustration of the proper
view. Defendant there ordered shingles from the agent, supposing him to be the owner. The goods were shipped direct
by the principal. Defendant was absent when they arrived
and he testified that no invoice was received which might have
shown the source of the shingles. He paid the agent for the
shingles; the agent failed to pay the principal whereupon the
latter sued defendant and recovered.

The court quoted from the leading English case of Baring v.
Corrie: [71] "The broker has not the possession of the goods and
so the vendee cannot be deceived by that circumstance; and
besides, the employing of a person to sell goods as a broker
does not authorize him to sell in his own name. If, therefore,
he sells in his own name he acts beyond the scope of his authority and his principal is not bound. But it is said that by
these means the broker would be enabled by his principal
to deceive innocent persons. The answer, however, is obvious,
that he cannot do so unless the principal delivers over to him
the possession and indicia of property."

It is believed that this puts the matter in the true light. No
doubt the defendant has acted reasonably and in good faith;
no doubt he is hurt. But the bricks were the principal's; the

[69] On setoff, see generally Ra-
bone v. Williams (1785) 7 T. R.
360, n. *a*; Ex parte Dixon (1876)
4 Ch. D. 133; Belfield v. National
Supply Co. (1899) 189 Pa. 189,
42 Atl. 131; Shine v. Kennealy
(1902) 100 Ill. App. 473; Deane v.
American Glue Co. (1909) 200
Mass. 459, 86 N. E. 890; F. T.
Banking Corp. v. Gerseta Corp.
(1923) 237 N. Y. 265, 142 N. E.
607, 31 A. L. R. 932; Fidelity Nat.
Bank v. Copeland (1929) 138 Okla.
19, 380 Pac. 273; Hammon v. Paine
(1932) 56 F.2d 19; annotation, 53
A. L. R. 414.

[70] (1883) 39 Ohio St. 100.

[71] (1818) 2 B. & Ald. 137.

defendant has them and the principal has not been paid. Familiar principles of agency must still govern: the third party has no claim valid against the principal unless he received such a claim from an agent empowered to give it. The agent here never had possession of the bricks, and he never had authority to receive payment. If the agent has appeared to defendant to be an owner of bricks it is because of the agent's own misrepresentations and not because of anything the owner has done or authorized the agent to do. It is the hard, familiar case of the third party who has been injured by the misconduct of an agent and the law of Agency does not make the principal responsible for the misconduct of the agent save in certain patterns not here traceable.

6. *Special Problems: Payment by Principal to Agent*

§ 184.   The English rule.   In the ordinary case of disclosed principal, where the principal, through the agent, has bought goods or otherwise incurred a liability to the third party the principal's liability is not discharged until the third party is paid. It is plainly no defense to the principal for him to say that he has paid the agent and that the third party should look to the agent. Should the case be different because the principal is undisclosed?

In a series of cases the English courts have ultimately decided that even in the case of undisclosed principal he is not discharged by paying or settling with the agent unless he does so in reliance on conduct of the third party which would make it inequitable for him now to insist that the principal pay; specifically, unless the third party has done "something to induce the defendant [principal] to believe that a settlement has already been made with the agent." [72] This view has in substance been adopted by the Restatement.[73]

---

[72] Brett, L. J., in Irvine v. Watson (1880) 5 Q. B. D. 414.

In Heald v. Kenworthy (1855) 10 Exch. 739, Parke, B., said: "The plea simply states, that, after the contract was entered into between the plaintiffs and a third party, the agent of the defendant, under circumstances which rendered the defendant liable upon it, the latter paid the agent. I am of opinion that this is no defence to the ac-

§ 185. Fradley v. Hyland. There is surprisingly little American authority on the point. Fradley v. Hyland [74] is considered the leading case and perhaps states the "American rule" if there is such a thing. The court after discussing the conflicting English cases relies upon Thomson v. Davenport [75] and states that the rule quoted above, i. e., that the principal is liable unless the third party has done something which would

tion. It is clear, that, if a person orders an agent to make a purchase for him, he is bound to see that the agent pays the debt; and the giving the agent money for that purpose does not amount to payment, unless the agent pays it accordingly. But there are no doubt cases and dicta, which, unless they be understood with some qualification, afford ground for the position taken by the counsel for the defendant. First, there is the dictum of Bayley, J., in Thomson v. Davenport, where that learned judge lays down the rule, that 'if the agent does make himself personally liable, it does not follow that the principal may not be liable also, subject to this qualification, that the principal shall not be prejudiced by being made personally liable, if the justice of the case is that he should not be personally liable.' And he then proceeds to say, 'If the principal has paid the agent, or if the state of accounts between the agent here and the principal would make it unjust that the seller should call on the principal, the fact of payment or such a state of accounts would be an answer to an action brought by the seller, where he had looked to the responsibility of the agent.' The expression, 'make it un-

just,' is very vague; but if rightly understood, what the learned judge said is, no doubt, true. If the conduct of the seller would make it unjust for him to call upon the buyer for the money; as, for example, where the principal is induced by the conduct of the seller to pay his agent the money on the faith that the agent and seller have come to a settlement on the matter, or if any representation to that effect is made by the seller either by words or conduct, the seller cannot afterwards throw off the mask and sue the principal. It would be unjust for him to do so. But I think that there is no case of this kind where the plaintiff has been precluded from recovering, unless he has in some way contributed either to deceive the defendant or to induce him to alter his position."

This view was rejected in Armstrong v. Stokes (1872) L. R. 7 Q. B. 598, but was reaffirmed in Irvine v. Watson, supra, and is taken to represent the present law of England

[73] Restatement, § 208.

[74] (1888) 37 Fed. 49.

[75] (1829) 9 B. & C. 78. The court relies on the language from this case quoted in the excerpt

122

make it inequitable for him to call on the principal for payment, while correct "when applied to cases in which the seller deals with the agent relying upon the existence of an undisclosed principal,[76] is not to be applied in those in which the seller has given credit solely to the agent, supposing him to be the principal. . . . Under such circumstances it is immaterial that the principal has not been misled by the seller's conduct or laches into paying or settling with his agent. It is enough to absolve him from liability that he has in good faith paid or settled with his agent."

§ 186. —— This view is perhaps a little less logical than the English and Restatement view; it may be that it is also a little more reasonable and consistent with actual business practices. One who has set up an agent in business under his own (the agent's) name will naturally expect the public to deal with him exclusively and to look to him for payment. Unless he has notice of facts which should put him on his guard it would seem that the principal has done his duty to customers of the agent if he has seen to it that the agent is properly kept in funds to meet his obligations. The customers have not relied on the principal's credit. Just as he is not entitled to enforce the contract when to do so would be inequitable to the third party, it seems that it should not be enforced against him when to do so is inequitable to him.

Such is no doubt the basis of the view taken in the Davenport and Fradley cases.[77]

7. The Partially Disclosed Principal

§ 187. **In general.** It remains to discuss briefly the case of the partially disclosed principal. That it may be done briefly is

from Heald v. Kenworthy, ante n. 72.

[76] I. e., what would now more accurately be referred to as a "partially disclosed" principal.

[77] The only other American case of importance appears to be South-ern Ry. Co. v. W. A. Simpkins Co. (1919) 178 N. C. 273, 100 S. E. 418, 10 A. L. R. 731. For discussion and collection of dicta in other cases see Note, 18 Miss. L. J. 436.

due to the fact that in most instances the law is self-evident, once the cognate undisclosed principal law is grasped.

§ 188. He has the rights and liabilities of any other principal. The partially disclosed principal is liable on the contract, and can enforce it, like any other principal. If his status is at all anomalous, it is less so than that of the undisclosed principal and it would be extraordinary if he were treated as less a party to the contract than an undisclosed principal.

§ 189. Election and merger. If it is surprising that by the prevailing view the third party may not treat undisclosed principal and agent as jointly and severally liable, it is even more so in the case of partially disclosed principal. The Restatement in fact appears to posit a joint and several liability. It is stated in Sec. 321 that "unless otherwise agreed" an agent contracting for a partially disclosed principal becomes a party to the contract.[78] And in Sec. 336 it is stated tnat where the agent of a partially disclosed principal is a party to the contract, he is not discharged by judgment against the principal. In Comment *c* it is said: "In making a contract through an agent for an unidentified principal, the other party to the contract has the same choice of selecting his debtors as where the principal is wholly disclosed. Since he knows the facts, he may at the time of entering the contract choose either the joint liability of the agent and the unidentified principal or their several liabilities. Unless otherwise agreed, he has cumulative and not alternative rights against agent and principal."

§ 190. —— That the third party has such a power of selection cannot be doubted. The cases, however, do not suggest that the third party often makes such an express election at the time the contract is formed. And, in the absence thereof, the tendency of the decisions is to treat the case exactly as if

---

[78] The rights and liabilities of the agent on a contract made for a principal, disclosed, partially disclosed or undisclosed, are discussed in Chapter X, post.

it were one of undisclosed principal. Thus in a leading English case [79] it is said: "Where an agent purports to make a contract for a principal, disclosing the fact that he is acting as an agent, but not naming his principal, the rule is that, unless a contrary intention appears, he makes himself personally liable on the authorized contract. It is presumed that the other party is unwilling to contract solely with an unknown man. He is willing to contract with an unknown man, and does so, but only if the agent will make himself personally liable, if called on, to perform the contract which he arranges for his principal. The agent is presumed to agree. The liability of the agent is not joint, nor is it contingent on default by the principal. Two contracts are made in identical terms, one with the principal and the other with the agent, and the opposite party, unless prevented by some election, can enforce either, but not both."

The few American decisions dealing with the situation seem to take a similar view.[80]

§ 191. **Prejudice to the third party.** Since, as will be seen,[81] the partially disclosed principal, to become an effective party to the contract, must answer any description of him that may have been given, and since a party who chooses to deal with an unidentified principal must be taken as pretty broadly waiving any objections to his possible identity, there is little room for the operation of the doctrine, discussed above, that the disclosure of the principal must not prejudice the third party. Given a proper situation, however, there is no reason to think that the doctrine would not apply.[82]

§ 192. **Apparent authority.** The doctrine of Watteau v. Fenwick,[83] though instances are rare, would seem equally applicable to the case of partially disclosed principal.[84]

[79] Benton v. Campbell, Parker & Co. [1925] 2 K. B. 410.

[80] See Cobb v. Knapp (1877) 71 N. Y. 348; Barrell v. Newby (1904) 127 Fed. 656; Pittsburgh Terminal Coal Corp. v. Williams (1934) 70 F.2d 65.

[81] Post, Chapter X.

[82] See Restatement, § 292, Comment c.

[83] Ante, n. 56.

[84] See Restatement, § 159, Comment d.

§ 193. Setoff. It has already been seen [85] that the third party cannot set off against the principal a claim against the agent if he knows or suspects that there is a principal, although he does not know of the principal's identity.

§ 194. Payment by the principal to the agent as a defense. It has been seen [86] that by the English view, adopted by the Restatement, payment to the agent by the undisclosed principal is no defense in a suit by third party against the undisclosed principal, unless the payment was made in reliance upon conduct of the third party indicating that he had already settled with the agent. A fortiori would this be true of payment to the agent by a partially disclosed principal.

By the so-called "American rule" [87] good-faith payment by the undisclosed principal is sufficient. However, in Fradley v. Hyland,[88] the leading case establishing the rule, it is expressly stated that the English rule should be applied in cases where the existence of a principal is known.[89]

[85] Ante, § 177.
[86] Ante, § 184.
[87] Ante, § 185.
[88] Ante, n. 74.
[89] See the quotation from Fradley v. Hyland, ante, § 185.

On the partially disclosed principal in general, see notes, 39 Yale L. J. 265 and 39 Ky. L. J. 208.

CHAPTER VIII

RATIFICATION: RATIONALE AND VOLUNTARY RATIFICATION

§ 195. **Introduction.** *Omnis ratihabitio retrotrahitur et mandato priori aequiparatur.* Every ratification is dragged back and treated as equivalent to a prior authority.

The doctrine expressed by this ponderous maxim is well settled in Agency law.[1] The subject, however, is a difficult and puzzling one. Just as in the case of undisclosed principal, recourse is often had to the adjective "anomalous." In the one case it is asked: How can you contract with someone you never heard of? In the other: How can a contract, admittedly not binding on the principal when made, become so at a later time by his mere assent, without new consideration, without the assent of the third party [as distinguished from his dissent] and indeed often without his knowledge?[2]

1. *Rationale of Ratification*

§ 196. —— One answer that might be given is that, just as in the case of undisclosed principal, the doctrine is more anomalous in theory than in practice. The issue of the agent's authority will not be settled until the matter is litigated, at a time substantially subsequent to the making of the contract;

[1] In Dempsey v. Chambers (1891) 154 Mass. 330, 28 N. E. 279, Holmes, J., in a learned opinion traces the history of the doctrine from the Roman law and attributes the modern form of the Latin maxim to Lord Coke.

[2] "As a general rule, only persons who are parties to a contract, acting either by themselves or by an authorized agent, can sue or be sued on the contract. A stranger cannot enforce the contract, nor can it be enforced against a stranger. That is the rule but there are exceptions. The most remarkable exception, I think, results from the doctrine of ratification as established in English law." Lord Macnaghten in Keighley, Maxsted & Co. v. Durant [1901] App. Cas. 240.

as a practical matter does it then make much difference *when* the principal expressed his willingness to be bound, as long as it is retroactively clear that at some time he has expressed it? The third party proceeded on the assumption that the contract bound the principal (as did the agent to the extent that his behaviour might be involved); the principal's assent, though subsequent, now merely makes it clear that the transaction is to be treated as what it appeared to be all along. Such a consequence is, if anything, less anomalous than the contrary one would be.

§ 197. ———— It is believed, however, that a more basic answer can be given. The difficulties and anomalies of the subject, it is suggested, arise chiefly from the difference between terminology and practice. The maxim, supra, and the various "requirements" of ratification as given in the books, sound largely in terms of a principal who wishes in cold blood to become bound on a contract made in his name but by a purported agent who lacked authority to bind the purported principal, at least in the way in question.

This is quite unrealistic and, so, misleading. Not one case in a hundred deals with such a situation. Discussion of the law applicable to it is largely academic. Rarely indeed is the principal trying to ratify; he is trying to escape from ratification.

§ 198. ———— A realistic statement of the problem that goes under the name of ratification might be this: What are the acts and facts by which a purported principal may be precluded from denying that the agent who purported to bind him had no authority to do so? As the statement suggests, estoppel, at least in the broad sense, is often involved. So is mistake. So is election; so is unjust enrichment. These are familiar topics and in no sense anomalous. Once the matter is put, for example, in terms of the proposition that ordinary principles of equity preclude a principal from retaining the consideration given in reliance on his promised performance and at the same time refusing to give the promised performance on the ground that the promise was unauthorized—all mystery, all anomaly disappears from the situation.

2. *The Conventional Requirements*

§ 199. —— First, a brief statement will be made of some of the more familiar requirements and limitations as found in the books. As suggested above, they tend to sound in terms of an intentional and willing affirmance; later discussion will deal with the matter from a somewhat different angle and it may then be considered how realistic these propositions are.

§ 200. **The contract must be one which would have been valid had A then been authorized.** Since the doctrine of ratification causes the transaction to be treated as if there had been authority in the first place, it follows (in logic, at least) that if the transaction would have been initially invalid, though authorized, ratification cannot subsequently make it valid. Since an unborn person can scarcely contract, it must follow that a contract purporting to bind a principal not yet born could not be ratified. (From a practical standpoint, it is not inconceivable that in such a case the purported principal might act in such a way as to be subject to liability.) The same would be true of a contract purporting to bind one then totally without contractual capacity but later acquiring it. A very common instance of this is a contract made by promoters on behalf of an as yet nonexistent corporation. Since by conventional dogma ratification is impossible, courts have been forced to exercise great ingenuity to find formulae permitting the corporation to be held when formed. Considerations of space forbid more than mentioning this problem here; reference must be made to authorities on corporation law.[3]

The contract likewise must have been a legal one when made.[4]

---

[3] Many cases on the problem are collected in 123 A. L. R. 726.

[4] See Zottman v. City and County of San Francisco (1862) 20 Cal. 96; Sanford v. Johnson (1877) 24 Minn. 172; Goldfarb v. Reicher (1934) 112 N. J. L. 413, 171 Atl. 149, aff'd (1934) 113 N. J. L. 399,

§ 201. P must have present ability. It is scarcely more than a truism to say that the principal must be legally competent at the time of ratification. Ratification is a jural act, having consequences as important as those of making a contract, and as much capacity is plainly necessary to ratify a contract as would have been necessary to authorize it in the first place.[5]

§ 202. Contract legal when made but illegal at time of ratification. More difficult is the question whether a contract may be ratified which was legal when made but illegal at the time of the attempted ratification. Here perhaps the criterion is the effect of ratification. If it would be to bind the parties to a performance now illegal, plainly there can be ratification. If, on the other hand, the result is simply to enforce obligations resulting from an agreement legal when made, the ratification may operate. The Restatement[6] illustrates this by saying that a contract to sell and deliver liquor, legal when made, but illegal at the time of the attempted ratification, plainly could not be ratified. On the other hand, if the liquor had been delivered (and perhaps consumed) at a time when such was legal, but payment for it had not been made, a ratification whereby the seller became entitled to payment would not be objectionable, since thereby the seller simply becomes entitled to payment for services which were legal when rendered, and does not attempt to enforce an act in violation of public policy.

§ 203. Contract must purport to be on behalf of a principal. A second proposition scarcely more than a truism is that a contract, ostensibly and actually made by a person solely on his own behalf, cannot be appropriated by another by "ratifying" it. There is nothing to ratify; it would be mere larceny of another's contract.

174 Atl. 507; Sullivan v. Hardin (Tex. Civ. App., 1937) 102 S.W.2d 1110; Board of Education v. Baugh (1941) 240 Ala. 391, 199 So. 822; Gilkison v. Roberts (1941) 154 Kan. 52, 114 P.2d 797; Jefferson Standard Life Ins. Co. v. Guilford County (1946) 226 N. C. 441, 38 S.E.2d 519.

[5] See Armitage v. Widoe (1877) 36 Mich. 124.

[6] Restatement, § 86.

More difficult is the question how far the contract must go in disclosing and identifying the principal. Is it enough that a party ostensibly binding himself and himself only privately intends to contract on behalf of a principal? Must it be *a* principal or a particular principal? May he simply be described in such a way as to permit identification or must he be named?

§ 204. ——— A substantial majority of the cases has refused to permit ratification where the contract as made in no way purports to bind a principal, although the agent privately intends to do so.[7] The law of Undisclosed Principal, it is said, is an anomaly; to permit him to ratify would be to add one anomaly to another.[8] Furthermore, it is said in the same case,

[7] See Mitchell v. Minnesota Fire Ass'n (1892) 48 Minn. 278, 51 N. W. 608; Keighley, Maxsted & Co. v. Durant [1901] A. C. 240, noted in 15 Harv. L. Rev. 221; Ferris v. Snow (1902) 130 Mich. 254, 90 N. W. 850; Knapp v. Baldwin (1931) 213 Iowa 24, 238 N. W. 542; Fay v. Doyle (1938) 95 F.2d 110; Valaske v. Wirtz (1939) 106 F.2d 450, 124 A. L. R. 889; Pullen v. Dale (1940) 109 F.2d 538; Gulf Refining Co. v. Travis (1947) 201 Miss. 336, 30 So.2d 398; Greene v. Golucke (1947) 202 Ga. 494, 43 S.E.2d 497; Hirzel Funeral Homes v. Equitable Trust Co. (1951) — Del. —, 83 A.2d 700. But it seems there can be ratification where the agent purports to be acting on the principal's behalf but is secretly acting on his own behalf: In re Tiedemann & Freres [1889] 2 Q. B. § 66.

[8] In Keighley, Maxsted & Co. v. Durant, supra, n. 7, Roberts bought wheat from plaintiff, intending to buy as defendants' agent, but without authority and without disclosing his intent. Defendants ratified but later refused to take the wheat. Judgment for defendant. Lord Davy said: "The argument seems to be that as the law permits an undisclosed principal, on whose behalf a contract has been made to sue and be sued on the contract, and as the effect of ratification is equivalent to a previous mandate, a person who ratifies a contract intended but not expressed to be made on his behalf is in the same position as any other undisclosed principal. Further, it is said that whether the intention of the contractor be expressed or not, its existence is mere matter of evidence, and once it is proved the conclusion ought to follow. Romer, L. J., held that on principle it ought to be held that ratification (in the case before the court) is possible, and that to hold the contrary would be to establish an anomaly in the law, and moreover a useless one. My

practical considerations forbid a rule which would require ascertaining the intent of the contractor at the time the contract is made.

A few jurisdictions have taken the contrary view, usually without discussion of the point.[9] It is to be noted that in a number of these cases the "ratification" found was based on the retention by P of benefits received by him under the unauthorized contract. In such cases, where P obviously must either restore the benefit received or keep it on the terms on which it is given, it seems not very material that in the original transaction no mention of a principal was made. Doubtless this is another of the "requirements" which presupposes an intentional ratification and makes little sense where the question is whether P has put himself in such a position as to equitably preclude him from disaffirming the contract.

§ 205. The same formality is required for ratification as for original authorization.

In the rare cases where authority must be given in some particular form, as under seal where it is to execute a specialty, or in writing where expressly required

Lords, I cannot agree. There is a wide difference between an agency existing at the date of the contract which is susceptible of proof, and a repudiation of which by the agent would be fraudulent, and an intention locked up in the mind of the contractor, which he may either abandon or act on at his own pleasure, and the ascertainment of which involves an inquiry into the state of his mind at the date of the contract. Where the intention to contract on behalf of another is expressed in the contract, it passes from the region of speculation into that of fact, and becomes irrevocable. In what sense, it may be asked, does a man contract for another when it depends on his own will whether he will give that other the benefit of the contract or not? In the next place, the rule which permits an undisclosed principal to sue and be sued on a contract to which he is not a party, though well settled, is itself an anomaly, and to extend it to case of a person who accepts the benefit of an undisclosed intention of a party to the contract would, in my opinion, be adding another anomaly to the law, and not correcting an anomaly."

[9] See Hayward v. Langmaid (1902) 181 Mass. 426, 63 N. E. 912 (with which cf. Allen v. Liston Lumber Co. (1933) 281 Mass. 440, 183 N. E. 747); Speer v. Campbell (1932) 167 Wash. 544, 9 P.2d 1100. Cases are collected in 124 A. L. R. 893.

by certain statutes of frauds, it is usually said that the same form is essential to effect a valid ratification.[10] This is reasonable; if authority to execute a land contract requires (under express statute) a written authorization, the written authorization must exist before the principal can be bound and this must be equally true whether authorization was given before or after the execution of the land contract.

However, in jurisdictions where seals still retain significance there is some tendency away from the rule that ratification must be under seal.[11] This is doubtless to be considered less as a matter of logic than as a revolt against the mediaeval ideas surviving in the law of the Seal.

§ 206. Principal must have knowledge of material facts.

One of the most common clichés of the subject is that there can be no ratification unless at the time of the ratification the purported principal had full knowledge of all the pertinent facts. This, if true, is curious. The doctrines of fraud and mistake give protection, but within rather narrow limits, to one who makes a contract or, in fact, to one who authorizes the making of one on his behalf. For the most part if he acts without knowledge of, or under mistaken assumptions as to, material facts, he does so at his own risk. Is the case really different with one who ratifies?

The Restatement states: [12] "In other consensual transactions, lack of knowledge by both parties as to the essential facts upon which the transaction is based constitutes a ground for rescission, but where manifestations of consent have been exchanged creating a contract, ordinarily the mistake of one of the parties not induced by a misrepresentation of the other

---

[10] See Stetson v. Patten (1823) 2 Greenleaf (Me.) 358; Halland v. Johnson (1919) 42 N. D. 360, 174 N. W. 874; Alleghany Gas Co. v. Kemp (1934) 316 Pa. 97, 174 Atl. 289; Dunbar v. Farnum (1937) 109 Vt. 313, 196 Atl. 237, 114 A. L. R. 996; Fulton County Fiscal Court v. Southern Bell Telephone & Tele- graph Co. (1942) 289 Ky. 159, 158 S.W.2d 437; Gulf Refining Co. v. Travis (1947) 201 Miss. 336, 30 So.2d 398; Wyman v. Utech (1950) 256 Wis. 234, 42 N.W.2d 603.

[11] See Moran v. Manning (1940) 306 Mass. 404, 28 N.E.2d 478.

[12] Restatement, § 91, Comment b.

is not a ground for rescission. A contract which results from ratification, however, may be rescinded by the person affirming, if he affirms under a unilateral mistake as to a material fact, unless he assumes the risk of mistake, or unless the third person has changed his position in reliance upon the ratification."

§ 207. —— The comment quoted gives no reason for this distinction, although it would seem that some reason is needed. It is believed that the common statement, and this expansion of it in the Restatement, are, if not erroneous, at least misleading. There appears to be only one type of situation where mistake does have the effect attributed; in the situations to which the statement would most naturally appear to be applicable, it appears not to be true. Two situations need to be considered.

§ 208. **Same: Mistake as to basic inducing fact.** First, suppose that P ratifies a contract, under some misapprehension as to factors affecting the wisdom of doing so, although not under such misapprehension as would justify a rescission for mistake if he were making rather than ratifying the contract. Is the ratification inoperative?

It would seem that this is the precise situation suggested by the customary statement, and by the language of the Restatement. It is believed however, that this ratification neither should or would be invalidated for P's failure to have knowledge of the material facts. No case so holding has been found. Such small authority as deals with the problem points in the opposite direction. Thus, in a well-known Pennsylvania case,[13] P's agent in this country without authority advanced P's money to a mutual friend, to enable her to save stock that she was carrying on a margin account. P, in Europe, on being informed of A's action, expressly approved. Later, however, he attempted to disavow the ratification on the ground that he

[13] Currie v. Land Title Bank & Trust Co., (1939) 333 Pa. 310, 5 A.2d 168.

had not realized in what a critical condition the friend's account was. The court denied this contention saying it was well settled that a principal could ratify without knowledge of material facts "if he intentionally and deliberately does so, knowing that he does not possess such knowledge and does not make further inquiry into the matter." This "exception" to the ordinary rule is often repeated; it would seem to cover nearly all cases where the facts would not warrant rescission for mistake.[14]

§ 209.   **Same: Ignorance of unauthorized term in a contract otherwise authorized.** The second situation to be considered, and the only one where any substantial number of cases can be found, purporting to apply the quoted rule, is that where P has approved a contract made for him but in ignorance of the fact that it contains an unauthorized provision. Thus, where a landlord approved a lease made on his behalf by his son, not knowing that the son had promised to make certain repairs, it was held that the landlord was not bound by the agreement to make repairs.[15]

So in a North Carolina case, P approved a sale of a note made for him by A, on the assumption (semble) that it was transferred without recourse; on learning that A had indorsed it in P's name, P was held not bound by ratification.[16] Other cases to this effect are cited in the note.[17] In a number of such

[14] See Haines v. Rumph (1921) 147 Ark. 425, 228 S. W. 46; Hill v. Tillman Co. Bank (1926) 117 Okla. 210, 245 Pac. 628; Miller v. Chatsworth Sav. Bank (1927) 203 Iowa 411, 212 N. W. 722.

[15] Lusco v. Jackson (1937) 27 Ala. App. 531, 175 So. 566.

[16] Sherrill v. Weisiger (1894) 114 N. C. 438, 19 S. E. 365.

[17] See Combs v. Scott (1866) 12 Allen (Mass.) 493; Valley Bank of Phoenix v. Brown (1905) 9 Ariz. 311, 83 Pac. 362; Thompson v. Laboringman's Mercantile & Man-

ufacturing Co. (1906) 60 W. Va. 42, 53 S. E. 908; Simonin's Sons, Inc. v. American Credit Indemnity Co. (1935) 318 Pa. 160, 177 Atl. 807; Barclay v. Dublin Lake Club (1938) 89 N. H. 500, 1 A.2d 633; Bank of America National Trust & Savings Ass'n v. Perry (1940) 41 Cal.App.2d 133, 106 P.2d 53; Broer v. Fenton's Vigortone Co. (1942) 231 Iowa 1276, 4 N.W.2d 416.

In some of these cases there were actual misrepresentations sufficient

cases, P is held to have ratified because of his carelessness in failing to avail himself of readily accessible information.[18]

§ 210. —— These cases, it is thought, do not require justification by any doctrine peculiar to ratification. They appear to be natural applications of fundamental contract law. Is there a meeting of minds? The part played by the agent makes it difficult to find an exact contractual analogue; is it too far-fetched to consider the case of the two good ships Peerless as in point? It seems reasonable to say that the supposed contract (in the ratification case) is made by the concurrence of the consent of the third party to the contract as proposed to him by the agent and the consent of the principal, as expressed by his ratification, to the contract as then presented to him. Plainly there has been no real *consensus ad idem* nor any apparent one. However the principal ratifies, it is not necessary to treat him as saying: "I ratify the proposition as made to T." He says: "I ratify the contract as I reasonably suppose it to be, in the light of my authorization and of the information given me by my agent." Since in all such cases the agent will normally have acted misleadingly if not fraudulently, it may be not inappropriate to compare them to. a famous Massachusetts illustration of the "Peerless" doctrine,

to invalidate an ordinary transaction.

"The argument that knowledge of Lyman was that of his principal, begs the question. It assumes his authority to act in the matter. 'The knowledge of an agent is the knowledge of his principal in regard to such matters only as come within the scope of the agent's employment.' Bohanan v. Railroad, 70 N. H. 526, 529. To the same effect, see Castonguay v. Company, 83 N. H. 1; Warren v. Hayes, 74 N. H. 355. The liability of an alleged principal cannot be enlarged by proof that his agent to do one act knew that he had done another act which was not authorized." Edelstone v. Salmon Falls Mfg. Co. (1930) 84 N. H. 315, 150 Atl. 545. Cf. Hyatt v. Clark (1890) 118 N. Y. 563, 23 N. E. 891, and comment thereon in Corbin, "Ratification in Agency Without Knowledge of Material Facts," 15 Yale L. J. 331, 338.

[18] See Holloway v. Arkansas City Milling Co. (1908) 77 Kan. 76, 93 Pac. 577; Payne Realty Co. v. Lindsey (1922) 91 W. Va. 127, 112 S. E. 306; Fisher v. Roper (1922) 183 N. C. 485, 111 S. E. 857; Hamilton v. Shredded Wheat

namely the bathhouse case, Vickery v. Ritchie,[19] where the architect fraudulently gave the contracting parties two different estimates, each naming a different price, on the basis of which the parties purported to contract. Obviously no contract was made; the court so held.

If these cases are in point, there appears to be no deviation from fundamental contract principles in holding that the P is not bound to the unknown term by his ratification.

§ 211. —— If the failure to achieve a meeting of minds prevents the formation of any contract and so relieves P of an obligation to perform with the unauthorized term included, does it not follow that T is likewise relieved of any obligation to perform with the unauthorized term excluded? Normally the answer would seem to be clear: yes. In a few instances, particularly where there has been part performance and change of position, equitable considerations may justify the principal in standing on the authorized contract and repudiating the unauthorized part. Such cases will be considered later in this chapter.[20]

3. Ratification of Tort

§ 212. **Dempsey v. Chambers.** May a person become a servant, or may the act of a servant not in the course of employment, become so, so as to charge a master, by a subsequent ratification on the part of the purported master? Such a proposition seems more anomalous than ratification by a principal, but the relatively few cases [21] are in agreement that there may be a ratification, as long as a supporting nexus is established by showing that the tortfeasor was intending to act for the

Sales (1934) 54 R. I. 285, 172 Atl. 614; Gordon v. Pettingill (1939) 105 Colo. 214, 96 P.2d 416.

[19] (1909) 202 Mass. 247, 88 N. E. 835.

[20] See post, § 242.

[21] See Forbes v. Hagman (1881) 75 Va. 168; Brown v. City of Webster City (1902) 115 Iowa 511, 88 N. W. 1070; Keedy v. Amherst (1915) 222 Mass. 72, 109 N. E. 817; Kirk v. Montana Transfer Co. (1919) 56 Mont. 292, 184 Pac. 987; Myers v. Shipley (1922) 140 Md. 380, 116 Atl. 645, 20 A. L. R. 1460; Jones v. Mutual Creamery Co.

purported master.[22] The leading case is Dempsey v. Chambers [23] where, under circumstances not stated, one not in fact defendant's servant was delivering, without his knowledge or consent, a load of coal plaintiff had ordered from defendant. In so doing he negligently broke plaintiff's window. With knowledge of these facts, defendant presented to plaintiff a bill for the coal and was paid. It was held (semble because of the demand for payment, though this is nowhere explicitly stated) that defendant had ratified the stranger's act, and Holmes, J., said that "consistency with the whole course of authority requires us to hold that the defendant's ratification of the employment established the relation of master and servant from the beginning, with all its incidents, including the anomalous liability for his negligent acts."

§ 213. —— Perhaps such a case can be justified by saying that coal delivering was defendant's business, that the law of *respondeat superior* makes him bear the cost of negligent delivery, and that there was no evidence to suggest that the interloper was more likely to be negligent than one of defendant's regular servants. On the other hand there seems to be no great inherent equity in the result. If one buys a horse with a warranty from an agent, it is unfair for the principal to keep the price and repudiate the warranty since that was part of the consideration for the price. It is less plausible to say that the price of the coal was in part paid on the understanding that defendant would be responsible for its careful delivery; *non constat* that plaintiff could have complained had defendant had the coal delivered by an independent contractor.[24]

(1932) 81 Utah 223, 17 P.2d 256, 85 A. L. R. 908.

[22] See Matulis v. Gans (1928) 107 Conn. 562, 141 Atl. 871; Ernshaw v. Roberge (1934) 86 N. H. 451, 170 Atl. 7; Bryan v. Pommert (1941) 110 Ind. App. 61, 37 N.E.2d 720; Restatement, § 85.

[23] (1891) 154 Mass. 330, 28 N. E. 279.

[24] An interesting and perplexing question that suggests itself in connection with such a case as Dempsey v. Chambers is this: what is the effect of the ratification on the relation between M & S? No doubt P can no longer treat the taking of a wagon as a conversion. However, if S had been originally M's servant, he would now be li-

§ 214. Approbation and retention in employ.

§ 214. **Approbation and retention in employ.** If the result of the Chambers case appears anomalous, what is to be said of the cases [25] holding a servant's assault ratified by the master's subsequent approval of it or by his retention of the servant in his employ? In a recent Federal case from Alaska [26]

able to indemnify M. Has M by ratifying both obligated himself to pay for the broken window, and lost his right of indemnity? Is there any reason why he should? S was originally liable to T; he does not appear to be prejudiced if M, having paid T, is subrogated to T's rights against S. Or it might be suggested that S's intent to act as M's servant, which is a prerequisite to ratification, carries with it an assumption of the liabilities of the position. The case is not such a one as Holloway v. Arkansas City Milling Co. (1908) 77 Kan. 76, 93 Pac. 577, where P's so-called ratification merely means that by his careless dealing with A, P has precluded himself from complaining *against A* of A's violation of instructions.

It must be admitted that the writer has found no authority to support the position suggested. And Secs. 416 and 430 of the Restatement appear to be inconsistent with it.

[25] See Gantt v. Belk-Simpson Co. (1934) 172 S. C. 353, 174 S. E. 1; Tanscher v. Doernbecher Mfg. Co. (1936) 153 Ore. 152, 56 P.2d 318; State v. Shain (1939) 345 Mo. 543, 134 S.W.2d 58, noted in 6 Mo. L. Rev. 99; Jameson v. Gavett (1937) 22 Cal.App.2d 646, 71 P.2d 937; McChristian v. Popkin (1946) 75 Cal.App.2d 249, 171 P.2d 85; Novick v. Gouldsberry (1949) 173 F.2d 496; Gindin v. Baron (1951)

11 N. J. Super. 215, 78 A.2d 297, aff'd (1951) 16 N. J. Super. 1, 83 A.2d 790.

In a number of the above-cited cases, it is said that punitive damages may be recovered against the master.

Cf. Gulf, C. & S. F. R. Co. v. Kirkbride (1891) 79 Tex. 457, 15 S. W. 495, where it is said: "We think it would be extending the doctrine of ratification too far to apply it to such a case as the one before us. Notwithstanding his one fault, the servant may be a useful and deserving one, and worthy of promotion and encouragement. We do not think it either just to the individual, necessary for the general good, or a wise public policy, to so arbitrarily punish the master for lenity to a servant, otherwise deserving, and perhaps penitent. The rule invoked might lead to the discharge of an innocent and useful servant, when wrongfully accused or suspected, because his employer might ascertain in advance what would be the result of a future trial, and, instead of taking the risk of being charged with a pecuniary liability for which he was not otherwise liable, might discharge the servant."

And see Judge Burch's masterful opinion in Kastrup v. Yellow Cab & Baggage Co. (1929) 129 Kan. 329, 282 Pac. 742.

[26] Novick v. Gouldsberry (1949) 173 F.2d 496.

defendant's barkeeper violently assaulted T, obviously from motives strictly personal. On encountering T subsequently defendant said to him: "If I had been there, I would have broke your God damn neck." From this statement and the fact that defendant did not discharge the barkeeper, the jury were allowed to find that he had ratified the assault.

What considerations of justice or policy justify such a decision, is hard to say. The result seems purely punitive. Defendant is punished for being a bad man and glorying in his servant's viciousness rather than condemning it and discharging the servant. Perhaps the most charitable thing that can be suggested is that the court is using ratification where they think the master should pay but where they find it difficult to put the assault in the course of employment.[27] As will be seen later [28] courts sometimes bolster a dubious case by a dubious holding that the master was at fault in hiring a servant whose bad qualities he knew or should have known. Here it may be that the master will be deterred from congratulating and retaining his vicious servant.

No doubt these tort cases are in a sense unimportant since they are infrequent and usually involve small amounts. However, they seem to the writer to be doctrinally significant as tending to substantiate the basic thesis of this chapter. The contract cases normally make good sense because normally they rest ultimately on solid principles of fair dealing and good sense; it is of little moment that they can be rationalized, after the fact, in terms of the mouth-filling maxim *omnis ratihabitio* and so on. The tort cases, on the other hand, mostly make no sense, and it is precisely because they rest on nothing but the maxim.

[27] A logical dilemma may be involved here. According to Sec. 85 of the Restatement, and the cases that have considered the point, there can only be ratification if the wrongdoer "intends or purports to perform [the act] as the servant" of the one ratifying. (See n. 22, supra.) In such a case modern authorities have little difficulty in considering the act as within the course of employment. See post, § 396.

[28] See post, § 403.

4. *Voluntary Ratification (Herein of Ratification by Silence)*

§ 215. Voluntary ratification: How made. It has already been suggested that in the great majority of instances ratification is simply the name given to the consequence when in some way the purported P has precluded himself from repudiating the transaction done by the purported agent. Such a ratification may be treated as involuntary, since it rests not on the principal's wish to be bound but on some other doctrine such as estoppel, unjust enrichment or the like. There are, however, some instances in which ratification can be based either on the expressed approval of the principal or something that can be treated as equivalent.[29] Some questions affecting such ratification will first be considered.

§ 216. To whom must expression of assent be made? The cases are few which deal with this problem. Logic seems to suggest that neither the agent nor the third party need be notified, and that the essence of the act is simply some unequivocal expression of intent to be bound.[30] It is equally clear that notification of the agent or third party would be the most unequivocal form of ratification and that statements to anyone else must be rather strictly scrutinized to be sure that P really meant to be bound.

§ 217. "Implied" ratification. It has been previously pointed out that in many instances courts in speaking of "implied" authority really mean only that, judging from appearances, there must have been authority. The authority thus found

[29] See Federal Garage v. Prenner (1934) 106 Vt. 222, 172 Atl. 622; Evans v. Ruth (1937) 129 Pa. Super. 192, 195 Atl. 163; Henry W. Savage, Inc. v. Friedberg (1948) 322 Mass. 321, 77 N.E.2d 213; Wittlin v. Giacalone (1948) 171 F.2d 147. And see the cases discussed, post, § 247 et seq., dealing with the principal's attempt to ratify where the third party wishes to repudiate the contract.

[30] See Bayley v. Bryant (1839) 24 Pick. (Mass.) 198; Rutland v. Burlington Ry. Co. (1857) 29 Vt. 206; Sheffield v. Ladue (1871) 16 Minn. 346; Shinn v. Smiley (1922) 1 N. J. Misc. 459, 122 Atl. 531; Restatement, § 95.

would of course be real. Rather similar are the cases in which courts speak of implied ratification, meaning apparently no more than that judging from appearances since the making of the contract, particularly the conduct of the supposed principal, there must have been authority when the contract was made. This again would be real authority—and no real ratification would be involved.[31]

§ 218. **Ratification by silence.** Suppose that P discovers that A, without authority, has purported to act, or is purporting to act, on his behalf; P does nothing. Does his silence amount to ratification?[32]

In DiLorenzo v. Atlantic National Bank,[33] plaintiff turned over to one Del Buono, as he had before, certain bankbooks in which Del Buono was to have the interest added. Del Buono, by forging the plaintiff's name, sold the books to defendant bank which bought them in good faith and proceeded to collect the amounts due. A few months later, plaintiff discovered what had happened. Thereafter, for four or five years, plaintiff negotiated with Del Buono, trying to get the money repaid, but never notified, nor made any demand on, the defendant. He now sues for conversion of the books. The case was tried to the court without a jury and the court found for defendant. This was affirmed, the court pointing out that there was no evidence of injury sustained by defendants by reason of plaintiff's delay, and so no basis for an estoppel, but

[31] See Haluptzok v. Great Northern Ry. Co. (1893) 55 Minn. 446, 57 N. W. 144; Kirkpatrick Finance Co. v. Stotts (1932) 185 Ark. 1089, 51 S.W.2d 512; Irving Tanning Co. v. Shir (1936) 295 Mass. 380, 3 N.E.2d 841; Boillin-Harrison Co. v. Lewis & Co. (1945) 182 Tenn. 342, 187 S.W.2d 17; St. Louis-San Francisco R. Co. v. Lee Wilson & Co. (1947) 212 Ark. 474, 206 S.W.2d 175; Gindin v. Baron (1951) 11 N. J. Super. 215, 78 A.2d 297, aff'd (1951) 16 N. J. Super. 1, 83 A.2d 790.

[32] Obviously, many of the cases discussed are not cases where P really wished to ratify. However, since some of them are nominally instances of the proposition that silence gives consent, they are lumped here for convenience as illustrations of voluntary ratification.

[33] (1932) 278 Mass. 321, 180 N. E. 148.

saying that on the evidence the court below could reasonably have found that plaintiff had "assented" to the wrongful act of his agent.

§ 219. —— Did plaintiff "assent"? Perhaps not, if all he did was procrastinate through shiftlessness and stupidity. More likely, he was unwilling to have his agent and friend prosecuted for forgery. Had plaintiff been asked by the bank: "Are you going to press your claim against us or are you going to be content with trying to get the money back from Del Buono?" and had he answered: "The latter," there could be little doubt of its being a ratification; perhaps what happened could reasonably be found to be the equivalent of this.

Should plaintiff be precluded if defendant has in fact sustained no injury? Probably not. The money is still equitably the plaintiff's and defendant cannot technically claim the position of bona fide purchaser. However, in spite of the court's statement, one is inclined to doubt the proposition that the defendant has sustained no injury. This seems taking a characteristically arbitrary and unrealistic view of what amounts to a change of position. To the present writer it seems that anyone who receives money in the good faith belief that he is entitled to it and, after a substantial lapse of time, is called upon to give it back, suffers a real injury. If the defendant here were an individual of modest means instead of a big city national bank, it is hard to doubt that he would regard it as a cruel hardship to be asked suddenly to produce five thousand dollars.

§ 220. **Same: Affirmance and estoppel.** The Restatement,[34] writers,[35] and occasionally courts,[36] have stressed the impor-

---

[34] Restatement, §§ 94 and 103.

[35] See Mechem, Agency (2d Ed. 1914) § 349.

[36] See Depot Realty Syndicate v. Enterprise Brewing Co. (1918) 87 Ore. 560, 170 Pac. 294, 171 Pac. 223, where defendant's agent, authorized to secure saloon-keepers who would sell defendant's beer exclusively, guaranteed, on defendant's behalf, the payment of rent by such a saloon-keeper. Defendant, being informed of this, did nothing. Moore, J., said: "Ratification by a principal of an unauthorized act of his agent has occa-

tance of distinguishing affirmance [37] by silence from estoppel. The distinction might be of practical importance; e. g., it might affect the measure of damages. If the unauthorized act is one which leads T to a series of reliances (as where P's name is forged or signed without authority to a guaranty) P as a matter of estoppel would be liable for injury suffered by T only after P knew of the unauthorized guarantee whereas it might be argued that he was liable for all T's losses if his silence is treated as a ratification.[38]

§ 221. **Same: Duty to speak.** If estoppel is to be talked, plainly we must posit a duty to speak. One cannot be responsible for the consequences of silence if one was under no obligation to speak. If on the other hand we are talking of "affirmance" or "assent" by silence ("Silence gives consent.") we are perhaps talking of psychology rather than duty. Silence binds the party not because he should have spoken but because under the circumstances the natural reaction is that his silence is tantamount to consent.

sionally been grounded upon the doctrine of an equitable estoppel. A clear distinction, however, exists between an estoppel in pais and ratification. 'The substance of ratification is confirmation of the unauthorized act or contract after it has been done or made, whereas the substance of estoppel is the principal's inducement to another to act to his prejudice. Acts and conduct amounting to an estoppel in pais may in some instances amount to a ratification; but on the other hand ratification may be complete without any elements of estoppel': 2 C. J. 469; 31 Cyc. 1247. In the case at bar, it is possible the extension of the term of the lease and the reduction of the monthly rent might be regarded as creating an equitable estoppel, but however that may be, we rest our decision upon an implied ratification by the defendant of its agent's unauthorized assumption of authority, by failing, when fully notified thereof, promptly to deny his power to consummate the agreement."

[37] "Acquiescence," "consent," "approval," and the like, are words used by courts as almost interchangeable in this context. By the Restatement, affirmance is the manifestation of an election to treat the act as authorized (Sec. 83) and ratification is the result of affirmance, whereby the act is given effect as if originally authorized (Sec. 82).

[38] See Note, 42 Harv. L. Rev. 124.

Whether or not this somewhat refined distinction is valid, the cases talk mostly in terms of duty. A few hold that there is in general no duty to speak and find no special factors creating such a duty.[39]

§ 222. Same: Myers v. Cook. One of the best known and best reasoned cases so holding is Myers v. Cook.[40] There it appeared that husband and wife lived apart. He bought logging equipment and gave a promissory note for the price, signing her name as surety. This was done without her knowledge or authority. The husband had never done it before or acted as her agent in any way. When she heard of the facts, she "grumbled" to some extent but gave no notice to the payee of the note. The court set aside a judgment against the wife, saying: "The husband acted for himself in the transaction, not the wife. He acted against her in signing her name to a note for his debt. The plaintiff was as well aware of that fact as he was. The former acted at his peril in taking the note without knowledge as to whether the husband had authority to bind his wife. He was bound to inquire and could not rely upon the supposed agent's representation. Rosendorf v. Poling, 48 W. Va. 621; Rohrbough v. Express Co., 50 W. Va. 155. The plaintiff omitted this duty, and, presumptively, wronged the wife by his acceptance of the note with her name on it. He could have ascertained by inquiry whether her signature was authorized, in time to have saved himself all she could have saved him by her disavowal. In other words, he could have done for himself what he thinks she should have done for him. To permit him to make her mere failure to do that prove ratification would allow him the benefit of his own wrong. If he had made the inquiry and she had induced him

---

[39] See Hortons & Hutton v. Townes (1835) 6 Leigh (Va.) 47; Kelly v. Phelps (1883) 57 Wis. 425, 15 N. W. 385; Merritt v. Bissell (1898) 155 N. Y. 396, 50 N. E. 280; Britt v. Gordon (1906) 132 Iowa 431, 108 N. W. 319; Shinew v. First Nat. Bank (1911) 84 Ohio St. 297, 95 N. E. 881; Myers v. Cook (1920) 87 W. Va. 265, 104 S. E. 593; Furst v. Carrico (1934) 167 Md. 465, 175 Atl. 442, 96 A. L. R. 375; O'Neill v. Niccolls (1949) 324 Mass. 382, 86 N.E.2d 522.

[40] (1920) 87 W. Va. 265, 104 S. E. 593.

to forego right of rescission by an express ratification or, possibly, by silence, when required to speak, and thus caused him loss, it would no doubt be otherwise. And, on the other hand, if she had disavowed the act, he could have asserted his rights against the husband at once. By rescission, he might have reacquired the property he had sold."

§ 223. **Same: Furst v. Carrico.** Also well-known, though it is not easy to characterize it as well-reasoned, is the case of Furst v. Carrico.[41] There defendant's name was forged to a guaranty of payment, in reliance on which plaintiff sold several bills of goods. Plaintiff notified defendant by registered mail of the supposed guaranty and that he was selling goods in reliance thereon, but defendant gave no answer; some of the goods were sold after the defendant had had ample time to answer. The forger was not defendant's agent and it is said there was no special relationship between him and defendant which might impose a duty to speak.[42] Defendant's demurrer was sustained below, and this action was affirmed. It was significant, the court said, that the failure was to answer a letter, rather than the failure to respond to an oral statement, since "men use the tongue much more readily than the pen." [43] And "the duties of strangers to transactions are duties of forbearance, not of exertion and assistance."

Other cases involving the same factual setup have unanimously reached a different conclusion.[44]

§ 224. **Same: The prevailing view.** By and large, juries have found duty, and so ratification, where one who "should in good conscience speak" fails to do so, and appellate courts have affirmed the finding.[45] It is often said that the duty to

---

[41] (1934) 167 Md. 465, 175 Atl. 442, 96 A. L. R. 375.

[42] It appears from the facts that the purported agent was also named Carrico. This might support an inference.

[43] Cf. Traders' Nat. Bank v. Rogers (1897) 167 Mass. 315, 45 N. E. 923.

[44] See Strauss Bros. v. Denton (1925) 140 Miss. 745, 106 So. 257; Furst & Thomas v. Smith (1939) 280 Ky. 601, 133 S.W.2d 941.

[45] In addition to cases already

speak is greater where the unauthorized act is done by one who is in fact P's agent or occupies some other close relationship to him.[46] This is no doubt true, but most of the cases are in fact of this type. Decisions involving a pure interloper are rare.

§ 225. **Ratification of forgery.** The guaranty cases, mentioned above, raise a problem which has been considerably discussed—perhaps more than it deserves, viz., the possibility of ratifying a forgery. The conventional view is that a forgery cannot be ratified because, by definition, the attempt does not satisfy the requirement that the actor purport to act as an

cited, see St. Louis Gunning Advertising Co. v. Wanamaker & Brown (1905) 115 Mo. App. 270, 90 S. W. 737; Argus v. Ware & Leland (1912) 155 Iowa 583, 136 N. W. 774; Seymour Improvement Co. v. Viking Sprinkler Co. (1928) 87 Ind. App. 179, 161 N. E. 389, noted in 42 Harv. L. Rev. 124; Greenwood v. Martin's Bank, Ltd. [1932] 1 K. B. 371, aff'd [1933] A. C. 51, noted in 11 Can. B. Rev. 632, 48 L. Q. Rev. 304, and 18 Va. L. Rev. 774; Watson v. Schmidt (1931) 173 La. 92, 136 So. 99; Renland v. First Nat. Bank (1931) 90 Mont. 424, 4 P.2d 488; Continental Supply Co. v. Palmer (1932) 19 La. App. 718, 140 So. 81; Sullivan v. Bennett (1933) 261 Mich. 232, 246 N. W. 90, 87 A. L. R. 791; McNeely v. Walters (1937) 211 N. C. 112, 189 S. E. 114; Gordon Const. Co. v. Pettingill (1939) 105 Colo. 214, 96 P.2d 416; Moe v. Zitek (1947) 75 N. D. 222, 27 N.W.2d 10.

[46] "A distinction has been made between the acts of an agent who has gone beyond his authority, and those of a mere stranger intermeddling in affairs with which he is in no way concerned. In the case of a stranger, it has been said that the act will not be binding upon the principal unless expressly ratified by him. Ward v. Williams, 26 Ill. 447. But the better opinion appears to be, that in this, as in the case where an agency exists, the approval of the principal may be inferred from his silence and acquiescence when informed of what has been done in his name. Philadelphia, Wilmington & Baltimore R. R. Co. v. Cowell, 28 Pa. St. 329; Ladd v. Heilderbrant, 27 Wis. 135. But all agree that the relations of the parties are of great consequence in determining the question of ratification, the presumption arising from acquiescence being very much stronger where the agency exists than in the case of a mere stranger. Story on Agency, § 256." Hallett, C. J., in Union Gold Mining Co. v. Rocky Mountain Nat. Bank (1873) 2 Colo. 248.

agent and not as a principal.[47] It is also said that to allow ratification would tend to stifle a criminal prosecution.

[47] "One who commits the crime of forgery by signing the name of another to a promissory note does not assume to act as the agent of the person whose name is forged. Upon principle there would seem to be no room to apply the doctrine of ratification or adoption of the act in such a case. Where the act done constitutes a crime and is committed without any pretense of authority, it is difficult to understand how one who is in a sense the victim of the criminal act may adopt or ratify it, so as to become bound by a contract to which he is to all intents and purposes a stranger, and which as to him was conceived in a crime and is totally without consideration. As has been well said, it is impossible in such a case to attribute any motive to the ratifying party but that of concealing the crime and suppressing the prosecution: 'For why should a man pay money without consideration when he himself has been wronged, unless constrained by a desire to shield the guilty party'?" Henry v. Heeb (1887) 114 Ind. 275, 16 N. E. 606.

Cf. Greenfield Bank v. Crafts (1862) 4 Allen (Mass.) 447, where the court, distinguishing a merely unauthorized signature from a forged signature, says: "In the first case, the actor has no authority any more than in the last. The contract receives its whole validity from the ratification. It may be ratified, where there was no pretense of agency. In the other case the individual who presents the note thus signed passes the same as a note signed by the promisor, either by his own proper hand, or written by some one by his authority. It was clearly competent, if duly authorized, thus to sign the note. It is, as it seems to us, equally competent for the party, he knowing all the circumstances as to the signature and intending to adopt the note, to ratify the same, and thus confirm what was originally an unauthorized and illegal act. We are supposing the case of a party acting with full knowledge of the manner [in which] the note was signed, and the want of authority on the part of the actor to sign his name, but who understandingly and unequivocally adopts the signature, and assumes the note as his own. It is difficult to perceive why such adoption should not bind the party whose name is placed on the note as promisor, as effectually as if he had adopted the note when executed by one professing to be authorized, and to act as an agent, as indicated by the form of the signature, but who in fact had no authority.

"It is, however, urged that public policy forbids sanctioning a ratification of a forged note, as it may have a tendency to stifle a prosecution for the criminal offense. It would seem, however, that this must stand upon the general principles applicable to other contracts, and is only to be defeated where the agreement was upon the understanding that if the signature was adopted the guilty party was not

Of the latter suggestion it seems reasonable to say that the question of the effect of a ratification on the criminal law is a rather remotely related one, which the criminal law should be quite adequate to handle. Of the former it may be suggested that it pays more attention to form than to substance. After all, one whose name has been forged to a document may have good reasons for electing to be bound by the document; or he may have acted in such a way as to make it clearly inequitable for him to deny the validity of the instrument. Either result should be attainable under the law. A number of cases frankly permit ratification [48] and more recognize the possibility that P may be "precluded" [49] or estopped from denying the validity of the instrument.[50]

to be prosecuted for the criminal offense."

[48] See Greenfield Bank v. Crafts (1862) 4 Allen (Mass.) 447; Montgomery v. Crossthwait (1890) 90 Ala. 553, 8 So. 498; Campbell v. Campbell (1901) 133 Cal. 33, 65 Pac. 134; Hogan v. Cooney (1931) 51 R. I. 395, 155 Atl. 240; Strader v. Haley (1943) 216 Minn. 315, 12 N.W.2d 608, 150 A. L. R. 970; Magid v. Drexel Nat. Bank (1947) 330 Ill. App. 486, 71 N.E.2d 898.

[49] Sec. 23 of the N. I. L. provides: "When a signature is forged or made without authority, it is wholly inoperative, and no right to retain the instrument or to give a discharge therefor, or to enforce payment thereof against any party thereto, can be acquired through or under such signature, unless the party against whom it is sought to enforce such right is precluded from setting up the forgery or want of authority." As to the meaning of this see Britton, Bills & Notes (1943) § 132.

[50] The typical cases are the ones in which, the present holder, *be-*

fore he acquired the instrument in question, e. g., a promissory note, inquired of the alleged maker if it was genuine, and being assured that it was, took it; or in which, while he may have taken the note without inquiry, he is induced by assurances of its genuineness, to give up or forbear from measures which he would otherwise have taken to protect himself. See Workman v. Wright (1878) 33 Ohio St. 405 (no estoppel found); Casco Bank v. Keene (1865) 53 Me. 103; Rudd v. Mathews (1881) 79 Ky. 479; Hefner v. Dawson (1872) 63 Ill. 403; Lynch v. Richter (1895) 10 Wash. 486, 39 Pac. 125.

As to fraudulent alteration, see Wilson v. Hayes (1889) 40 Minn. 531, 42 N. W. 467; Montgomery v. Crossthwait (1889) 90 Ala. 553, 8 So. 498.

And see Greenwood v. Martin's Bank, Ltd. [1932] 1 K. B. 371, aff'd [1933] A. C. 51, noted in 11 Can. B. Rev. 632, 48 L. Q. Rev. 304, and 18 Va. L. Rev. 774; annotation, 150 A. L. R. 978.

CHAPTER IX

FURTHER OF RATIFICATION: INVOLUNTARY RATIFI-CATION, RATIFICATION AGAINST UNWILLING THIRD PARTIES, AND RATIFICATION AS AFFECTING THE AGENT

5. *Involuntary Ratification*

§ 226. In general. As has already been pointed out, the generality of cases to which the tag "ratification" is applied are not cases where the principal with full knowledge of the consequences, deliberately elects to ratify; they are cases where the principal has not the least wish to ratify but where he has put himself (or chosen to remain) in a situation where he cannot equitably refuse to treat the contract as ratified.

To such cases the name "involuntary ratification" has herein been given and the next few sections will be devoted to an analysis of the problem and an attempt to classify the cases.

§ 227. A partially executed transaction is usually involved. If the contract is wholly executory, the only likely basis for holding P will be that he has ratified by silence or has estopped himself from denying ratification. (The latter, obviously, is a case of involuntary ratification but for reasons given above it has been lumped with ratification by silence, commonly assumed to be a form of voluntary ratification.) On the other hand, since we mean by "the contract" the unauthorized contract or, as is more likely, the authorized contract with unauthorized terms, if the contract is completely executed that will mean that P has performed, although not bound so to do, and hence will normally neither wish to nor be in a position to object to the unauthorized contract or the unauthorized portion of it. Hence the problem will chiefly arise where the contract is partly executed, the unexecuted portion naturally being the performance by P, promised by A but without authority.

§ 228. Problem usually one of election. In such a case the position of P will be, basically, very much like that of a defrauded person. True, the third party is not assumed to have done any deliberate wrong but, ex hypothesi, he has chosen to deal with an agent who had neither real nor apparent authority, and hence he has no rights on which he can stand. It is perhaps fair to say that his position, legally, is no better than that of a contracting party guilty of fraud.

The injured party, in a fraud case, normally has an election. He is not compelled to repudiate the transaction; he may affirm it and (what is not pertinent to the present analogy) sue for damages. On the other hand he may, if he chooses, disaffirm; in such a case he is entitled to the return of any performance rendered on the assumption that the contract was valid and would stand, and must normally himself return any performance under the contract. The latter requirement is plainly based on principles of unjust enrichment: if he were allowed to terminate the contract and receive back what he has given, and at the same time to keep what he has received, he would be unjustly enriched to the extent of the benefit retained.

§ 229. ——— It is to be remembered that in the ratification case just as in the fraud case, there is only one contract involved: that actually made between T and A.[1] Since it was in whole, or in part, unauthorized, P need not be bound by it. If he elects to affirm, however, he can only affirm the contract as made; he cannot affirm, i. e., enforce, the authorized part, and not affirm the unauthorized part. To do so would be forcing on T a contract he never made.

It follows, thus, that in the typical case of the partly executed contract, the P has two choices and two only. He may disaffirm,

---

[1] Rarely the case is presented where A has made several authorized contracts at the same time or where, although there is nominally only one contract, it is clearly and fairly severable. In such a case one of the contracts, or a severable part, may be ratified. See Meeks v. Adams Louisiana Co. (1943) 49 F. Supp. 489.

in which case he must return what he has received. Or he may affirm, in which case he necessarily ratifies the unauthorized part of the contract. In the latter case the typical result is to bind him to perform the unauthorized part of the contract, which he had hoped to repudiate, although retaining the benefit of the third party's performance.

§ 230. How election made. In the fraud cases the election to affirm (and, in both the fraud and the ratification cases, it is the election to affirm which is more decisive and more vital) is commonly made in one of two ways: (a) by affirmance in pais and (b) by affirmance by suit.[2] The same is commonly true of election to ratify.

§ 231. Affirmance in pais. By this is simply meant conduct inconsistent with the obligation of the party to disaffirm, if he ever means to do so, promptly on his discovery of his right to elect. Plainly rescission is more drastic and more upsetting to the other party than affirmance (and this is particularly true in the ratification cases since there, as distinguished from the fraud case, the ratification imposes no burden but on the contrary leaves the other party in the situation he has all along assumed he was entitled to be in) and plainly each day during which the dominant party fails to make his choice to rescind adds to the actual or possible hardship to the other party. Hence courts are rather quick to find that P's failure, either to return what he has received or to demand a rescission, justify treating him as having affirmed.

§ 232. —— So where the agent of a lumber company without authority contracted to buy standing timber and the lumber company contracted to sell it to a third party in the form of lumber, had part of it milled and delivered to the third party,

---

[2] There can, of course, be an express affirmance just as there can be an express ratification, but this is not pertinent in the present context.

it was held too late for the company to insist that the contract of purchase was unauthorized.[3]

And so where the manager of plaintiff's racing stable sold a race horse without authority, and some months later, after the horse in the hands of its new owner had won several races, plaintiff challenged the sale as unauthorized and demanded a return of the horse (but without tendering a return of the price) it was held that he had ratified.[4]

And so where plaintiff corporation's agent, authorized to rent property but not for more than two years, leased it to defendant for four years, the lease being put in plaintiff's safe although plaintiff never bothered to examine it, and plaintiff accepted rent from defendant for nearly two years, it was held that plaintiff must be charged with having ratified and could not eject defendant at the termination of two years.[5]

§ 233. Land contracts induced by unauthorized misrepresentations. In a previous section [6] there has been considered the liability of a principal for the misrepresentations of a real estate broker. It was there pointed out that as the broker is only authorized to find a possible buyer, with whom the principal then negotiates, it is assumed that statements as to the character and attributes of the land will be made by the principal in person while negotiating; it follows that the incidental or apparent authority of the broker to make representations is very limited and scarcely goes beyond identifying the land. Where the broker has thus no power to bind the principal by his representations, it follows that the principal cannot be held liable for them in tort. A majority of cases however (and the Restatement), to prevent unjust enrichment of the principal, allow the third party to rescind in such a case.

[3] Wilkins v. Waldo Lumber Co. (1931) 130 Me. 5, 153 Atl. 191.

[4] Watson v. Schmidt (1931) 173 La. 92, 136 So. 99.

[5] Payne Realty Co. v. Lindsey (1922) 91 W. Va. 127, 112 S. E. 306. See also Sargent v. Drew-English, Inc. (1942) 12 Wash.2d 320, 121 P.2d 373; Marian v. Peoples-Pittsburgh Trust Co. (1942) 149 Pa. Super. 653, 27 A.2d 549; Cannon v. Blake (1944) 353 Mo. 294, 182 S.W.2d 303.

[6] Restatement, § 139.

Suppose that the third party, on discovering that he has been deceived, demands a rescission from the principal; the principal refuses and says that he stands on the contract. Will this have the effect of ratifying the representations so as to make the principal liable in tort?

§ 234. —— An affirmative answer might be expected. In other situations courts are quick to say that a principal cannot retain the benefits of a transaction and at the same time disavow the means by which the benefits have been obtained. A little authority applies this view here. Thus in Light v. Chandler Improvement Company,[7] the court says that the buyer, on discovering the fraud, may go to the seller and offer to rescind. "If the owner, after due notice of the fraud and offer of rescission, insists upon holding the purchaser to his bargain, he will then be deemed to have ratified the alleged representations of the agent and the purchaser may pursue as against such owner any remedy which he would have had, had the false representations been made by the owner in person."[8]

§ 235. —— In most instances, however, it seems to be assumed that the purchaser is adequately protected by his right to rescind and that the seller's unwillingness to rescind will not be treated as an affirmance. It is not quite clear what is the basis of this attitude. Perhaps it is thought that in such a case since the sale itself is as authorized (i. e., the agent was unquestionably authorized to find a buyer) and the principal has performed all *promises* made on his behalf, the principal is not keeping anything to which he is not entitled by the contract. Such an argument is plainly fallacious, however, particularly where the loss of bargain theory of damages is applied, since his liability is the same as if he had promised

[7] (1928) 33 Ariz. 101, 261 Pac. 969, 57 A. L. R. 107.
[8] And see Lewis v. McClure (1932) 127 Cal.App.2d 9, 15 P.2d 166; Daum v. Urquhart (1933) 61 S. D. 431, 249 N. W. 738; Gower v. Wieser (1934) 269 Mich. 6, 256 N. W. 603; Smith v. Miller (1938) 225 Iowa 241, 280 N. W. 493.

to sell a property of the type represented, which he plainly has not done. In substance the case seems to be like one involving an unauthorized warranty, where, as already seen, retention or attempt to enforce will normally be treated as ratification. Perhaps, in view of the traditional reluctance of courts to hold an innocent principal for fraud, it can be said that they are simply expressing a feeling that the third party should have known better and is given all the protection he deserves by being given a right to rescind.

§ 236. **Restitutionary relief based on receipt of benefits.** In a number of cases a principal who has received money as the result of the unauthorized act of his agent, is held liable to T in an action of assumpsit for money had and received. In such cases it is seldom said that the defendant's liability rests on a theory of ratification. It is apparent, nevertheless, that the basis of the liability is the same as would exist in slightly different circumstances where it would be said that defendant had ratified. The retention of benefits is the basic operative fact charging defendant with liability; what form, technically, the relief takes is relatively immaterial.

A typical instance is afforded by the case of First National Bank v. Oberne,[9] where defendant, a Chicago firm dealing in hides and pelts, had an agent in Las Vegas who was authorized to draw checks, for their business, on their account in plaintiff, a Las Vegas bank. The agent received a note from J. S., for a personal debt; he indorsed and guaranteed payment of the note in defendant's name, discounted it with the bank, and put the proceeds into defendant's account. Thereafter he withdrew the money on various checks, two of which, amounting to $560.27, were given in payment for pelts bought for defendant and which, apparently, were shipped to them and used by them in the ordinary course of their business. The guaranty of the note was conceded to be outside the authority of the agent, but defendant was held liable to the extent of $560.27, namely the extent to which they received the proceeds of the

---

9 (1886) 121 Ill. 25, 7 N. E. 85.

unauthorized act. The court said that they could not "be permitted to repudiate a contract made in their name by an assumed agent, on the ground of a want of authority in the agent to make it, without restoring the money received by them under the contract, and as the result of an agent's act." [10]

§ 237. —— It is clear that in such a case this is more realistic than to speak of ratification. Defendants have neither prospectively nor retrospectively approved the conduct of their agent; this is, however, in the case of money (in the form of pelts) received by their agent, ostensibly on their behalf, and if they elect to keep it, it can be argued that they are as much obligated to account for it as if it had been in fact received on their account.

The question might be asked: suppose defendant's account with the bank was overdrawn because of improper drafts on it made by the A, so that the pelts in fact represented payment by A to P for prior improper transactions—could it then be argued that the value was received in payment of an antecedent debt, making defendant a bona fide purchaser for value? It could be asked: is defendant barred from asserting such a claim by virtue of the knowledge of the agent who was the active party? These and other questions involving restitution, bona fide purchase, and the like, can only be suggested here, and a few typical cases cited.[11] Any more detailed discussion must be sought in works on Equity and Restitution.

[10] See also Seifert v. Union Brass & Metal Mfg. Co. (1934) 191 Minn. 362, 254 N. W. 273, noted in 19 Minn. L. Rev. 318; Duffy v. Scott (1940) 235 Wis. 142, 292 N. W. 273, 129 A. L. R. 487.

[11] See Thacher v. Pray (1873) 113 Mass. 291; Baldwin v. Burrows (1872) 47 N. Y. 199; Bailey v. Hamburg (1919) 106 Wash. 177, 179 Pac. 88; Arkansas Valley Bank v. Kelley (1928) 176 Ark. 387, 3 S.W.2d 53, 58 A. L. R. 808; Citizens Banking Co. v. American Bakeries Co. (1930) 41 Ga. App. 89, 151 S. E. 824, noted in 8 Tenn. L. Rev. 278; Massachusetts Bonding & Insurance Co. v. Pittsburg Pipe & Supply Co. (Tex. Civ. App., 1939) 135 S.W.2d 818, noted in 18 Tex. L. Rev. 502; Blumberg v. Taggard (1942) 213 Minn. 39, 5 N.W.2d 388, noted in 41 Mich. L. Rev. 1184; Newco Land Co. v. Martin (1948) 358 Mo. 99, 213 S.W.2d 504.

§ **238. Affirmance by suit.** As already pointed out, there is in these cases only one contract: the contract as made by the agent. It is not possible to sue on part of a contract. Hence, a suit brought by the principal on the contract can only be taken as a suit brought on all the contract; it is necessarily brought on the (hitherto) unauthorized portion as well as on the authorized portion. This, it should be stressed, is not the same as saying that P has evinced his wish to affirm. Quite the contrary. No doubt in most instances he is either deliberately taking a chance or acting in ignorance of probable consequences. A party with an election must make it sooner or later; sooner, in fairness to the other party. And when he has taken an unequivocal step which is only consistent with an affirmance it is difficult to say that he can escape the consequences by showing that he did not intend them.

§ **239. Same: Instances.** The party who has affirmed by bringing suit may have had only the alternative of suing or not suing, or he may have had a choice of several remedies, one or more of which would not necesarily have been an affirmance.

In a Minnesota case the agent of plaintiff corporation had sold T shares of plaintiff's stock, taking his note therefor, and promising that plaintiff would employ him as local representative, and furnish him with a place of business and equipment; the latter part of the agreement was unauthorized. Without furnishing the place of business or equipment (although a certificate of stock had been given) plaintiff sued T on the note. It was held that the effect was to ratify the unauthorized portion of the contract; plaintiff was then necessarily in default, having neither given the promised consideration nor evinced any readiness and willingness to do so.[12]

[12] Independent Harvester Co. v. Malzohn (1920) 147 Minn. 145, 179 N. W. 727. Cf. Robie v. Holdahl (1930) 180 Minn. 226, 230 N. W. 641, where a corporation made a deed of its property to plaintiff as trustee for its creditors, and plaintiff liquidated the assets and applied them pro rata among the creditors. Thereafter he was appointed receiver and brought an action to enforce the stockholders' statutory liability. Defense, that one Lacy, who had negotiated the deed of

---

§ 240. —— In a well-known Connecticut case [13] plaintiff was a dealer in musical instruments; his agent sold and delivered a piano to defendant, the latter to pay for the same by cancelling certain brokerage debts which the agent owed or expected to owe him. Such a sale was of course unauthorized; when plaintiff discovered the sale he repudiated it and brought an action of assumpsit to recover the price of the piano. The court said that they could have recovered the piano in replevin or its value in trover. "But, knowing the terms of the sale, they elected to sue in assumpsit on the contract for the agreed price, and thereby they affirmed the contract and ratified the act of the agent, precisely as if it had been expressly approved upon being reported to them by the agent or the defendant. . . . The argument for the plaintiff (though it is not so stated) seems really to involve the fallacious assumption that the plaintiffs could affirm the contract in part and repudiate it in part; that is, that the contract is to be treated as good for the agreed price but bad as to the agreed mode of payment. But the law requires a contract to be affirmed or repudiated in its entirety. There was no contract at all relative to the piano except the one made by Day as their agent; and when the plaintiffs, knowing the facts, sued on that contract, they affirmed it in every essential particular, both as to price and as to the terms of paying the price."

trust, had secured it on the agreement that the creditors would waive the stockholders' liability. Held, no ratification. "The evidence discloses no other benefit to the creditors of the company except a part payment of their debts, something they were legally entitled to receive and retain irrespective of any contract."

See generally Eadie, Guilford & Co. v. Ashbaugh (1876) 44 Iowa 519; Kelley v. Isensee (1930) 60 N. D. 149, 233 N. W. 245; General Paint Corp. v. Kramer (1932) 57 F.2d 698; Crookum v. Ketchum (1935) 174 Okla. 468, 50 P.2d 710;

Tway v. Southern Methodist Hospital (1936) 48 Ariz. 490, 62 P.2d 1318; Texas Pacific Coal & Oil Co. v. Smith (Tex. Civ. App., 1939) 130 S.W.2d 425; King v. Continental Casualty Co. (1940) 110 F.2d 950; Walter v. Baldwin (1937) 126 Pa. Super. 589, 193 Atl. 146; Hardware Mutual Casualty Co. v. Lieberman (1941) 39 F. Supp. 243; Halsey v. Robinson (1942) 19 Cal.2d 476, 122 P.2d 11; Perkins v. Benguet Consolidated Mining Co. (1943) 55 Cal.App.2d 720, 132 P.2d 70.

13 Shoninger v. Peabody (1889) 57 Conn. 42, 17 Atl. 278.

§ 241. —— Of the two cases just stated the first at least seems to reach an eminently satisfactory result. Plaintiff's attempt to enforce the contract without the authorized term failed. In effect the result was a rescission, leaving the parties where they should be, unless plaintiff were willing to be bound by the contract as made by their agent. The result of the second is more questionable. It leaves defendant with a piano to which, as against plaintiff, he had no claim; plaintiff is out a piano, not from any attempt to be grasping or to force on defendant a contract he never made, but solely because of a mistake of law as to the proper form of relief to be invoked. Perhaps plaintiffs should be allowed to dismiss and start again, or to amend. However, where the action is brought with knowledge of the facts [14] it is hard to say how far the court should go in allowing a plaintiff to change his ground because of his own mistake as to the merits of the course of action he has deliberately chosen.[15]

[14] A later hearing in the case (1890) 59 Conn. 588, 22 Atl. 437, suggests that P may not really have known what contract he was ratifying.

[15] The doctrine of the Shoninger case appears to be approved by the Restatement. See Sec. 97, Illustration 1. It may be suggested that in the fraud cases the party presumably gets something of value, whichever alternative he elects; here he just elected himself out of his piano.

Instructive to contrast with the Shoninger case is United Australia, Ltd. v. Barclays Bank [1941] A. C. 1, [1940] 4 All. E. R. 20. "E. was the secretary and a director of the plaintiff company. Without authority, he indorsed a cheque, made payable to his company, to M. F. G. Trust, Ltd. The defendant bank accepted it for collection, and credited the proceeds to the account of M. F. G. Trust, Ltd. Subsequently, the plaintiff company commenced an action against M. F. G. Trust, Ltd., to recover the value of the cheque as a loan, or, in the alternative, as money had and received. Before final judgment, M. F. G. Trust, Ltd., went into liquidation. The plaintiffs put in a proof for the sum alleged to be due in the liquidation, but the proof was not admitted, as the funds to meet the demands of creditors were merely trivial. They then brought the present action against the bank for wrongful conversion of the cheque. The defense pleaded was, inter alia, that the plaintiffs had ratified E.'s indorsement of the cheque by suing the M. F. G. Trust, Ltd., and had, therefore, waived the tort." This defense was successful below, but was denied by the House of Lords, which held that there was no election or ratification. Lord Atkin

§ 242. Change of position. The election angle of ratification has been stressed because of its usefulness in explain-

said: "I will deal with election later, but at present I wish to deal with the waiver of the tort which is said to arise whenever the injured person sues in contract for money received. If the plaintiff in truth treats the wrongdoer as having acted as his agent, overlooks the wrong, and, by consent of both parties, is content to receive the proceeds, this will be a true waiver. It will arise necessarily where the plaintiff ratifies, in the true sense, an unauthorized act of an agent. In that case, the lack of authority disappears, and the correct view is, not that the tort is waived, but that by retraction of the ratification it has never existed. In the ordinary case, however, the plaintiff has never the slightest intention of waiving, excusing, or in any kind of way palliating the tort. If I find that a thief has stolen my securities and is in possession of the proceeds, when I sue him for them, I am not excusing him. I am protesting violently that he is a thief, and, because of his theft, I am suing him." . . . "Concurrently with the decisions as to waiver of tort, there is to be found a supposed application of election, and the allegation is sometimes to be found that the plaintiff elected to waive the tort. It seems to me that in this respect it is essential to bear in mind the distinction between choosing one of two alternative remedies and choosing one of two inconsistent rights. As far as remedies were concerned, from the oldest time the only restriction was on the choice between real and personal actions. If you chose the one, you could not claim on the other. Real actions have long disappeared, and, subject to the difficulty of including two causes of action in one writ, which has also now disappeared, there has not been, and there certainly is not now, any compulsion to choose between alternative remedies. You may put them in the same writ, or you may put one in first and then amend and add or substitute another." . . . "On the other hand, if a man is entitled to one of two inconsistent rights, it is fitting that, when, with full knowledge, he has done an unequivocal act showing that he has chosen the one, he cannot afterwards pursue the other, which, after the first choice, is by reason of the inconsistency, no longer his to choose. Instances are the right of a principal dealing with an agent for an. undisclosed principal to choose the liability of the agent or the principal, the right of a landlord whose forfeiture of a lease has been committed to exact the forfeiture or to treat the former tenant as still tenant, and the like." . . . "I think, therefore, that, on a question of alternative remedies, no question of election arises until one or other claim has been brought to judgment." . . . "Verschures Creameries v. Hull & Netherlands S. S. Co. [1921] 2 K. B. 608, upon which both the

ing certain cases otherwise hard, if not impossible, to explain. This involves the matter of change of position. A person wishing to rescind normally must restore what he has received. This is obviously because of the unjust enrichment that would otherwise accrue to the rescinding party. However, there may be cases in which forcing him to restore would in fact unjustly enrich the other party. In such a case P should be able to rescind, i. e., repudiate the unauthorized agreement or portion thereof, without restoration.

Among other instances given in Sec. 99 of the Restatement, is this: "4. Purporting to represent P but without power to bind him thereby, A contracts with T to deliver to P a case of grapefruit. P, supposing that the grapefruit came as a gift from a friend in Florida, eats some of them and the rest are destroyed in a fire before he learns the facts. There is no affirmance."

Plainly in such a case to make P pay would be to unjustly impoverish P. He has in fact received no substantial benefit from the grapefruit. And T would be unjustly enriched by escaping a loss resulting from his own carelessness and which, as between him and P, T should bear.

§ 243. **Unauthorized promises to repurchase stock.** A not uncommon case involves the agent of a corporation who travels selling its stock. He is likely to be carrying blank certificates which he is authorized to fill in and deliver. In such a situation an unscrupulous agent, dealing with a housewife or other possible purchaser little familiar with business

courts below founded their decision, has, with great respect, very little bearing on the matter. A firm of carriers, being authorized by the plaintiffs to carry goods to A, delivered them to B. The plaintiffs invoiced the goods to B, sued him for the price, recovered judgment, and took bankruptcy proceedings against him. They afterwards sued the carriers for misdelivery. It was the plainest case of ratification of an act done by the carriers purporting to deliver on behalf of the plaintiffs, and, as such, there could be no complaint against the carriers for breach of authority."

The Barclays Bank case is discussed by E. S. Thurston in 45 Mich. L. Rev. 935, 948, and is the subject of an article by Lord Wright in 57 L. Q. Rev. 184.

practices, is likely to clinch the sale by making the obviously [16] quite unauthorized promise that at the end of a period the company will on request repurchase the stock at a named price, usually its par value or even more. The salesman thereby earns a commission and expects to be on another job in another part of the country before the named time elapses and the company discovers what has been done.

§ 244. —— Practically all possible solutions may be found in the cases dealing with such a practice. The principal may be held on a theory of apparent authority [17] or of ratification; [18] the principal may be held on a quasi-contractual theory; [19] the principal may not be held on any theory.[20] The last solution seems most readily justified on a change of position theory. The matter will not come to light for a period of years after the sale. The company will long since have spent the money.

[16] Obvious, that is, to a lawyer or business man, but not likely to be so to the unsuspecting victim.

[17] See Wright v. Iowa Power & Light Co. (1938) 223 Iowa 1192, 274 N. W. 892, noted in 22 Marq. L. Rev. 107.

[18] See Davies v. Montana Auto Finance Corp. (1930) 86 Mont. 500, 28 Pac. 267.

[19] In Seifert v. Union Brass & Metal Mfg. Co. (1934) 191 Minn. 362, 254 N. W. 273, noted in 19 Minn. L. Rev. 318, the purchaser was allowed to recover the purchase price back in a quasi-contractual action. The court said: "The findings establish that Mr. Michel had no authority to bind defendant by offer of monthly bonus or to repurchase. But, nevertheless, that agreement was both term and condition of the supposed contract under which plaintiff parted with his money. Defendant cannot affirm in part and repudiate in part. Failure of the agreement to bind defendant according to its terms makes a clear case of no contract. Plaintiff did not get what he paid for; there was failure of consideration for his payment, and so he is entitled to recover it in order to prevent the unjust enrichment of defendant which otherwise would result. One of the long-recognized heads for such recovery is 'where the money was paid under a mistake as to the creation, existence, or extent of an obligation.' Keener, Quasi-Contracts, 112. This is just such a case."

See also Plate v. Detroit Fidelity & Surety Co. (1924) 229 Mich. 482, 201 N. W. 457; Downs v. Jersey Central Power & Light Co. (1934) 115 N. J. Eq. 348, 174 Atl. 887, noted in 33 Mich. L. Rev. 1241.

[20] See Schuster v. North American Hotel Co. (1921) 106 Neb. 672, 184 N. W. 136, 186 N. W. 87.

The purchaser naturally will not be seeking to enforce the agreement unless the stock is now worth less than the promised price. The election presented now between rescission and affirmance is now purely nominal, since either way the company will have to pay out for the stock more than its value. In the light of these circumstances it seems that the purchaser has no compelling equity against the company. Rescission is assumed to mean no loss to either party, but here one party or the other has to take the loss in value and it seems fair to put it on the one who allowed himself to be tricked by the agent.

§ 245. **The Johnson case.** The case of Johnson v. City Company [21] affords a striking instance of change of position in a situation analogous to those just discussed. In November of 1929 defendant's agent sold plaintiff certain stock for $450 a share, warranting that its market value would be $650 a share within three days. The warranty was fantastic, except perhaps in the hysteria of the moment; it was plainly unauthorized. Three days later the value of the stock had gone, not up but down, two hundred dollars a share. Plaintiff sued for his loss, alleging among other things, that defendant could not retain the benefits of the transaction and at the same time repudiate the authority of the agent to make it. Such a doctrine, the court replied, does not apply where the principal has changed his position before learning of the agent's unauthorized act.

§ 246. **The Northwestern Sleigh case.** To be contrasted with this is the famous case of Wheeler v. The Northwestern Sleigh Company.[22] P's agent, authorized to sell P's stock, did so but, without authority, threw in a sale of a dividend already declared on the stock and so not normally passing with a sale of the stock. P was allowed to enforce the sale of the stock without the dividend, making T pay for the stock alone the price he had agreed to give for the stock *and*

[21] (1935) 78 F.2d 782.
[22] (1889) 39 Fed. 347.

163

the dividend. No facts appear which would warrant a justification of the decision in terms of change of position. Less
than three months elapsed between the sale and P's discovery
of the unauthorized term. It is not suggested that the value of
the stock had changed significantly; indeed there is no suggestion that it had changed at all. This decision and some
others like it appear to overlook the fundamental equities of
the problem, and it is believed that they must be treated as
unsound.

6. *Ratification Against an Unwilling Third Party*

§ 247. In general. The case sometimes, though infrequently, arises, where a principal, finding out about the unauthorized contract and thinking it a profitable one, wishes to
ratify, but the third party (perhaps for the same reason that
the principal wishes to ratify) repudiates the contract and
insists he is not bound. Can the principal effectively ratify
in such a case?

The few cases on this point illustrate three different views.

§ 248. The English view. The English cases have applied
the maxim *omnis ratihabitio* with strict logic.[23] Since the

[23] In Bolton Partners v. Lambert
(1889) 41 Ch. D. 295, noted in 5
L. Q. Rev. 440, plaintiff's manager, Scratchley, without authority
leased defendant property belonging to plaintiff. Later, defendant
attempted to withdraw from the
contract; thereafter plaintiff ratified. Specific performance was
granted. Lopes, L. J., said: "If
there had been no withdrawal of
the offer, this case would have been
simple. The ratification by the
plaintiffs would have related back
to the time of the acceptance of
the defendant's offer by Scratchley, and the plaintiffs would have

adopted a contract made on their
behalf.

"It is said that there was no
contract which could be ratified,
because Scratchley at the time he
accepted the defendant's offer had
no authority to act for the plaintiffs. Directly Scratchley on behalf and in the name of the plaintiffs accepted the defendant's
offer, I think there was a contract
made by Scratchley assuming to
act for the plaintiffs, subject to
proof by the plaintiffs that Scratchley had that authority.

"The plaintiffs subsequently did
adopt the contract, and thereby

effect of the ratification is to treat the contract as if it had been authorized in the first place, and since the third party was plainly willing to be bound by the contract at the time it is made, it follows automatically that, once the contract is ratified, the third party must be treated as being as much bound as if there had been authority originally. This seems reasonable and, unless a long time has elapsed (and the later English cases say that P must ratify within a reasonable time),[24] there seems no great hardship on the third party.

American courts have been slow to follow this view, however, and it has been rigorously criticized by writers. Thus Mr. Seavey says [25] that the effect "is to worship the fiction of relation back as a transcendental shrine and justifies the harshest language used by the critics of the doctrine. It creates an offer when none was intended and imposes upon the mistaken party an obligation not imposed upon an offeror. The English court creates before ratification a contract subject to disaffirmance, a one-sided obligation created elsewhere only where it has been paid for, where protection is afforded to a dependent class, or where there is fraud."

§ 249. The Wisconsin view.

The extreme opposite view has been taken by some early Wisconsin cases, supposed still to be law. In Dodge v. Hopkins,[26] where the principal sought to enforce a land contract made by an agent whose power of attorney, the court found, did not authorize the sale in question, the court said that if (at the time the purported

---

recognized the authority of their agent Scratchley. Directly they did so the doctrine of ratification applied and gave the same effect to the contract made by Scratchley as it would have had if Scratchley had been clothed with a precedent authority to make it.

"If Scratchley had acted under a precedent authority the withdrawal of the offer by the defendant would have been inoperative,

and it is equally inoperative where the plaintiffs have ratified and adopted the contract of the agent. To hold otherwise would be to deprive the doctrine of ratification of its retrospective effect."

[24] See In re Portuguese Consolidated Copper Mines (1890) 45 Ch. D. 16.

[25] 29 Yale L. J. 859, 891, Studies in Agency, 104.

[26] (1861) 14 Wis. 630.

contract is made) "either party neglects or refuses to bind himself, the instrument is void for want of mutuality, and the party who is not bound cannot avail himself of it as obligatory on the other." Furthermore "no subsequent act of the party, who has neglected to execute it can render it obligatory on the party who did execute it without his assent. . . . The principal in such case may, by his subsequent assent, bind himself; but if the contract be executory, he cannot bind the other party. The latter may, if he chooses, avail himself of such assent against the principal which, if he does, the contract, by virtue of such mutual ratification, becomes mutually obligatory." [27]

§ 250. —— On this view the principal's attempted ratification amounts virtually only to an offer, which the third party may accept or not as he chooses. Under it ratification becomes a one-sided proposition by which a principal may bind himself but not the other party. If the English view seems to carry Agency doctrines to their logical extreme at the expense of contract concepts, it may be said that the Wisconsin view carries Contract doctrines to their logical extreme at the expense of Agency concepts. Of course the Wisconsin view could be justified as taking the blunt and realistic view that there really is no such doctrine as ratification; there are only cases where equitable considerations preclude someone, usually the principal from relying on the agent's lack of authority. No strong equitable considerations appear to require that an unwilling third party be held bound where the principal originally was not; hence there is no occasion for lumping this situation with others really unlike it, and invoking the name "ratification." As already appears the present writer would find little difficulty in agreeing with this. However, if we are to continue to assume that the maxim *omnis ratihabitio* and so on really expresses something in the nature of a rule

[27] See also Atlee v. Bartholomew (1887) 69 Wis. 43. A note in [1947] Wis. L. Rev. 394 remarks: "This unique view has not been repudiated by any later Wisconsin decision. But neither has it been reiterated in recent years."

of law it is hard to think of the Wisconsin cases as anything but deviations.

§ 251. The "prevailing" view. Insofar as the few American cases permit speaking of a majority rule, it would seem to be a compromise between the English and the Wisconsin doctrines. The principal may ratify if he does so before the third party withdraws from the contract.[28] On this view the original purported contract is in substance an offer by T to P; like any other offer it may be accepted before, and only before, withdrawal.

This view is thus expressed in Sec. 88 of the Restatement: "To constitute ratification, the affirmance of a transaction must be before the third party has manifested his withdrawal from it either to the purported principal or to the agent, and before the offer or agreement has otherwise terminated or been discharged."

As is often the case with compromises, this position seems to have no particular logic to recommend it. Either the English or the Wisconsin view appears more logical. However, as a matter of policy and psychology, it eliminates the lack of mutuality characteristic of the English view and at the same time does not completely repudiate the doctrine of ratification or prevent the principal in most instances from taking advantage of it.[29]

§ 252. Ratification of insurance after loss. Suppose insurance on the principal's property to be effected by one purporting to be but not in fact authorized to do so. May the principal, after loss has occurred, ratify so as to collect the insurance? Under the English rule as to ratification against an unwilling third party, the insurance company's objection is no defense, and a line of cases, mostly dealing with marine

[28] See McClintock v. South Penn Oil Co. (1892) 146 Pa. St. 144, 23 Atl. 211; Baldwin v. Schiappacasse (1896) 109 Mich. 170, 66 N. W. 1091; Steinfeld v. Broxholme (1922) 59 Cal. App. 623, 211 Pac. 473; Masonic Temple v. Ebert (1942) 199 S. C. 5, 18 S.E.2d 584; Equity Mutual Ins. Co. v. General Cas. Co. (1943) 139 F.2d 723.

[29] See generally F. R. Mechem, "A Question of Ratification," 24

insurance, has settled it that the principal may ratify after loss.[30] Conversely, under the Wisconsin view, there could be no ratification unless the company was willing, which it would scarcely be likely to be. Under the prevailing American view there could be no ratification if the company learned of the lack of authority and withdrew before the principal ratified, but if the principal attempts to ratify before the company withdraws the weight of the scant authority is that he may.[31]

One striking consequence is that this permits the principal to do by ratification what he could not do directly, namely, insure lost property.[32] The result, however, is not as anomalous or as hard on the insurance company as it might seem to be at first sight. The premium will have been paid (or must be accounted for); the transaction, from the standpoint of the insurance company, will be completely routine and will present none of the apparent hardship there is in the case of an individual third party forced to pay a claim that might have been averted had the agent's lack of authority been known.[33]

Am. L. Rev. 580; Wambaugh, "A Problem as to Ratification," 9 Harv. L. Rev. 60.

[30] See Hagedorn v. Oliverson (1814) 2 M. & S. 485; Williams v. North China Ins. Co. (1876) 1 C. P. D. 757; Grover & Grover, Ltd. v. Mathews [1910] 2 K. B. 401.

[31] See Watson v. Southern Ins. Co. of New Orleans (Miss., 1902) 31 So. 904; Bontwell v. Globe & Rutgers Fire Ins. Co. (1908) 193 N. Y. 323, 85 N. E. 1087; Marqusee v. Hartford Fire Ins. Co. (1912) 198 Fed. 475, 1023, cert. den. (1912) 299 U. S. 621, 33 S. Ct. 1049, 57 L. Ed. 1355, noted in 11 Mich. L. Rev. 163; Farrar v. Western Assurance Co. (1916) 30 Cal. App. 489, 159 Pac. 609; Norwich Union Fire Ins. Society v. Paramount Famous Lasky Corp. (1931)

50 F.2d 747, noted in 32 Col. L. Rev. 139.

Cf. Kline Bros. & Co. v. Royal Ins. Co. (1911) 192 Fed. 378, noted in 25 Harv. L. Rev. 729 (opinion by L. Hand, J.).

See generally Robinson, Ratification After Loss in Fire Insurance, 18 Corn. L. Q. 161.

[32] See Mallard v. Hardware Indemnity Ins. Co. of Minn. (Tex. Civ. App., 1948) 216 S.W.2d 263.

[33] In the Marqusee case, ante, n. 31, it is said: "Before ratification an unauthorized contract is not binding, because it is not mutual. The party discovering the lack of authority may therefore withdraw. When he has done so there is nothing to ratify. What shocks us at first blush is that one may ratify an unauthorized con-

§ 253. —— The Restatement does not subscribe to this view. By Sec. 89 ratification is not effective, at the third party's election, "if it occurs after the situation has so materially changed that it would be inequitable to subject him to liability thereon." [34] Comment *c* indicates that this is thought to be true in the insurance cases, unless the consideration has been paid before loss. Query, whether this factor has much to do with the fairness of the matter, since the principal will naturally have to pay or account before receiving the insurance.

7. *Ratification as Affecting the Agent*

§ 254. To the third party. The agent, as will be seen hereafter,[35] is liable to the third party for any injury to him resulting from lack of the authority which the agent purports to have and exercise; in the modern cases this liability is most commonly put on the theory of the breach of an implied warranty by the agent that he has the authority he purports to exercise. If the principal ratifies before harm is done to the third party, plainly the agent is subject to no liability.[36] The cases are not numerous, however, and it is not very clear as to the circumstances under which the agent is relieved. The basic proposition

tract after he knows that it is to his own advantage to do so, and so bind the other party to his apparent disadvantage. Further reflection, however, causes this apparent unfairness to disappear. The other party, having agreed to be bound by this contract and not having withdrawn from it, has no ground to complain if compelled to perform; the original lack of authority having been cured."

[34] See Cook v. Tullis (1874) 18 Wall. 332, 21 L. Ed. 933; Pollock v. Cohen (1877) 32 Ohio St. 514; Kempner v. Rosenthal (1891) 81 Tex. 12, 16 S. W. 639; Norton v. Alabama Nat. Bank (1893) 102 Ala. 420, 14 So. 892; Graham v.

Williams (1902) 114 Ga. 716, 40 S. E. 790; People ex rel. Goldschmidt v. Board of Education (1916) 217 N. Y. 470, 112 N. E. 167; Taslich v. Industrial Commission (1927) 71 Utah 33, 262 Pac. 281, noted in 41 Harv. L. Rev. 792; Forrest v. Hawkins (1938) 169 Va. 470, 194 S. E. 721; Pape v. Home Ins. Co. (1943) 139 F.2d 231.

[35] Post, § 322 et seq.

[36] See Sheffield v. Ladue (1871) 16 Minn. 388; Berger's Appeal (1880) 96 Pa. St. 443; Chieppo v. Chieppo (1914) 88 Conn. 233, 90 Atl. 940; Henry v. Savage, Inc. v. Friedberg (1948) 322 Mass. 321, 77 N.E.2d 213.

is stated in Sec. 338 of the Restatement without any attempt to
state its limits save as Illustration 2 states and A would not
be relieved from liability to T by a ratification made after
T has instituted action against A. Query, as to A's liability
for inconvenience and delay caused T before ratification, although T has not got to the point of bringing suit.

§ 255. **To the principal.** There is little authority as to
the effect of ratification on the agent's liability to the principal. It is in general clear that after ratification the principal
can scarcely complain (against the agent) of the exercise of
the authority as such. The effect of the ratification is to make
the case as if the authority had existed from the start. Thus
in Holloway v. Arkansas City Milling Company [37] the agent
sold P's flour at $2.75 a barrel instead of $2.75 per hundred
weight. This appeared in documents relating to the sale, immediately forwarded by A to P, but which P did not bother to
examine. Five months later, on discovering the mistake, P
attempted to hold A liable for the difference but the court
said it was P's duty to examine the transaction immediately
and that by his failure to do so he had ratified the sale and
released A from any liability. [38]

[37] (1908) 77 Kan. 76, 93 Pac.
577.

[38] And see Bank of Owensboro
v. Western Bank (1877) 13 Bush.
(Ky.) 526; Wilson v. Dame (1878)
58 N. H. 392; Hazard v. Spears
(1868) 4 Keyes (N. Y.) 469, 2 Abb.
353; Appeal of Berger (1880) 96
Pa. 443; Lingenfelder v. Leschen
(1895) 134 Mo. 55, 34 S. W. 1089;
Shepherd v. Gibbs (1891) 85 Mich.
85, 48 N. W. 179; Smith v. Cologan
(1787) 2 T. R. 188, n.; Goss v.
Stevens (1884) 32 Minn. 472, 21
N. W. 549; Brewer v. Sparrow
(1827) 7 B. & C. 310; Frixione v.
Tagliaferro (1856) 10 Moore's Pr.
Coun. Cas. 175.

See generally, Restatement,
§ 416.

And cf. the discussion of Dempsey v. Chambers, ante, § 212.

CHAPTER X

PRINCIPAL AND AGENT: TERMINATION OF AGENT'S POWER

§ 256. **Introduction.** Two questions arise: (a) What acts or facts, as between P and A, terminate A's authority to represent P? (b) To what extent and under what circumstances is notice to third parties of the termination essential to put an end to A's *power* to bind P, although his authority to do so has admittedly ceased?

Of these the second question is much more difficult.

§ 257. **Termination of authority: In general.** The books usually mention a number of ways in which, as between the parties, the relation may come to an end. Many of these are almost too obvious to require comment.

Generally speaking, methods of termination may be roughly classified under two heads:

1. Termination by the act of the parties.
2. Termination by operation of law (or, as it may be put, by the happening of events).

1. *Termination by Act of the Parties*

§ 258. **In general.** Taking these up in order we see first that the authority may be terminated by the act of the parties either (a) because of some limitation or condition which the parties, expressly or by implication, attached to the agency at the time of its creation; or (b) by some act done by one or both of them at a later time with a view to terminate the relation. Shortly stated, then, termination by act of the parties may be either—

(a) By force of their original agreement; or
(b) By the subsequent act of one or both of them.

§ 259. **Prior agreement of the parties.** When the authority
is given it may be expressly provided or understood that the
authority is to terminate at a certain time [1] or on the happening of a certain event.[2] There is normally no reason why the
parties should not so agree or why their agreement should not
be given effect. Where there is no express agreement it is
ordinarily taken that the authority was to last for what was
a reasonable time in the light of all the circumstances.[3]

§ 260. **Accomplishment of the object.** Very often the authority given is to accomplish a certain object, e. g., the sale of
the principal's property. When this object is accomplished the
authority will normally terminate as a matter of course, since
there is no reason for assuming the continued existence of
authority to do something which can no longer be done.[4]

It will normally be unimportant whether the object has been
accomplished by the agent in question, another agent, or the
principal in person. The question of the necessity of notice
to third persons is discussed below.[5] It is also possible that
the completion of the object, otherwise than by the agent,
might be a violation of his rights which, though not preventing
the termination of the agency, might give him a cause of
action against the principal. The situation in which this possibility is most litigated is discussed in a later section.[6]

[1] See Danby v. Coutts (1885)
L. R. 29 Ch. Div. 500; Gundlach
v. Fischer (1871) 59 Ill. 172;
Rundle v. Cutting (1893) 18 Colo.
337, 32 Pac. 994; Herd & Son v.
Bank of Buffalo (1896) 66 Mo.
App. 643.

[2] See Ballard v. Travelers' Ins.
Co. (1896) 119 N. C. 187, 25 S. E.
867; Burelson v. Northwestern Mutual Life Ins. Co. (1890) 86 Cal.
342, 24 Pac. 1064; Barkley v. Ol-
cutt (1889) 52 Hun. (N. Y.) 452, 5
N. Y. S. 525.

[3] See Marquam v. Ray (1913)
65 Ore. 41, 131 Pac. 523.

[4] See Macbeath v. Ellis (1828) 4
Bing. 578; Moore v. Stone (1875)
40 Iowa 259; Marbury v. Barnet
(1896) 17 Misc. 386, 40 N. Y. S.
76; Short v. Millard (1873) 68 Ill.
292; Campbell v. Chase (1908) 78
Kan. 593, 96 Pac. 949; Marquam
v. Ray (1913) 65 Ore. 41, 131 Pac.
523; Williams' Estate v. Tuch
(1942) 313 Ill. App. 230, 39 N.E.2d
695; Fleming v. Fleming (1944) 49
D. & C. (Pa.) 663.

[5] See post, § 282 et seq.
[6] See post, § 568.

§ 261. By mutual consent. Plainly, as between themselves, principal and agent may at any time, by mutual consent, put an end to the relationship, whether it is based on contract or not.

§ 262. Revocation by the principal or renunciation by the agent. It is one of the basic concepts of the subject that no one can be forced to be a principal or agent against his will, and that either one may at any minute, without the consent of the other, terminate the relationship. The position of principal is inherently precarious; his possible liabilities are great; he may see his most precious interests being hazarded, not by his own acts but by those of an agent whose conduct he is unable to control. Plainly the principal should always be able, for any or no reason, to withdraw his affairs from further control by the agent (if the agent has not yet acted).[7] Likewise, though the proposition is less conspicuous and less important, there are burdens and responsibilities connected with the position of agent which he should not be called on to carry unwillingly.[8]

This, as stated above, the law recognizes.[9] It should be noted, however, that we are speaking of a power and not a right. The renunciation of the agent or the revocation by the principal may well violate contractual or other rights of

---

[7] Of course, if the authority has been executed, or the agent has entered into a legally binding contract, the authority, though otherwise revocable, cannot be revoked so as to affect these acts already done. If the authority has been executed in part only, and the residue be severable, the authority as to such residue may be revoked as in other cases.

[8] This does not mean, of course, that the agent may at his whim renounce his agency, with its resulting fiduciary obligations, and proceed to complete the transaction

for his own benefit and to the principal's detriment. As to the duration of the agent's fiduciary obligation, see post, Chapter XVI.

[9] "But the power to revoke is not to be confused with the right to revoke, under a contract such as is before us, without incurring liability to the opposite party for its breach. 2 C. J. S., Agency, § 74 (a); Williston, Contracts, §§ 1293, 1293a; Mechem, Agency, § 568. From the last cited authority we quote: 'Distinction may be made in these cases between the power to revoke and the right to

the other, and in such a case the law may (and does) say that the existence of a power to terminate does not carry with it the right to terminate in violation of vested obligations.

Only one type of authority, infrequent and far from well-defined, is irrevocable; this, often referred to as "a power coupled with an interest" or "a proprietary power" is discussed at length in later sections of this chapter.[10]

§ 263. How revocation or renunciation effected.

There is little law as to the manner in which revocation or renunciation is effected. Since authority is normally created by the principal's expression of willingness to the agent that he act on his (principal's) behalf, and the agent's expressed or implied assent thereto, revocation or renunciation can normally be effected in the same way.[11] Unless a statute expressly requires it, no formality is necessary. Thus, it is said, authority under seal can be revoked by simple writing or even orally.[12]

revoke; the principal always having the power to revoke but not having the right to do so in those cases wherein he has agreed not to exercise his power during a certain period. If, in the latter case, he does exercise his power, he must respond in damages.'" Piper v. Wells (1938) 175 Md. 326, 2 A.2d 28.

See also Clark v. Marsiglia (1845), 1 Denio (N. Y.) 317; State v. Walker (1885) 88 Mo. 279, aff'd 125 U. S. 339, 8 S. Ct. 929, 31 L. Ed. 769; Owen v. Frink (1864) 24 Cal. 171, 178; Lord v. Thomas (1876) 64 N. Y. 107; Burke v. Priest (1892) 50 Mo. App. 310; Brookshire v. Voncannon (1845) 28 N. Car. (6 Ired.) 231.

[10] Post, § 265 et seq.

[11] What would be the effect of notice of revocation made, not to A but to T? In Robert Simpson Co. v. Godson [1937] 1 D. L. R.

454, noted in 15 Can. B. Rev. 196, defendant had opened an account with plaintiff, and had expressly authorized his wife to buy there on his credit. Later, becoming dissatisfied with her extravagance, he notified plaintiff to give her no further credit, but gave no notice to his wife of the attempted revocation. He was held liable for further purchases made by the wife "on the short ground that Mrs. Godson had authority to purchase, and her authority had never been terminated." The court below, reaching the same result, had remarked that "the husband could not thus stand by and permit her to become personally liable for her purchases."

Cf. Restatement, § 119; Seavey, Rationale of Agency, 29 Yale L. J. 859, 892, Studies in Agency, 105.

[12] See Brookshire v. Brookshire (1847) 30 N. C. (8 Ired.) 74:

The agent may renounce expressly, such renunciation taking effect on notice being given to the principal.[13] Not infrequently renunciation results from some breach of duty by the agent, which justifies the principal in treating the agency as terminated.[14]

2. *Irrevocable Authority*

§ 264. Contract not to revoke. P may contract with A that he will employ A for a specified time, and that A shall represent him within certain limits (or work for him in a specified manner) for the specified time. Such contracts are common, perfectly legal, and, while neither party can be compelled to perform,[15] a breach by either party subjects him to liability for damages.[16] Suppose that, in addition, P contracts not to revoke the authority within the limited time. Plainly this adds nothing to the contract; such an obligation was implicit in the original contract. P may still revoke, subject to liability for breach. A fortiori, the fact that the agency is stated to be "irrevocable" will not make it so.[17]

Restatement, § 119, Comment *a*.

[13] See Bergner v. Bergner (1907) 219 Pa. 113, 67 Atl. 999.

[14] See State ex rel. Mountain Grove Creamery Co. v. Cox (1926) 315 Mo. 619, 286 S. W. 368, noted in 11 Mo. L. Rev. 177; Allen v. Adams (1928) 16 Del. Ch. 77, 140 Atl. 694.

[15] See Alworth v. Seymour (1890) 42 Minn. 526, 44 N. W. 1030; Harlow v. Oregonian Publishing Co. (1904) 45 Ore. 520, 78 Pac. 737; Rudolph v. Andrew Murphy & Son (1931) 121 Neb. 612, 237 N. W. 659. Cases in which a kind of negative enforcement is given of contracts of employment by injunction (such as the famous case of Lumley v. Wagner (1852) 1 De G. M. & G. 604) are outside

the scope of this work. Treatment of this type of relief can be found in any of the standard works on Equity.

[16] See Missouri v. Walker (1888) 125 U. S. 339, 8 S. Ct. 929; Durkee v. Gunn (1889) 41 Kan. 496, 21 Pac. 637; Standard Oil Co. v. Gilbert (1890) 84 Ga. 714, 11 S. E. 491; Wilcox & Gibbs Sewing Machine Co. v. Ewing (1891) 141 U. S. 627, 12 S. Ct. 94, 35 L. Ed. 882; Cannon Coal Co. v. Taggart (1891) 1 Colo. App. 60, 27 Pac. 238; Security Ins. Co. v. Ellsworth (1906) 129 Wis. 349, 109 N. W. 125.

[17] See Blackstone v. Buttermore (1866) 53 Pa. St. 266, where it is said: "A mere power like a will is in its very nature revocable

§ 265. Irrevocable authority. As stated above, there is one type of authority which may not be revoked. The cases here are neither numerous nor clear. To understand the idea involved it may be useful to reconsider what was stated above as to the reasons why authority in the ordinary situation is always revocable. Briefly, they inhere in the fact that in the ordinary agency the agent is charged with the management of some part of the principal's business. It should be, it is thought, always in the power of the principal to manage his own business. This includes, if necessary, the power of the principal to reassume the control of his own business which he has delegated to the agent.

There is no rule of law or policy, however, which prevents a person from getting rid of his business. He may sell and convey it. He may also mortgage it, or otherwise create a security interest in it in some third party. What if this is in substance what is intended, but that the transaction takes the form of a power to deal with P's property in a certain way in certain circumstances? Should the substance or the form of the transaction be regarded?

§ 266. —— Suppose, for example, that A renders services to P and in return P authorizes A to sell P's land Blackacre

when it concerns the interest of the principal alone, and in such a case even an express declaration of revocability will not prevent revocation." See also McGregor v. Gardner (1862) 14 Iowa 326; Chambers v. Seay (1882) 73 Ala. 373; Walker v. Denison (1877) 86 Ill. 142.

A statute, of course, may make a certain type of authority irrevocable. An interesting instance of this is the New York statute (also found elsewhere) making the Secretary of State agent for service of process on a nonresident motorist. In Leighton v. Roper (1950) 300 N. Y. 434, 91 N.E.2d

876, it is said: "It is urged that the decedent's designation of the Secretary of State was not binding because the agency created by the statute terminates on the death of the principal. But this is to ignore not only the fact that it was an agency created, not for the benefit of the principal, but for the benefit of third persons, Restatement, Agency, §§ 120, 139, as well as the State, in the orderly regulation of its highways, and the additional fact that the Legislature has seen fit to make the agency irrevocable, thus annulling any common-law rule to the contrary."

and pay himself with or out of the proceeds. Or suppose that P borrows money from A and as security authorizes A to sell Blackacre, if the loan is not repaid, and pay himself from the proceeds. It is clear that in such a case there is no more reason why P should be allowed to revoke than if he had formally conveyed or mortgaged Blackacre to A, and that it would be most unwarranted and unfair to A to allow P to revoke. It is also clear that the reason the case is not properly governed by the considerations (set forth above) normally making an agency revocable is that it is not in reality a case of agency at all. In a genuine agency case the power is given to the agent to enable him to do something for the principal; here it is given him to enable him to do something for himself.

§ 267. **Hunt v. Rousmanier.** The leading case in this area and one which has unfortunately done much to becloud the issue, is Hunt v. Rousmanier's Administrators.[18] There a lender was given a power of attorney to sell certain ships of the borrower, by way of security. The borrower died with the debt unpaid. As stated and discussed later in [19] connection with revocation by operation of law, it is, for rather obvious reasons, the ordinary rule that authority is terminated by the death of the principal (or agent). It was held that P could not have terminated it during his lifetime. "Where a letter of attorney forms a part of a contract, and is a security for money, or for the performance of any act which is deemed valuable, it is generally made irrevocable in terms, or if not so, is deemed irrevocable in law." This, while doubtless sound insofar as it suggests that the power is irrevocable because it was given not for P's benefit but as security to A, only inferentially makes such a suggestion and for the rest appears to rely on doctrines that could only be called dubious.

§ 268. —— The Court said, however, that the power was nevertheless and necessarily terminated by P's death. This was put on the ground that the power created in A no "inter-

[18] (1823) 8 Wheat. 174, 5 L. Ed. 589.
[19] See post, § 275.

est or estate" which would permit him to convey in his own name. Failing this, the conveyance must be in the name of the principal. ". . . and it would be a gross absurdity," said Marshall, C. J., "that a deed should purport to be executed by him, even by attorney, after his death; for the attorney is in the place of the principal, capable of doing that alone which the principal might do." [20]

Of this reasoning it must be said, with all respect to the great Chief Justice, that it is purely technical, and suggests no awareness of the merits involved.

§ 269. —— The fame of the case and the reputation of the judge who wrote the opinion, has led to the assumption, stated in cases and texts, that it states that law of the subject. This is, it is said, that a power coupled with security is irrevocable by the grantor but does not survive his death; only a power coupled with an interest is irrevocable either by the grantor or by operation of law. Nevertheless the writer believes it doubtful that this states current law on the question.[21] No good reason appears for the distinction taken. It is like saying that

[20] The unfortunate plaintiff was never able to realize on what he had supposed was his security. In a later appeal ((1828) 1 Peters 1, 7 L. Ed. 1) the court refused to reform the instruments for mistake, saying: "Where the parties, upon deliberation and advice, reject one species of security, and agree to select another, under a misapprehension of the law as to the nature of the security so selected, a Court of Equity will not, on the ground of such misapprehension, and the insufficiency of such security, in consequence of a subsequent event, not foreseen, perhaps, or thought of, direct a new security, of a different character, to be given, or decree that to be done which the parties supposed would have been effected, by the instrument which was finally agreed upon.

[21] The Rousmanier case and the later authorities are acutely analyzed by Mr. Seavey in "Termination by Death of Proprietary Powers of Attorney," 31 Yale L. J. 283, Studies in Agency, 109. He remarks (at 287) that it "is remarkable for the almost unanimous acceptance of its reasoning by the American courts and for the avoidance of its effects by many of them. It has become a tradition and, because of the great names associated with it, will always be cited. But it has had far more good fortune than it deserves. The authorities relied on were far from conclusive; it has curious inconsistencies; and the result

a mortgage is revoked by death while a deed is not. "Interest" in the technical sense seems to be irrelevant; "security" is slightly too narrow, in the technical sense, to state the considerations which should make the power irrevocable by death in either case. No adjective appears completely satisfactory in expressing the idea involved. Perhaps Mr. Seavey's phrase,[22] a "proprietary" power, is as good as any.

§ 270. **Modern law.** The Restatement[23] repudiates the distinction taken in the Rousmanier case and puts irrevocable powers into one category: "Powers given as security." Such powers are said to be "created in the form of an agency authority, but held for the benefit of the power holder or a third person and given to secure the performance of a duty or to protect a title, either legal or equitable, such power being given when the duty or title is created or given for consideration."

This is scarcely a very lucid definition but perhaps the subject matter is one not permitting completely lucid definition. It has, however, been quoted in modern cases, and they tend to apply the proprietary power idea without distinction between security and interest.[24]

---

reached was unfortunate both because justice was not done in the particular situation and because it has caused great confusion."

[22] See his article, cited in the preceding note.

[23] Restatement, §§ 138 and 139.

[24] See Knapp v. Alvord (1843) 10 Paige (N. Y.) 205; Hutchins v. Hebbard (1865) 34 N. Y. 24; Merry v. Lynch (1878) 68 Me. 94; Montague v. McCarroll (1897) 15 Utah 318, 49 Pac. 418; Mulloney v. Black (1923) 244 Mass. 391, 138 N. E. 584, noted in 37 Harv. L. Rev. 261; Sphier v. Michael (1924) 112 Ore. 299, 229 Pac. 1100, noted in 19 Ill. L. Rev. 596; Lane Mortgage Co. v. Crenshaw (1928) 93 Cal. App. 411,

269 Pac. 672, noted in 17 Geo. L. J. 156 and 39 Yale L. J. 110; Shornhorst v. Peoples Savings & Trust Co. (1930) 301 Pa. 519, 152 Atl. 569; In re Ferrara (1931) 109 N. J. Eq. 49, 156 Atl. 265, noted in 30 Mich. L. Rev. 963; Superior Oil Co. v. Stanolind Oil Co. (Tex. Civ. App., 1950) 230 S.W.2d 346; Cox v. Freeman (1951) 204 Okla. 138, 227 P.2d 670.

Cf. Halloran-Judge Trust Co. v. Heath (1927) 70 Utah 124, 258 Pac. 342, 64 A. L. R. 368; O'Connell v. Superior Court (1935) 2 Cal.2d 418, 41 P.2d 334, 97 A. L. R. 918; Marchand v. Gulf Refining Co. (1937) 187 La. 1002, 175 So. 647; Mairs v. Central Trust Co. (1945)

§ **271.** —— Thus in Chrysler v. Blozic,[25] one dying of tuberculosis executed a power of attorney authorizing the hospital where he was confined to collect his insurance and apply it on his hospital bill. It was held that the power "was coupled with an interest" and not revoked by the death of the principal.

So, under a liability policy which provided "that the sole right of settlement and defense was in the hands of the insurance carrier" it was held that the insured had created "a power coupled with an interest" so that he could neither "revoke nor control the exercise of the power." [26]

On the other hand, it has been consistently held that a contract by which the agent is to have, as compensation, a specified percent of the property sold or secured by his services does not render the agency irrevocable.[27]

---

127 W. Va. 795, 34 S.E.2d 742; Marnon v. Vaughan Motor Co. (1950) 189 Ore. 339, 219 P.2d 163.

The English law on the point is thus stated in 1 Halsbury's Laws of England (2d Ed. 1931) Tit. "Agency," § 497: The authority of an agent is irrevocable under the following circumstances: "(1) Where the agency is created by deed, or for valuable consideration, and the authority is given to effectuate a security or to secure an interest of the agent. Thus if an agreement is entered into on a sufficient consideration whereby an authority is given for the purpose of securing some benefit to the donee of the authority, such authority is irrevocable, on the ground that it is coupled with an interest. So an authority to sell in consideration of forbearance to sue for previous advances, an authority to apply for shares to be allotted on an underwriting agreement, a commission being paid for the underwriting, and an authority to

receive rents until the principal and interest of a loan have been paid off, or to receive money from a third party in payment of a debt, have been held irrevocable. On the other hand, an authority is not irrevocable merely because the agent has a special property in or a lien upon goods to which the authority relates, the authority not being given for the purpose of securing the claims of the agent." [Citations omitted.]

25 (1934) 267 Mich. 479, 255 N. W. 399.

26 Hayes v. Gessner (1944) 315 Mass. 366, 52 N.E.2d 968. See also Rollins v. Bay View Auto Parts Co. (1921) 239 Mass. 414, 132 N. E. 177; MacDonald v. Gough (1950) 326 Mass. 93, 93 N.E.2d 260, noted in 49 Mich. L. Rev. 755.

27 See Taylor v. Burns (1906) 203 U. S. 120, 27 S. Ct. 40, 51 L. Ed. 116; In re Lohnert's Estate (1930) 137 Misc. 442, 243 N. Y. S. 757; Bowman v. Ledbetter (1935)

§ 272. **Powers of sale in mortgages.** Two types of cases, of frequent occurrence, perhaps deserve special mention. In a number of states it is permissible to insert in a mortgage a power of sale in the mortgagee, taking effect on default in payment. Is such a power revoked by the death of the mortgagor? In a great majority of states, both those where the mortgage is said to pass a legal title and those where it creates a lien, the power is held to be irrevocable.[28] This, at least in the case of the mortgage thought to pass legal title, would seem to be consistent with the terminology of the Rousmanier case; nevertheless, as has been suggested by a learned writer on mortgages,[29] it seems more realistic to treat of the matter as having its real roots in mortgage law and being only superficially a problem of agency law. From this standpoint it is self-evident that the power of sale must survive.

173 Okla. 345, 48 P.2d 334; In re Buller's Estates (1939) 192 La. 643, 188 So. 728. Cf. Capital Nat. Bank v. Stoll (1934) 220 Cal. 260, 30 P.2d 411, noted in 34 Col. L. Rev. 359 and 19 Corn. L. Q. 267.

[28] See Reilly v. Phillips (1894) 4 S. D. 610, 57 N. W. 780; Carter v. Slocomb (1898) 122 N. C. 475, 29 S. E. 720; Stewart v. Smalling (1927) 33 N. M. 39, 261 Pac. 814; Denver Joint Stock Land Bank of Denver v. Preston (1937) 52 Wyo. 132, 70 P.2d 584. Cf. Wilkins v. McGehee (1891) 86 Ga. 764, 13 S. E. 84. Cases are collected in 56 A. L. R. 224.

[29] "One approach to the . . . problem is to treat a mortgagee's power of sale as governed by the principles applicable to powers conferred upon an agent. This view makes survival of the power upon death or insanity depend upon whether it satisfies the murky test of 'power coupled with an interest.' At the opposite extreme, they are likened to powers of appointment creating springing future interests or powers of sale or appointment given to a trustee by will. Criticism of the agency theory by an exponent of this second view is sound. [The author here in a note quotes from Walsh, Mortgages, 343.] However, it also is open to objection as being too narrow and resting upon the wrong foundation. The power conferred upon an agent and the power to appoint real property are merely specialized instances of the use of one of the fundamental conceptions of the law. When employed in certain types of transactions, definite bodies of rules, principles and standards developed which governed its exercise in that particular field. Familiar instances of this are to be found in the law of agency regulating the powers given to an agent and quite different from it, the technical law of powers of appointment of real property. A power of

§ 273. Cognovit notes. In a number of states a valid power to confess judgment on nonpayment may be put in a negotiable promissory note; the resulting instrument is often spoken of as a "cognovit" note.[30] Again the question arises: Is the power irrevocable? The common answer appears to be that the power cannot be revoked by the maker and is not revoked by his insanity or other incapacity but is revoked by his death.[31] Again there is apparent conformity to the doctrines of the Rousmanier case. It may be suggested however that the distinction can readily be explained in terms of common sense, without recourse to the rather arbitrary technicalities of the Rousmanier case. Plainly the maker cannot repudiate the power he has given nor does there seem any very compelling reason why it should be terminated by his incapacity. The rights given by the power are procedural, however, rather than substantive: the purpose is to eliminate the necessity of litigation. When the maker dies, such necessity disappears. His estate passes almost automatically [32] into the control of a court, under the administration of a person whose functions include that of receiving and passing on claims. It

sale given to a mortgagee is separate and distinct in its purpose and use from either of these examples. It is *sui generis* and should be so treated rather than assimilated into a category whose rules were formulated for other ends. It is given to the mortgagee as an integral part of his security and should no more be lost to a mortgagee by reason of the death or insanity of the mortgagor than any other incident of it which is necessary to its realization." Osborne, Mortgages (1951) pp. 995, 996. (The author's citations are omitted.)

[30] See Britton, Bills & Notes (1943) § 39.

[31] See Johnson v. National Bank of Mattoon (1926) 320 Ill. 389,

151 N. E. 231, 44 A. L. R. 1306; Stucker v. Shumaker (1927) 290 Pa. 348, 139 Atl. 114; Acker v. Cecil Nat. Bank (1931) 162 Md. 1, 157 Atl. 897, noted in 16 Minn. L. Rev. 874; In re Kohl's Guardianship (1936) 221 Wis. 385, 266 N. W. 800; Schuck v. McDonald (1938) 58 Ohio App. 394, 16 N.E.2d 619; Frey v. Cleveland Trust Co. (1944) 143 Ohio St. 319, 55 N.E.2d 416; United Trading Corp. v. Schautz (1947) 59 D. & C. (Pa.) 231; Haggard v. Shick (1949) 151 Ohio St. 535, 86 N.E.2d 785. Cases are collected in 44 A. L. R. 1310.

[32] It is true that estates often can be and are settled without formal administration. However it is almost always a prerequisite to such a settlement that all claims

may be suggested that in any event the power to confess judgment is a substantial convenience only when no challenge of the validity of the note is likely to be made. In such a case it is very likely quite as convenient for the holder of the note to file and secure allowance of the claim as it would be to confess judgment.[33]

3. *Termination by Operation of Law*

§ 274. **In general.** So much for termination by the act of the parties. We now turn to consideration of the second basic form of revocation. Of a number of facts it is commonly said that they revoke authority instantly, irrespective of the intent of the parties and by operation of law. Of these the more important are the death or other legal incapacity of the principal (or agent), the bankruptcy of the principal, war between the country of the principal and that of the agent, and destruction or disposition of the subject matter of the agency. These will be taken up in turn.[34]

§ 275. **Death of the principal or agent.** It is obvious that the death of the agent will normally terminate the agency.[35] The principal has a right to an agent of his own choice; there is nothing to suggest that he would or should expect the authority to pass to the agent's heirs or personal representative. Furthermore, in the case of the death of the agent it is very unlikely that any question of notice could arise.

have been attended to. In such a situation it is likely that the holder of the note will be able to get it paid more quickly and easily than if he were able to confess judgment.

[33] Should it be suggested that confessing judgment is quicker, the answer is obvious: even a judgment will normally have to be filed as a claim and will not be paid until all such claims are paid. Nor, should the estate be insolvent, will it have any preference over other judgments based on like consideration.

[34] On this topic generally see Note, Termination of Authority by Operation of Law, 44 Harv. L. Rev. 265.

[35] See Love v. Peel (1906) 79 Ark. 366, 95 S. W. 998; Adriance v. Rutherford (1885) 57 Mich. 170, 23 N. W. 718; Tyson v. George's Creek Coal & Iron Co. (1911) 115 Md. 564, 81 Atl. 41.

It is almost equally obvious that the death of the principal will also terminate the agency.[36] True, the principal's affairs must be wound up, or even, in rare cases, carried on for a time, but these interests now in reality belong to someone else, the quasi-entity known as P's estate, and the law has provided for the situation by setting up a personal representative, vested with full authority to handle the liquidation of P's affairs. It is for him to say what shall be done about the business originally delegated by P to A; if A is to continue the business it must be by the personal representative's authority and as his agent.

This analysis, it may be suggested, ties in with that of the proprietary power, just discussed. That is not revoked by the principal's death for the precise reason that it really involves the affairs, not of the principal but of the agent; it is no more revoked by the principal's death than any other interest or estate which he has granted to a third party.

It is apparent that it is not unlikely that the principal's death will not be known for some time by the agent, the third party or both, and that they may reasonably and naturally proceed to do business in his name, ignorant of his death. To prevent hardship, should innocent parties acting reasonably be protected as to acts done in ignorance of the principal's death? This troublesome question is discussed in a following section.[37]

§ 276. **Death of a master.** It is commonly said that the same rule applies in case of the death of one technically a master rather than a principal. Where the relationship is at

[36] In addition to the cases cited, ante, §§ 265–273 (dealing with the possibility of creating irrevocable powers), see Wallace v. Cook (1804) 5 Esp. 117; Graham v. Hoke (1941) 219 N. C. 755, 14 S.E.2d 790; Ferguson v. Pilling (1942) 231 Iowa 530, 1 N.W.2d 662; Gallup v. Barton (1943) 313 Mass. 379, 47 N.E.2d 921; Parker v. First Citizens Bank & Trust Co. (1948) 229 N. C. 527, 50 S.E.2d 304; In re Garland's Will (1950) — Misc. —, 97 N.Y.S.2d 442.

The death of one of joint principals revokes the authority: Ferguson v. Pilling, ante. Cf. In re Chapal's estate (1943) 182 Misc. 402, 45 N.Y.S.2d 237.

[37] See post, § 287 et seq.

all personal in nature this is necessarily true.[38] The servant
has a right to work for a master of his own choice and the
estate should not be compelled to keep a servant not of its
own selection where the relationship is personal or the work
involves discretion. There are, however, some cases in which,
because of the nature of the work, the death of the employer
has been held not to terminate the employment. So, where
the employment was to do the assessment work on twelve mining claims for a year.[39] And so where it was to serve as clerk
in a tobacco warehouse during the tobacco season.[40]

[38] See Lacy v. Getman (1890)
110 N. Y. 109, 23 N. E. 452. It is
there said: "If in this case, Lacy
had died on that day in July, his
representative could not have performed his contract. McMahan,
surviving, would have been free to
say that he bargained for Lacy's
services, and not for those of another selected and chosen by
strangers, and either the contract
would be broken or else dissolved.
I have no doubt that it must be
deemed dissolved, and that the
death of the servant, bound to
render personal services under a
personal control, ends the contract,
and irrespective of the inquiry
whether those services involve
skilled or common labor. For, even
as it respects the latter, the servant's character, habits, capacity,
industry, and temper, all enter into
and affect the contract which the
master makes, and are material
and essential where the service
rendered is to be personal and subject to the daily direction and
choice and control of the master.
He was willing to hire Lacy for a
year; but Lacy's personal representative, or a laborer tendered by
him, he might not want at all and

at least not for a fixed period,
preventing a discharge. And so it
must be conceded that the death
of the servant, employed to render
personal services under the master's daily direction, dissolves the
contract.

"But if that be so, on what
principle shall the master be differ-
ently and more closely bound? And
why shall not his death also dis-
solve the contract? There is no
logic and no justice in a contrary
rule. The same reasoning which
relieves the servant's estate relieves also the master's for the
relation constituted is personal on
both sides and contemplates no
substitution. If the master selects
the servant, the servant chooses
the master."

See also Yerrington v. Greene
(1863) 7 R. I. 589; Marvel v. Phillips (1894) 162 Mass. 399, 38 N. E.
1117.

[39] Dumont v. Heighton (1912) 14
Ariz. 25, 123 Pac. 306.

[40] Hall v. Durham Loan & Trust
Co. (1931) 200 N. E. 734, 158 S.
E. 388. Cf. Levy v. Wilmes (1926)
239 Ill. App. 229; In re Estate of
Mallory (1929) 99 Cal. App. 96,
278 Pac. 488, noted in 28 Mich. L.

§ 277. **Insanity of principal or agent.** The insanity of the agent presumably terminates his authority, although cases on the point are hard to be found.[41] The insanity of the principal likewise will terminate the authority, particularly if there has been an adjudication of insanity.[42] As pointed out later the insanity will not normally terminate as to third parties unaware of it, particularly as to transactions benefiting the principal or his estate.[43]

§ 278. **Bankruptcy of principal or agent.** The bankruptcy of either party to the relation will normally terminate the authority for most purposes.[44] As in the case of the death of the principal, authority to look after his affairs is transferred by operation of law, here to the trustee. However, insofar as the authority relates to a matter where the principal's property or power to act on his own behalf is not affected by the bankruptcy, the authority is not necessarily terminated.[45] The authority of an agent to collect is terminated by his bankruptcy and does not pass to the trustee.[46]

§ 279. **War.** It is sometimes said that where principal and agent are residents or nationals of different countries, the outbreak of war between the two countries will automatically terminate the agency.[47] A learned writer in the Harvard Law

Rev. 445; Graves v. Cohen (1929) 46 T. L. R. 121, noted in 4 Ans. L. J. 141.

[41] See Restatement, § 122.

[42] See Matthiessen Co. v. McMahon (1876) 38 N. J. L. 536; Yonge v. Toynbee [1910] 1 K. B. 215; Lewis v. Commission of Banks (1934) 286 Mass. 570, 190 N. E. 790; Warwick v. Addicks (1931) 5 W. W. Harr. (Del.) 43, 157 Atl. 205; Fischer v. Gorman (1937) 65 S. D. 453, 274 N. W. 866; Restatement, § 122.

[43] See post, § 290.

[44] See Hudson v. Granger (1821)

5 B. & Ald. 27; Warwick v. Hardingham (1880) 15 Ch. Div. 339; Audenried v. Betteley (1864) 90 Mass. 302; Hall v. Bliss (1875) 118 Mass. 554; Renshaw v. Creditors (1888) 40 La. Ann. 37, 3 So. 403; Restatement, § 124, Comment c.

[45] See Dixon v. Ewart (1817) 3 Mer. 322.

[46] See Florance v. Kresge (1938) 93 F.2d 784.

[47] See New York Life Ins. Co. v. Davis (1877) 95 U. S. 425, 24 L. Ed. 453; Mutzenbecher v. Ballard (1935) 266 N. Y. 574, 195 N. E.

Review [48] says that this is the "best" rule, since only thus can intercourse between residents of belligerent countries be absolutely precluded. Nevertheless, it is believed that the statement is inaccurate. At most it should be said that in many instances the outbreak of war will render carrying out the purpose of the agency impossible or illegal and so result in its termination, and that the question should be treated as one to be decided on the facts of the particular case.

§ 280. —— In opposition to the arbitrary position mentioned above, it may be stated that in many cases the outbreak of war has been held not to terminate the agency. They are mostly cases where a local agent was looking after the interests of a nonresident, now become an enemy. In a leading supreme court case [49] it is held that a power of attorney to sell land in the District of Columbia was not revoked by the fact that the principal became a member of the Confederate army. And in a recent Delaware case [50] it was held that proxies to vote stock in a Delaware corporation were not revoked by the fact that the principals subsequently became alien enemies. The court said that the authorities "indicate certain characteristics which agencies must have in order not to be terminated

206, noted in 3 U. Chi. L. Rev. 137.

[48] Note, 31 Harv. L. Rev. 637. It is there said: "The cessation of agency by war depends not upon the consent of the parties, but upon the broader ground of public policy. That policy forbids all intercourse between residents of opposing belligerent countries. If there were revocable agencies which offered by no possibility a necessity of communication between the parties to the relation, the distinction taken by some of the American cases cited above would be sound enough. But such a relation cannot be conceived. There is always the pos-sibility that the principal may desire to revoke his authority, which of course requires communication. Furthermore the agent owes a duty of loyalty which may at any time require him to notify his employer of change in circumstances affecting his powers. The best rule, therefore, is to regard war as, at once and without regard to the knowledge or consent of the parties, terminating the relation."

[49] Williams v. Paine (1897) 169 U. S. 55, 18 S. Ct. 279, 42 L. Ed. 658.

[50] Albridge v. Franco-Wyoming Securities Corp. (1943) 27 Dela. Ch. 80, 31 A.2d 246.

or suspended by the event of war. These seem of equal rank of importance. Of course the acts authorized must be of such character that they would be unobjectionable if the principal were not an enemy. The agency, or doing of the acts authorized, must not require and must not be attended by communication or intercourse, direct or indirect, with an enemy. The circumstances must disclose the principal's assent, express or implied, to the continuance of the authority upon the occurrence of war. As to this, 'where it is the manifest interest of the principal that the agency, constituted before the war, should continue, the assent of the principal will be presumed.' " [51]

§ 281. **Destruction, loss or sale of subject matter.** The destruction of the subject matter of the agency, or of the principal's interest therein, must generally terminate the agency as a matter of necessity. So, as has been seen, authority to sell a particular piece of property is usually held to be terminated by the sale of that property by the principal himself or by some other agent, subject to considerations of notice or estoppel.[52]

4. *Notice of Termination*

§ 282. **General considerations.** The rough generalization is sometimes encountered that notice of termination is necessary where the termination results from the act of the parties but not where it results from operation of law. The generalization is obviously subject to criticism. In some instances what is classified as revocation by operation of law results in fact

---

[51] See also Sutherland v. Mayer (1926) 271 U. S. 272, 46 S. Ct. 538, 70 L. Ed. 943, where it is said: "Agencies, created before the war, and not requiring intercourse across the enemy's frontier, such as for the collection of debts, preservation of property, and so forth, are not terminated by war"; Tingley v. Muller [1917] 2 Ch.

144 (with which cf. Marshall v. Glanvill [1917] 2 K. B. 87); Pipe v. The La Salle (1943) 49 F. Supp. 662; United States v. Grain Importers (1944) 144 F.2d 921; Restatement, § 115.

[52] See Jones v. Hodgkins (1872) 61 Me. 480; Ahern v. Baker (1885) 34 Minn. 98, 24 N. W. 341; Cooper v. Cooper (1921) 206 Ala. 519, 91

from a party's act, as where the principal goes into voluntary bankruptcy or himself disposes of the property that is the object of the power. Again, some revocations by act of the principal are held to require no notice and in some instances parties without notice are protected where there has been a revocation by operation of law. Nevertheless, the generalization is not without use; it illustrates what is in most instances a significant difference.

§ 283. **By act of parties: Special agents.** It is said that ordinarily no notice is required of the revocation of a special agent.[53] This is based primarily on two ideas: first, that notice is not necessary since no habit of dealing with the agent or appearance of continuing authority will have been created, and secondly, that there is no group of people, viz., those who have been accustomed to deal with the agent, to whom it is feasible to require the giving of notice.

These considerations automatically suggest certain exceptions to the proposition that no notice of termination is necessary or possible in the case of a special agent. Thus P may have specially accredited A to a certain T; e. g., he may have written or telephoned T that A will visit him with reference to a certain transaction, and will be authorized to represent him. In such a case it is both feasible and fair for P to notify T of any change in A's authority. This is likewise true where A, though not specially accredited, has to P's knowledge begun to deal with a particular T.[54] Finally, if P has given A a written power of attorney or some other indicium of authority on which a third party will naturally rely, P cannot escape liability if T in good faith deals with A in reliance on the power although as between P and A the authority has been revoked. It is no defense to P, it seems, that he cannot locate A or recapture the indicium; as between P and T this risk should be on P.[55]

So. 82; Walsh v. Grant (1926) 256 Mass. 555, 152 N. E. 884.

[53] See Morgan v. Harper (Tex. Civ. App., 1922) 236 S. W. 71; Restatement, § 132.

[54] See Florida Central R. Co. v. Ashmore (1901) 43 Fla. 272, 32 So. 832; Kelly v. Brennan (1897) 55 N. J. Eq. 423, 37 Atl. 137.

[55] See Williams v. Birbeck

It should be noted that in the cases mentioned it is the obligation of P to bring home to the mind of T the fact that the authority has been terminated. Constructive notice, as by publication in a paper not actually seen by T, will not do.[56]

§ 284. **By act of parties: General agents.** In the case of a general agent there will normally result a custom of dealing with him as such, and an appearance in him of a continuing authority. Fairness to those who have dealt with him or who rely on his appearance of continuing authority requires that they be informed of the termination of his authority. On the other hand the law will not require the impossible of P; it will not ask him to give personal notification to those whose identity or existence he has no way of ascertaining.

Here the cases have worked out a compromise, based on practical considerations. Those who have previously dealt with the agent, giving or receiving credit (as distinguished from those who may have merely bought or sold for cash), will normally be on the books of the business; it will not be difficult to ascertain their names and addresses and it is not unfair to ask the principal to see that they are in fact informed.[57] As to others it is said the principal must do the best he can; he must give public notice. This is doubtless best and most commonly done by advertising in a local paper, but other forms

(1840) Hoff. (N. Y.) 359; Beard v. Kirk (1840) 11 N. H. 397; George v. Sandel (1866) 18 La. Ann. 535; Morgan v. Harper (Tex. Civ. App., 1922) 236 S. W. 71; Keller v. N. J. Fidelity Ins. Co. (1930) 299 Pa. 315, 149 Atl. 482.

[56] See Union Bank & Trust Co. v. Long Pole Lumber Co. (1912) 70 W. Va. 558, 74 S. E. 674.

[57] In a leading case, Claflin v. Lenheim (1876) 66 N. Y. 301, it is said: "It is a familiar principle of law that when one has constituted and accredited another his agent to carry on his business, the authority of the agent to bind his principal continues, even after an actual revocation, until notice of the revocation is given; and, as to persons who have been accustomed to deal with such agent, until notice of the revocation is brought home to them. The case of such an agency is analogous to that of a partnership, and the notice of revocation of the agency is governed by the same rules as notice of the dissolution of a partnership. As to persons who have been previously in the habit of dealing with the firm, it is requisite that actual

of notice will satisfy the requirement if they appear to the court reasonable under the circumstances.[58]

It should be noted that these rules are similar to those developed by courts as to the requirement of notice on dissolution of a partnership.[59]

§ 285. **Undisclosed principal.** In Morris v. Brown,[60] it is held that the undisclosed principal of a general agent need not give notice of the termination of the authority. "The

notice should be brought home to the creditor, or at least, that the credit should have been given under circumstances from which notice can be inferred. Where the circumstances are controverted, or where notice is sought to be inferred as a fact, from circumstances, the question is for the jury; they must determine, as a question of fact, whether the party claiming against the partnership or the principal, did have notice of the dissolution or revocation; and there being some evidence of the fact of notice, the court, in the present case, properly submitted to the jury this question of fact."

See also Acme Cement Co. v. Greensboro Plaster Co. (1911) 156 N. C. 455, 72 S. E. 569; Montana Reservoir & Irrigation Co. v. Utah Junk Co. (1924) 64 Utah 60, 228 Pac. 201; Carr v. Moragne (1926) 136 S. C. 218, 131 S. E. 424, 43 A. L. R. 1212; Bernhagen v. Marathon Finance Corp. (1933) 212 Wis. 495, 250 N. W. 410; Don G. McAfee, Inc. v. Great American Indemnity Co. (1939) 289 Mich. 143, 286 N. W. 189; Ohio Oil Co. v. Smith-Haggard Lumber Co. (1941) 288 Ky. 278, 156 S.W.2d 111; Baum v. Rice-Stix Dry Goods Co. (1942)

203 Ark. 581, 157' S.W.2d 767.

[58] This requirement is commonly stated in the cases and in the treatises, is adopted by Sec. 136 of the Restatement, and is no doubt the law, but the present writer has found no cases clearly and explicitly applying it.

[59] Uniform Partnership Act, § 35: "(1) After dissolution a partner can bind the partnership . . .

"(b) By any transaction which would bind the partnership if dissolution had not taken place, provided the other party to the transaction

"(I) Had extended credit to the partnership prior to dissolution and had no knowledge or notice of the dissolution; or

"(II) Though he had not so extended credit, had nevertheless known of the partnership prior to dissolution, and, having no knowledge or notice of dissolution, the fact of dissolution had not been advertised in a newspaper of general circulation in the place (or in each place if more than one) at which the partnership business was regularly carried on."

[60] (1932) 115 Conn. 389, 162 Atl. 1. See Uniform Partnership Act, § 35 (2), providing in substance

liability of the defendant as an undisclosed principal cannot be predicated upon a course of conduct in holding himself out as a principal because the plaintiffs had no knowledge of such conduct, and therefore could not, and did not, rely on it." This is significant as emphasizing what must ordinarily be true, namely that the liability of the principal to a former dealer who has no knowledge of the revocation of the authority of the general agent is based on apparent authority. Thus it should be part of the burden of proof of a non-former dealer seeking to hold the principal that while he had never before dealt with the agent, he knew that he was such and relied on the fact in entering into the transaction in question.

On the other hand the doctrine asserted in Morris v. Brown cannot be one of unlimited validity; in some situations it would conflict with the rule in Watteau v. Fenwick.[61]

§ 286. Termination by operation of law: In general. It is commonly stated that no notice is necessary where revocation is by operation of law; when a reason is given it is likely to be that the events which cause the termination are events of public notoriety so that the third party will either know of them or may be fairly charged with notice. This explanation, it would seem, is too glib. It is doubtless valid as to the outbreak of war. It is less valid as to the principal's bankruptcy, still less valid as to his death, and, it would seem, scarcely valid at all in the case where the principal revokes by selling the subject matter of the agency. Accordingly the necessity of notice in each of these cases will here be considered separately.

§ 287. Death. The possible circumstances, and the possible relations between P and T, are so infinitely various that it would seem impossible to state that there was any presumption that T would or would not know of P's death. Hence, even considering modern facilities of communication, a presumption that T does know of P's death would seem quite

that secret partners need give no notice of retirement to protect themselves from further liability.

[61] See ante, § 174 et seq.

unwarranted. Nevertheless, on the basis of such a presumption or for other reasons not stated, the prevailing rule is that the agency is revoked by P's death immediately, and that T's (or A's) lack of knowledge thereof is irrelevant.[62]

The possible hardship to P's estate of holding it bound by A's act in a case where P's death was unknown to T when he contracted with A, do not seem very serious. Since, *ex hypothesi*, A was authorized up to the moment of P's death, any claim against the estate resulting from treating the agent's act as still authorized would not appear likely to be more onerous than the claims incurred by P in person. On the other hand if A's authority is held revoked by P's death, although T neither knew nor had reason to know of it, the consequences to T are likely to be serious. He will be forced, e. g., to pay a debt already paid once in good faith. The humane rule would seem to be that there should be apparent authority as to T until he knew of P's death or at least until such a time had elapsed that a reasonable presumption would exist that the death was known.

§ 288. ——— It is noteworthy, however, that while it appears from the Proceedings of the American Law Institute that the then reporter, Mr. Seavey, thought the rule "shocking," [63] it nevertheless, out of deference to precedent, is embodied in the Restatement.[64] It is also noteworthy that in 1939 the New York Law Revision Committee considered the question carefully, collected the authorities, and reported that the hardships of the rule did not seem great enough to warrant suggesting any change in the law.[65]

---

[62] See Harper v. Little (1822) 2 Me. 14; Davis v. Windsor Sav. Bank (1874) 46 Vt. 728; Weber v. Bridgman (1889) 113 N. Y. 600, 21 N. E. 985; Ohlandt v. Craven (1927) 146 S. C. 450, 144 S. E. 162; Gallup v. Barton (1943) 313 Mass. 379, 47 N.E.2d 921.

[63] (1934) 11 Proc. Am. L. Inst. 85 et seq.

[64] Restatement, § 120.

[65] (1939) Report of the Law Revision Commission for 1939, 687 et seq. In the preliminary "Communication" the Commission thus states its position: "Upon completion of a study of the question, transmitted herewith, the Commission has concluded that a remedial statute changing the law would not

§ 289. Death: Minority view. In a number of states the prevailing view has been changed, either by statute [66] or decision,[67] and it is held that the authority continues until T has notice of P's death. Some of the common-law cases vouch the civil-law rule to this effect; in others the proposition is bottomed simply on common sense and fairness. Thus, in the leading case of Cassiday v. McKenzie,[68] it is said: "Thus, if

be desirable, for several reasons. The instances of injustice under the present law are extremely rare and there is consequently little demand for a change. The New York rule is in accord with the majority of jurisdictions.

"A changed rule would give rise to the possibility of fraud or collusion between the agent and a third person and there would be danger of injustice in holding the principal's estate on contracts made by agents who, unknown to the representative of the estate, have authority outstanding and whose authority cannot be disproved by the representative. Any extension of the time during which an agent's authority is valid as to third persons without notice, for a period after death, would not necessarily eliminate the possibility of injustice but would merely extend the period and set another arbitrary date after which injustice might also be done. Furthermore, there are procedural difficulties to be considered, such as delay in the settlement of estates and in the final accounting of executors and administrators, difficulties in proof, conflicts in jurisdiction between the Supreme Court and the Surrogate's Court."

With all respect to the learned Commission it would seem to the

present writer that they have both underestimated the real dangers of the present rule and gone out of their way to imagine unlikely dangers in a different one.

[66] The statutes are collected in the 1939 Report of the New York Law Revision Commission (ante, n. 65) 715 et seq. Nine states are listed there as having statutes of this type, mostly applicable to all situations but sometimes limited to certain situations. (Thus the Pennsylvania statute, Purdon's Penna. Stats. Ann., Tit. 21, § 304, applies only to authority to sell land.)

[67] See Drew v. Nunn (1879) 4 Q. B. 661; Cassiday v. McKenzie (1842) 4 Watts & S. 282; Dick v. Page (1852) 17 Mo. 234; Ish v. Crane (1858) 8 Ohio St. 521. See generally notes, 44 Harv. L. Rev. 265; 12 Mo. L. Rev. 50; annotation, 67 A. L. R. 1419.

[68] Ante, n. 67. It may be slightly questionable whether this case is still law in Pennsylvania. However, it does not appear ever to have been expressly overruled. See Kern's Estate (1896) 176 Pa. 373, 35 Atl. 23; Provident Life & Trust Co. v. Spring Garden Ins. Co. (1913) 53 Pa. Super. 66.

In the Cassiday case Rogers, J., makes a pertinent answer to a contention often advanced, namely, that where the act must be done

a man is the notorious agent for another to collect debts, it is but reasonable that debtors should be protected in payments to the agent until they are informed that the agency has terminated. But this, it is said, is only true of an agency terminated by express revocation, and does not hold, of an implied revocation by the death of the principal. It would puzzle the most acute man to give any reason why it should be a mispayment when revoked by death, and a good payment when expressly revoked by the party in his lifetime." In some cases the doctrine seems to apply to any agency; [69] by others it is limited to particular cases, as to payment to an agent [70] (by far the most common instance under any rule) or to payment of a check after the death of the drawer.[71]

§ 290. **Insanity, bankruptcy and war.** These cases are lumped together because they are infrequent and the applicable rules somewhat uncertain. The Restatement appears to state that in each case there is termination without notice.[72] Cases can be found, however, in which T has been protected where he acted in good faith ignorance of the fact terminating the agency.[73]

in the name of the principal, it cannot be done after his death: "It will be observed that the reason is purely technical. How can a valid act be done in the name of a dead man? And it might with as much propriety be asked, how can a valid act be done by an agent whose authority is revoked by his principal?"

[69] This is probably true of all the cases cited in n. 67, ante.

[70] See DeWeese v. Muff (1898) 57 Neb. 17, 77 N. W. 361; Catlin v. Reed (1929) 141 Okla. 14, 283 Pac. 549, 67 A. L. R. 1015.

[71] The leading case holding that payment of a check by a bank in ignorance of the drawer's death is good against the drawer's estate

is Glennan v. Rochester Trust & Safe Deposit Co. (1913) 209 N. Y. 12, 102 N. E. 537: "It would be utterly impracticable for business to be done if, before the bank could safely pay checks, it must delay to find out whether the drawer is still living." For full citation of authorities on the point, see Britton, Bills and Notes (1943) § 182.

[72] See Restatement, §§ 127, 133.

[73] See Drew v. Nunn (1879) 4 Q. B. D. 661; Matthiessen & Weichers Refining Co. v. McMahon (1876) 38 N. J. L. 536; Merritt v. Merritt (1899) 43 App. Div. 68, 59 N. Y. S. 357; Witherington v. Nickerson (1926) 256 Mass. 351, 152 N. E. 707; Watkins v. Hagerty (1920)

§ 291. **Destruction, loss or sale of subject matter.** Where
the subject matter of the authority—e. g., the property
which A has been authorized to sell—has been destroyed or
disposed of by the principal, it is plain that it can in fact
no longer be sold by the principal, personally or through an
agent. A person however may contract to sell property which
he does not own or which does not exist and may be liable for
breach of the contract. There is thus no legal impossibility in
saying that A's authority to bind P may last although the
property is destroyed or disposed of. The scanty authorities
seem to imply that since this is a case of revocation by operation of law, no notice is necessary.[74] Clearly, however, this
is a situation where the presumption is very slight that the
third party will know what has happened. If he contracts in
good faith in ignorance of the facts it would seem he should
be protected. The Restatement appears to favor this position
although it is far from clear on the point.[75]

104 Neb. 414, 177 N. W. 654; War-   [74] See Ahern v. Baker (1885) 34
wick v. Addicks (1931) 5 W. W.   Minn. 98, 24 N. W. 341.
Harr. (Del.) 43, 157 Atl. 205.   [75] See Restatement, § 133.

CHAPTER XI

PRINCIPAL AND AGENT: PARTIES TO CONTRACTS MADE BY AN AGENT AND AGENT'S LIABILITY TO THIRD PARTIES

§ 292. Introduction. Prior discussion has been focused almost exclusively on the question of A's authority or power to bind P. It has been assumed without comment that the contract has been integrated in such a form as to bind P, assuming that A has the requisite authority or power so to do.

It is apparent, however, that the parties, for reasons satisfactory to themselves, may wish to frame their contract so as to create some other version of liability. T may wish to have, and A be willing to give him, A's liability as well as that of P's; or, it may be, T wishes to have A's liability instead of P's. Or, in some instances, inept bargaining may lead to an unanticipated variation from the norm.

The cases further suggest that where the contract is written, technical rules as to the making and interpretation of contracts may result in the imposition or nonimposition of liability otherwise than precisely as intended by the parties. The rule most likely to lead to such a result is the so-called parol evidence rule; also involved may be the Statute of Frauds, the Negotiable Instruments Law, and the common-law rules relating to sealed instruments.

§ 293. —— Or, reverting again to the matters hitherto most discussed, suppose that investigation proves that the agent had neither power nor authority to bind his purported principal; is that the end of the problem? Obviously not; it would seem clear that A should be under some liability to T; the difficult questions concern the exact nature and extent of that liability.

Finally, it is to be remembered that while it is the master's liability which is most litigated where a servant has injured

197

a third party in the course of his employment, the servant himself is liable if he has committed a tort. Is the nature of that tort liability affected by the fact that the actor is a servant?

This question, it is admitted, is logically rather far removed from those arising under contracts made by agents. It does involve the liability of A to T, however, and is considered here for convenience.

The topics just mentioned form the subject matter of this chapter.

1. *The Normal Liability of Parties to a Contract Made by an Agent*

§ 294. **The normal contract: Undisclosed principal.** Plainly the situation where the existence of the principal is unknown is neither the commonest nor the most important of the situations involving a principal. On the other hand, it is the one where the considerations governing the incidence of liability are simplest and most obvious. It is clear that both the principal and the agent are parties to the contract. The agent has purported to be dealing on his own behalf and he has deliberately used language whose natural and only reasonable interpretation is to bind himself as a contracting party. The simplest and most basic contract principles make the agent liable [1] and preclude him from repudiating liability on the ground that privately he didn't mean to bind himself but to bind another. By the same token he may enforce the contract save to the extent that his fiduciary obligations to

[1] See Davenport v. Riley (1822) 2 McCord. (S. Car.) 198; Murphy v. Helmrich (1884) 66 Cal. 69, 4 Pac. 958; Cochran v. Rice (1910) 26 S. Dak. 393, 128 N. W. 583; Winsor v. Griggs (1849) 59 Mass. (5 Cush.) 210; Holt v. Ross (1873) 54 N. Y. 472; Amans v. Campbell (1897) 70 Minn. 493, 73 N. W. 506; Patrick v. Bowman (1892) 149 U. S. 411, 13 S. Ct. 811, 866, 37 L. Ed. 790; Alexander Eccles & Co. v. Strachan Shipping Co. (1924) 21 F.2d 653; Hospelhorn v. Poe (1938) 174 Md. 242, 198 Atl. 582, 118 A. L. R. 682; Grommes v. Anderson (1941) 67 S. D. 650, 297 N. W. 687; Banks v. Chas. Kurz Co. (1946) 69 F. Supp. 61.

his principal compel him to respect the principal's wishes as to how and by whom the contract shall be enforced.[2]

The liability of the undisclosed principal plainly does not rest on simple or basic contract principles. Quite the contrary. It rests on the application of basic agency principles to a situation where the application leads to results that are, from the standpoint of the law of Contract, abnormal. Where an authorized agent makes a contract for his principal, the law of Agency says that the principal is a party. The law of Undisclosed Principal says this is true although it results in a contract between two persons who have never agreed to be so bound, and who may never have seen or heard of each other.

The rationale of undisclosed principal, the precise nature of the principal's liability, and the duty of the third party to elect between enforcing the liability of the principal or that of the agent, has been discussed in an earlier chapter[3] and need not be reconsidered here.

§ 295. Partially disclosed principal. Where the existence but not the identity of the principal is known it is usually held that the agent is bound as well as the principal.[4]

---

[2] See Allen v. Dailey (1928) 92 Cal. App. 308, 268 Pac. 404; Franklin Fire Ins. Co. v. Shadid (Tex. Civ. App., 1931) 45 S.W.2d 769.

As to the principal's right to control the suit, see Restatement, § 370.

[3] Chapter VII, ante.

[4] Argersinger v. McNaughton (1889) 114 N. Y. 535, 21 N. E. 1022; Annes v. Carolan, Graham, Hoffman, Inc. (1929) 336 Ill. 542, 168 N. E. 637, noted in 16 Va. L. Rev. 504; Raff Co. v. Goeben (1932) 116 Conn. 83, 163 Atl. 462; Smith v. Pendleton (1933) 53 R. I. 79, 163 Atl. 738; State ex rel. Bronson v. Superior Court (1938) 194 Wash. 339, 77 P.2d 997; Schelly v. Gribben (1947) 161 Pa. Super. 20, 53 A.2d 862; Note, 33 Harv. L. Rev. 591.

In Argersinger v. McNaughton, ante, it is said: "When there is in fact a principal, the agent may ordinarily relieve himself from personal liability upon a contract made in his behalf by disclosing his name at the time of making it. Upon such disclosure, however, the party proceeding to deal with the agent may or may not, as he pleases, enter into contract upon the responsibility of the named principal; but to permit an agent to turn over to his customer an undisclosed, and, to the latter, unknown principal, might have the effect to

This is superficially to be explained by the fact, pointed out in an earlier chapter, that courts have been accustomed to apply the same rules to partially disclosed principals as to wholly undisclosed ones.[5] More realistic and fundamental is the consideration that T will not normally wish to extend credit to someone unknown: he will wish and expect the credit of the person he knows, and whose credit and reliability he is in a position to gauge. That person, obviously, is A. The rule is analogous to that formerly in force, though now said to be obsolete, that where the principal dwelt in a foreign country, T expected to have the liability of the agent.[6]

§ 296. Disclosed principal.

The contract most commonly made by an agent is executed or phrased by him in some such form as this: "John Jones, per H. F. Smith, agent." Or "H. F. Smith, as agent for John Jones." In such a case the intent and consequence is to bind Jones. It is his contract as much as if he had executed it in person.

By the same token, Smith is not a party to it. Assuming him empowered to bind Jones, he has fulfilled his function in doing so. He may have rights against P for compensation for performing this function; as against T he has neither rights

deny to the customer the benefit of any available or responsible means of remedy or relief founded upon the contract. The rule is no less salutary than reasonable that an agent may be treated as the party to the contract made by him in his own name, unless he advises the other party to it of the name of the principal whom he assumes to represent in making it, where that is unknown to such party."

[5] See State ex rel. Bronson v. Superior Court, ante, n. 4, involving suit against the agent of a partially disclosed principal, referred to consistently by the court as an "undisclosed" principal. Plaintiff sought discovery, inter alia, of the principal's identity; this was denied by a majority of the court on the ground that the discovery statute did not warrant a "mere fishing bill" and that in a suit against the agent, the principal's identity was not material.

[6] See Oelricks v. Ford (1859) 23 How. 49, 16 L. Ed. 534; Miller, Gibb & Co. v. Smith & Tyrer [1917] 2 K. B. 141; McKeen v. Boothby (1930) 129 Me. 324, 152 Atl. 53; Marano v. Granata (1942) 147 Pa. Super. 558, 24 A.2d 148; Fegan, "Foreign Principals," 80 U. Pa. L. Rev. 858.

nor liabilities. He cannot sue or be sued on the contract.[7] By making it he has not warranted that P can or will perform. His only warranty [8] which is, *ex hypothesi,* irrelevant in this context, is that he is authorized to bind P and (perhaps) that P is capable to contract.

§ 297. Disclosed principal: Variations.

Even where the principal is disclosed, the parties are of course quite free to alter by agreement the normal incidence of liability; this "normal incidence" results either from what they have said or from what it is to be supposed they would naturally intend. If they intend something else their intent will be given effect, if legal (and if the contract is not in writing and their intent does not conflict with the legal interpretation of the writing). Thus the parties may agree that only A shall be liable, or that P and A shall both be liable, jointly or with A (or P) in the position of a surety.

Where such an agreement is clear and explicit, no difficulty is normally to be expected; this doubtless explains why cases dealing with such agreements are rare. Where litigation does result it is usually from dispute whether it was agreed that A's liability should be substituted for that of P. Such a dispute may arise from, among other things, a misapprehension of the law, T's claimed ignorance of P's connection with the transaction, or the ambiguity often inherent in oral contracts.

---

[7] See Bickerton v. Burrell (1816) 5 M. & S. 383; Fairlie v. Fenton (1870) L. R. 5 Exch. 169; Wakefield v. Duckworth & Co. [1915] 1 K. B. 218; Goodenough v. Thayer (1882) 132 Mass. 152; Huffman v. Newman (1898) 55 Neb. 713, 76 N. W. 409; Hoon v. Hyman (1921) 87 W. Va. 659, 105 S. E. 925; Inland Printing & Binding Co. v. Elam (Mo. App., 1922) 240 S. W. 823; Henry W. Savage, Inc. v. Friedberg (1948) 322 Mass. 321, 77 N.E.2d 213; Firestone Tire & Rubber Co. v. Robinson (1948) 225 Minn. 493, 31 N.W.2d 18. In Wilkins v. Leach (1951) 229 Ind. 114, 95 N.E.2d 836, it is held that the agent has no standing to appeal from a judgment granting specific performance against the principal. In Rich v. Bongiovanni (1949) 4 N. J. Super. 243, 66 A.2d 888, it is held that the agent cannot join with the principal in bringing the suit.

[8] See post, § 327 et seq.

§ 298. **Williamson v. Barton.** Thus, in a well-known English case [9] hay was sold at auction and bid in by one Barton. He was in fact acting for a contractor working in the neighborhood, who wanted the hay for his horses. His relationship to the contractor was known to T, who was present at the auction and who had previously sold other goods to him through Barton. The auctioneer did not know this and when he asked the buyer's name the latter simply said "Barton" which was written down as the buyer's name by the auctioneer's clerk. Four distinguished judges [10] divided equally as to Barton's liability.

§ 299. **Paterson v. Gandesequi.** In another well-known English case, Paterson v. Gandesqui,[11] a different conten-

[9] Williamson v. Barton (1862) 7 H. & N. 899.

[10] Bramwell, B., Channell, B., Pollock, C. B., and Wilde, B.

Wilde, B., said: "Supposing, then, it was competent to the jury, on the above evidence, to find that the plaintiff actually knew that the defendant was buying for Smith, the question would still remain, whether the defendant, by what he did, made himself the contracting party. To my mind it is clear that he did. He communicated to no one that he was acting as agent; he did nothing by word or act to indicate that he was not contracting himself, and for himself. There is not a single incident, however slight, in his conduct at the sale, to distinguish it from that of a man who was buying for himself. It was the ordinary conduct in all respects of a buyer at an auction. There was nothing, therefore, on which the jury could properly be invited to find that he did not make himself a contracting party. It is not too much to ask or expect of a man who walks into an auction room and becomes a purchaser, that when he gives his own name he should protect himself from being taken as the contracting party."

Pollock, C. B., said: "I think, if the plaintiff was present, and perfectly well knew that the defendant, from his position in life, could not be, and therefore was not, bidding for himself, and the defendant had no intention of bidding for himself, but gave his name because he was asked what his name was, whatever may have been the impression or intention of the auctioneer, no contract was, in point of fact, made between the plaintiff and the defendant. The defendant did not mean to sell to the defendant, but to his principal only. I think there were circumstances from which the jury might infer that such was the real state of things, and if the jury had any evidence, I am not disposed to disturb their verdict."

[11] (1812) 15 East. 62.

tion was involved. Defendant, a Spanish merchant, while in London employed the Larrazabal firm of London to purchase various goods for him. Larrazabal applied to the plaintiff who sent them a supply of samples. Defendant was present at Larrazabal's counting house, inspected the samples and picked out the ones desired. An order was sent, signed by Larrazabal, the invoices were made out and sent to Larrazabal, who debited defendant with the amount, and (semble) the goods were sent to Larrazabal. Larrazabal then became insolvent and plaintiff sues defendant to collect the price. Lord Ellenborough left to the jury the question whether plaintiff had known that defendant was Larrazabal's principal. If not, he was an undisclosed principal and liable when discovered; if so, it was clear that plaintiff had elected to take Larrazabal as their debtor and so had precluded himself from recovering against the principal.

As to such cases the most that can profitably be said is that they raise an issue of fact to be determined in the light not only of what was said by the parties, but of all the surrounding circumstances.[12]

2. Types of Written Contracts and the Liability of Parties Thereto

§ 300. Determination of the parties as governed by the form of the contract: (a) Simple written contracts. Where a contract is integrated (which, for most practical purposes, means simply being put into writing) it is familiar law that it cannot be varied or contradicted by evidence of some understanding of the parties not put into the integration. This rule

[12] See Jones v. Gould (1910) 200 N. Y. 18, 92 N. E. 1071; Hess v. Kennedy (1918) 171 N. Y. S. 51; Hurricane Milling Co. v. Steel & Payne Co. (1919) 84 W. Va. 376, 99 S. E. 490, 6 A. L. R. 637; F. R. Conant Co. v. Lavin (1924) 124 Me. 437, 126 Atl. 647; Lucas v. Bode (1928) 94 Pa. Super. 248; Silvers v. Greene (1939) 280 Ky. 299, 133 S.W.2d 84; Rochell v. Moore-Handley Hardware Co. (1940) 239 Ala. 555, 196 So. 143; Jackson v. Farmers Union Livestock Commission (1944) 238 Mo. App. 449, 181 S.W.2d 211; Fuller v. Melko (1950) 5 N. J. 554, 76 A.2d 683.

finds frequent application in contracts made by agents.

A point of caution needs to be emphasized at the start. In many instances the interpretation of the contract seems to turn on the form of the signature made by the agent. This, however, is not because of any rule that the interpretation of the contract as to parties must be based solely on the form of the signature; it results from the fact that in many instances the body of the contract is inexpressive or indecisive on the point and the solution has to be found in the signature. Very often, however, the problem can be solved by interpretation of the whole paper or papers comprising the contract. Such cases will first be considered.

§ 301.   **Interpretation as found in the whole contract.**   In a well-known supreme court case [13] an order for machinery was sent as follows:

"Our company being so far organized, by direction of the officers we now order from you [the machinery in question.]

Charles Wyman
Edward P. Perry
Carlton L. Storrs.
Prudential Committee
Grand Haven Fruit Basket Co."

It was sought to hold the three signers on the contract on the theory, discussed, post,[14] that the phrase "Prudential Committee" and so on, was simply *descriptio personarum*, saying who were the three men who legally signed as individuals and bound themselves. The court, however, held that the contract must be found not only in this document but in the letter sent by plaintiff accepting the order. The latter was addressed to the company and did not mention the names of the committeemen. This fact, the court said, coupled with the statement in the order that it was sent "by direction of the officers" made it "entirely clear that both parties under-

---

[13] Whitney v. Wyman (1879) 101   [14] See § 306 et seq.
U. S. 392, 25 L. Ed. 1050.

stood and meant that the contract was to be, and in fact was, with the corporation and not with the defendants individually." [15]

§ 302. —— A simple instance of interpretation leading to the contrary result is found in Schwab v. Getty [16] where the suit was based on a letter as follows:

"Referring to our talk at the depot yesterday, regarding the one thousand dollars worth of stock, Mr. Summers and I both agree to take back same Jan. 1st, 1924, after that time you do not wish to keep it, providing you give us 15 days notice.
Yours very truly,
Yakima Shoe Company,
Geo. A. Getty, Pres.
P. S. Summers, Sec."

In a suit against the individuals they claimed that the obligation was that of the corporation but the court held that the use of the language "Mr. Summers and I both agree" outweighed the apparent corporate signature. It was further pointed out that the parties were presumed to know that the corporation was not authorized to buy its own stock, and that they must be taken to have intended to make a legal and effective agreement.[17]

§ 303. **Types of signatures: (1) Naked signatures.** In the leading case of Higgins v. Senior,[18] a sold note, stating "We have this day sold to . . ." and containing in its body nothing to identify the parties, was signed:

"John Senior & Co.
William Senior."

[15] See also People's Bank v. National Bank (1879) 101 U. S. 181, 25 L. Ed. 907; Downs v. Bankhead (1915) 44 App. D. C. 101; Zehr v. Wardall (1943) 134 F.2d 805; Geyer v. Huntington County Agricultural Ass'n (1949) 362 Pa. 74, 66 A.2d 249.

[16] (1927) 145 Wash. 66, 258 Pac. 1035, 54 A. L. R. 1382.
[17] See also Walford v. McNeill (1938) 100 F.2d 112.
[18] (1841) 8 M. & W. 834.

Defendant William Senior, an iron merchant trading under
the name of John Senior & Co., offered evidence that he was
in fact contracting as agent of the Varteg Co. and that this was
known and understood by both parties. The evidence was
rejected and defendant held liable, the court saying that
"to allow evidence to be given that the party who appears
on the face of the instrument to be personally a contracting
party, is not such, would be to allow parol evidence to contradict
the written agreement, which cannot be done."

This view has been universally followed in similar cases.[19]

§ 304. —— Would the evidence rejected in the Higgins
case have been admitted, not to discharge Senior, but to charge
Varteg as principal? At the first thought it would seem not.
The evidence, if not contradicting the writing, at least alters
or adds to it; a contract binding a principal (and an agent)
is very different from one binding only the agent. In Calder
v. Dobell,[20] however, the evidence was held admissible to
charge the principal. The court relied on the rule that such
evidence is necessarily admissible in the case of an undisclosed
principal; if not, such a principal could never be held where
the contract was in writing. And, the court said, they could
see no distinction between such a case and the present one.

In Chandler v. Coe,[21] the court pointed out a distinction. In
the case of the undisclosed principal, it is said there, the
admission of evidence as to the existence of the principal
does not violate at least the "spirit of the rule" since the
third party is not showing that he wrote one thing and meant
another; not knowing of the existence of the principal, he
could not have meant to hold him. Where the existence of
the principal was known and where it was intended that he
be a party to the contract, the case is different. "Parol evi-

[19] See Meyer v. Redmond (1912)
205 N. Y. 478, 98 N. E. 96 (with
which cf. Hernandez v. Brookdale
Mills (1920) 194 App. Div. 369, 185
N. Y. S. 485); Shaughnessy v.
D'Antoni (1938) 100 F.2d 422,
noted in 37 Mich. L. Rev. 975;
Otis Elevator Co. v. Berry (1938)
28 Cal.App.2d 430, 82 P.2d 704;
John Minder & Son v. L. D. Schrei-
ber (1947) 73 F. Supp. 477; Bru-
netto v. Ferrara (1950) 167 Pa.
Super. 568, 76 A.2d 448.
[20] (1871) L. R. 6 C. P. 486.
[21] (1874) 54 N. H. 561.

dence, therefore, if admitted in such a case, does show that the contract which the parties intended to make was not what the writing indicates but different."

This distinction would appear to be valid. However, most of the cases,[22] and the Restatement,[23] adopt the rule of Calder v. Dobell.

§ 305. —— It would seem that under the rule of Calder v. Dobell it could be shown that one who had signed in such a form to indicate his agency (e. g., "Smith, as agent of Jones") was in fact intended to be a party. This, as in Calder v. Dobell, would simply be adding a liability apparently negatived by the form of the contract. This, however, is denied.[24]

Likewise, even under Calder v. Dobell, the contract may be signed in such a form, as to preclude showing the liability of the undisclosed principal. Thus in Sladovich v. Glaser [25] an offer to buy land was accepted by a writing as follows: "I, the owner of the above property, accept the above offer. [Signed] George Sladovich." The George Sladovich who signed the acceptance was in fact acting as the agent of his son, George Sladovich, Junior. The son was not allowed to enforce the contract, the court saying: "Parol evidence would not be admissible to contradict the statement that the senior George Sladovich acted in the capacity of owner of the property, or to prove that he was acting in the capacity of agent for an undisclosed principal." [26]

[22] Barbre v. Goodale (1896) 28 Ore. 465, 43 Pac. 378; Marshall v. Bernheim (1923) 64 Cal. App. 283, 221 Pac. 401, noted in 12 Calif. L. Rev. 206; Bankers' & Shippers' Ins. Co. v. Murdock (1934) 72 F.2d 292; State v. Bennett (1949) — Utah —, 201 P.2d 939; Newfield v. National Cash Register Co. (1951) 186 F.2d 883; Note, 33 Harv. L. Rev. 591.

[23] Restatement, § 149.

[24] See Bray v. Kettel (1861) 1 Allen (Mass.) 80; Heffron v. Pol-

lard (1889) 73 Tex. 96, 11 S. W. 165; Heringer v. Schumacher (1928) 88 Cal. App. 349, 263 Pac. 550; Dover v. Burns (1938) 186 Ga. 19, 196 S. E. 785; Stoefen v. Brooks (1939) 66 S. D. 587, 287 N. W. 330; Stern v. Lieberman (1940) 307 Mass. 77, 29 N.E.2d 839; Restatement, § 323.

[25] (1922) 150 La. 918, 91 So. 297.

[26] See also Crowder v. Yovovich (1917) 84 Ore. 41, 164 Pac. 576; Pope v. Landy (1938) 39 Del. 437,

§ 306. (2) Qualified signatures. The agent may sign the contract neither in his own unqualified name, nor yet in such a form as to indicate beyond doubt that he signs as and for a named principal, but in an intermediate form, as "John Smith, Agt.," or "John Smith, Agent of Tom Brown," or "John Smith, Chairman of the Board, Grand Haven Fruit Basket Co." In such cases two familiar questions arise: Is Smith a party to the contract? Is his named (or suggested) constituent a party to the contract?

"To the eye of common sense" (adopting the language and quite probably the thought, of Cardozo, J., in the New Georgia Bank case) [27] the answers would seem clear. A layman, unlearned in the subtleties of the law of Agency, would take it for granted that Smith, by signing in such a form, meant to indicate that he was not binding himself personally but meant to bind the named (or unnamed) constituent.

Unfortunately, common sense was not very conspicuous in the older cases. It was ordinarily said that the above-mentioned words (that is, those in addition to the agent's name) were mere *descriptio personae*—description of the person, and were added merely to state who the agent was, but not to indicate his intention not to be personally bound.

Two situations must be distinguished.

§ 307. —— According to the Restatement,[28] the addition of the word "agent" to the agent's personal signature, while prima facie to be construed as making the agent a party to the contract, nevertheless renders the contract ambiguous and permits of extrinsic evidence showing that the intent was to bind P and not T. This appears to be a reasonable view, and is supported by a number of cases.[29] Others of the not very numerous cases involving the point hold simply that A has bound

---

1 A.2d 589; Heart of America Lumber Co. v. Belove (1940) 111 F.2d 535, 130 A. L. R. 658; Allemania Fire Ins. Co. v. Keller Diamond Corp. (1950) — Misc. —, 101 N.Y.S.2d 9, rev'd (1951) 278 App. Div. 899, 104 N.Y.S.2d 875.

27 New Georgia Nat. Bank v. J. & G. Lippman (1928) 249 N. Y. 307, 164 N. E. 108, 60 A. L. R. 1344, discussed, post, § 313.

28 See Restatement, §§ 156, 323 (2).

29 See Haile v. Peirce (1870) 32

himself [30] (though of course parol evidence may also be used to make P a party under Calder v. Dobell).

§ 308. —— According to the Restatement [31] where the signature is in such a form as "Smith, agent of Jones," the instrument is interpreted as the instrument of P, "in the absence of a manifestation to the contrary therein." This appears to be an even more reasonable view but one by no means universally supported by the authorities, particularly the older ones. Thus in a well-known Massachusetts case [32] decided by Holmes, J., a published offer of reward was signed: "X, Y, Z, Selectmen of Milton." It was held that "the mere addition of their office" would not exonerate the three signers from personal liability. It will be observed that in the nature of the case extrinsic evidence of intent would not be available. However, where such evidence is forthcoming it is usually held that the signature is sufficiently ambiguous to permit the admission of the evidence to show the real intent. [33]

§ 309. **Determination of the parties as governed by the form of the contract: (b) Negotiable instruments.** It is not surprising that the most numerous and most troublesome problems of this type have arisen in connection with negotiable

Md. 327; Deering v. Thom (1882) 29 Minn. 120, 12 N. W. 350; Rhone v. Powell (1894) 20 Colo. 41, 36 Pac. 899; Clark v. Talbott (1913) 72 W. Va. 46, 77 S. E. 523; Griffin v. Union Savings & Trust Co. (1915) 86 Wash. 605, 150 Pac. 1128; Solomon v. New Jersey Indemnity Co. (1920) 94 N. J. Law 318, 110 Atl. 813.

See generally, Note, 36 Geo. L. J. 238.

[30] See Anthony v. Comstock (1851) 1 R. I. 454; Norfolk County Trust Co. v. Green (1939) 304 Mass. 406, 24 N.E.2d 12; Bissonnette v. Keyes (1946) 319 Mass. 134, 64 N.E.2d 926, noted in 45 Mich. L. Rev. 206; Dorsey v. Martin (1945) 58 F. Supp. 722.

[31] See Restatement, § 156, Comment a.

[32] Brown v. Bradlee (1892) 156 Mass. 28, 30 N. E. 85.

[33] See Page v. Wight (1867) 14 Allen (Mass.) 182; Anderson v. English (1905) 105 App. Div. 400, 94 N. Y. S. 200; Hay v. McDonald (1917) 33 Cal. App. 572, 165 Pac. 1030; International Stove Co. v. Barnes (Mo. App., 1928) 3 S.W.2d 1039; Falsten Realty Co. v. Kirksey (1931) 103 Fla. 225, 137 So. 267; Stern v. Lieberman (1940) 307 Mass. 77, 29 N.E.2d 839.

paper. Where an instrument is designed to pass from hand
to hand and where it is not unusual, but the contrary, for the
instrument to end in the hands of one who knows nothing
either of the original parties or of the circumstances surrounding the execution of the instrument, it is natural that the law
go rather far in insisting that the instrument be self-explana-
tory and be construed in terms of what, and what only, appears
on its face.

§ 310. —— Three consequences of this have been most conspicuous in the cases: (1) the principal cannot be liable on
the instrument unless his name appears thereon; (2) the
agent, if unauthorized, will be held liable not on the basis
of implied warranty as in the case of other unauthorized
agents,[34] but as the maker of the instrument; (3) the agent
will be held to be a party unless it unmistakably appears not
only that he does occupy a representative capacity but that
he is acting in it.

These three propositions will be taken up in order.

§ 311. (1) The principal cannot be held liable unless his
name appears on the instrument. Plainly the person who
takes negotiable paper in a business transaction wishes to
know with whom he is dealing; in particular he wishes to know
who is liable on the instrument. From this follows the rule
that the instrument must name someone as liable—and the
corollary (perhaps not inevitable) that no one whose name
does not appear on the instrument can be held liable. This
rule is stated unequivocally both in the N. I. L.,[35] in the new
Uniform Commercial Code,[36] and in the Restatement.[37] Most
cases have followed it where it is clear that the suit is strictly
on the instrument [38] although in a few instances it has been

[34] See post, § 325.

[35] N. I. L., § 18.

[36] Uniform Commercial Code,
§ 401.

[37] Restatement, § 152.

[38] See Williams v. Robbins (1860)
16 Gray (Mass.) 77; Webster v.
Wray (1886) 19 Neb. 558, 27 N. W.
644; Richards v. Warnekros (1913)
14 Ariz. 488, 131 Pac. 154; Huntington Finance Co. v. Young (1928)
105 W. Va. 405, 143 S. E. 102,
noted in 35 W. Va. L. Q. 92; Lady
v. Thomas (1940) 38 Cal.App.2d
688, 102 P.2d 396; Naas v. Peters
(1945) 388 Ill. 505, 58 N.E.2d 530.

ignored or explained away on dubious grounds.[39] The inequity of such a result is apparent, where the principal has received the benefit of the consideration, and it is not surprising that in many cases the principal has been held liable, not on the instrument but in quasi contract or "on the original consideration." [40]

§ 312. (2) Liability of the unauthorized agent. As explained in later sections of ⁺his chapter [41] an agent who makes a contract on behalf of a principal but who fails to bind him because of lack of power to do so, is liable to the

In Webster v. Wray, ante, it is said: "As between the unnamed principal and a subsequent holder, the reason for the rule in question seems perfectly clear and satisfactory; but as between the immediate parties to the transaction, does the reason for its application exist? For example, an agent purchases goods, discloses the name of his principal, and having express authority gives the vendor a negotiable promissory note for the price, signing it with his own name alone, without any addition, or, let us say, with the addition of the word 'agent' to his signature. In such a case it is held that the payee cannot recover against the principal upon the instrument, because it is negotiable and his name is not disclosed upon it; but what material difference does it make whether the instrument is negotiable when it has not been negotiated? But it must be confessed that the weight of authority, if not of reason, is in favor of the rule excluding all oral evidence, even as between the immediate parties to the transaction. It is held that, although the party executing the instrument describes himself as 'agent' yet, if the name of the principal is not disclosed upon the face of it, all evidence *dehors* the instrument, for the purpose of holding him thereon, is to be excluded. It is wholly immaterial, therefore, that the agent had full authority to make it in behalf of his principal; that the consideration was exclusively received for his benefit; that the plaintiff knew the agent's principal, and accepted the note as the promise of the principal."

[39] See Burkhalter v. Perry & Brown (1906) 127 Ga. 438, 56 S. E. 631; Harding v. Harding-Coor Co. (1914) 223 Fed. 323; Flower v. Commercial Trust Co. (1915) 223 Fed. 318.

[40] See Coaling Coal & Coke Co. v. Howard (1908) 130 Ga. 807, 61 S. E. 987; Gordon v. Anthracite Trust Co. (1934) 315 Pa. 1, 172 Atl. 114, 93 A. L. R. 1160; Johnson v. Maddock (1935) 119 Fla. 777, 161 So. 842; Bank of America Trust & Savings Ass'n v. Cryer (1936) 6 Cal.2d 485, 58 P.2d 643; Bride v. Stormer (1938) 368 Ill. 524, 15 N.E.2d 282.

[41] See § 322 et seq., post.

third party. This liability was often explained in the earlier cases on the theory that the agent, not binding the principal, necessarily bound himself as a party to the contract. Recently the cases have more commonly reasoned that the agent, by purporting to bind the principal, impliedly warrants that he has power to bind him; the agent is thus held for breach of implied warranty, and the measure of damages is different in theory and sometimes in fact from that appropriate where the agent is sued for breach of the purported contract.

One reason for the modern reluctance to hold the agent as a party to the contract is the incongruity of holding him for failing to perform something which in most instances he could not possibly have performed and which he certainly never intended to agree to perform. On the other hand there is no incongruity in holding the agent as a party to negotiable paper, since the promise is necessarily only to pay money. Accordingly there was authority, prior to the N. I. L., that the unauthorized agent was liable as a party to the paper; there was also authority to the contrary.

§ 313. —— The much-discussed Sec. 20 of the N. I. L. provides: "Where the instrument contains or a person adds to his signature words indicating that he signs for or on behalf of a principal or in a representative capacity, he is not liable if he was duly authorized; . . ." It is thought by the draftsman of the act, most commentators, and a majority of the cases, that the effect of this is to make the agent liable on the instrument if he has signed without authority. In a leading New York case,[42] Cardozo, Ch. J., after commenting on the "subtle distinctions" that had existed before the passage of the act, says:

"The statute, as we read it, sweeps these subtleties away. Whenever the form of the paper is such as fairly to indicate to the eye of common sense that the maker signs as agent or

[42] New Georgia Nat. Bank v. J. & G. Lippman (1928) 249 N. Y. 307, 164 N. E. 108, 60 A. L. R. 1344, noted in 9 B. U. L. Rev. 206; 28 Col. L. Rev. 821; 13 Corn. L. Q. 429; 27 Mich. L. Rev. 806; 6 N. Y. U. L. Rev. 495; 77 U. of Pa. L. Rev. 926; 2 St. John's L. Rev. 227; 3 So. Cal. L. Rev. 59; and 4 Wis. L. Rev. 492.

in a representative capacity, he is relieved of personal liability, if duly authorized. But along with this relief there goes a new burden, the corrective of an exemption too broad if unrestrained. By hypothesis, the signer has not meant to contract as an individual. Accordingly, there was need to make provision for the case where the agent or representative, though indicating an intention to contract otherwise than personally, had acted without authority. For this the proviso was inserted. As the price, so to speak, of relief from liability when authority exists, there is to be liability on the instrument when authority fails. Unless this was meant, the interjection of the proviso becomes an irrelevant futility." The learned judge goes on to point out that according to some decisions the cause of action for breach of warranty does not pass with the negotiation of the instrument; hence on any other interpretation of the statute the holder might be left without a remedy where the agent was unauthorized.

Courts have generally followed the view adopted in the New Georgia Bank case.[43]

§ 314.   (3) The agent as a party. It is not strange that courts have been strict in holding agents to be parties to negotiable paper, not only when there would otherwise be no liability on the instrument but when the instrument, reasonably construed, did not clearly show the agent's intent not to assume personal liability. The cases, however, tended to go well beyond what was reasonable and to hold the agent personally bound in situations where it would be clear to any business man that no such liability was intended.

Thus in Heffner v. Brownell,[44] where a note was signed:

"Independence Mf'g Co.
D. I. Brownell, Pres.
D. B. Sanford, Secy."

the court said, in a suit against the president: "There is nothing

[43] For full discussion and citation of authorities see Britton, Bills & Notes (1943) § 166; Brannan, Negotiable Instruments Law (6th Ed., 1938) 296 et seq.

[44] (1887) 70 Iowa 591, 31 N. W. 947, (1888) 75 Iowa 341, 39 N. W. 640.

on the face of the note which indicates that the defendant
signed it as president of the manufacturing company and for
it. . . . There is no ambiguity in the language of the contract, but it clearly expresses the undertaking of the parties."
It was accordingly held that parol testimony showing the intent
of the parties that the president be not bound was inadmissible,
and judgment was rendered against the defendant.

Quaere, if any business man would not have said that it
was at least more probable than not that the intention was
not to bind the president.

§ 315. ——— Section 20 of the N. I. L. has been quoted above,
in connection with the New Georgia Bank case, to the effect
that the authorized agent is not liable on an instrument where
he adds to his signature "words indicating that he signs for
or on behalf of a principal or in a representative capacity."
The section concludes: "but the mere addition of words describing him as an agent, or as filling a representative character, without disclosing his principal, does not exempt him
from personal liability." This section has been much discussed, mostly unfavorably. It is thought that it was intended
to liberalize the rule as to the liability of the agent, but it
is hard to see how the language can be construed as necessarily,
or even reasonably, leading to that result. The agent has never
been liable where his signature indicates that he signs on
behalf of a named principal; the question, which Sec. 20
seems not to touch, is what words are necessary so to indicate.
The last clause might help except that it seems to be limited
to the case where the principal is not disclosed, in which case
the agent not only was usually liable before the Act[45] but
still normally would be under the Act unless he used some
language which left nobody bound on it.[46]

[45] Compare Hobson v. Hassett (1888) 76 Cal. 203, 18 Pac. 320, with Keidan v. Winegar (1893) 95 Mich. 430, 54 N. W. 901.

[46] In Kegel v. McCormack (1937) 225 Wis. 19, 272 N. W. 650, 111 A. L. R. 643, a note (containing no reference to any principal) was signed:

"Jas. L. McCormack, Pres.
N. J. Savignac, Sec. & Treas."

It was held that, absent reforma-

§ 316. —— Nevertheless, Sec. 20 has to a considerable extent served its supposed purpose. However little it may mean logically, it has been used by courts to justify a relaxation of the rule. Thus the court that decided Heffner v. Brownell,[47] forty years later held the officers not liable in an almost identical case,[48] relying on the N. I. L.

Typical of the modern approach under Sec. 20 is Canton Provision Co. v. Chaney,[49] where defendant Chaney was sued on a check signed "Finer Foods Jack Chaney." The court held the signature ambiguous, and defendant was permitted to show that, as known to the payee, he signed simply as agent of one J. S., who conducted a grocery store under the name of "Finer Foods." The cases taking such a position are very numerous.[50]

tion in equity (which the court held impossible in the instant case) McCormack & Savignac were liable, in spite of their proved intent to bind only their principal. The N. I. L. and Sec. 324 of the Restatement were relied on.

Cf. Bieser v. Irwin (1937) 101 Colo. 210, 72 P.2d 271, 113 A. L. R. 1360. For extensive collection of authorities, see Brannan, Negotiable Instruments Law (6th Ed. 1938) 310 et seq.; Britton, Bills & Notes (1943) § 164.

[47] Ante, n. 44.

[48] Consumers' Twine Co. v. Mount Pleasant Thermo Tank Co. (1923) 196 Iowa 64, 194 N. W. 290, noted in 22 Mich. L. Rev. 156. In this case the court said: "If their signatures had been preceded by the word 'by' there could be no possible question but that the designation of their representative capacity would be sufficient. The abbreviation 'Pres.,' affixed to the signature of Felsing, and 'Sec'y' to the signature of Waterbury, imme-

diately following the name of the corporation, as clearly and definitely indicates their representative, capacity as though their signatures were in fact preceded by the word 'by' . . . it is difficult to perceive how anyone could be misled [into thinking that personal liability was intended] where the name of a corporation is followed by signatures to which are affixed the proper abbreviations of the officers usually and customarily signing the obligations of such corporation."

[49] (Ohio App., 1945) 46 Ohio Abs. 513, 70 N.E.2d 687.

[50] See Jump v. Sparling (1914) 218 Mass. 324, 105 N. E. 878; Austin, Nichols & Co. (1923) 98 Conn. 782, 120 Atl. 596; Charles Nelson Co. v. Morton (1930) 106 Cal. App. 144, 288 Pac. 845, noted in 18 Calif. L. Rev. 536; Dormont Savings & Trust Co. v. Kommer (1940) 338 Pa. 548, 13 A.2d 525, noted in 7 U. of Pitt. L. Rev. 67; Fricke v. Belz (1944) 237 Mo. App. 861, 177

§ 317. —— Section 3–403 (2) of the new Uniform Commercial Code provides: "An authorized representative who signs his own name to an instrument is also personally obligated unless the instrument names the person represented and shows that the signature is made in a representative capacity. The name of an organization preceded or followed by the name and office of an authorized individual is a signature made in a representative capacity." This is doubtless a step in the direction of clarification but it hardly seems complete or completely lucid. Is an individual principal an "organization" or is agency an "office"? It would seem not. It would seem that "Jones, President of Omega Oil Co." would bind the company but "Jones, Agent of Smith" would bind Jones. Why such a distinction? And, if intended, why not make it so clearly as to leave no room for speculation?

§ 318. Determination of the parties as governed by the form of the contract: (c) Sealed instruments. The law of Sealed Instruments is happily obsolescent. Roughly speaking the rules as to parties are similar to the common-law rules governing negotiable paper. The principal cannot be held unless not only his name appears on the instrument but it appears unequivocally that the instrument is signed and sealed in his name and as his instrument.[51] Description of the maker

S.W.2d 702. In the last-cited case, plaintiff claimed to be a holder in due course, but the court denied her claim, saying: "She could see what anyone else could see, that there was an apparent ambiguity as to the signatures on the note, and it was her duty to inquire, if in fact she was a purchaser for value."

See also Hawthorne v. Austin Organ Co. (1934) 71 F.2d 945, cert. den. in Austin Organ Co. v. Hawthorne (1934) 293 U. S. 623, 55 S. Ct. 237, 79 L. Ed. 710. And see Note, 33 Mich. L. Rev. 766.

[51] In the leading case of Lessee of Clarke v. Courtney (1831) 5 Pet. 319, 8 L. Ed. 140, the deed recited the named principals had appointed Carey L. Clarke their agent to convey the land in question; it further recited that "I, the said Carey L. Clarke, attorney as aforesaid" conveyed the land; it was executed: "In witness whereof the said Carey L. Clarke, attorney as aforesaid, has hereunto subscribed his hand and seal . . ." This was held to be the deed of the agent and not of the principal. On the other hand where the lease stated

as "agent" or as "agent of" a named principal will not relieve him from liability, if the instrument otherwise appears to be executed as his act. In a jurisdiction where seals still have some significance but the instrument in question is by common-law rules valid without a seal, there is some difference of opinion as to the rule applicable where the instrument is in fact executed under seal. Common sense would suggest that the instrument be treated as unsealed, and some cases support this view.[52] Other cases insist that since the instrument in fact is sealed it must be governed by the rules applicable to sealed instruments.[53] Where seals have been abolished it would seem that sealed instruments must be treated as simple written contracts, and the weight of the sparse authority supports this view,[54] but in Texas it has been held that the

that it was the lease of the principal it was held adequate to bind him when executed "John Hammond for B. B. Mussey." Mussey v. Scott (1851) 7 Cush. (Mass.) 215.

See also Briggs v. Partridge (1876) 64 N. Y. 357 (as to which see Crowley v. Lewis (1925) 239 N. Y. 264, 146 N. E. 374, noted in 13 Geo. L. J. 400, 9 Minn. L. Rev. 580, 34 Yale L. J. 782); Borcherling v. Katz (1883) 37 N. J. E. 150; Ramsey v. Davis (1927) 193 N. C. 395, 137 S. E. 322; Harp v. First Nat. Bank (1931) 173 Ga. 768, 161 S. E. 355; United States v. New Amsterdam Casualty Co. (1931) 52 F.2d 148.

[52] See Kirschbon v. Bonzel (1886) 67 Wis. 178, 29 N. W. 907; Lancaster v. Knickerbocker Ice Co. (1893) 153 Pa. 427, 26 Atl. 251; Horner v. Beasley (1907) 105 Md. 193, 65 Atl. 820; Harris v. McKay (1924) 138 Va. 448, 122 S. E. 137, 32 A. L. R. 156 (with annotation).

[53] See Walsh v. Murphy (1897) 167 Ill. 228, 47 N. E. 354; Van Dyke v. Van Dyke (1905) 123 Ga. 686, 51 S. E. 582; Seretto v. Schell (1923) 247 Mass. 173, 141 N. E. 871. In New England Dredging Co. v. Rockport Granite Co. (1889) 149 Mass. 381, 21 N. E. 947, it is said: "Assuming that, if it clearly appeared from the face of the document that the contract was intended to bind one who by the technical rules applied to sealed instruments was not bound, the seal, if unnecessary, might be disregarded in some cases, still, when the instrument discloses no such intent, is complete on its face, and is framed throughout as a deed only intended to bind those whom it purports to bind, it would overthrow the distinction between specialty and parol if the seal could be rejected in order to charge an undisclosed principal upon any fact alleged in this bill."

[54] See J. B. Streeter, Jr., Co. v. Janu (1903) 90 Minn. 393, 96 N. W. 1128; Donner v. Whitecotton (1919) 201 Mo. App. 443, 212 S. W. 378.

rule under which an undisclosed principal cannot be shown to be a party to a sealed instrument has not been changed by the statute providing inter alia that the addition or omission of a seal shall not "in any way affect the force and effect" of the instrument.[55]

§ 319. **Determination of the parties as governed by the form of the contract: (d) The Statute of Frauds.** The Statute of Frauds requires that certain types of contracts be evidenced by a memorandum signed by the party to be charged or his agent thereunto lawfully authorized. Difficult questions arise as to the form of memorandum, executed by an agent, which will satisfy this requirement.[56] Here as in so many contexts, the existence of the law of Undisclosed Principal has tended to confuse the issue.

§ 320. —— The conventional rule has been that the memorandum must, in terms, bind either the principal or the agent. The statute is satisfied, of course, if the signature is in the conventional form, naming and binding the principal. If A is named as the contracting party, the statute is again satisfied, since A is bound; by the law of Undisclosed Principal, the

---

[55] Sanger v. Warren (1898) 91 Tex. 472, 44 S. W. 477 (and see Farrier v. Hopkins (1938) 131 Tex. 75, 112 S.W.2d 182). In the Sanger case the court says: "It is true the statute renders it unnecessary to place a seal upon a deed, but it does not undertake to give one executed without a seal a different status from what it would have had before if executed with a seal. On the contrary, it provides that the addition or omission of a seal shall not 'in any way affect the force and effect of the same.' In order for the omission of a seal not to in any way affect its force or effect, the deed must be allowed to retain

the only status it had before. When we adopted the common law, its settled rules relating to the construction and effect of deeds became a party of our system. To them we were compelled to resort to determine the nature and extent of the estate conveyed by the deeds, as well as of the covenants therein contained, and who were bound or benefited thereby. It was not the intention of said statute to abolish them."

[56] This is to be distinguished from the question, discussed ante, § 27, whether the agent must be authorized in writing, to bind the principal.

existence and liability of an unmentioned principal may be established.[57]

If, however, the memorandum, without naming and binding the principal, is signed by the agent but in such terms as not to bind him as a party to the contract, then the memorandum on its face binds no one, and is insufficient. Thus in Follender v. Schwartz,[58] where a land contract was signed: "Samuel Pesin, Agent," it was held that the principal could not be held. The court said: "The rule seems to be that, where the contract on its face appears to be one between two parties who are named therein, it may be enforced, and proof, aliunde, may be introduced as to the principal, if one of the parties, in truth, acted as agent but where the memorandum disclosed upon its face that it is signed by one of the apparent parties as an agent for an undisclosed principal, then the memorandum does not conform to the requirements of . . . our statute." [59] Quaere, if the agent was bound.

§ 321. ——— The Restatement,[60] which has been followed by some recent cases,[61] states a more liberal rule. By this rule the memorandum is sufficient to bind the principal if "signed by a properly authorized agent with or without indication of the existence or identity of the principal." This appears reasonable; it is certainly anomalous to hold that a principal not suggested at all by the instrument can be held, whereas one cannot be held because his existence or identity is suggested without actually naming him as a party.

---

[57] Waddill v. Sebree (1892) 88 Va. 1012, 14 S. E. 849; Irvmor Corp. v. Rodewald (1930) 253 N. Y. 472, 171 N. E. 747, 70 A. L. R. 192; Kohagen-Mendenhall Co. v. Joyce (1945) 221 Minn. 83, 31 N.W.2d 232.

[58] (1930) 107 N. J. E. 451, 151 Atl. 55.

[59] The leading modern case to this effect is Irvmor Corp. v. Rodewald (1930) 253 N. Y. 472, 171 N. E. 747, 70 A. L. R. 192. See

also Ades v. Supreme Lodge (1947) 51 N. M. 164, 181 P.2d 161.

[60] Restatement, § 153.

[61] See Estate of Kaiser (1935) 217 Wis. 4, 258 N. W. 177; Penn Discount Corp. v. Sharp (1937) 125 Pa. Super. 171, 189 Atl. 749; Dodge v. Blood (1941) 299 Mich. 364, 300 N. W. 121, 138 A. L. R. 322, noted in 42 Col. L. Rev. 475, 40 Mich. L. Rev. 900, 5 U. Det. L. J. 62.

3. *Liability of the Unauthorized Agent*

§ 322. History and analysis. As far as the writer knows
it has never been doubted that one who purports to contract as
agent, but proves in fact unable to bind the purported principal, should be liable to the third party for the injury done
him thereby; there has nevertheless been considerable dispute
and uncertainty as to the precise form which this liability
should take. At least three somewhat plausible theories can
be suggested: (a) the agent is liable on the contract; (b) the
agent is liable for misrepresentation; (c) the agent is treated
as having by reasonable implication warranted his authority
and is accordingly liable for breach of warranty.

§ 323. (a) The agent is liable on the contract. Since the
agent has clearly purported to bind someone it is not difficult to say that, failing to bind the named principal, he
must have bound himself. This view was stated in a considerable number of early cases [62] and may still be the law
in some jurisdictions.[63] The tendency today is to criticize it
and it is obviously illogical in holding the agent to a promise
he never meant to make. On the other hand it is simple to

---

[62] See, e. g., Mott v. Hicks (1823)
1 Cow. (N. Y.) 513; Layng v. Stewart (1841) 1 Watts & S. (Pa.) 222;
Edings v. Brown (1845) 1 Rich.
Law (S. C.) 255. In the last-cited
case it is said: "It is objected, that
by holding the deed to be the deed
of the agent, the intention apparent in the terms of the execution
of it, that he should be party only
as agent, and his nominal principal
bound to the stipulation of the instrument, is violated. The intention of the other and innocent contracting party is defeated, if he
has not that security which the
agent professed and undertook to
give. In this alternative, the

wrong-doer cannot complain that
he should be substituted to that
contract which he imposed on the
other party, by undertaking to execute in the name of a principal
whom he had no authority to obli-
gate. Such substitution is only a
fair and reasonable indemnity."

[63] See Weare v. Gove (1862) 44
N. H. 196; Kroeger v. Pitcairn
(1882) 101 Pa. 311 (with which cf.
Mott v. Kaldes (1927) 288 Pa. 264,
135 Atl. 764, and Tramontina v.
Bacher (1950) 71 D. & C. (Pa.)
574); Terwilliger v. Murphy (1885)
104 Ind. 32, 3 N. E. 404; Coral
Gables v. Palmetto Brick Co. (1937)
183 S. C. 478, 191 S. E. 337.

apply [64] and probably does justice save in the rare case where (because, e. g., of P's insolvency) it makes T better off than he would have been had A been authorized.

§ 324. (b) The agent is liable for misrepresentation. No doubt the agent is liable in tort in any jurisdiction, when he makes a misrepresentation actionable within ordinary tort principles, i. e., where he makes a deliberate material misrepresentation which is relied on by T to his detriment.[65] In a few jurisdictions it is said that the agent is liable *only* in tort.[66] This again is simple and workable but may in some instances involve the court in a dilemma; either the innocent third party is to be denied relief or the agent, who has made no conscious misrepresentation, must be held liable in defiance of ordinary tort rules. It is apparent, for example, in Massachusetts, where the only relief is said to be in tort, that the court is very liberal in construing the requirements for a cause of action.[67]

§ 325. (c) The agent is liable for breach of implied warranty. In 1857 was decided the important case of Collen v. Wright.[68] Here defendant's [testator] was a land agent

[64] In Layng v. Stewart, ante, n. 62, it is said: "It is not worth while to be learned on very plain matters. The cases cited show that, if an agent goes beyond his authority and employs a person, his principal is not bound, and in such case the agent is bound."

[65] See Flora v. Hoeft (1922) 71 Colo. 273, 206 Pac. 381.

[66] See Foster v. Featherston (1935) 230 Ala. 268, 160 So. 689. And see the Massachusetts cases cited in the following note.

[67] See Jefts v. York (1852) 10 Cush. (Mass.) 392, where Shaw, C. J., said: "If one falsely represents that he has an authority, by which another, relying on the representa-

tion, is misled, he is liable; and by acting as agent for another, when he is not, though he thinks he is, he tacitly and impliedly represents himself authorized without knowing the fact to be true, it is in the nature of a false warranty, and he is liable. But in both cases his liability is founded on the ground of deceit, and the remedy is by action of tort." And see Mendelsohn v. Holton (1925) 253 Mass. 362, 149 N. E. 38, 42 A. L. R. 1307, noted in 35 Yale L. J. 625, and 26 Col. L. Rev. 224; Henry W. Savage, Inc. v. Friedberg (1948) 322 Mass. 321, 77 N.E.2d 213.

[68] (1857) 8 E. & B. 647. See discussion in 10 Col. L. Rev. 567 and

and made an agreement to execute a 12-year lease on behalf of his principal, the agreement being signed: "Robert Wright, agent to William Dunn Gardner Esquire, Lessor." The principal refused to execute the lease; specific performance was sought and refused on the ground that Wright was not authorized to contract for so long a lease. It was held that defendant was liable for "money laid and costs of Chancery suit."

Willes, J., said: "I am of opinion that a person who induces another to contract with him as the agent of a third party by an unqualified assertion of his being authorized to act as such agent, is answerable to the person who so contracts for any damages which he may sustain by reason of the assertion of authority being untrue. This is not the case of a bare misstatement by a person not bound by any duty to give information. The fact that the professed agent honestly thinks that he has authority affects the moral character of his act; but his moral innocence, so far as the person whom he has induced to contract is concerned, in no way aids such person or alleviates the inconvenience and damage which he sustains. The obligation arising in such a case is well expressed by saying that a person, professing to contract as agent for another, impliedly if not expressly, undertakes to or promises the person who enters into such contract, upon the faith of the professed agent being duly authorized, that the authority which he professes to have does in point of fact exist."

This view has been followed ever since in England,[69] is adopted by the Restatement,[70] and is said to be the prevailing view in this country.[71] However, as has been pointed out by

23 Harv. L. Rev. 478.

[69] See In re National Coffee Palace Co. (1883) 24 Ch. D. 367; Rainbow v. Hawkins [1904] 2 K. B. 323; Yonge v. Toynbee [1910] 1 K. B. 215.

[70] Restatement, § 329.

[71] See Moore v. Maddock (1929) 251 N. Y. 420, 167 N. E. 572, 64 A. L. R. 1189, noted in 2 Dak. L. Rev. 459, 43 Harv. L. Rev. 324, 7 N. Y.

U. L. Rev. 541 and 16 Va. L. Rev. 164; Forrest v. Hawkins (1938) 169 Va. 470, 194 S. E. 721; Brawley v. Anderson (1947) 80 Ohio App. 15, 74 N.E.2d 428; Robinson v. Pattee (1949) 359 Mo. 584, 222 S.W.2d 786, noted in 16 Mo. L. Rev. 59; Bregman Screen & Lumber Co. v. Bechefsky (1951) 16 N. J. Super. 35, 83 A.2d 804.

a careful writer,[72] the cases are in considerable confusion and it is reckless to make too definite statements.

§ 326. Implied warranty: Where T knows or suspects the lack of authority. Where the third party knows or has reason to know that the agent lacks authority, he cannot fairly claim that he assumed that the agent was warranting his authority, and the agent, according to most of the cases, is not liable.[73] Likewise, the agent may avoid liability by an express disclaimer of authority [74] or by fully and fairly laying all the facts concerning his authority before the other party so that he may decide for himself.[75]

§ 327. Scope of the warranty. Normally, where there is an existing and competent principal, the full scope of the warranty is that the agent is authorized to make the contract. It is clear that the agent does not by implication (though of course he may expressly) warrant that the principal is honest, solvent, or that he will perform the contract.[76] Where the principal is undisclosed the third party has the agent's liability and there can scarcely be an implied warranty. Where the principal is disclosed, the third party must make his own decision as to the wisdom of contracting with him. The agent represents only that he is authorized to contract for him if the third party so desires.

[72] See Abel, Some Spadework on the Implied Warranty of Authority, 48 W. Va. L. Q. 96.

[73] See Swearingen v. Bulger & Son (1915) 117 Ark. 557, 176 S. W. 328; Boelter v. Hilton (1927) 194 Wis. 1, 215 N. W. 436; Christenson v. Nielson (1929) 73 Utah 603, 276 Pac. 645; R. D. Johnson Milling Co. v. Brown (1938) 173 Md. 366, 196 Atl. 100.

[74] See Halbot v. Lens [1901] 1 Ch. 344.

[75] As where the agent signed, adding the words "by telegraphic authority of" a named principal, which words, in that market, were habitually used to show that the agent did not assume responsibility for the correctness of the telegram. Lilly v. Smales [1892] 1 Q. B. 456.

And see Newport v. Smith (1895) 61 Minn. 277, 63 N. W. 734; Thilmany v. Iowa Paper Bag Co. (1899) 108 Iowa 357, 79 N. W. 261; Kansas Nat. Bank v. Bay (1901) 62 Kan. 692, 64 Pac. 596; Dillon v. MacDonald (1901) 21 New Zeal. 45; Blower v. Van Noorden [1909] Transv. L. R. (S. C.) 890.

[76] See Restatement, § 328.

There are cases, however, where the difficulty arises not so much from a question of authority, as from the fact that the principal is nonexistent or legally incapable. Suppose, e. g., that the purported principal is a corporation not fully organized or one that has been dissolved, or that the principal is dead, or that he is legally incompetent, e. g., for mental incapacity. These facts may or may not be known to the agent.

On principle, it would seem that the agent should be liable, at least where the incapacity or limited capacity was not known to the third party. It should be his responsibility to know who or what he is representing. He is normally in a better position than the third party to know whether there is or ever was a principal, and whether he is still alive and capable. The warranty should be taken to include all the facts which are functionally essential to the act done by the agent; that is, one who purports to act on behalf of a named principal naturally implies both that he is authorized and that there is an existing and legally competent principal who could authorize him. In fact, however, as appears in the following sections, the scope of the warranty often appears to be held less broad than that just suggested.

§ 328. **Associations lacking capacity to contract.** A common situation involves the agent who purports to bind an association never or not now capable of contracting, as an unincorporated club or the like, a proposed corporation, or one once duly organized but for some reason dissolved. In such a case it is probably more likely than not that the status of the supposed principal is known to both parties; this eliminates the possibility of holding the agent either for misrepresentation or on a warranty. In such a case the agent is often held on a special variant of the on-the-contract theory. ". . . it would be a legal absurdity to assume that an agent intended to bind a principal who was not in existence. Under such circumstances, the agent having entered into a contract which as a matter of legal presumption he intends can be enforced, and it being manifestly impossible to enforce the contract against a principal who has no existence, it is assumed that the agent intended that the contract should be enforced

against him." [77] This basis of liability has been applied even
where the agent was ignorant of the principal's incapacity.
"The theory of the action is, of course, the personal liability
of individuals holding themselves out as agents for a principal
in whose behalf they had no power to act. . . . Assuming
that defendants in good faith made the purchases on behalf
of a supposedly legal corporation, it was the actual and not
the supposed situation that controlled the matter of liability." [78]

§ 329. **Contract ultra vires the corporate principal.** It
might plausibly seem to follow that an agent would be bound
who made a contract on behalf of an existing corporation, but
one in excess of its corporate powers. A majority of the cases
dealing with this problem, however, have not held the agent
liable.[79]

[77] Hagan v. Asa G. Candler, Inc.
(1939) 189 Ga. 250, 5 S.E.2d 739,
126 A. L. R. 108, noted in 53 Harv.
L. Rev. 1042. See also Lewis v.
Tilton (1884) 64 Iowa 220, 19 N. W.
911; Medlin v. Ebenezer Methodist
Church (1925) 132 S. C. 498, 129
S. E. 830; Forsberg v. Zehm (1928)
150 Va. 756, 134 S. E. 284, 61 A. L.
R. 232; Wexler v. Poe (1929) 245
Mich. 442, 222 N. W. 715, noted in
27 Mich. L. Rev. 713; Hosey v.
Southport Petroleum Co. (1943)
244 Ala. 45, 12 So.2d 93. Cf. Weiss
v. Baum (1926) 218 App. Div. 83,
217 N. Y. S. 820, noted in 12 Corn.
L. Q. 192, 40 Harv. L. Rev. 780
and 36 Yale L. J. 709.

In Kelner v. Baxter (1866) L. R.
2 C. P. 174, a written contract to
buy a stock of wines was made by
the defendant, "On behalf of the
proposed Gravesend Royal Alex-
andra Hotel Company, Limited."
The corporation was organized but
shortly collapsed and defendant
was held personally liable on the

contract. Willes, J., said that the
words "on behalf, etc." would operate no more than if a person
should contract for a quantity of
corn "on behalf of my horses."
And see O'Rorke v. Geary (1903)
207 Pa. 240, 56 Atl. 541. But see
McQuiddy Printing Co. v. Head
(1913) 7 Ala. App. 384, 62 So. 287;
Shawnut Waxed Paper Co. v. Ton-
dreau (1938) 135 Me. 515, 199 Atl.
426; McEachin v. Kingman (1940)
64 Ga. App. 104, 12 S.E.2d 212.

Cases on nonexistent principals
are collected in 126 A. L. R. 114.

[78] Studerus Oil Co. v. Bienfang
(1939) 122 N. J. L. 238, 4 A.2d
787.

[79] As to the agent's liability
where a contract made on behalf of
a corporation is ultra vires, see
Thilmany v. Iowa Paper Bag Co.
(1899) 108 Iowa 357, 79 N. W. 261;
Brown v. Hare (1932) 112 W. Va.
648, 166 S. E. 362; Hill v. Daniel
(1936) 52 Ga. App. 427, 183 S. E.
662; Jenkins v. City of Hender-

§ 330. Human principal dead or incompetent.

Where the principal is *non compos mentis* or an infant, the cases are few and unsatisfactory. This would seem, between agent and third party, peculiarly a situation where the agent should take the risk. The cases do not take this view, however. Thus the Restatement [80] says that in the case of one who lacks full contractual capacity or capacity to enter the particular contract, the agent is not liable "unless he contracts or represents that the principal has capacity or unless he has reason to know of the principal's lack of capacity and of the other party's ignorance thereof."

On the other hand, where the principal is dead or completely lacking in capacity, the few authorities [81] and the Restatement [82] indicate that the agent is liable for breach of warranty.

§ 331. Measure of damages.

The measure of damages in a suit for breach of implied warranty of authority is analytically very different from that applicable were the principal bound by the contract and the third party suing him for breach, though in practice the result is doubtless much the same in both instances. The gist of the warranty action is the injury accruing to the third person not from the breach but from the want of authority. Crudely put, the damages are measured by the amount to which T would have been better off if that agent had been authorized. This may in many instances be roughly equivalent to the damages recoverable in a suit for breach of the purported contract. On the other hand it is

son (1938) 214 N. C. 244, 199 S. E. 37. Cf. Seeberger v. McCormick (1899) 178 Ill. 404, 53 N. E. 340.

[80] Restatement, § 332. As to the liability of the agent of an infant principal, see Patterson v. Lippincott (1885) 47 N. J. L. 457, 1 Atl. 506; Goldfinger v. Doherty (1934) 153 Misc. 826, 276 N. Y. S. 289, affirmed without opinion (1935) 244 App. Div. 779, 280 N. Y. S. 778, noted in 4 Brooklyn L. Rev. 352, 35 Col. L. Rev. 279, 48 Harv.

L. Rev. 1016, 20 Minn. L. Rev. 97 and 44 Yale L. J. 1240. See also Seavey, Agency Since the Restatement, 23 A. B. A. J. 503, 505–507, Studies in Agency (1949) 161.

[81] See Smout v. Ilbery (1842) 10 M. & W. 1; Yonge v. Toynbee [1910] 1 K. B. 215, noted in 23 Harv. L. Rev. 478; Cheda v. Grandi (1950) 97 Cal.App.2d 513, 218 P.2d 97.

[82] See Restatement, § 329, Comment *b*.

possible that T has lost little or nothing through the agent's lack of authority. Thus if the principal is insolvent, an enforceable contract against him might be worth little or nothing.[83] Or if the contract, though authorized, would have been unenforceable as where it was oral and within the Statute of Frauds, the third party has in fact suffered no loss from the agent's lack of authority.[84]

[83] In In re National Coffee Palace Co. (1883) 24 Ch. D. 367, defendant brokers, mistakenly thinking themselves authorized, subscribed on behalf of the supposed client, for 50 shares, at 1 pound each, in a newly organized corporation. The corporation, which had no assets, was liquidated; the liquidator was allowed to recover 50 pounds from defendants. Brett, M. R., said that in various cases it had been decided that "the measure of damages was what the plaintiff actually lost by losing the particular contract which was to have been made by the alleged principal if the defendant had had the authority he professed to have; in other words, what the plaintiff would have gained by the contract which the defendant warranted should be made. If that be the measure of damages, it does not depend upon the amount which would have been awarded to him in an action against the alleged principal if the contract had been broken by him; that may not be the same amount as what the plaintiff had actually lost. We may test it in this way. If the action were brought against the principal because he had broken the contract, the amount actually recovered would be quite different if he were solvent and if he were insolvent;

if he were solvent the plaintiff would recover the whole loss, if he were insolvent he might not recover a shilling. Therefore it is what the plaintiff actually lost, not what the verdict of a jury would have given him, for the execution might have produced nothing." See further, as to measure of damages, Baltzen v. Nicolay (1873) 53 N. Y. 467; Oliver v. Bank of England [1901] 1 Ch. 652, [1902] 1 Ch. 610, [1903] App. Cas. 114; Kennedy v. Stonehouse (1904) 13 N. D. 232, 100 N. W. 258; Tedder v. Riggin (1913) 65 Fla. 153, 61 So. 244; Flora v. Hoeft (1922) 71 Colo. 273, 206 Pac. 381; Harriss v. Tams (1932) 258 N. Y. 229, 179 N. E. 476, noted in 9 N. Y. U. L. Q. Rev. 488 and 6 St. John's L. Rev. 401.

"The detriment caused by the breach of a warranty of an agent's authority, is deemed to be the amount which could have been recovered *and collected* from his principal if the warranty had been complied with, and the reasonable expenses of legal proceedings taken, in good faith, to enforce the act of the agent against his principal." [Italics added.] Calif. Civ. Code (Deering, 1949) § 3318.

[84] See Dung v. Parker (1873) 52 N. Y. 494; Baltzen v. Nicolay (1873) 53 N. Y. 467; Rainbow v. Howkins [1904] 2 K. B. 323.

4. *Liability of Agent for Money Received*

§ 332. Liability of agent who has received money from third person: In general. A number of questions may arise concerning the right of a third person, who has paid money to one as agent for another, to reconsider and regain the money so paid from the one to whom as such agent it had been thus paid.[85]

§ 333. No recovery of money properly paid to which principal was entitled. Where a third person intentionally and voluntarily pays money to an authorized agent for a principal entitled to receive it, he cannot recover it from the agent, and the fact that the agent, in violation of his duty to his principal, has not paid the money over to the latter, does not justify a recovery of it by the third person from the agent. That is a matter for his principal.[86]

§ 334. When money voluntarily paid by mistake may be recovered. Where a third person has, by mistake or without consideration, or by the fraud of the principal alone, voluntarily paid money to one as agent for the use of his principal (and which the third person could therefore recover from the principal), the agent will not be liable to the person paying it, if, before notice of the mistake, he has paid it over to his principal.[87] That is the very thing the payer expected him to do with it. The action should be against the principal.

If, however, before he has paid it over or changed his position to his prejudice, he is notified of the mistake, etc., and

---

[85] See Restatement, §§ 339–342; annotation 82 A. L. R. 307.

[86] See Gulf City Const. Co. v. Louisville & N. R. Co. (1898) 121 Ala. 621, 25 So. 579; Huffman v. Newman (1898) 55 Neb. 713, 76 N. W. 409.

[87] See Hauenstein v. Ruh (1905) 73 N. J. L. 98, 62 Atl. 184; Lang v. Friedman (1912) 166 Mo. App. 354, 148 S. W. 992; Owen v. Cronk [1895] 1 Q. B. 265; Cabot v. Shaw (1889) 148 Mass. 459, 20 N. E. 99; Bromfield v. Gould (1935) 289 Mass. 80, 193 N. E. 796; Weiner v. Roof (1942) 19 Cal.2d 748, 122 P.2d 896; Cannon v. Clayton (1946) 59 York (Pa.) 144. And see City of Kiel v. Frank Shoe Mfg. Co. (1944) 245 Wis. 292, 14 N.W.2d 164, 152 A. L. R. 691.

directed not to pay the money over, the case is altered. Here, if the third person could recover the money from the principal if he had received it, he is usually permitted to intercept and recover it from the agent, and if the agent pays it to the principal after such notice, the agent will ordinarily be liable notwithstanding.[88] The principal who has received it might ordinarily be held, at the option of the payer.

§ 335. —— Equivalent to a payment over, within the foregoing rules, would be a settlement with the principal upon the basis that this payment was good, or a release of securities, or the incurring of a binding obligation upon the same basis, under such circumstances that the agent would be prejudiced, by having the original payment now called in question;[89] but not a mere statement of accounts or merely placing the amount to the credit of his principal.[90]

§ 336. —— Where, however, the agency was not known, and therefore there could be no implied permission or consent to his paying it over, the agent will be liable even though he has paid the money to his principal.[91]

§ 337. **Money obtained illegally.** An agent who has obtained money from third persons illegally, as by practicing

[88] See Smith v. Binder (1874) 75 Ill. 492; Herrick v. Gallagher (1871) 60 Barb. (N. Y.) 566; Gosslin v. Martin (1910) 56 Ore. 281, 107 Pac. 957; Globe Indemnity Co. v. Thayer County Bank (1938) 135 Neb. 484, 282 N. W. 400; General Exchange Ins. Corp. v. Driscoll (1944) 315 Mass. 360, 52 N.E.2d 970. Cf. Marks v. Jos. H. Rucker & Co. (1921) 53 Cal. App. 568, 200 Pac. 655; Francis v. Blache (La. App., 1944) 17 So.2d 29.

[89] See Buller v. Harrison (1777) 2 Cowp. 565; Langley v. Warner (1850) 3 N. Y. 327; LaFarge v. Kneeland (1827) 7 Cow. (N. Y.) 456; Union Mutual Casualty Ins. Corp. v. Insurance Budget Plan, Inc. (1935) 291 Mass. 62, 195 N. E. 903, 98 A. L. R. 1422.

[90] See Smith v. Binder, ante; Buller v. Harrison, ante; Garland v. Salem Bank (1812) 9 Mass. 408.

[91] See Smith v. Kelly (1880) 43 Mich. 390, 5 N. W. 437; Oppenheimer v. Harriman Nat. Bank & Trust Co. (1936) 85 F.2d 582. And see Wartman v. Shockley (1944) 154 Pa. Super. 196, 35 A.2d 587.

fraud, compulsion or extortion,[92] or by joining in the fraud or other wrong of his principal, will be liable to the person paying it, although he has paid it over to his principal.

At his option, the other party might ordinarily bring his action against the principal.[93]

§ 338. Liability where principal's right terminated after payment.

Where money has been properly paid to the known agent of a principal then entitled to receive it, but the principal's right to keep it is later terminated—for example, by rescission or failure of conditions—it is generally held that an action for its recovery must be brought against the principal, and not against the agent, even though the agent has not yet paid it over.[94] It became the principal's money when it was paid, and he is the proper person from whom to demand it.

§ 339. Where agent is mere stakeholder.

Where the person to whom the money was paid was not really the agent of either party, but a mere stakeholder, authorized to hold the money until an agreed event is determined, and then is to pay it over to the person entitled, and he pays it over in violation of the agreement, or before the event is determined, the party who is entitled may recover it from him.[95]

---

[92] See Ripley v. Gelston (1812) 9 Johns. (N. Y.) 201; Grover v. Morris (1878) 73 N. Y. 473; Lilienthal v. Carpenter (1912) 148 Ky. 50, 146 S. W. 2; Moore v. Shields (1889) 121 Ind. 267, 23 N. E. 89; Larkin v. Hapgood (1884) 56 Vt. 597; Hardy v. American Exp. Co. (1902) 182 Mass. 328, 65 N. E. 375; Millsap v. National Funding Corp. (1943) 57 Cal.App.2d 772, 135 P.2d 407.

[93] See Grover v. Morris, ante.

[94] See Ellis v. Goulton [1893] 1 Q. B. 350; Kurzawski v. Schneider (1897) 179 Pa. 500, 36 Atl. 319; Bleau v. Wright (1896) 110 Mich.

183, 68 N. W. 115; Wilson v. Wold (1899) 21 Wash. 398, 58 Pac. 223; Union Mutual Casualty Ins. Corp. v. Insurance Budget Plan, Inc. (1935) 291 Mass. 62, 195 N. E. 903, 98 A. L. R. 1422; Garrison v. Edward Brown & Sons (1944) 25 Cal.2d 473, 154 P.2d 377.

Compare Smith v. Binder (1874) 75 Ill. 492.

Agent liable where he acted for an undisclosed principal: Pancoast v. Dinsmore (1909) 105 Me. 471, 75 Atl. 43.

[95] See Read v. Riddle (1886) 48 N. J. L. 359, 7 Atl. 487.

§ 340. **Money delivered to agent by principal for third person.** Where money has been delivered to an agent by the principal with instructions to pay it to a third person, this creates ordinarily only a revocable agency, and the principal may countermand the order to pay, and recover the money from the agent, at any time before the situation has been changed,[96] as where the agent has either paid it over to the third person, or assumed an obligation to such third person to pay it to him.

So long as it remains a mere revocable agency, the third person may not ordinarily recover the money from the agent, though the cases are in great conflict.[97] If the agent has assumed a legal obligation to pay it to the third person, the latter may recover it accordingly.[98]

§ 341. —— But there may be more than a mere revocable agency between the principal and the agent: there may be a *contract* between them that the agent shall pay the money to the third person. Whether the third person may sue for and recover it in such a case from the agent is not certain. It is held in a good many cases that a person for whose benefit a contract was made but who was not a party to it, cannot maintain an action at law upon it. Many other cases—doubtless a majority—recognize the right of the beneficiary under a contract, though not a party to it, to sue upon and enforce it.[99]

[96] See Beers v. Spooner (1838) 9 Leigh (Va.) 153; Clark v. Cilley (1860) 36 Ala. 652; Brockmeyer v. Washington Bank (1888) 40 Kan. 744, 21 Pac. 300; Tiernan v. Jackson (1831) 30 U. S. (5 Pet.) 580, 8 L. Ed. 234; McDonald v. American Nat. Bank (1901) 25 Mont. 456, 65 Pac. 896.

[97] See Williams v. Everett (1811) 14 East. 582; Seeman v. Whitney (1840) 24 Wend. (N. Y.) 260; Burton v. Larkin (1887) 36 Kan. 246, 13 Pac. 398; Nolan v. Manton (1884) 46 N. J. L. 231; Mish v. Schindel (1933) 164 Md. 164, 164 Atl. 166.

Compare Hall v. Marston (1822) 17 Mass. 575; Keene v. Sage (1883) 75 Me. 138.

[98] See Goodwin v. Bowden (1867) 54 Me. 424; Wyman v. Smith (1849) 2 Sandf. (N. Y.) 332; Crowfoot v. Gurney (1832) 9 Bing. 372; Walker v. Rostron (1842) 9 Mees. & Wels. 411; Griffin v. Weatherby (1868) L. R. 3 Q. B. 753.

[99] See Williston, Contracts (Rev. Ed., 1936) §§ 347–403.

This, however, is a question for a treatise on the law of Contract.

§ 342. ——— So, again, instead of being a mere revocable *agency,* or a *contract* to pay to the third person, the money may be put into the hands of the so-called agent *in trust* for the benefit of the third person. If the so-called agent, i. e., the trustee, accepts the trust, the beneficiary may have such remedies, equitable or legal, as he may have in such cases under the law of Trusts; [100] but that also is foreign to the present subject.[101]

5. *The Agent's Tort Liability*

§ 343. **In general.** The basic proposition concerning the agent's or servant's [102] tort liability is simple and readily stated: it is normally unaffected by the fact that he is an agent or servant. ". . . for a misfeasance an action will lie against a servant or deputy, but not quatenus as deputy or servant, but as a wrongdoer." [103] It cannot be a defense to an action for battery that defendant was acting at the behest of or in the service of another [104] whatever may be the effect of that fact on that other.[105] The same is true of other torts involving affirmative misconduct, such as fraud,[106] slander,[107] and of course negligence.[108]

[100] See McKee v. Lamon (1895) 159 U. S. 317, 16 S. Ct. 11, 40 L. Ed. 165; Rogers Locomotive Works v. Kelley (1882) 88 N. Y. 234.

[101] See Scott, Trusts, (1939) § 530.

[102] The differences (and likenesses) between agents and servants can profitably be recalled. See §§ 12 and 13, ante. However, while this distinction is of vital importance on the question of the principal or master's vicarious liability, it is ordinarily not of great significance in the present context.

[103] Holt, C. J., in Lane v. Cotton (1701) 12 Mod. 488.

[104] See Scott v. Watson (1850) 46 Me. 362; New Ellerslie Fishing Club v. Stewart (1906) 123 Ky. 8, 93 S. W. 598.

[105] The master's vicarious liability is the subject of the chapters immediately following.

[106] See Endsley v. Johns (1887) 120 Ill. 469, 12 N. E. 247; Peterson v. McManus (1919) 187 Iowa 522, 172 N. W. 460; Seestedt v. Jones (1925) 230 Mich. 341, 202 N. W. 984.

[107] Miles v. Louis Wasmer, Inc.

There are, however, a number of special problems, often extremely difficult ones, involving the agent's tort liability. A few of these will be touched on briefly here.

§ 344. **As affected by the immunities of the principal.** There are situations where, for some reason connected with identity or status, the principal is immune to liability for what would otherwise be tortious conduct; the question arises whether the agent, acting on behalf of the principal, shares the immunity. In some instances he does, in others not. He does not, according to the Restatement [109] where the immunities are "personal" to the principal, though it may be questioned whether this affords any clue to what immunities are personal.

Thus where the principal is T's spouse, parent or child, and so, by the law of the jurisdiction, immune to suit by T, the immunity is nevertheless personal and A may be liable to T.[110] Likewise the immunity to suit of a municipality is not shared by its employee, acting on its behalf.[111] On the other hand it has been held that a statute making a car owner immune to suit by a guest, unless the injury was intentional or resulted from intoxication or gross negligence, applies to shield the owner's servant from liability.[112] Similarly, the servant of a land occupier owes to persons on the land, e. g., trespassers

(1933) 172 Wash. 466, 20 P.2d 847.

[108] See Humphreys Co. v. Frank (1909) 46 Colo. 524, 105 Pac. 1093; Southern Ry. Co. v. Grizzle (1905) 124 Ga. 735, 53 S. E. 244; Southern Ry. Co. v. Reynolds (1906) 126 Ga. 657, 55 S. E. 1039; Hewett v. Swift (1862) 85 Mass. (3 Allen) 420; Breen v. Field (1892) 157 Mass. 277, 31 N. E. 1075; Corliss v. Keown (1910) 207 Mass. 149, 93 N. E. 143; Johnson v. Barber (1849) 10 Ill. 425; Bennett v. Bayes (1860) 5 H. & N. 391; Horner v. Lawrence (1874) 37 N. J. L. 46.

[109] Restatement, § 347.

[110] See Pepper v. Morrill (1928) 24 F.2d 320. For the interesting converse question, i. e., can a wife sue her husband's master, see post, § 421.

[111] See Florio v. Jersey City (1925) 101 N. J. L. 535, 129 Atl. 470, 40 A. L. R. 1353; Meads v. Rutter (1936) 122 Pa. Super. 64, 184 Atl. 560.

[112] See Herzog v. Mittleman (1937) 155 Ore. 624, 65 P.2d 384, noted in 50 Harv. L. Rev. 1324.

or licensees, only the duty owed them by the occupier him-self.[113]

§ 345. **The agent's liability for conversion.** A number of cases deal with the situation where an agent, on behalf of and under instructions from his principal, takes possession of, transfers, or otherwise deals with property in a way which would be a conversion if he were doing it on his own behalf. The line here is difficult to draw. Where the agent, however innocently, negotiates the transaction, it is said, which involves taking possession of the goods or otherwise exercising do-minion over them, he is liable to the owner. On the other hand if all he does is innocently to receive or transport the goods, he is not liable.[114]

A special situation to be noted is that where the subject matter is a negotiable instrument, a chattel obtained by a fraudulently-induced sale, or any other piece of property, the holder of which, by the applicable law, has the power to pass good title to a bona fide purchaser. In such a case a sale by an innocent agent on behalf of the wrongful holder is not a conversion.[115]

§ 346. **Managing agents.** Granting that an agent is liable where he personally commits or participates in a tort, difficulty is often encountered in determining whether in fact he has done so. The difficulty is particularly great where the party is a foreman or other managing agent who is in charge of the work though not a manual participant in the harmful act. Thus in an action for obstructing lights one of the defendants was the other defendant's foreman; he had been in charge, had given all the orders for the construction of the offending buildings, and had been repeatedly warned of the harm that

---

[113] Restatement, Torts, § 382. See also Harding v. Ohio Casualty Ins. Co. (1950) 230 Minn. 327, 41 N.W.2d 818; Employers' Fire Ins. Co. v. United Parcel Service (1950) 89 Ohio App. 447, 99 N.E.2d 794.

[114] See Prosser, Torts (1941) 103. Cf. Restatement, § 349.

[115] See First Nat. Bank of Blairs-town v. Goldberg (1941) 340 Pa. 337, 17 A.2d 377; Restatement, § 349, Comment g.

was being done. Both defendants were held liable.[116] On the other hand it is clear that a foreman or superintendent is not as such liable for the torts of other servants, although he is in charge of them, and even if he himself (properly) hired them on behalf of his principal; he will not be liable unless he is taking an immediate part in the work or exercising immediate control.[117]

§ 347. **Misfeasance and nonfeasance.** By far the most difficult question as to the agent's tort liability is that of his responsibility to third parties for injury resulting from his failure to perform a duty which nominally he owes only to his principal. Suppose, e. g., that the agent is put in control of the principal's property and charged with keeping it in safe condition. In violation of this duty he allows the property to get and remain in a dangerous condition; in consequence a third party is injured. In a famous Louisiana case [118] the agent was held not liable; the court used language often quoted: "At common law, an agent is personally responsible to third parties for doing something which he ought not to have done, but not for not doing something which he ought to have done, the agent, in the latter case, being liable to his principal only. For nonfeasance, or mere neglect in the performance of duty, the responsibility therefor must arise from some express or implied obligation between particular parties standing in privity of law or contract with each other. . . . No man increases or diminishes his obligations to strangers by becoming an agent."

§ 348. —— The view stated above has not become obsolete. It is still true that one is not liable to another to whom he owes no duty. There has, however, been a gradual expansion of

[116] Wilson v. Peto & Hunter (1821) 6 Moore 47.

[117] See Stone v. Cartwright (1795) 6 Term Rep. 411; Brown v. Lent (1848) 20 Vt. 529; Brown & Sons Lumber Co. v. Sessler (1913) 128 Tenn. 665, 163 S. W. 812; White v. Maconbray (1932) 309 Pa. 266, 163 Atl. 521; Jackson v. Gordon (1935) 173 Miss. 759, 163 So. 502.

[118] Delaney v. Rochereau & Co. (1882) 34 La. Ann. 1123.

the duty concept as a matter of tort law. Modern cases tend
to hold that one who takes control of a piece of property
or a situation thereby comes under an obligation to use reasonable care to see that the property or situation does not become
harmful to third parties. As put in Baird v. Shipman [119] the
agent is under a "common-law obligation to so use that which
he controls as not to injure another." Thus in a leading case [120]
it was held that a railroad section foreman, whose duties
included keeping the right of way free of inflammable materials, was liable to a third party whose property was destroyed by fire in consequence of a foreman's failure to do his
duty.[121]

It is obviously beyond the scope of this work to go thoroughly
into so profound and difficult a question of modern tort law.
The reader can only be referred to tort authorities, particularly
to Mr. Seavey's classic article.[122]

[119] (1890) 132 Ill. 16, 23 N. E.
384.

[120] Atlantic Coast Line v. Knight
(1933) 48 Ga. App. 53, 171 S. E.
919.

[121] See also Ellis v. McNaughton
(1889) 76 Mich. 237, 42 N. W.
1113; Mollino v. Ogden & Clarkson
(1927) 243 N. Y. 450, 154 N. E.

307, 49 A. L. R. 518; Wachovia
Bank & Trust Co. v. Southern Ry.
Co. (1936) 209 N. C. 304, 183 S. E.
620; Brooks v. Jacobs (1943) 139
Me. 371, 31 A.2d 414.

[122] The Liability of an Agent in
Tort, 1 So. L. Q. 16, Studies in
Agency 1.

CHAPTER XII

THE MASTER'S TORT LIABILITY: RATIONALE

§ 349. **Basic proposition.** *Respondeat superior.* Let the master respond (i. e., in damages). Or, to put the matter more specifically: the master is liable for the torts of his servant, committed in the course of employment.

This has been well-settled law for 250 years; if any trend is observable, it is in the direction of increasing the scope and vigor of the doctrine. In connection with it, three questions primarily suggest themselves. One is an important question of policy; two are difficult questions of legal analysis. The first: *why* is the master liable for the torts of his servants, committed in the course of employment? The second: given a defendant who may be a master, what are the criteria that determine whether or not the actor was "his servant"? The third: when is a servant "in the course of employment"? It is proposed to discuss the first briefly in this chapter; the other two will be the subjects of following chapters.

§ 350. **Notable dissenters from the proposition.** A number of notable persons have been inclined to doubt that there is any good reason for the master's liability. Mr. Justice Holmes remarked in a well-known passage: "I assume that common sense is opposed to making one man pay for another man's wrong, unless he actually has brought the wrong to pass according to the ordinary canons of legal responsibility—unless, that is to say, he has induced the immediate wrongdoer to do acts of which the wrong, or at least, wrong, was the natural consequence under the circumstances known to the defendant . . . I therefore assume that common sense is opposed to the fundamental theory of agency." [1]

[1] The History of Agency, 4 Harv. L. Rev. 345, 5 Harv. L. Rev. 1, 14 (reprinted in 3 Select Essays in Anglo-American Legal History, 368, 404).

Mr. Baty, in his well-known book on Vicarious Liability says that the master's liability is based on no considered theory; in fact the real explanation is: "the damages are taken from a deep pocket." [2]

Likewise, the author of the first edition of this book appears to have some doubts as to the propriety of the rule, remarking that "the actual results reached are often harsh, if not absolutely unjust." Nevertheless he concedes that "there seems to be no tendency to mitigate its application." [3]

§ 351. **Some supporters of the view.** On the other hand, some far from inconsiderable modern thinkers have approved the doctrine. Professor (now Mr. Justice) Douglas,[4] the late Mr. Laski,[5] and Professor Seavey [6] have all written acutely of the doctrine and each, in his own slightly different way, has found it not only sound on principle but almost a necessity in our modern highly-commercialized civilization.

The present writer ventures to share this opinion and to believe that the rule is a sound and reasonable one, producing a far more just result than would be reached in its absence. The failure of common-law rules to give anything like adequate protection to employees injured in their employment led to the passage of the (as it then seemed) drastic legislation known as Workmen's Compensation Laws. It is believed that if the common-law rules of the master's liability to third parties had not developed as they did there would ultimately have been irresistible pressure for similar legislation to achieve the result.

It is hard to believe that a rule which has been in force for 250 years, which is currently subject to no criticism, and which the tendency of decisions and legislation is, if any, to strengthen, can lack any substantial basis. Unreasonable common-law rules occasionally persist—vide the absurd rule of Matthew

[2] Baty,   Vicarious   Liability (1916) 29.

[3] Mechem, Outlines of Agency (3d Ed. 1923) p. 326.

[4] Vicarious Liability and the Administration of Risk, 38 Yale L. J. 584.

[5] The Basis of Vicarious Liability, 26 Yale L. J. 105.

[6] Speculations as to Respondeat Superior, Harv. Legal Essay (1934) 433, Studies in Agency (1949) 129.

v. Ollerton [7]—but usually the common law, like any other
running stream, tends to purify itself. The rule of *respondeat
superior*, it is believed, must satisfy some instinct of public
policy, else it would not have survived so long and so vigor-
ously.

§ 352. **Justifications.** A number of explanations or justifications for the rule have been offered. Mr. Justice Holmes who,
as seen above, thought the rule opposed to common sense,
in his book on the Common Law expresses the view that
it is largely a survival of the earlier liability of the master for
the act of his slave.[8] It is sometimes said that as the principal
or master has the power of control, he should take the responsibility. It has been said that as he is to get the benefit of the
act, he should bear the burdens of it. It is said that, although
the principal or master may be personally innocent, so also is
the person injured, and that even as between two equally innocent persons, that one should bear the loss who initiated the
enterprise. It is said that making the principal or master liable
will induce him to greater care, from which the public will
benefit. It is said that since the principal or master is likely
to be of greater financial responsibility than the agent or servant—although the latter is liable—and since public policy demands that injuries shall not go uncompensated, the best results are promoted by giving a remedy against the principal.
(This is the deep-pocket principle, regarded by Baty as odious
and socialistic.)

§ 353. —— None of these reasons is completely satisfying,
though many of them contain elements of truth. With all
respect to the learned historical investigations of Mr. Justice
Holmes and Mr. Wigmore,[9] it is difficult to think of *respondeat
superior* as being to any substantial extent a survival of ancient
law. If any historical analogy be appropriate it would seem

[7] (1693) Comberbach 218. It is
absurd, at least, in its persistence.
[8] Lecture I.
[9] Wigmore, Responsibility for

Tortious Acts: Its History, 7 Harv.
L. Rev. 313, 315, 442, reprinted 3
Select Essays in Anglo-American
Legal History 474.

to be that just as the *mandatum* developed to meet the needs of commercialized and prosperous Rome, so *respondeat superior* blossomed spontaneously in the fertile surroundings of eighteenth and nineteenth century England. The nonhistorical explanations tend to be rationalizations rather than explanations. Some of them, while consistent with *respondeat superior,* would lead to extraordinary results if applied literally in other contexts. Thus the proposition that as between two equally innocent persons, he who initiated the enterprise must bear the loss, while often stated, would virtually eliminate negligence as a basis for tort liability and substitute for it liability without fault.

§ 354. **The master furnishes the facilities.** A slightly altered version of the last-stated proposition has often seemed to the writer significant, if scarcely to be offered as a complete justification. In most instances the master gives the servant facilities for doing harm which he would not otherwise have. Largely the modern law is a law of harm done with machines: trucks, locomotives, steamboats, streetcars, winches, drills, and the like. (In older days it was largely horses and carts.) The economic status of the ordinary servant would not permit him to employ these instrumentalities for his own pleasure or business; the master by entrusting him with such equipment enormously increases his potentialities for doing harm. Likewise, although no instrumentalities are involved, the nature of the job may increase the individual's capacity to make trouble. Take the average person of average stupidity and poor judgment and make him floorwalker, charged among other things, with spotting and dealing with shoplifters, and you increase his capacity for mischief just as you do if you make him a motorman and set on him the way to becoming so infuriated with the insouciance of pedestrians that ultimately he doesn't care whether he kills them or not.

§ 355. **The Missouri anomaly.** In a well-known Missouri case,[10] the Western Union Company was held not liable for

[10] Phillips v. Western Union Tel. 711, noted in 45 Harv. L. Rev. 376.
Co. (1917) 270 Mo. 676, 195 S. W.

the negligence of its messenger boy who, while hurrying along the public street on his own legs delivering a telegram, ran into the plaintiff and knocked her down. The rationale of the decision is not wholly clear but apparently the court thought that a master's liability did not arise where the servant was using only his own legs and hurrying down a street like anyone else. "Had this boy," the court said, "been furnished by the defendant with a horse to ride or an automobile to transport him in the performance of his duties, his management of these facilities would have been the management of his master, which would have been liable for his acts and omissions in such management."

No doubt this case is bad law, and it has been virtually overruled in its own jurisdiction,[11] and repudiated elsewhere.[12] It nevertheless seems to express the court's instinctive feeling that there is something abnormal about treating as a risk of the telegraph business the conduct of a boy doing no more than running down a public street like a thousand other boys. This instinctive feeling, the writer believes, may be true to the basic philosophy of agency, however inconsistent it may be with developed technical doctrines of the subject.

§ 356. **Unauthorized instrumentalities.** Again, conceivably the numerous cases which refuse to hold the master liable where the servant has employed an unauthorized instrumentality— e. g., the messenger expected to use a bicycle uses a car [13]— may indicate the same instinct. I. e., a master who has not furnished, or authorized the use of, some mechanism involving risk cannot be saddled with the risk since it is the use of the mechanism rather than the employment in general on which liability is posited.

[11] Salmon v. Dun & Bradstreet (1942) 349 Mo. 498, 162 S.W.2d 245, where the Phillips case was distinguished on the ridiculous ground that here the messenger carelessly caught plaintiff in a revolving door and so caused the injury by the use of an instrumentality, though not one furnished by his master.

[12] See Hobb v. Postal Tel. Cable Co. (1943) 19 Wash.2d 102, 141 P.2d 648; Annis v. Postal Tel. Co. (1944) 114 Ind. App. 543, 52 N.E.2d 373, noted in 32 Geo. L. J. 308; 20 Ind. L. J. 187.

[13] See post, § 380.

§ 357. **The problem of the travelling salesman and his car.**
Again, the group of cases which refuses to treat the travelling
salesman or insurance agent, using his own car, as a servant,[14]
may reflect the same instinct, although, paradoxically, involving the permitted use of a dangerous machine. That is, the
insurance salesman, driving his car across the country is no
different from any one of the millions of other people doing
the same thing; his car is an average car, he is an average
driver (and, incidentally, probably up to average in his ability
to pay a judgment). How is it possible to treat that as a case
where the job increases the servant's potentiality of doing
harm?

§ 358. **The Workmen's Compensation analogy.** Workmen's
Compensation may furnish some slight analogy. It was definitely not the idea of Workmen's Compensation just to protect
workmen as a class; the idea was to protect them from the
extreme risks resulting from their exposure to dangerous machinery in their own hands or those of irresponsible co-workers.
(Vide the fact that in some states compensation applies only
to ultrahazardous industries; in most it does not apply to
domestic employment.) If workmen as a class had suffered
primarily from fallen arches, fatigue, tuberculosis, indigestion
and old age, Workmen's Compensation would never have been
thought of. On the contrary it was created to give protection
against the added risk thrust on the workman by his job; likewise, it could be argued, *respondeat superior* was invented to
give protection against the added risk thrust on the public
by the job.

§ 359. **The Entrepreneur Theory.** The explanation or justification of master's liability which undoubtedly finds the widest
acceptance today is one that goes under the rather pretentious
name of the Entrepreneur Theory.[15] Every industry, it is sug-

---

14 Post, § 446.

15 The writer does not know why
this is more accurate or impressive
in French, but it is seldom referred
to as the "Enterpriser" Theory.

According to Douglas (art. cit.,
ante, n. 4, 584 n) the Entrepreneur Theory was first articulated,
and presumably named, by the late
Underhill Moore.

gested, takes a regular and more or less predictable annual toll, both in property and in flesh and blood. If, e. g., the records of the Shantytown & Southern Railroad were examined and subjected to a statistical computation, it could be predicted with considerable accuracy how many people would be killed and maimed in the coming year, how many cars wrecked, and the like. Restaurants doubtless have an accounting item named "breakage"; this is breakage, too, if on a bigger and more distressing scale. On whom should the replacement cost fall? Unlike the restaurant, the railroad can get new victims without cost; to do so, however, leaves a tragic list of innocent and uncompensated victims. Why not treat it as a cost of the business, as the restaurant does? If the railroad pays, it will easily be able to spread the cost by raising its charges. The expense then ultimately rests, like other expenses of running a railroad, on that part of the public which needs, patronizes, and presumably profits by the existence of, a railroad. The cost, to each individual member of the railroad-interested public, is, per accident, insignificant; if left to lie on the victim of the particular accident it may be ruinous.[16]

Thus, in the light of the Entrepreneur Theory, *respondeat superior* achieves an allocation of the loss which is fair and reasonable; no better justification, it is thought, could be needed.

§ 360. **Should society as a whole share the loss?** Why not, it might be asked, go a step further and put the burden on society as a whole; more specifically, on the state? The state is interested in the welfare of its citizens; it is interested in the industry without which it could not grow to be great. Why not say that industrial accidents are affected with a public interest, and that all persons injured shall be compensated from a fund to be raised by taxation, perhaps general or perhaps on industry as a whole?

Most people would regard this as going too far. The dreadful word "socialism" would be hurled, forgetful of the obvious

---

[16] For a slightly different statement of this theory, and comment on it, see Morris, The Torts of an Independent Contractor, 29 Ill. L. Rev. 339.

truth that socialism is anything which is a little too social for the particular time or the particular speaker. After all, in the light of the Entrepreneur Theory, is not the law of Master and Servant a small piece of mild and well-accepted socialism? Labels aside, however, there seem practical reasons against such an extension. While the effect of *respondeat superior* may be in a broad sense to put the loss on the industry, as long as there is competition within the industry, there will be a strong profit motive in keeping the accident loss low. With a state-supported pool a particular entrepreneur would have so little to gain by accident prevention in his own plant that he would have little zeal in seeking to attain it. It is quite otherwise when the cost is important as a competitive item. One of the best things about *respondeat superior* is the pressure it exerts on the individual entrepreneur to keep his accident cost low.[17] State insurance against injury by motor car may be a development of the next few years; however, there seems little probability of the extension of such an idea to industrial accidents in general.

§ 361. **The effect of the wide extension of corporate activity.** Finally, it should be noted that the present status of the corporation as the dominant factor in modern business nearly furnishes an automatic justification of *respondeat superior*. The corporation could not exist without the law of Principal and Agent. A corporation can only act through agents; no one would deal with it if it were not bound by the acts of its agents. The case is somewhat different where torts are involved. A corporation could bind and be bound by agent-made contracts and still bear no liability for the torts of its servants. (In the case of fraud the results would be curious: the corporation would be bound by the promises but not the representations of its agents.) At one time there was a judicial tendency to reach such a result on the premise that a corporation being a creature with strictly limited powers, could not be bound

---

17 Morris and Seavey (arts. cit., ante) both stress this point: Seavey calls attention to the fact that insurance companies "have learned that it pays to educate the persons they insure" and that industrial mortality has decreased under Workmen's Compensation.

ultra vires—and surely a corporation had no authority to commit torts.

§ 362. —— Common sense has never taken any such attenuated view. To common sense it is apparent that the corporation is a real thing which can and does act. If the man in the street is run over by the Standard Oil truck he indulges in no abstractions about *respondeat superior* or corporate metaphysics; it is quite clear to him and his wife and his friends that he has been run down by the Standard Oil Company which at the moment was driving its truck in a shockingly reckless fashion. The man in the street would seem, in this instance, to be quite right. To the eye of pragmatism it is apparent that the corporation can both make contracts and commit torts. No justification is necessary for the obvious.

Since such a great share of the world's business is done by corporations, it is not surprising to find applied to noncorporate enterprisers the same rule of liability. If the normal enterprise is liable for the torts of those who work for it, why give immunity to a similar enterprise just because it is owned, not by a corporation, but by an individual or a partnership?

§ 363. **Conclusion.** The present writer has observed elsewhere that if there were no law of Agency it would be necessary to invent one. Large scale business would be impossible without it. Thus the rule of *respondeat superior* is congenial to and consistent with our industrial civilization. It may need no other justification.

CHAPTER XIII

THE MASTER'S TORT LIABILITY: COURSE OF EMPLOYMENT

§ 364. **The questions.** The master, however, is liable only for the torts of the servant committed in the course of the employment. This raises two questions: (a) Why this limitation? (b) What is the course of employment?

1. *Rationale of Course of Employment*

§ 365. **Why is the master liable only for torts committed in the course of employment?** This question is relatively simple and easy to answer. If the purpose of *respondeat superior* is to put on the business, for the purpose of allocation, the risks of the business, that plainly means just the risks of carrying on the business; it does not include the risks of the personal conduct of all connected with the business, simply because they are connected with the business. If the coal company's truck-driver drives the truck carelessly while delivering coal, that is a risk of the business; if he goes home after work and beats his wife, that is a risk of life or of matrimony but certainly not a risk of the coal business. To say that the coal company should pay for all damage done by coal company employees whenever and however committed and whether or not it had any connection with the coal business would be an advanced and apparently not very rational form of social insurance; it has never been thought that the law of Master and Servant embodies any such doctrine. It imposes liability only where it can fairly be said that the injury resulted from some activity incidental to the carrying-on of the business.

§ 366. **Course of employment: Analysis.** No completely successful analysis of the "course of employment" concept has ever been made; doubtless it is not susceptible of any such

246

analysis and none will ever be made. Most attempts, however, have tended to state in some form or other two requirements:

(a) an intent on the part of the servant to serve the master rather than to seek the servant's own ends, and

(b) a way of doing the master's work that does not vary too much from the norm, i. e., from the expectable ambit of servant conduct.[1]

§ 367.   **Intent to serve the master.** It seems plausible to say that M will not be liable unless S's act was intended to benefit M. It is the risks of M's business we wish to put on M, not the risks of S's business. Things done by S with intent to further his own ends and not those of M can hardly be considered within the risks of M's business.

Examination of specific instances, however, shows that the idea of intent may be rather elusive. The driver of the coal truck mentioned above, driving the truck down the road to deliver his master's coal to a customer may be taken as the archtype of the servant in the course of employment. An X ray of his mind, however, might disclose no trace of his master; he is thinking of his breakfast, his girl friend, his debts— anything but his master. His absorption in his thoughts, in fact, may be the cause of the accident. Nevertheless no one doubts that he was in the course of employment. If then, we say that he was intending to serve the master we can only mean that

---

[1] "The act of the servant complained of is regarded as outside the relation and as that of a stranger: (a) if he did not assume to act within the scope of his employment; or (b) if what he did was a thing so remote from his duty as to be altogether outside of, and unconnected with, his employment." Isaacs, J., in Bugge v. Brown (1919) V. L. R. 264, 26 C. L. R. 110.

"A tort is within such scope [of employment]—(1) if A, in doing the act in the doing of which the tort was committed, was motivated in part at least by a desire to serve his employer; and (2) if it further appears that the act in the doing of which the tort was committed was not an extreme deviation from the normal conduct of such employees." Powell's Tiffany (1924) § 38. Mr. Powell states that examination of the cases shows that liability is imposed where these two factors are present, but he does not attempt to rationalize them.

And see Restatement, §§ 228,

he was consciously carrying on a course of activity designed to achieve the master's ends.

§ 368. —— In other words we may have to determine his intent from what he was doing, rather than as an independent factor. This rather casts doubt on the value of "intent" as a clue or test. The difficulty can perhaps be eliminated if we adopt a statement like this: the servant following a pattern designed to achieve the master's ends will be taken to be intending to serve the master unless for the time being he is conspicuously and unmistakably seeking a personal end. I. e., if he speeds up his truck to run over a dog that has snapped at him [2] or a girl who has deceived him, we say that quite clearly an intent to serve a personal end has for the time being quite superseded any thought of serving the master.

§ 369. —— This is not difficult, nor is the case where he is clearly in no sense following a pattern designed to serve his master's ends. E. g., he takes the master's truck without permission to visit his girl, or, while using the master's truck on the master's business, he parks it for a while and goes in to enjoy a beer.[3] Much more difficult and characteristic are the cases where the servant has several intents, even patternwise. Thus driving the truck towards the proper destination, he plans

229 (2) (a) (i), 230, Comment *c*, 233, 234, 235 and 236.

[2] Cf. Columbus Ry. Co. v. Woolfolk · (1907) 128 Ga. 631, 58 S. E. 152, where a petition was sustained charging that defendant's motorman wilfully speeded the trolley car in order to kill plaintiff's dog. The opinion suggests that M was held because S was at the very moment doing his job, i. e., driving D's trolley. It is doubtful that the case can be regarded as correctly decided. Cf. Hoppe v. Deese (1950) 232 N. C. 698, 61 S.E.2d 903, where a telephone employee on a business mission attacked the lady of the house. "According to the allegation of the complaint, the male defendant assaulted the feme plaintiff to conduct an independent and licentious purpose of his own, and not to accomplish the business mission entrusted to him by the corporate defendant. This being true, the ruling [sustaining] the demurrer was correct for it appears upon the face of the complaint that the wrongful act of the male defendant was outside the scope of his employment."

[3] Though M might be liable for

to stop en route to visit his mother. Perhaps we handle this
by saying that but for the master's business he wouldn't be
seeing his mother; hence his real or chief or primary intent is
to serve the master. But suppose the mother's house is not on
the direct route; the servant must deviate one or two or five
or ten miles. What of his intent while so doing? Is it affected
by the question whether he makes a right angle turn or follows
an arc? [4]

These simple instances show some of the difficulties inherent
in trying to use intent as a test.

§ 370. Excessive deviation.

Suppose the master asks the
office boy to run down the short two blocks to the post office
and mail a letter. The office boy elects to take the big truck
which he has never tried to drive before. Disaster ensues.

Here plainly the master's business was being done and the
boy was intending to do it. Nevertheless we are likely to feel
that this was not in the course of employment. How rationalize this feeling?

We may say we are charging M with the risks of the business
and "risk" is a word of prospective operation, meaning harms
likely to happen. The boy's whim was unforeseeable. However,
this is probably mere sophistry. If a business is to bear its
breakage costs, it should not matter that a given loss happened
in quite a novel and unforeseen fashion.

§ 371. ——

More reasonably we say that it must be M's
privilege to set, at least roughly, the limits of his business. If
he is a householder and employs a chauffeur to drive his car
he cannot be responsible if the chauffeur, though with the best
of intentions, attempts to put car and master into the business
of delivering dynamite. Similarly the master must be able to
determine, within limits, the manner in which his business is
to be done. Trucks are to be used only for hauling heavy goods
and to be driven only by truckdrivers. In the absence of spe-

the negligent parking of the truck,   [4] For cases dealing with such
see Dolinar v. Pedone (1944) 63   problems, see post, § 391.
Cal.App.2d 169, 146 P.2d 237.

cific instructions, the normal routine of such a business is to be followed. Thus we say that for the servant to be in the course of employment he must be (within limits) doing the business in which the master has embarked, using the means and methods selected by the master, and respecting the normal routine of such a business.[5]

§ 372. —— "Within limits." That is the rub. The law necessarily takes cognizance of human frailty and realizes that servants will disobey instructions. In fact the doctrine of *respondeat superior* assumes this, since it cannot be assumed that a master ever authorizes negligence. The difficult question of fact always remains, however, at what point the servant's deviation takes him out of the job as distinguished from simply evidencing the bad doing of the job, for which the master is liable.

§ 373. **The judicial process in course-of-employment cases.** It is believed that in fact the judicial process in course-of-employment cases is not unlike that in "causation" cases. In novel instances, the court decides on the basis of intuition or hunch; where similar instances increase, there is a tendency for a rule to crystallize.

This approach will be followed herein and little attempt to generalize will be made. Instead a number of the most typical and difficult problems will be considered, and an endeavor made to discuss the approach to them made by courts.

[5] "Both cases assert that the employee was acting in furtherance of the master's business. This alone is not enough. It also must appear that the means of furtherance have been expressly or impliedly entrusted to the employee. If a servant is employed only as a helper on a truck, implied authority to drive the truck on the public highways is not a warrantable inference from such hiring. To find that operation of the truck is within the scope of such service ant's employment, it must be shown to be included in the general type of service in which the servant is engaged. . . . The intention of the servant to further the master's business, however laudable, may not make the master responsible for the servant's torts unless committed while acting within the bounds of duties expressly or impliedly entrusted to him." Haining v. Turner Centre System (1930) 50 R. I. 481, 149 Atl. 376.

2. *Negligent Torts*

§ 374. **The servant's personal habits and needs.** Is eating, going to the toilet, smoking, chewing gum or powdering the nose within the course of employment? It is plain that (excluding such characters as professional cigarette testers and the like) the servant is not hired to do these things. It is also plain that, as incidental to the job he is hired to perform, the servant will naturally or perhaps necessarily do some things he is not precisely hired to do. The janitor is hired to mop the floor and the like and not to walk, but clearly he is in the course of employment while walking (or taking the elevator) from one part of the premises to another to reach the next floor that needs mopping. Is it any less essential to his mopping that he go to the toilet when the need arises? Apparently not, at least so far as he is using toilet facilities on the premises and within an express or implied permission.[6]

In most instances the servant is given time off for lunch; he is free to eat where and what he wishes and no doubt, even if he chooses to eat in the master's cafeteria, he is not in the course of employment.[7] In some employments, however, particularly domestic and agricultural ones, the time-off concept is not applicable and the servant may well be in the course of employment while eating. Thus in a familiar Australian case,[8] two ranch servants, sent off for the day to a remote part of the

6 See J. C. Penney Co., Inc. v. McLaughlin (1939) 137 Fla. 594, 188 So. 785.

7 Davidson v. Harris (1949) 79 Ga. App. 788, 54 S.E.2d 290.

8 Bugge v. Brown (1919) V. L. R. 264, 26 C. L. R. 110. Cf. General Foods Corp. v. Coney (1950) 35 Ala. App. 492, 48 So.2d 781; McIntyre v. Straussen (1950) 365 Pa. 507, 76 A.2d 220; Fowser Fast Freight v. Simmont (1951) — Md. —, 78A.2d 178.

In Adams v. American President Lines (1944) 23 Cal.2d 681, 146 P.2d 1, defendant was held liable for an injury sustained by plaintiff when he stepped on an orange peel, presumably thrown away by a crew member after a meal. "(A seaman's) employment requires him to spend his entire time on the vessel while it is at sea. His time is never wholly his own. On his hours off he is subject to call to duty in an emergency. Necessary incidents of life therefore, such as sleeping, eating, washing, etc., are contemplated to be within the scope of the employment." The

ranch to work and furnished with chops and a frying pan to
cook lunch, were held in the course of employment while cook-
ing the lunch (which they did carelessly, thereby burning the
plaintiff's property).

§ 375. **Smoking.** In the situations discussed in the preceding paragraph, the activities in question could properly be
described as necessary incidents of a long day's work. Suppose
the servant on the job smokes cigarettes or a pipe and sets
fire to something? The cases agree that prima facie the master
is not liable: smoking is not part of the employment. Thus
where a salesman while telephoning his employer on business
started a fire by lighting a cigarette and tossing the match
away, unextinguished, the master was held not liable.[9]

§ 376. —— There are, however, several groups of cases in
which the master has been held liable. In one, the master has
been held liable on nonagency principles where it has been
more or less plausibly found that the master knew of the
servant's propensity to smoke in a careless way or under circumstances where any smoking was dangerous, and was negligent in not taking steps to prevent a continuation of the dangerous conduct.[10]

In a more important one, liability has been imposed on agency
principles on a theory seldom made explicit by the cases and

numerous cases cited by the court
were mostly, if not all, workmen's
compensation cases.

[9] Kelly v. Louisiana Oil Refining
Co. (1933) 167 Tenn. 101, 66
S.W.2d 997. "The act of lighting
the cigarette was not incident to
the telephoning and had no relation to it. It did not render the
act of telephoning hazardous, nor
did it create any causal relation
between the service he was employed to render the defendant
and the injury sustained by the
plaintiff." See also Williams v.

Jones (1865) 3 H. & C. 602; Adams
v. Southern Bell Telephone & Telegraph Co. (1924) 295 Fed. 586;
Herr v. Simplex Paper Box Corp.
(1938) 330 Pa. 129, 198 Atl. 309,
noted in 18 Ore. L. Rev. 261; Tom-
linson v. Sharpe (1946) 226 N.
C. 177, 37 S.E.2d 498.

[10] See Keyser Canning Co. v.
Klots Throwing Co. (1923) 94 W.
Va. 346, 118 S. E. 521, 31 A. L. R.
283; Triplett v. Western Public
Service Co. (1935) 128 Neb. 835,
260 N. W. 387; Palmer v. Keen
Forestry Ass'n (1921) 80 N. H.

somewhat difficult to rationalize but which can perhaps be explained by saying that, considering the nature of the job, the smoking cannot be thought of independently but must be thought of rather as a (bad) way of doing the job.[11] If a truckdriver uses both hands to light his pipe and loses control of the truck, we do not exonerate the master by saying that smoking is not within the course of employment; we say that driving is, and that this was a bad way of driving. On the other hand if the driver throws away the match and ignites the neighboring field, presumably the master is not liable; that is not a way of driving a truck at all.

§ 377. —— In the cases under discussion the servant is most commonly one employed to handle gasoline or some other highly inflammable substance. When his cigarette ignites the gasoline, we do not say it was a poor way to smoke—but smoking is no part of the employment; we say it was a poor way to pour gasoline. Thus we distinguish the case of the telephoning employee; we do not instinctively think of smoking as a poor way to telephone, though it turned out to be such in the particular instance.

68, 112 Atl. 798, 13 A. L. R. 995; Allen v. Pasterknack (1932) 107 Pa. Super. 332, 163 Atl. 336.

It often appears to be implied in the cases that the master would be liable if it were shown that he had authorized the servant to smoke. Save in the situation illustrated by the foregoing cases, it is not believed that this implication is the basis of authority, nor that it is sound. The fact that the master allows his truckdriver to smoke a pipe, chew tobacco, or whistle as he drives, does not make these acts part of the job. See Restatement, § 229, Comment c.

[11] See Maloney Tank Mfg. Co. v. Mid-Continent Petroleum Corp. (1931) 49 F.2d 146; Century Ins. Co. v. N. or H. Ireland Sc. Board, (1942) A. C. 509, 1 All E. Rep. 491; Bluestein v. Scoparino (1950) 277 App. Div. 534, 100 N.Y.S.2d 577. In the last-cited case the court said: "Strictly speaking, an employee who smokes on the job for his own pleasure or satisfaction does something that cannot be regarded as furthering the master's interest. Nevertheless, the courts have on occasion held that where the circumstances are such that the smoking increases the danger of conflagration, the act of smoking is merely incidental to the general employment and the master is liable because his work is being negligently performed."

Another and more basic rationalization would be to say that careless smoking is a conspicuous risk of some businesses; in those cases and those only, the cost should be put on the business.

No instances have been found of harm done by the gum-chewing stenographer or the clerk patronizing the refreshment-vending machine supplied or sanctioned by the employer. Should such cases arise it seems likely they would be governed by the considerations applicable to smoking.

§ 378. **Unauthorized delegation.** The master may, of course, authorize the servant to use a helper at his own or the master's expense, who becomes a subservant or simply another servant of the master, and charges him by the negligent performance of his job. The troublesome cases are those where the servant, without express authorization, procures someone to help him. In such cases, where the work to be performed is obviously beyond the power of the unaided servant, or (more rarely) where some sudden emergency makes it such, courts are willing to say that there is implied authority to procure help.[12]

Absent necessity resulting in implied authority, the rule of the books is that the servant has no power to charge the master by employing a helper.[13] *Delegatus non potest delegare.* The rationale of this is obvious: a master who by law is liable for the negligence of his servants has a right not to have servants thrust on him without his consent.

[12] As to the circumstances amounting to necessity on emergency sufficient to warrant the implication of authority, see Gwilliam Twist [1895] 2 Q. B. 84; Kirk v. Showell, Fryer & Co. (1923) 276 Pa. 587, 120 Atl. 670; White v. Consumers Finance Service (1940) 339 Pa. 417, 15 A.2d 142; Burkhalter v. Birmingham Elec. Co. (1942) 242 Ala. 388, 6 So.2d 864; Schiano v. McCarthy Freight System (1947) 72 R. I. 455, 53 A.2d 527; Hanis v. Railway Exp. Agency (1949) 178 F.2d 8; Sandefur v. Sandefur (Tex. Civ. App., 1950) 232 S.W.2d 111; annotation, 76 A. L. R. 963.

[13] Cooper v. Lowery (1908) 4 Ga. App. 120, 60 S. E. 1015; Weatherman v. Handy (Mo. App., 1917) 198 S. W. 459; Great A. & P. Co. v. Compton (1932) 164 Miss. 553, 145 So. 105; Kosick v. Standard Properties, Inc. (1935) 13 N. J. Misc. 219, 177 Atl. 428.

§ 379. —— In a number of instances, however, where the work requires no particular skill or discretion and where it would not seem that the master attached particular significance to the identity of the servant, delegation has been allowed on one theory or another. This is particularly true where the delegate is acting under the immediate supervision of the servant and the fault results from the nature of the act directed rather than from the manner of its doing. Thus in a well-known New York case [14] a servant, directed to remove the snow from the master's roof, got a friend to help him; they did the job by throwing the snow into the street. The court held it immaterial whether the snow that struck the plaintiff was thrown by the servant or by the delegate.[15]

§ 380. Unauthorized instrumentality. The courts have been strict—perhaps surprisingly so—in refusing to impose liability where the servant has altered the risk by using an unauthorized instrumentality. Thus where the servant, authorized to go on foot, rides or drives a horse or uses a bicycle, or where one authorized to use a bicycle, uses an automobile, the master is not responsible for his negligence in using the unpermitted form of transportation.[16] Or the authorization may be limited

---

[14] Althorf v. Wolfe (1860) 22 N. Y. 355.

[15] See also Leavenworth Ry. Co. v. Cusick (1899) 60 Kan. 590, 57 Pac. 519; Letterstrom v. Brainerd Ry. Co. (1903) 89 Minn. 262, 94 N. W. 882; Levin v. Omaha (1918) 102 Neb. 328, 167 N. W. 214; Malloy v. Svoboda (1928) 29 Ohio App. 331, 163 N. E. 579, noted in 29 Col. L. Rev. 221; Ada-Konawa Bridge Co. v. Cargo (1932) 163 Okla. 122, 21 P.2d 1.

[16] See Goodman v. Kennell (1827) 3 Car. & P. 167, where Park, J., said: "I cannot bring myself to go the length of supposing, that if a man sends his servant on an errand, without providing him with a horse, and he meets a friend who has one, who permits him to ride, and an injury happens in consequence, the master is responsible for that act. If it were so, every master might be ruined by acts done by his servant without his knowledge or authority"; Stretton v. City of Toronto (1887) 13 Ont. 139 (servant, expected to go on foot, took a horse and buggy); St. Louis, I. M. & S. Ry. v. Robinson (1915) 117 Ark. 37, 173 S. W. 822 (boy sent to call employees unnecessarily and unauthorizedly used a bicycle); Miller v. Western Union Tel. Co. (1939) 63 Ohio App. 125, 25 N.E.2d 466 (messenger boy, "engaged strictly as a bicycle mes-

to a particular vehicle, as in the rather obvious case of the use of a car not covered by insurance in place of one that is.[17]

In all these cases, it would seem that the risk is increased. Quaere whether the master would be relieved from liability where the instrumentality, though unauthorized, involved a lesser risk, as if a servant authorized to use a car went on foot instead.

§ 381. **Characteristic automobile problems: (a) The unauthorized driver.** It is not surprising to find that a very large proportion of current litigation over course of employment involves the driving of automobiles by servants. Three problems have been especially conspicuous. The first concerns the servant who lets a friend drive for him.

At first sight this would seem merely to be a version of the delegation problem and since the risk is palpably great it might be expected that nonliability of the master would be the normal result. In fact the case is usually treated as a separate one and in a large number of cases the master has been held liable on one theory or another.[18] Only a sprinkling of cases hold the contrary.[19]

senger," used an automobile); Hughes v. Western Union Tel. Co. (1931) 211 Iowa 1391, 236 N. W. 8 (same).

In Rankin v. Western Union Tel. Co. (1946) 147 Neb. 411, 23 N.W.2d 676, 166 A. L. R. 873, the court refused to differentiate between a "racing" bicycle and an "ordinary" bicycle and the company was held.

[17] See Lambert v. M. Satsky Trucking Co. (1937) 118 N. J. L. 485, 193 Atl. 702, noted in 11 So. Calif. L. Rev. 377; Lockart v. Stinson & C. P. R. (Ont. A. C. 1939) [1940] 1 D. L. R. 23, noted in 18 Can. B. Rev. 205. Cf. Canadian Pacific Ry. Co. v. Lockhart [1942] A. C. 591, noted in 8 Camb. L. J. 211. And see Ingle v. Bay City

Transit Co. (1945) 72 Cal.App.2d 283, 164 P.2d 508, where the bus driver took out a bus although his foreman, discovering him to be drunk, had forbidden it.

[18] See Jones v. Lozier (1922) 195 Iowa 365, 191 N. W. 103; Grant v. Knepper (1927) 245 N. Y. 158, 156 N. E. 650, 54 A. L. R. 845; Conway v. Pickering (1933) 111 N. J. L. 15, 166 Atl. 76; Potter v. Golden Rule Grocery Co. (1935) 169 Tenn. 240, 84 S.W.2d 364; Siciliano v. U. S. (1949) 85 F. Supp. 726.

Courts have been slower to impose liability where the servant was not in the car with the substitute when the accident occurred. See White v. J. E. Levi & Co.,

§ 382. **Grant v. Knepper.** In this field by far the most influential opinion has been that written by Cardozo, C. J., while on the New York Court of Appeals, in Grant v. Knepper.[20] In this case defendant sent out a truck with a driver and a salesman to deliver merchandise. The driver allowed the salesman, who had no operator's license, to drive, and he negligently ran into plaintiff's parked car. The court said that while the substitution was unauthorized, defendant might be liable for the (original) driver's negligence in turning the truck over to an incompetent driver and in failing to control his driving. The incompetence of the substitute was proved (it was said) by his failure to have a license and "the very nature of the accident"; his negligence in control was shown by his failure to control the driving at a rate of speed "presumptively excessive."

§ 383. —— Of these bases of liability it may be suggested, with all respect for the great Chief Justice, that, at least as a practical matter, they are of somewhat doubtful validity. No doubt one may be in the course of employment in abandoning it temporarily; e. g., the truckdriver who leaves the truck parked on a hill inadequately braked or leaves the team untied while he goes in for a beer.[21] In these days of universal car-driving, however, the cases are likely to be rare where it will realistically be said that the new driver was such a bad risk as to make it negligent to allow him to drive the car. It does

(1911) 137 Ga. 269, 73 S. E. 376; Simon v. City Cab Co. (1935) 78 F.2d 506, noted in 24 Geo. L. J. 178; cf. Emison v. Wylam Ice Cream Co. (1927) 215 Ala. 504, 111 So. 216, noted in 11 Minn. L. Rev. 670. A number of cases involve the incidence of the liability, where a "prospect" driving a dealer's car, negligently does harm; see Kantola v. Lovell Auto Co. (1937) 157 Ore. 534, 72 P.2d 61; Archambault v. Holmes (1939) 125 Conn. 167, 4 A.2d 420; annotation, 50 A. L. R. 1391.

[19] Butler v. Mechanics Iron Foundry Co. (1927) 259 Mass. 560, 156 N. E. 720, 54 A. L. R. 849; Copp v. Paradis (1931) 130 Me. 464, 157 Atl. 228, noted in 6 U. of Cin. L. Rev. 359; Rose v. Gisi (1941) 139 Neb. 593, 298 N. W. 333.

[20] (1927) 245 N. Y. 158, 156 N. E. 650, 54 A. L. R. 845.

[21] See Whatman v. Pearson (1868) L. R. 3 C. P. 422; Loomis v. Hollister (1903) 75 Conn. 718, 55 Atl. 561; Hayes v. Wilkins (1907) 194 Mass. 223, 80 N. E. 449.

not appear in the Grant case that there was really evidence
which would support a finding of negligence had the master
himself, e. g., allowed the substitute to drive.

§ 384. —— Again, resting the matter on the negligence of
the servant in "controlling" the substitute is likely to seem unrealistic. One can control the driver one is sitting next to, but
one seldom does. It is submitted that in the Grant case and in
most where the Cardozoan formula is applied there is really
no more than a finding that since the substitute drove carelessly and caused harm he must have been incompetent and
the servant must have failed to use care in controlling him.
Thus the formula turns out in practice to be merely a way of
evading the issue.[22]

§ 385. **Suggested rationale.** It is submitted that if the
master is to be held in these cases, and courts seem inclined
so to do, it should be put on the honest and forthright basis
that experience shows that drivers will let their friends drive
the master's truck, in spite of all that can be done to prevent
it, and that thus the risk of the substitute's careless driving

[22] But cf. Copp v. Paradis
(1931) 130 Me. 464, 157 Atl. 228,
noted in 6 U. of Cin. L. Rev. 359,
where the court expressed approval
of the doctrine of the Knepper case
but sustained the lower court's
nonsuit, saying: "The evidence does
not support the charge that Carpenter (the substitute) was an incompetent driver. No witness
testifies as to his knowledge or
experience with automobiles and
we are not impressed with the view
that a legitimate inference of incompetency can be drawn from
the incidents of this accident. The
cars met at night on or near a
culvert where the road was fifteen
feet wide. The rear end of the
truck undoubtedly hit the left forward wheel of the plaintiff's car.
The plaintiff's assertion that his
car was at the right of the middle
of the traveled part of the road
warrants an inference that Carpenter was negligent and no more.
A competent driver might well
have been as remiss in his duty
and brought the same misfortune
to the plaintiff. Incompetency is
a matter of conjecture.

"Nor can the defendant's driver
be deemed negligent because of his
failure to supervise his assistant's
operation of the car. There is
nothing in the evidence to indicate
that a collision was anticipated by
either party. The course of the
two cars or their relative positions
on the highway just before the

becomes one of the normal risks of the business, to be borne
by the master along with the others. Or, if fictions are to be
employed, it is perhaps easier to say simply that the servant
is really doing the driving (vicariously, because he "controls"
the driving, as does the owner who sits by the guest who is
driving with his permission) [23] than to go further and insist
that he must have been exercising control negligently.

§ 386. Characteristic automobile problems: (b) The un-authorized passenger.

The second conspicuous problem caused
by the servant driving the enterpriser's truck is that of the
unauthorized passenger, taken aboard on the invitation of or
by consent of the driver, and injured by the latter's negligent
driving. Here the strong tendency of courts has been not to
hold the master.[24] The theory appears to be that the risk of
injury to passengers is one the master has not assumed
and which the servant cannot thrust on him without authority.
As stated by Holmes, J., in a "horse and cart" precursor of the
present cases: "The defendant was not bound to expect or look
out for people falling from his cart, where they had no business
to be, and persons who got into it took the risk of what might
happen as against him." [25]

accident is not shown with any
degree of certainty. The facts attending the collision, which do appear, are consistent with the sudden and unexpected swerve of the
truck or a like failure to turn it
away from the plaintiff's car sufficiently to clear the rear end.
There is no determining factor in
the case which leads to a contrary
conclusion. Under the rule, if the
operator's act of negligence was so
sudden or unexpected that the
driver had no reason to foresee it
nor opportunity to avert it, he
cannot be deemed negligent. Nor
can liability attach to the employer."

[23] See post, § 414.

[24] In addition to cases cited in
following notes, see Dearborn v.
Fuller (1919) 79 N. H. 217, 107
Atl. 607; Thomas v. Magnolia
Petroleum Co. (1928) 177 Ark. 963,
9 S.W.2d 1, noted in 2 U. of Cin.
L. Rev. 440 and 13 Minn. L. Rev.
156; Mayhew v. DeCoursey (1932)
135 Kan. 184, 10 P.2d 10, noted in
32 Col. L. Rev. 1074; Hicks v.
Swift & Co. (1950) 81 Ga. App.
145, 58 S.E.2d 256; Conca v. Cush-
man's Sons, Inc. (1950) 277 App.
Div. 360, 100 N.Y.S.2d 212.

[25] Driscoll v. Scanlon (1896) 165
Mass. 348, 43 N. E. 100. See also
Houghton v. Pilkington [1912] 3
K. B. 308.

§ 387. "**Wilful and wanton negligence.**" In perhaps a majority of the cases the position has been rationalized in terms
of the passenger's being a trespasser on the truck and the
master's duty being only to abstain from injuring him by wilful
and wanton negligence.[26] This seems to be an unfortunate
application of deplorable tort law. The idea that one aware
of the presence of an intruder on his property needs to limit
his own activities only to the extent of not wilfully or wantonly
injuring the intruder, is an outrageous anachronism, ameliorated, in the jurisdictions where it prevails, only by the willingness of juries to find wilful and wanton negligence on rather
slight provocation. Applying it in the present context allows
a servant negligently to imperil the life of a human being
without even the flimsy justification that that human being is
an intruder on the servant's property; it also leads to the
illogical result that the master is more likely to be liable the
closer the servant gets to the limits of his authority. I. e., the
master is presumably not liable if the servant deliberately injures the passenger but he is liable if, and only if, the servant
is wilfully and wantonly negligent, which is the next thing to
committing deliberate injury.

[26] See Higbee Co. v. Jackson
(1920) 101 Ohio St. 75, 128 N. E.
61, 14 A. L. R. 131; Perry Supply
Co. v. Brown (1930) 221 Ala. 290,
128 So. 227; Stefan v. New Process Laundry Co. (1936) 323 Pa.
373, 185 Atl. 734 (and comments by
Eldredge, 12 Temp. L. Q. 32, 46,
47); Shrimplin v. Simmons Auto
Co. (1940) 122 W. Va. 248, 9
S.E.2d 49; Reynolds v. Knowles
(1947) 185 Tenn. 337, 206 S.W.2d
375, noted in 20 Tenn. L. Rev. 290.

The Higbee case, ante, has been
repudiated by a later case in Ohio,
Union Gas & Elec. Co. v. Crouch
(1930) 123 Ohio St. 81, 174 N. E.
6, 74 A. L. R. 160, noted in 5 U. of
Cin. L. Rev. 357. The court there
says: ". . . the relation of [the
passenger] to the owner of the car
must be held to be that of trespasser, to whom no duty is owing
except not to wilfully injure him."
The meaning of this is obscure; the
owner knows nothing of the passenger's existence and can scarcely
intend to injure him, and if the
servant intended to injure him he
would thereby have left the course
of employment.

Cf. Mayhew v. DeCoursey, ante,
n. 24, where, with reference to the
suggestion that M might be liable
for S's wilful and wanton negligence, the court says: "An examination of the above cases shows that
the liability is based on knowledge
on the part of the employer of the
position in which the injured party

§ 388. Minority view. A tiny sprinkling of authority takes the view that the master is liable to the passenger for ordinary negligence.[27] The writer ventures to believe this the sounder view. If the prevailing view in this type of case be compared with that in those just discussed (the unauthorized driver) it would appear that the proper order of liability has been reversed. Obviously the act of the servant in allowing an unauthorized person to drive both is a greater deviation from normal behavior and more greatly increases the risk than the act of the servant in allowing a friend to ride with him. If the master is to be held liable in either case, it would seem it should be in the case involving the lesser deviation and the lesser increase of risk. Where the servant uses an unauthorized instrumentality, the master is exposed to a type of risk he has not contemplated or assumed; where the driver is unauthorized, he is asked to be responsible for the control of a dangerous machine by one whose character and capabilities he has had no opportunity of checking. In the case of the unauthorized passenger, however, the master has voluntarily assumed the risk of the harm that this particular servant using this very instrumentality may do to the car itself and the persons and property of the public at large; it is surely a very trifling

finds himself. We have seen that the rider on the vehicle, who is there on the invitation or the license of a servant who had no authority to extend the invitation, is a trespasser, that is, the invitation to ride is not the invitation of the employer. It is the invitation of the employee. Now, if this is true, the consequences of having extended this invitation, which put the injured one in a place of peril, are those of the employee alone and not of the employer. . . . As a matter of fact, as far as appellants are concerned, they knew nothing of the presence of appellee on that truck. It is true the driver knew of it and the jury found that he drove wantonly, but all this time he was acting for himself, not for his employer, as far as appellee is concerned."

[27] See Pitman v. Merriman (1920) 79 N. H. 492, 111 Atl. 751; Kuharski v. Somers Motor Lines, Inc. (1945) 132 Conn. 269, 43 A.2d 777. In the latter case, the court said: "In permitting Sophie to board the truck, Nihill was acting outside of his employment, but in then continuing his trip he was again in the course of it. The defendant was responsible for the results of negligent acts performed by him while in the performance of his master's business."

increase of risk to say that the master may be liable for the
servant's negligent driving not only to other cars and people
using the street—a veritable horde—but also to the passenger
riding in the car without the master's permission.

§ 389. **Characteristic automobile problems: (c) Frolic and
detour.** In Joel v. Morison,[28] Baron Parke gave the law of
Agency one of its most famous phrases when he said: "If the
servants, being on their master's business, took a detour to
call upon a friend, the master will be responsible, . . . but if
[the servant] was going on a frolic of his own, without being
at all on his master's business, the master will not be liable."
Servants are very prone to deviate from the direct route with
a view to take a loaf of bread to their mothers or to call on
their girls or to buy a pack of cigarettes; nothing has given
rise to more common and troublesome litigation than the question whether the deviation in question was simply a detour
or rose to the status of being a frolic.

§ 390. —— Some cases permit of decision on the basis of
purely arbitrary and geometrical considerations. Thus the
servant starting from the master's headquarters may proceed
in a straight line towards the master's objective and then, on
the same or another line, towards a private one beyond. Three
questions arise. (a) The accident may happen before S reaches
M's objective but while he definitely purposes to go beyond
it to his own. Here the master is usually held, on the theory
that the servant was doing his master's business, though intending to do some strictly of his own. As Cardozo, J., said in
Clawson v. Pierce-Arrow Motor Car Company:[29] "The unful-
filled intention of passing the repair shop and returning did
not transform the trip in its entirety, and vitiate that part of
the service which was legitimate and useful." (b) The accident

[28] (1834) 6 C. & P. 501.
[29] (1921) 231 N. Y. 273, 131 N.
E. 914. See also Perry v. Haritos
(1924) 100 Conn. 476, 124 Atl. 44;
Ford v. Reinoehl (1935) 120 Pa.
Super. 285, 182 Atl. 120. And see

Linam v. Murphy (1950) 360 Mo.
1140, 232 S.W.2d 937. But the
master is not liable where the primary purpose of the trip is personal to the servant and he is only
incidentally doing something for

may happen after S passes M's objective but before he reaches his own. Here M is probably not liable.[30] It is too difficult to regard the master's business as, for the time being, even incidental to the journey. (c) He has performed his unauthorized mission, turned around, and started back towards home but has not yet passed the original authorized destination. "His thoughts are homeward bound."[31] This is the most difficult question and with other questions of re-entry will be discussed in a following section.

§ 391. —— In many cases the geography of the trip does not permit these useful, if rather arbitrary, distinctions. The servant will take a circuitous route, conforming to no particular pattern. The most important factor will usually be the relative extent of the deviation. If a servant, sent on an errand involving the going round three sides of the same block, takes a six-block trip to buy himself cigarettes, it is likely to be considered a frolic and not a detour.[32] On the other hand in a case where the servant drove around three sides of a block (unnecessarily, from the standpoint of the authorized mission) to buy himself a paper, the jury was allowed to find it only a detour.[33]

the master. United States v. Eleazer (1949) 177 F.2d 914; Mc-New v. Puget Sound Pulp Co. (1950) 37 Wash.2d 495, 224 P.2d 627.

[30] See McCarthy v. Timmins (1901) 178 Mass. 378, 59 N. E. 1038; Brand v. Vinet (La. App., 1941) 5 So.2d 200; Master Auto Service Corp. v. Bowden (1942) 179 Va. 507, 19 S.E.2d 679; Freeza v. Schauer Tool & Die Co. (1948) 322 Mich. 293, 33 N.W.2d 799.

[31] Cardozo, J., in Fiocco v. Carver (1922) 234 N. Y. 219, 137 N. E. 309.

[32] See Healey v. Cockrill (1918) 133 Ark. 327, 202 S. W. 229.

[33] Loomis v. Hollister (1903) 75 Conn. 718, 55 Atl. 561. And see generally Thomas v. Lockwood Oil Co. (1921) 174 Wis. 486, 182 N. W. 841; Drake v. Norfolk Steam Laundry (1923) 135 Va. 354, 116 S. E. 668; De Bello v. Reep & Blackford (1925) 101 N. J. L. 218, 127 Atl. 522; Gordoy v. Flaherty (1937) 9 Cal.2d 716, 72 P.2d 538; Carter v. Bessey (1939) 97 Utah 427, 93 P.2d 490; Retail Merchants Ass'n & Associated Retail Credit Men of Tulsa v. Peterman (1940) 186 Okla. 560, 99 P.2d 130; Wibye v. United States (1949) 87 F. Supp. 830.

See Smith, "Frolic and Detour," 23 Col. L. Rev. 444 and 716.

§ 392. **Re-entry.** One of the most troublesome angles of the general "frolic and detour" problem has been that involving the determination of the point at which the servant, concededly having deviated, returns to or re-enters the employment. In the simple case referred to in § 391, ante, where the servant, for his own purposes goes on in a straight or angling line beyond his proper destination and returns in the same line, it would seem easy and reasonable to treat the whole unauthorized trip as outside the course. Some courts have done so.[34]

In the leading New York case of Riley v. The Standard Oil Company,[35] the driver, sent to a freight yard, did his business there and then picked up some sticks and drove on four blocks to give them to his sister. Returning, but before passing the freight yard, he negligently ran into plaintiff. The court held the master liable, saying that when there is a temporary abandonment, "the master again becomes liable for the servant's acts when the latter once more begins to act in his business. Such a re-entry is not effected merely by the mental attitude of the servant. There must be that attitude coupled with a reasonable connection in time and space with the work in which he should be engaged."

This language is obviously the source of Sec. 237 of the Restatement: "A servant who has temporarily departed from the scope of employment does not re-enter it until he is again reasonably near the authorized space and time limits and is acting with the intention of serving his master's business."

§ 393. —— Other courts have carried this idea to what is perhaps its logical conclusion by holding that the servant re-enters the employment as soon as he starts to return.[36]

---

[34] See Curry v. Bickley (1923) 196 Iowa 827, 195 N. W. 617; Peters v. Pima Mercantile Co. (1933) 42 Ariz. 454, 27 P.2d 143; Southwest Dairy Products v. DeFrates (1939) 132 Tex. 556, 125 S.W.2d 282; Pesot v. Yanda (1939) 344 Mo. 338, 126 S.W.2d 240, noted in 6 Mo. L. Rev. 333; Public Service Co. v. Illinois Industrial Commission (1946) 395 Ill. 238, 69 N.E.2d 875.

[35] (1921) 231 N. Y. 301, 132 N. E. 97, 22 A. L. R. 1382.

[36] See Meyn v. Dulaney-Miller Auto Co. (1937) 118 W. Va. 545, 191 S. E. 558; Mancuso v. Hurwitz-Miutz Furniture Co. (La. App.,

It should be noticed that there is no problem of return either where the whole trip is with the master's permission, or where it is completely unauthorized. If the master allows the servant to take the master's car for the servant's business, the servant should be on the same footing as any other borrower, and not a servant either going or coming.[37] Likewise, if the servant has taken the master's car for his own purposes and without permission, or, probably, if he is engaged in a very gross frolic, he does not become a servant merely because he is bringing the car back to the place from which he took it.[38]

3. *Wilful Torts*

§ 394. Generally. It was at one time supposed that the master would not be liable for the wilful torts of his servant, save as to such as he expressly authorized or sanctioned. This distinction was explained in a leading case [39] as follows: "The dividing line is the wilfulness of the act. If the servant makes a careless mistake of omission or commission, the law holds it to be the master's business negligently done. It is of the very nature of business that it may be well or ill done. We frequently speak of a cautious or careless driver in another's employment. Either may be in the pursuit of his master's business, and negligence in servants is so common, that the law will hold the master to the consequences, as a thing that he is bound to foresee and provide against. But it is different with a wilful act of mischief. To subject the

1938) 181 So. 814; Cain v. Marquez (1939) 31 Cal.App.2d 430, 88 P.2d 200; United States v. Johnson (1950) 181 F.2d 577.

[37] See Fletcher v. Meredith (1925) 148 Md. 580, 129 Atl. 795, 45 A. L. R. 474; Kunkel v. Vogt (1946) 354 Pa. 279, 47 A.2d 195.

[38] See Fleischner v. Durgin (1911) 207 Mass. 435, 93 N. E. 801; Cannon v. Goodyear Tire & Rubber Co. (1922) 60 Utah 346,

208 Pac. 419; Martin v. Lipschitz (1930) 299 Pa. 211, 149 Atl. 168; Krolak v. Chicago Express (1950) 10 N. J. Super. 60, 76 A.2d 266; Skapura v. Cleveland Elec. Illuminating Co. (1950) 89 Ohio App. 403, 100 N.E.2d 700; McNeill v. Spindler (1950) 191 Va. 685, 62 S.E.2d 13.

[39] Wright v. Wilcox (1838) 19 Wend. (N. Y.) 343.

master in such a case, it must be proved that he actually assented, for the law will not imply assent."

This view, however, is now obsolete, at least as an arbitrary limitation on the possible liability of the master. The modern cases fully recognize that the master may be liable for the wilful torts of his servant; they also recognize, however, that it is less likely that a wilful tort will properly be held to be in the course of employment and that the liability of the master for such torts will naturally be more limited.[40]

In following sections an attempt is made to classify and summarize the authorities.

§ 395. **Injuries to person and property.** The cases in which the master has been held liable for the servant's wilful injury to person or property (aside from the few in which it may fairly be said that the master has authorized the specific tort) [41] can mostly be put into one of three rather broad categories: (a) torts incident to a custodial job where the use of force is a natural incident; (b) torts resulting from wrongful means used to promote the master's business, and (c) torts resulting from friction naturally engendered by the master's business.

§ 396. **(a) Torts incident to a custodial job where the use of force is a natural incident.** If one is employed as a bouncer in a saloon, it is to be expected that one will use such means

---

[40] In Son v. Hartford Ice Cream Co. (1925) 102 Conn. 696, 129 Atl. 778, it is said: ". . . it now seems plain enough that the liability of a master for his servant's torts is quite independent of the master's assent to or approval of the tortious act; and also that the rule *respondeat superior* is not applicable upon any theory which does not make it applicable to a wilful as well as to a negligent tort. It may be more difficult for a plaintiff to sustain the burden of proving that a willful, as distin- guished from a negligent, injury was inflicted while the servant was upon the master's business, and acting within the scope of his employment; but when these conditions are shown to exist there is no satisfactory reason for holding a master, who is himself free from fault, liable for his servant's lapses of judgment and attention, which does not also apply to the servant's lapses of temper and self-control."

[41] See, e. g., Janvier v. Sweeney [1919] 2 K. B. 316.

as are necessary to bounce an unruly customer. It is a job calling more for force than finesse; if a jury finds that more force was used than the situation quite warranted, and so a tort was committed, it seems neither unlikely nor unreasonable that such a happening will be considered one of the risks of the saloon business and that the tort, though wilful, will be treated as committed in the course of employment.[42] The same is true of a caretaker who tortiously prevents the plaintiff from mooring his boat at the master's dock in a storm.[43] And the same has been held true in many cases when the servant was, generally or for the time being, in a custodial capacity, and the act, though tortious, was not surprising, considering the nature of the job.[44]

§ 397. (b) Torts resulting from wrongful means used to promote the master's business. In a well-known Ohio case,[45] defendant's janitor, engaged in cleaning up a room, wished to move a table so that he could finish the job. Plaintiff, an electrician, was working on a stepladder he had placed on the table; he refused to get off, to accommodate the janitor, whereupon the latter shoved the table out of his way. The court reversed a directed verdict for defendant, holding that the jury could return a verdict for plaintiff if they found that the janitor's motive was not to injure the electrician but to do his job. So, in a Mississippi case,[46] the jury was allowed to

[42] See Stewart v. Reutler (1939) 32 Cal.App.2d 195, 89 P.2d 402; Chuck's Bar v. Wallace (1946) 198 Okla. 152, 176 P.2d 484.

[43] Ploof v. Putnam (1910) 83 Vt. 252, 75 Atl. 277.

[44] See Ciarmataro v. Adams (1931) 275 Mass. 521, 176 N. E. 610, 75 A. L. R. 1171; Pilipovich v. Pittsburgh Coal Co. (1934) 314 Pa. 585, 172 Atl. 135; Simmons v. Kroger Grocery Co. (1937) 340 Mo. 1118, 104 S.W.2d 357; Metzler v. Layton (1940) 373 Ill. 88, 25 N.E.2d 160. And see Horton v.

Jones (1950) 208 Miss. 257, 44 So.2d 397.

[45] Nelson Business College v. Lloyd (1899) 60 Ohio St. 448, 54 N. E. 471.

[46] Singer Sewing Machine Co. v. Stockton (1934) 171 Miss. 209, 157 So. 366; and see Buchanan v. Western U. Tel. Co. (1920) 115 S. C. 433, 106 S. E. 159. Cf. Smothers v. Welch Furnishing Co. (1925) 310 Mo. 144, 274 S. W. 678, 40 A. L. R. 1209; Allen v. National Peanut Corp. (1947) 321 Mass. 665, 75 N.E.2d 240; Bradley v. Stevens

find that defendant's salesman laid his hands unlawfully on the female plaintiff in the effort to sell her a sewing machine. And so competing busdrivers or jockeys have been held in the course of employment when they attempted to win for their employer by pushing the competitor off the road.[47] The cases of this type are numerous; as in those discussed in the preceding section they can be rationalized by saying that the servant was only doing his job, if in an undesirable way.[48]

§ 398. **(c) Torts resulting from friction naturally engendered by the master's business.** A third type of case has become increasingly common in recent years. This may be typified by the recent Michigan case of Guipe v. Jones.[49] Here defendant's bartender engaged in an argument with a customer who refused to pay for a drink he claimed he had not ordered. On the customer's continuing refusal to pay, the bartender struck him. The court allowed a recovery, saying that the undisputed testimony showed "that the bartender was acting within the scope of his employment in seeking to enforce payment." It may be suggested, with deference to the court, that while the bartender's act may have resulted from an attempt to enforce payment, it can scarcely be regarded as a way of enforcing payment.

§ 399. —— In Carr v. Crowell,[50] the employee of defendant, a building contractor, became engaged in an altercation with plaintiff, the employee of a subcontractor, over the method

(1951) 329 Mich. 556, 46 N.W.2d 382.

[47] See Limpus v. Landon General Omnibus Co. (1862) 1 H. & C. 526; McKay v. Irvine (1882) 10 Fed. 725.

[48] See generally Jackson v. American Telephone & Telegraph Co. (1905) 139 N. C. 347, 51 S. E. 1015; Singer Sewing Machine Co. v. Phipps (1911) 49 Ind. App. 116, with which cf. Moskins Stores, Inc. v. L. Hart (1940) 217 Ind. 622, 29

N.E.2d 948; Noland v. Morris & Co. (1922) 212 Mo. App. 1, 248 S. W. 627; Francis v. Barbazon (1931) 16 La. App. 509, 134 So. 789; Magnolia Petroleum Co. v. Guffey (Tex. Comm. App., 1936) 95 S.W.2d 690, noted in 15 Tex. L. Rev. 253.

[49] (1948) 320 Mich. 1, 30 N.W.2d 408.

[50] (1946) 28 Cal.2d 652, 171 P.2d 5.

of laying a floor; to conclude the argument defendant's employee threw a heavy hammer at plaintiff, injuring him severely. In holding defendant liable the court said that it was not necessary to show that the throwing of the hammer was a way of forwarding defendant's business. "It is sufficient . . . if the injury resulted from a dispute arising out of the employment. . . . In the present case, defendant's enterprise required an association of employees with third parties, attended by the risk that someone might be injured."

In these cases,[51] it may be suggested that courts are tending in the direction of the broad test usually found in compensation statutes, namely that the injury arise in and out of the employment.

§ 400. **False imprisonment and malicious prosecution.** Masters operating stores are very frequently held liable for excessive zeal manifested by clerks and floorwalkers in the prevention of alleged pilfering by customers. This liability is obviously closely akin to that discussed above, re the activity of custodians, with the difference, however, that there the stress was on direct physical injury. Women and children unaware of their legal rights are often taken to an office for questioning in an attempt to secure a confession; not infrequently the police are summoned. In such cases if the act constitutes false imprisonment or leads to malicious prosecution, the liability of the master is clear.[52]

[51] And see generally Dilli v. Johnson (1939) 107 F.2d 669; Plotkin v. Northland Transp. Co. (1939) 204 Minn. 422, 283 N. W. 758, noted in 23 Minn. L. Rev. 981; Porter v. Grennan Bakeries (1944) 219 Minn. 14, 16 N.W.2d 906; Shannesy v. Walgreen Co. (1945) 320 Ill. App. 590, 59 N.E.2d 330; Schultz v. Purcell's Inc. (1947) 320 Mass. 579, 70 N.E.2d 526; Fields v. Sanders (1947) 29 Cal.2d 834, 180 P.2d 684, 172 A. L. R. 525, noted in 28 Ore. L. Rev. 83;

Guipe v. Jones (1948) 320 Mich. 1, 30 N.W.2d 408; Conney v. Atlantic Greyhound Corp. (1950) 81 Ga. App. 324, 58 S.E.2d 559.

[52] See J. J. Newberry Co. v. Judd (1935) 259 Ky. 209, 82 S.W.2d 359; Lamm v. Charles Stores Co. (1931) 201 N. C. 134, 159 S. E. 444, 77 A. L. R. 923; McDemott v. W. T. Grant Co. (1943) 313 Mass. 736, 49 N.E.2d 115; Manuel v. Cassada (1950) 190 Va. 906, 59 S.E.2d 47.

§ 401. **Libel and slander.** In a number of cases [53] the curious idea appears that a master, particularly a corporate master, *cannot* be liable for slander committed by a servant. This is perhaps the result of a number of misconceptions, engendered by old-fashioned pleading: since the master is charged with having committed the offense (though by his servant) and since malice is a part of the offense, plainly the master cannot be liable since it is conceded that he had (and, if a corporation, could have) no malice towards the plaintiff.

A majority of cases have now abandoned this anomaly, whatever may be its origin, and hold that a master may be liable for slander committed in the course of employment, just as in the case of other torts.[54] The master's liability for libel committed in the course of employment seems never to have

---

[53] See Singer Mfg. Co. v. Taylor (1907) 150 Ala. 574, 43 So. 210; Duquesne Distributing Co. v. Greenbaum (1909) 135 Ky. 182, 121 S. W. 1026; Flaherty v. Maxwell (1915) 187 Mich. 62, 153 N. W. 45; Sims v. Miller's, Inc. (1935) 50 Ga. App. 640, 179 S. E. 423.

In Singer Mfg. Co. v. Taylor, ante, it is said: "The liability of the principal for the torts of the agent, when not based upon a breach of duty arising out of contract, as in the case of common carriers, is based upon principles of public policy. It is essential to such liability that the tort of the agent, if not authorized or ratified by the principal, should be committed by the agent in the course of the business of the principal and of the agent's employment. By reason of the fact that the offense of slander is the voluntary and tortious act of the speaker, and is more likely to be the expression of momentary pas- sion or excitement of the agent, it is, we think, rightly held that the utterance of slanderous words must be ascribed 'to the personal malice of the agent, rather than to an act performed in the course of his employment and in aid of the interest of his employer, and exonerating the company unless it authorized or approved or ratified the act of the agent in deferring the particular slander.'"

[54] See Mills v. W. T. Grant Co. (1917) 233 Mass. 140, 123 N. E. 618; West v. F. W. Woolworth Co. (1939) 215 N. C. 211, 1 S.E.2d 546; Keller v. Safeway Stores (1940) 111 Mont. 28, 108 P.2d 605; Britt v. Howell (1935) 208 N. C. 519, 181 S. E. 619; Hand v. Industrial Life & Health Ins. Co. (1936) 174 Miss. 822, 165 So. 616; Wisemore v. First Nat. Life Ins. Co. (1938) 190 La. 1011, 183 So. 247; Gillis v. Great A. & P. Tea Co. (1943) 223 N. C. 470, 27 S.E.2d 283, 150 A. L. R. 1330.

been doubted,[55] though it is hard to see any distinction between libel and slander for this purpose. Obviously the most common instance is the liability of the newspaper; under modern conditions it is unlikely that the liability of a newspaper for defamation will be other than vicarious. Perhaps the most common other instances of the master's liability for defamation involve overzealous clerks accusing customers of pilfering [56] and salesmen who make derogatory remarks about the credit or honesty of competitors. A somewhat troublesome problem arises when the occasion is conditionally privileged but the servant is actuated by personal malice; the tendency appears to be that the servant in writing maliciously is serving both his own and the master's ends so that the latter is liable.[57]

§ 402. **Liability based on nonagency principles.** There are a number of rather ill-defined situations in which masters have been held liable for wilful torts of servants but on principles that are not strictly agency principles. In one such group of cases where the master offers services and facilities to the public on a contractual, or at least a business, basis it is held that where the plaintiff accepts the invitation and avails himself of the master's services and facilities he is entitled to be protected by the master from the depredations of his servants, whether strictly in the course of employment or not. It is clear that such a duty rests on carriers and innkeepers; it is less clear in the cases of others in a somewhat similar category, as, e. g., restaurant keepers, storekeepers, taxicab operators and telegraph companies.[58]

[55] See Bruce v. Reed (1883) 104 Pa. 408; Solow v. General Motors Truck Co. (1933) 64 F.2d 105; Rickbeil v. Grafton Deaconess Hospital (1946) 74 N. D. 525, 23 N.W.2d 247.

[56] See § 401, ante.

[57] See Crane v. Bennett (1904) 177 N. Y. 106, 69 N. E. 274; Pion v. Caron (1921) 237 Mass. 107, 129 N. E. 369; Solow v. General Motors Truck Co. (1933) 64 F.2d 105, cert. den. (1933) 290 U. S. 629, 54 S. Ct. 48, 78 L. Ed. 547, noted in 33 Col. L. Rev. 1461; Hooper-Holmes Bureau v. Bunn (1947) 161 F.2d 102; Atlanta Journal Co. v. Doyal (1950) 82 Ga. App. 321, 60 S.E.2d 802.

[58] See, as to:

(a) Carriers: Goddard v. Grand Trunk Ry. (1869) 57 Me. 202;

§ 403. Negligence in employment. In another group of cases the master's liability is based on (or, in many instances, bolstered by) a finding that the master was negligent in employing a servant with known or discoverable dangerous proclivities. Highly typical is the case of Davis v. Merrill.[59] There, defendant's crossing gateman, who had left the gates down though no train was approaching, was asked by plaintiff to raise the gates so he could pass through. The gateman suddenly became incensed and shot plaintiff. Recovery was allowed on two grounds. First, the act was in the course of employment. "The contention arose over the raising of the gates at a late hour of the night, a matter admittedly within the scope of the gateman's employment and duty, and as an immediate result thereof the gateman shot and killed the deceased. The two acts constitute parts of one and the same transaction." Second, that the gateman had been employed without any investigation of his character, although a check would have disclosed that he had a police record as a drunkard and that he had "spells" and would become dangerously angry on slight provocation.

Undoubtedly it is actionable negligence to put a man in a position where his known dangerous habits make him an unreasonably great source of danger to the public. However, in

Barad v. New York Rapid Transit Corp. (1937) 162 Misc. 458, 295 N. Y. S. 901; Yazoo & M. V. R. Co. v. Smith (1940) 188 Miss. 856, 196 So. 230; Hairston v. Greyhound Corp. (1942) 220 N. C. 642, 18 S.E.2d 166.

(b) Innkeepers: Mayo Hotel Co. v. Danciger (1930) 143 Okla. 196, 288 Pac. 309; Ledington v. Williams (1935) 257 Ky. 599, 78 S.W.2d 790.

(c) Restaurant and tavern keepers: Curran v. Olson (1903) 88 Minn. 307, 92 N. W. 1124; Davidson v. Chinese Republic Restaurant Co. (1918) 201 Mich. 389, 167 N. W. 967; Schell v. Vergo (1938) 166 Misc. 839, 4 N.Y.S.2d 644.

(d) Storekeepers: Mallach v. Ridley (1888) 9 N. Y. S. 922; Robinson v. Sears Roebuck & Co. (1939) 216 N. C. 322, 4 S.E.2d 889, noted in 18 N. C. L. Rev. 163.

(e) Taxicab operators: Jenkins v. General Cab Co. (1940) 175 Tenn. 409, 135 S.W.2d 448.

(f) Telegraph companies: Dunn v. Western Union Tel. Co. (1907) 2 Ga. App. 845, 59 S. E. 189.

And see generally, Note, The Growth of Vicarious Liability for Wilful Torts Beyond the Scope of the Employment, 45 Harv. L. Rev. 342.

[59] (1922) 133 Va. 69, 112 S. E. 628.

some of the cases of this group, the evidence of negligence is slight, and the feeling is inescapable that the court is using the negligence theory to reinforce a case that is slightly dubious if only course of employment is to be relied on.[60]

4. Procedure Problems

§ 404. Joinder—Election—Res judicata. In most jurisdictions master and servant can be sued together.[61] Whether they are technically "jointly" liable is a mooted question, yet one not of great significance today when the word "joint" is so loosely and variously used in speaking of tort liability. For present purposes it is enough to say that master and servant are jointly liable at least to the extent that the term imports the proposition that they may be joined as defendants and that judgment in full may be given against both.

Not infrequently a sympathetic jury will find against the master and in favor of the servant, or will find against both but assess a lesser amount of damages against the servant than the master. Such a result is plainly a logical impossibility, since the master is liable only if the servant has committed a tort and only for the tort committed by the servant. By the prevailing view such a verdict cannot stand,[62] but a few hold

[60] See generally, F. & L. Mfg. Co. v. Jomark, Inc. (1929) 134 Misc. 349, 235 N. Y. S. 551; Hamilton Bros. Co. v. Weeks (1929) 155 Miss. 754, 124 So. 798; Argonne Apartment House Co. v. Garrison (1930) 42 F.2d 605; Priest v. F. W. Woolworth Co. (1933) 228 Mo. App. 23, 62 S.W.2d 926; Spear v. Koshelle (1934) 150 Misc. 305, 269 N. Y. S. 391; Wishone v. Yellow Cab Co. (1936) 20 Tenn. App. 229, 97 S.W.2d 452; Crockett v. United States (1940) 116 F.2d 646, noted in 26 Iowa L. Rev. 896; Fleming v. Bronfin (1951) 80 A.2d 915; Bradley v. Stevens (1951) 329 Mich. 556, 46 N.W.2d 382.

[61] See Cravens v. Lawrence (1936) 181 S. C. 165, 186 S. E. 269; Lasko v. Meier (1946) 394 Ill. 71, 67 N.E.2d 162; annotation, 98 A. L. R. 1057.

[62] See Pollard v. Coulter (1939) 238 Ala. 421, 191 So. 231; Kinsey v. William Spencer & Son Corp. (1937) 165 Misc. 143, 300 N. Y. S. 391, aff'd (1938) 255 App. Div. 995, 8 N.Y.S.2d 529; Monumental Motor Tours, Inc. v. Eaton (1945) 184 Va. 311, 35 S.E.2d 105; Ferne v. Chadderton (1949) 363 Pa. 191, 69 A.2d 104; aliter, of course, where the master is liable on an independent basis. See Humphrey

that if the plaintiff is willing to take the verdict, the defendant master cannot complain.[63]

§ 405. —— Since the liability is in the nature of joint and several liability, it is usually permissible to sue the parties severally, even in jurisdictions where they may be joined; a few jurisdictions require that they be sued severally and do not permit joinder.[64] The latter view is said to result from the fact that at common law trespass lay against the servant and case against the master, and that the two forms of action could not be joined. This, it seems, should be irrelevant under modern pleading.

Where the parties may be treated as jointly and severally liable, a judgment against one, it has been held, does not bar a suit against the other.[65] In jurisdictions where the liability is taken to be several only, there are a number of decisions indicating that the liability of the master and servant is alternative; thus T must elect and a judgment against either amounts to an election.[66]

Where election is not involved, questions of res judicata may arise. Here it has been held in a number of cases that a judgment in favor of the master bars a subsequent suit against

v. Virginian Ry. (1948) — W. Va. —, 54 S.E.2d 204.

[63] See Illinois Cent. Ry. v. Murphy's Adm'r (1906) 123 Ky. 787, 97 S. W. 729; with which cf. Blue Valley Creamery Co. v. Cronimus (1937) 270 Ky. 496, 110 S.W.2d 286; Bennett v. Eagleke (1930) 8 N. J. Misc. 37, 148 Atl. 197, noted in 78 U. of Pa. L. Rev. 904. See also note, 45 Harv. L. Rev. 1230.

[64] See Parsons v. Winchell (1850) 5 Cush. (Mass.) 592; Warax v. Cincinnati, N. O. & T. P. Ry. (1896) 72 Fed. 637; Betcher v. McChesney (1917) 255 Pa. 394, 100 Atl. 124 (with which cf. Brennan v. Huber (1934) 112 Pa. Super. 299, 171 Atl. 122; East Broad Top

Transit Co. v. Flood (1937) 326 Pa. 353, 192 Atl. 401.

[65] Maple v. Cincinnati, H. & D. R. Co. (1883) 40 Ohio St. 313; Gadsden v. Crafts (1918) 175 N. C. 358, 95 S. E. 610; Verhoeks v. Gillivan (1928) 244 Mich. 367, 221 N. W. 287; Brennan v. Huber (1934) 112 Pa. Super. 299, 171 Atl. 122, noted in 9 Temp. L. Q. 94.

[66] See McNamara v. Chapman (1923) 81 N. H. 169, 123 Atl. 229, 31 A. L. R. 188; Raymond v. Capobianco (1935) 107 Vt. 295, 178 Atl. 896, 98 A. L. R. 1051, noted in 36 Col. L. Rev. 324 and 45 Yale L. J. 920, with which cf. Jones v. Valisi (1941) 111 Vt. 481, 18 A.2d 179.

the servant,[67] even though in the second suit the third party would be able to rely on admission by the servant, held inadmissible in the first suit. A fortiori a prior judgment for the servant will bar a later suit against the master.[68] And there is the further consideration that if suit were allowed against the master after a judgment for the servant, the master, if held liable, might have a cause of action for indemnity against the servant, and the anomaly would be presented that the servant could be liable to the master though not to the third party.

§ 406. —— If the first judgment is *for* the third party, the party not sued is presumably not bound.[69] He has had no day in court, no opportunity to present his own evidence tending to show nonliability. And in other suits involving a master or servant who was a party to the original transaction but not to the prior suit, it is usually held that res judicata does not operate.[70]

5. Crimes

§ 407. **In general master not liable for crimes of servant.** The master will often be held civilly liable in tort for a wrongful act by a servant, which is also a crime. Thus no doubt in the Merrill case, discussed in the preceding section, the act of the gateman in shooting the plaintiff was murder or manslaughter. The master, however, could not have been prosecuted criminally for the wrong; criminal liability is ordinarily based on fault and it would be inconsistent with the theory and policy of the criminal law to prosecute a man for a crime when he did not and could not have the intent to commit it. Thus it

---

[67] Wolf v. Kenyon (1934) 242 App. Div. 116, 273 N. Y. S. 170; Jones v. Valisi (1941) 111 Vt. 481, 18 A.2d 179; Silva v. Brown (1946) 319 Mass. 466, 66 N.E.2d 349. Cf. Myers v. Brown (1933) 250 Ky. 64, 61 S.W.2d 1052.

[68] See Portland Gold Mining Co. v. Stratton's Independence (1907) 158 Fed. 63; Good Health Dairy Products v. Emery (1937) 275 N.Y. 14, 9 N.E.2d 758; Restatement, Judgments, § 96, Illustration 1.

[69] See Jones v. Valisi (1941) 111 Vt. 481, 18 A.2d 179.

[70] See Elder v. New York & P. Motor Exp., Inc. (1940) 284 N.Y. 350, 31 N.E.2d 188; 133 A. L. R. 176; Gentry v. Farrugia (1949) — W. Va. —, 53 S.E.2d 741.

is usually said that the principal will not be held criminally liable for the crimes of his agent or servant, unless he has in some way directed, participated in, or approved the act. Unless, that is, he is guilty by conventional doctrines of criminal law, having nothing to do with *respondeat superior*.

§ **408. Exceptions.** There are, however, several situations, usually involving conduct which the layman might be apt not to identify as criminal at all, in which vicarious liability has been imposed. Thus it is commonly held that the owner of property may be held liable for use of that property amounting to a public nuisance, although the use is that of his servant, neither authorized by nor known to the owner.[71] This has been rationalized on the ground that the proceeding, though criminal in form, was essentially civil in nature and so should be governed by tort principles.[72] It is also apparent that the primary purpose of the proceeding is to put an end to the wrongful use of the premises, and that there is little hope of success if the owner can achieve immunity by sedulously remaining unaware of what use is being made of his premises.

§ **409.** —— A more important exception has resulted from the modern prevalence of regulatory legislation, prohibiting certain types of conduct and making violation a misdemeanor irrespective of intent. Typical are statutes regulating the sale of liquor, the purity and branding of foods, and the accuracy and range of prices and weights. Such statutes sometimes expressly provide for vicarious liability. Thus, in a recent California case,[73] the statute made guilty of a misdemeanor every person "who by himself or his employee or agent" sold

---

[71] See Queen v. Stephens (1866) L. R. 1 Q. B. 702; State v. James (1940) 177 Tenn. 21, 145 S.W.2d 783; annotation, 121 A. L. R. 643.

[72] See Mellar, J., in Queen v. Stephens (1866) L. R. 1 Q. B. 702, 710.

[73] In re Marley (1946) 29 Cal.2d 525, 175 P.2d 832, noted in 35 Calif. L. Rev. 583. See also New York Cent. R. R. v. United States (1908) 212 U. S. 481, 29 S. Ct. 304, 53 L. Ed. 613; State v. Lundgren (1913) 124 Minn. 162, 144 N. W. 752; Commonwealth v. Sacks (1913) 214 Mass. 72, 100 N. E. 1019; State v. Wenberg (1943) 74 Ohio App. 91, 55 N.E.2d 870.

any commodity at short weight. The owner was convicted and sentenced to 90 days in jail, although he was not present in the store when the sale was made and had never instructed the clerk to give short weight. A majority of the court held the statute constitutional and affirmed the conviction.

§ 410. —— Even where the statute makes no provision for vicarious liability courts have frequently felt that the lack of any requirement of criminal intent and the strong policy of protecting the public warranted punishing the master for the misdemeanor of his servant. Thus, in a recent federal case, defendant employed one Helfrich to process and distribute certain goods supplied by defendant. Unknown to defendant, Helfrich did this by the use of a deleterious substance which amounted to an adulteration under the Federal Food, Drug and Cosmetic Act. In affirming defendant's conviction the court said of defendant's argument that Helfrich was an independent contractor: "But we are not concerned with any distinction between independent contractors and agents in the ordinary sense of those words. It is clear that defendant was engaged in procuring the manufacture and distribution of the article in interstate commerce. . . . The liability was not incurred because defendant consciously participated in the wrongful act, but because the instrumentality which it employed, acting within the powers which the parties had mutually agreed should be lodged in it, violated the law. The act of the instrumentality is controlled in the interest of public policy by imputing the act to its creator and imposing penalties upon the latter." [74]

§ 411. —— In some such cases it is said that while the master's knowledge or consent need not be shown, it will be

[74] United States v. Parfait Powder Puff Co. (1947) 163 F.2d 1008. And see State v. Brown (1914) 73 Ore. 325, 144 Pac. 444; State v. Sobelman (1937) 199 Minn. 232, 271 N. W. 484; Lunnsford v. State (1945) 72 Ga. App. 700, 34 S.E.2d 731. But see Boos v. State (1914) 181 Ind. 562, 105 N. E. 117; Lovelace v. State (1941) 191 Miss. 62, 2 So.2d 796; United States v. Food & Grocery Bureau (1942) 43 F. Supp. 966; State v. Pinto (1942) 129 N. J. L. 255, 29 A.2d 180;

a defense that the servant acted in direct violation of express instructions given him.[75] In others it seems to be sufficient that the act, even if specifically forbidden, was done while the servant was performing the function for which he was hired.[76]

Lauding v. United States (1950) 179 F.2d 419.

[75] See John Gund Brewing Co. v. United States (1913) 204 Fed. 17; Commonwealth v. Jackson (1941) 146 Pa. Super. 328, 22 A.2d 299, aff'd memorandum decision (1942) 345 Pa. 456, 28 A.2d 894.

[76] See Allen v. Whitehead [1930] 1 K. B. 211; State v. Kittelle (1892) 110 N. C. 560, 15 S. E. 103; Dezarn v. Commonwealth (1922) 195 Ky. 686, 243 S. W. 921.

See generally Sayre, Criminal Responsibility for the Acts of Another, 43 Harv. L. Rev. 689.

The topic under discussion shades almost insensibly into another important and highly specialized one, viz., the criminal liability of corporations. It is obviously impracticable to attempt any discussion of this here; some of the better known treatments are Canfield, Corporate Responsibility for Crime, 14 Col. L. Rev. 469; Edgerton, Corporate Criminal Responsibility, 36 Yale L. J. 827; Lee, Corporate Criminal Liability, 28 Col. L. Rev. 1, 181; Winn, The Criminal Responsibility of Corporations, 3 Camb. L. J. 398.

CHAPTER XIV

THE MASTER'S TORT LIABILITY: SERVANT OR NOT?

§ 412. **Analysis of the problem.** The basic proposition, as already stated, is: the master is responsible for the torts of his servant, committed in the course of employment. What is meant by, and included in, the course of employment, has been discussed in the preceding chapter. What is meant by "his servant" is the topic for consideration here. The question may be presented in one or both of two forms: (a) Is the actor in question a servant at all (as distinguished, e. g., from an independent contractor)? If he is no one's servant, *cadit questio.* (b) If he is a servant, whose servant is he? E. g., if one borrows one's neighbor's car and driver for the afternoon, and an accident occurs, whose servant is the driver, his regular employer's or that of the borrower? (Or the servant of both?) [1]

These questions are, in practice, exceedingly difficult to answer. In fact it is believed that, with the considerable crystallization of course-of-employment rules that has taken place, more decided cases now involve the question whether the tortfeasor was a servant, and, if so, whose, than involve the question whether he was acting in the course of employment. The importance and complexity of the problem has been lately augmented by the fact that under various types of social legislation it is essential to determine whether the claimant is a "servant." Such legislation is not treated in this book, but some typical decisions involving the problem under various types of legislation are cited in the note.[2]

---

[1] See Dunmore v. Padden (1918) 262 Pa. 436, 105 Atl. 559.

[2] See Halverson v. Sonotone Corp. (1947) 71 S. D. 568, 27 N.W.2d 596; Graystone Ballroom, Inc. v. Baggott (1947) 319 Mich. 87, 29 N.W.2d 256; National Veneer & Lumber Co. v. Crisp (1947) 117 Ind. App. 370, 72 N.E.2d 576; Hargis v. Wabash R. Co. (1947) 163 F.2d 608; United States v. Silk (1948) 331 U. S. 704, 67 S. Ct.

1. *The Concept Analyzed*

§ 413. What is a servant? A servant is defined in the Restatement [3] as "a person employed to perform service for another in his affairs and who, with respect to his physical conduct in the performance of the service, is subject to the other's control or right to control."

Does "employed" imply that there must be a hiring? It would seem so, but the Restatement elsewhere [4] states the well-established rule that no compensation is essential. Nor need there be a contract. An amusing and extreme instance of these propositions is found in a recent New Jersey case [5] where defendant, sitting at the wheel of his car, directed his sister-in-law, sitting to his right, to close the car door. She closed it, negligently, on the finger of plaintiff, who was entering the car. It was held that she was, pro tem, defendant's servant, so as to make him liable.

§ 414. What is "control"? Similar are the numerous cases in which it is held that the owner of a car, riding in it but allowing a friend or member of the family to drive, becomes the driver's master.[6] Aliter, if the owner is not in the car, since then there is no control and the driver is just a bailee.[7]

1463, 91 L. Ed. 1757, noted in 16 Geo. Wash. L. Rev. 586 and 32 Minn. L. Rev. 414; Feller v. New Amsterdam Casualty Co. (1950) 363 Pa. 483, 70 A.2d 299.

[3] Restatement, § 220.

[4] Restatement, § 225.

[5] Winkelstein v. Solitaire (1942) 129 N. J. L. 38, 27 A.2d 868.

[6] See Scott v. Schisler (1931) 107 N. J. L. 397. 153 Atl. 395, noted in 44 Harv. L. Rev. 1292; Gochee v. Wagner (1931) 257 N. Y. 344, 178 N. E. 553; Mazur v. Klewans (1950) 365 Pa. 76, 73 A.2d 397.

Otherwise, when the husband is driving the wife's car—at least in Pennsylvania, where the husband is still head of the family and brooks no control. Rodgers v. Saxton (1931) 305 Pa. 479, 158 Atl. 166, 80 A. L. R. 280.

In jurisdictions where a minor is not responsible for the torts of his servant, he may still be liable if he is in the car on the theory that the car is "in contemplation of law" under the direction (i. e., control) of the minor. McKerall v. St. Louis-San Francisco Ry. Co. (Mo. App., 1924) 257 S. W. 166.

[7] See Nash v. Lang (1929) 268 Mass. 407, 167 N. E. 762, noted in 10 B. U. L. Rev. 62, 43 Harv. L.

These cases seem rather imperàtively to call for an answer to the question: what precisely is this control, that is so important (or, at least, is treated as being so important) in these cases?

§ 415. —— Clearly, it does not mean that the master is actively or actually controlling the servant. That is unlikely in most cases and impossible in some. Then it must be, as so often put, the *right* to control. That, however, seems to be a conclusion of law. Perhaps it is most accurately described as a matter of intuition, viz., a sense, on the part of the hypothetical observer, that considering normal usages and particular circumstances, the relationship is one in which it is taken for granted that the actor is to respect the wishes of the constituent as to the manner of doing the job.[8]

§ 416. **Further of control: The supervisory servant.** It should further be noted that mere control is not the test; it is performing a service for another subject to control. An important instance of this is furnished by the foreman or manager who is supervising one or more employees. He is undoubtedly controlling them, but they are not his servants.[9] This can be rationalized by saying, according to the Restatement test, that they are not working *for* him or in *his* affairs, but for his employer. Or it can be said that since control must be unitary, the real control is that of the employer who exercises it through his control of the foreman.

Rev. 502, 24 Ill. L. Rev. 603 and 78 U. of Pa. L. Rev. 1009.

[8] When one asks a friend to drive, one does not add: "And do it the way I wish." On the other hand, one expects one's wishes to be respected.

Were it objected that this describes the frame of mind of a mere bailee, it might be answered that the limitations on the behavior of a bailee are usually both broader and more typical. I. e., the borrower of a car is not supposed to use it in a way that any owner would object to, i. e., a way likely to prove harmful to the car. He does not, however, expect to be told at what speed to drive or what routes to take. If he were, he might respond: "What do you think I am, your servant"?

[9] See Patterson v. Barnes (1945) 317 Mass. 721, 60 N.E.2d 82. And see Lehigh Valley Coal Co. v. Yensavage (1914) 218 Fed. 547; Smith

2. *Capacity*

§ 417. The servant. The capacity of the servant raises no problems. The power of a person to act as servant appears to be limited only by his own personal mental and physical limitations. Even a lunatic or a very young child could doubtless be a servant; to the extent that his mental and physical limitations permitted him to perform according to the master's instructions, he would bind the master.[10]

§ 418. The master. Authority is very sparse but it is probable that a lunatic cannot be a master; hence he is not liable for the torts of his purported servant.[11] Since it is commonly said that a lunatic is liable for his own torts, it is probable that he would be liable for the acts of one who acted under his immediate direction.

At common law a married woman lacked contractual capacity and therefore was considered incapable of being a principal or master. This incapacity has been widely removed by statute and it is doubtful if there remain any jurisdictions where a married woman may not be a master.[12] It is a commonplace to find the wife treated as the servant of the husband, or vice versa, as for example where the wife drives the husband's car.[13]

§ 419. The infant master. The most important, most doubtful and most commonly litigated problem is whether an infant can be a master. There is no doubt that a majority of the cases have denied that he can.[14] It is often said that as an infant's contract is void, his attempt to appoint a servant is void. This is believed to involve both an erroneous proposi-

v. Howard Crumley & Co. (La. App., 1936) 171 So. 188.

[10] See Restatement, §§ 21, 25.

[11] See Gillet v. Shaw (1912) 117 Md. 508, 83 Atl. 394; Reams v. Taylor (1906) 31 Utah 288, 87 Pac. 1089.

[12] Although the contrary may have been true in Florida as late as 1932. See Potter v. Florida Motor Lines (1932) 57 F.2d 313.

[13] Question of capacity to be principal or agent has been dealt with previously. See ante, Chapter II.

[14] For collection of cases see

tion of law and a logical non sequitur. Mr. Williston says that at the present time in most instances the contract of an infant is simply voidable.[15] Further, we have already seen that the relation of master and servant does not rest on contract, but that it is a status, requiring the continuing assent of the parties.

The attempt to solve the problem in terms of contract law is believed to be misguided. No effort is being made to hold the infant to the performance of a promise he has made. The question is simply one as to the legal consequences of a status assumed by the infant, one that there is no doubt that he can assume in fact. If it be said that the relationship is voidable, that is of course true. As has been seen, the relationship of principal and agent or master and servant is always terminable at any moment at the will of either party, with or without reason. The fact of the purported master's infancy can add nothing to his power to avoid the existing relationship, since it is already complete. If what is meant is that the infant may avoid the consequences of an act already committed by his purported servant, that is a proposition of law finding no support in the voidability of an infant's contracts.

§ 420. —— Plainly a simple question of policy is presented. The law feels that minors should not be held to their promises; the law likewise feels that a minor should be liable for his wilful torts, regardless of age, and for his negligence, at least to the extent that he has failed to use the degree of care fairly to be expected of one of his age and experience. Now a third question confronts us : what shall the law do about a minor who makes no promise, commits no tort in person, but sets a third party to carrying on his business, in the course of which he commits a tort ?[16] It is not an easy question

Gregory, Infant's Responsibility for His Agent's Tort, 5 Wis. L. Rev. 453; annotation, 103 A. L. R. 487.

[15] Contracts (Rev. Ed. 1936) § 226.

[16] It is suggestive to notice that an infant has been held liable for his negligence in entrusting a car to a drunken driver (Harrison v. Carroll (1943) 139 F.2d 427) and for the negligence of his bailee under a statute making the owner of a car liable for the negligence of one driving a car with the own-

to answer but at least it should not be confused by irrelevant considerations, drawn from contract law.

To the writer there seems no apparent reason why infants should be freed from the liability of other masters. Infants do not commonly carry on large enterprises; it is not likely that they will be swamped by liabilities beyond expectation. The bulk of recent cases involve cars driven for infants. The infant old enough to own or possess a car will probably be liable for his own negligence in driving it; why should he not be liable for the negligence of someone doing it on his behalf and under his control?

A number of thoughtful recent cases take this view.[17]

§ 421. **The relation as affected by the personal immunity of the servant.** In a prior chapter [18] the question has been considered: how far may the servant's liability be affected by the existence of some immunity enjoyed by the master? Here the converse question is considered, namely, is the master's liability affected by the fact that the servant has a personal immunity which frees him from liability though not from culpability? The case most commonly arising involves a suit against the master where the wrong-doing servant is the spouse, parent, or child of the plaintiff. If the jurisdiction is one which, because of this relationship, would not allow a suit against the servant, does the immunity extend to the master?

Two arguments have commonly been advanced to support the proposition that the master is immune.

§ 422. —— (a) The master's liability, it is said, is derivative, and fails when there is no primary liability from which it can derive. This, it is believed, is a pure quibble. The master's liability results not from the liability of the servant but

---

er's consent. (Lind v. Eddy (1943) 232 Iowa 1328, 6 N.W.2d 427, 146 A. L. R. 695.)

[17] See Scott v. Schisler (1931) 107 N. J. L. 397, 153 Atl. 395, noted in 44 Harv. L. Rev. 1292; Carroll v. Harrison (1943) 49 F. Supp. 292. And see Woodson v. Hare (1943) 244 Ala. 301, 13 So.2d 172.

[18] See ante, § 344.

from his fault in carrying on the master's enterprise. The fact that the servant is, for reasons not affecting his fault, personally immune to suit should no more protect the master than the fact that the servant has fled the jurisdiction or is judgment-proof.

(b) It is said that since a master, forced to pay for his servant's fault, has a right of indemnity against the servant, the result will be that the master will collect over from the servant and the servant will thus indirectly be forced to pay, the very thing his immunity is intended to prevent.

§ 423. —— It cannot be denied that this is a possibility. Thus, in a Pennsylvania case [19] the defendant was a large oil company, the plaintiff the daughter of its president, and the servant her husband. Under the local practice the defendant joined the servant and recovered judgment against him for indemnity in the same suit in which the daughter recovered judgment against the defendant. In such a case the economic position of the parties makes it seem likely that the [indemnity] judgment will be paid. However, this is a very unusual situation and it is believed that in the ordinary case there is no more likelihood that the defendant will attempt to collect from the servant than that the plaintiff will. Experience shows that, for obvious economic reasons, the latter contingency is rather remote. In practice, judgment will ordinarily be rendered against the master, his insurer will pay, and the servant will be no more likely to be sued or discharged than if the plaintiff had not been his wife or minor child.[20] Thus the

[19] Koontz v. Messer (1935) 320 Pa. 487, 181 Atl. 792, noted in 84 U. of Pa. L. Rev. 791, 10 Temp. L. Q. 221, and 14 Tex. L. Rev. 558.

[20] In Chase v. New Haven Waste Material Corp. (1930) 111 Conn. 377, 150 Atl. 107, 68 A. L. R. 1497, allowing a recovery by a minor child against its father's master, Wheeler, C. J., says: "The argument against recovery rests upon

the fallacious assumption that since the employer has an action over against his employee it will merely result in the employee paying back to him the recovery from the employer less the expenses of the litigation. The recovery for the wrong done the wife or child by the employer does not belong to the husband or father but to the wife or child. The recovery by the em-

family harmony, thought to be protected by the immunity rule, will not be threatened.

Surely the supposed policy of *respondeat superior* dictates a recovery. Harm has been done by the enterprise no less than if the plaintiff were unrelated to the servant.

These considerations (most authoritatively stated by Judge Cardozo in the Schubert case) [21] have led a substantial majority of courts to hold that the master is not protected by the servant's immunity.[22]

ployer from his employee will diminish his own property, it will not in the eye of the law diminish the property belonging to his wife or child. The assumption is also fallacious in that it assumes there will be an actual recovery in fact against the employee. Instances where such a recovery has been actually paid by the employee have not been called to our attention. Economic conditions, of which courts cannot avoid taking notice, would deter the employer from attempting to procure an uncollectible judgment against his negligent employee; by itself this fact of life very largely destroys the presumption upon which the conclusion of these cases is based." With the Chase case, cf. Myers v. Tranquility Ditch Co. (1938) 26 Cal.App.2d 385, 79 P.2d 419, noted in 5 U. of Pitt. L. Rev. 54 and 12 S. C. L. Rev. 218; Graham v. Miller (1944) 182 Tenn. 434, 187 S.W.2d 622, 162 A. L. R. 571, noted in 46 Col. L. Rev. 148 and 19 Tenn. L. Rev. 88.

[21] Schubert v. Schubert Wagon Co. (1928) 249 N. Y. 253, 164 N. E. 42, 64 A. L. R. 293.

[22] See Smith v. Moss [1940] 1 All. E. R. 469, noted in 18 Can.

B. Rev. 230; Miller v. Tyrholm (1936) 196 Minn. 438, 265 N. W. 324, noted in 21 Iowa L. Rev. 804, 20 Minn. L. Rev. 566 and 4 U. of Chi. L. Rev. 132; Hudson v. Gas Consumers' Ass'n (1939) 123 N. J. L. 252, 8 A.2d 337, noted in 88 U. of Pa. L. Rev. 265; Broaddus v. Wilkenson (1940) 281 Ky. 601, 136 S.W.2d 1052. In the leading authority for the contrary view, Maine v. Maine & Sons Co. (1924) 198 Iowa 1278, 201 N. W. 20, 37 A. L. R. 161, noted in 10 Iowa L. Bull. 228, the court says: "Unless the servant is liable, there can be no liability on the part of the master. This has been repeatedly held in cases where both were sued and the verdict was against the employer only. Where the only negligence alleged against the employer is that of the servant or employee, the former is not liable as a joint wrongdoer, as he did nothing, save through the employee; but his liability arises because of his responsibility for the act of his servant. . . . It has been held that one associated with the husband as a joint tortfeasor in the infliction of a personal injury upon the wife cannot be held liable to her. Abbott v. Abbott, supra, [67 Me.

3. *Master by Estoppel or Ratification*

§ 424. Apparent or ostensible master. It has been seen [23] that in the law of Principal and Agent, apparent or ostensible authority, based on estoppel or objective contract, is of prime importance; in fact few cases involving the power of the agent to bind the principal fail to involve to some extent the element of apparent authority.

The converse is true in the master and servant field. A little reflection shows the reason: it is seldom that an injured person can say that he was led to be injured by his reliance on the appearance that the tortfeasor was defendant's servant. One struck by a truck seldom knows, let alone relies on, the real or apparent identity of the owner.

§ 425. —— In rare cases, estoppel is a factor. (Here there can be no argument that it is objective contract; no contract on any theory is involved.) Thus a person could conceivably be induced to enter premises, relying on the reputation of the apparent owner as a guarantee of the safety of the premises.[24] Even more plausibly one might be induced to accept services or buy goods,[25] relying on the reputation of the apparent owner of the business. Thus, in several instances a department store has been held liable for negligence in the operation of a dental establishment or beauty parlor operated in the store and apparently by the store, but in reality by an independent enterpriser leasing space in the store.[26] So a com-

---

304]; Libby v. Berry, 74 Me. 286. We think there are more cogent reasons for saying that she has no right of action against the employer of her husband for his negligent injury to her person, where any liability on the part of the employer must depend on the liability of the husband, than there are for denying her a right of action against one who actually inflicts an injury upon her, because he acted in association with her husband."

And see Riegger v. Bruton Brewing Co. (1940) 178 Md. 518, 16 A.2d 99, 131 A. L. R. 307, noted in 4 U. of Detroit L. J. 122.

[23] Ante, Chapter V.

[24] See Lord v. Lowell Institution (1939) 304 Mass. 212, 23 N.E.2d 201.

[25] See Rubbo v. Hughes Provision Co. (1941) 138 Ohio St. 178, 34 N.E.2d 202.

[26] See Hannon v. Siegel-Cooper Co. (1901) 167 N. Y. 244, 60 N. E.

pany which advertises its taxicabs in the daily press, whose (supposed) cabs bear its name, and which takes orders for cabs under a phone number listed in its own name, is liable for the negligence of the driver of the cab, although the cabs are owned by the drivers themselves, whose relation to the company is really that of independent contractor.[27]

§ 426. Master by ratification. The question of the circumstances under which, and the extent to which, one not a master at the time of the commission of the tort may become liable therefor by ratification, have been previously discussed in the chapter on ratification and need not be gone into again here.

4. *Independent Contractor*

§ 427. The concept in general.[28] The conventional independent-contractor concept is one readily stated in conventional language. He is one performing a physical service for an employer, but not as a servant. Not as a servant—because he is not under the control of the employer, and because he is engaged not in the employer's enterprise but one of his own.

This concept is like some others: easy to apply in easy cases. For example, the man who comes to fix your radio is plainly an independent contractor. You would not dream of telling him how to do it; you can only pray that behind his uncontrolled operations lies the skill and knowledge he purports to

597; Fields, Inc. v. Evans (1929) 36 Ohio App. 153, 172 N. E. 702, noted in 29 Mich. L. Rev. 640; Manning v. Leavitt Co. (1939) 90 N. H. 167, 5 A.2d 667.

[27] Rhone v. Try Me Cab Co. (1933) 65 F.2d 834, noted in 47 Harv. L. Rev. 344. Cf. Marchetti v. Olyowski (1950) 181 F.2d 285, noted in 4 Vand. L. Rev. 375. See generally annotation, 2 A.L.R.2d 406.

[28] Much has been written on in-dependent contractor and allied concepts. Among others, see Douglas, Vicarious Liability and the Administration of Risk, 38 Yale L. J. 584; Harper, The Basis of the Immunity of an Employer of an Independent Contractor, 10 Ind. L. J. 1094; Morris, The Torts of an Independent Contractor, 29 Ill. L. Rev. 339; Steffen, Independent Contractor and the Good Life, 2 U. of Chi. L. Rev. 501.

have. Equally plainly, he is in the radio repair business and
you are not. If he drops a monkey wrench out of the window
on the head of some unsuspecting pedestrian, it is obviously
no liability of yours.

The definition, it will be noted, is throughout in the negative. One who works for you—but *not* as a servant. Why not?
Because, at least according to the Restatement, he is "not controlled by the other [i. e., the employer] nor subject to the
other's right to control with respect to his physical conduct
in the performance of the undertaking." [29]

The consequence is likewise in the negative: the employer
is not liable for the contractor's torts. Why not? Because
he is not a servant. Presumably the reasons most commonly
given for the master's liability do not normally, or at least
necessarily, apply to the employer of an independent contractor. There is no strong presumption that his is the deeper
pocket; he does not usually furnish the equipment with which
the work is done; it is more likely to appear that the contractor is carrying on an enterprise of his own than that he
should appear to be a part of the employer's enterprise.

§ **428. A caveat.** Hence it is possible to say that the employer is not liable for the contractor's torts because there appears
neither any accepted nor any good reason why he should be.
A caveat to the last phrase is necessary, however. It is probably still true that in general no considerations indigenous to
master and servant suggest that the employer be liable; courts,
however, tend increasingly to feel that in certain types of work,
involving a hazard to the public, the owner or employer has a
duty to the public which he cannot avoid by turning the work
over to a contractor. Thus the employer may be held, not
because simply he is the employer, not for the normal risks
of his general business, but because he cannot by employing
an independent contractor escape possible liability for special
risks inherent in a particular project.

Liability based on this theory will be discussed in the following chapter. For the purpose of the present discussion we

[29] Restatement, § 2 (3).

proceed on the conventional assumption that the employer of an independent contractor is not, as such, liable for the contractor's torts.

§ 429. Attributes of the independent contractor. A number of things can be stated which are normally true of an independent contractor; few, if any of them, however, are essential to the capacity. Thus a contractor normally works for compensation under a contract. However, in spite of the language of the Restatement [30] ("An independent contractor is a person who contracts with another to do something for him . . .") it is thought that it is not necessary that there be either contract or compensation to constitute an independent contractor. The watchmaker who repairs your watch is an independent contractor; he would not seem less so because he is doing it just for fun or friendship. It is characteristic that the work be performed for a lump sum, but this is certainly not essential.[31] It is characteristic that the contractor carries on some independent business or profession of his own, but this would not normally be said of a travelling salesman, who, under some decisions [32] is treated as a contractor and not as a servant. The contractor, it is said, agrees to produce a result and the employer reserves no control over the manner of producing it. This is no doubt true, but the proposition that the employer reserves no control in a given case is likely to be a conclusion of law.

§ 430. —— It is characteristic of the contractor that he possesses skill and experience in the work required, that the employer does not, and so would not be able to supervise the work; however, the relationship is not altered by the fact that the employer is himself skilled.[33] Thus a surgeon who employs another to operate on his wife is not employing the second

[30] Restatement, § 2 (3).
[31] Cf. Griffin's Case (1945) 318 Mass. 282, 61 N.E.2d 142.
[32] See post, § 446 et seq.
[33] See Immaculate Conception

Church v. Industrial Commission (1947) 395 Ill. 615, 71 N.E.2d 70; Gill v. Northwest Airlines (1949) 228 Minn. 164, 36 N.W.2d 785.

surgeon as a servant, nor is the family cook rendered an independent contractor by the fact that she is more expert than her mistress. The contractor normally furnishes his own equipment, and often his own place to work, but it is not impossible to do work with the employer's tools and on the employer's premises and still be an independent contractor. Cases often say that a contractor has power to delegate and a servant does not.[34] No doubt, in the ordinary case where one contracts to have a job done, the nature of the job makes it the natural assumption that the contractor is not expected to do it in person and hence that he is authorized to do it by competent members of his staff. Suppose, however, that one employs Signor Raphael to paint one's portrait; is it to be supposed either that he is authorized to do it through an assistant or that he becomes one's servant?

§ 431. —— The illustrations above suggest that it is impossible to frame any definition of independent contractor which is of universal validity. It is believed that the most that can be done is to use a sophisticated discretion, that is, one based on a study both of business usages and of decided cases, and to ask one's self the question: was the actor here carrying on what, according to the habits of the locality would be thought of by a reasonable man as rising to the dignity of a trade or profession, and was he hired by defendant to do a job for him under circumstances which could fairly be regarded as suggesting that defendant intended only to contract for the achieving of a result and did not mean to dictate the methods or to control the doing of the job?

In the leading case of Hexamer v. Webb,[35] Burford, "who was engaged in the roofing and cornice business, was employed by the defendant to do the work, which was intended to obviate a difficulty caused by pigeons making their nests under the eaves of the roof of [defendant's] hotel. . . . Burford was a mechanic engaged in a particular kind of business which

[34] See La Bree v. Dakota Tractor & Equipment Co. (1939) 69 N. D. 561, 288 N. W. 476.

[35] (1886) 101 N. Y. 377, 4 N. E. 755.

qualified him for the work which he was employed to do. By the arrangement with the defendant he was an independent contractor engaged to perform the work in question, he was employed to accomplish a particular object by obviating the difficulty which he sought to remove. The mode and manner in which it was to be done and the means to be employed in its accomplishment were left entirely to his skill and judgment. Everything connected with the work was wholly under his direction and control. No right was reserved to the defendant to interfere with Burford or the conduct of the work. It was the result which was to be attained, that was provided for by the contract, without any particular method or means by which it was to be accomplished. So long as the contractor did the work the defendant had no right to interfere with his way of doing it."

This case, it is believed, is typical of the employer-independent contractor relation; it is also typical of the language used in characterizing it.

In the following sections a few special problems are stated and discussed.

5. *Servant or Independent Contractor: Characteristic Problems*

§ 432. **Medical persons.** May a doctor treating a patient or a surgeon performing an operation properly be regarded as anyone's servant? Certainly he is not the patient's servant. No stronger case can be imagined in which the doctor (at least as far as the patient is concerned) is thought of as carrying on a dignified and independent profession and as being wholly free from any control by the patient. May he be the servant of the hospital on whose staff he is or of the clinic by which he is employed?

It was formerly thought that he might not. This view was largely based on two important cases.

§ 433. **The Hillyer case.** In Hillyer v. St. Bartholomew's Hospital,[36] plaintiff was put under an anaesthetic for a medical

---

[36] C. A. [1909] 2 K. B. 820.

examination; during the operation he was burned, due (as he claimed) to the negligence of the surgeon or the attending nurses. The hospital was a "public," i. e., charitable, hospital, liable for its torts under English law; [37] plaintiff was a non-paying patient of the surgeon; it is simply said that he was a "consulting surgeon attached to the hospital." Farwell, L. J., said: "It is, in my opinion, impossible to contend that Mr. Lockwood, the surgeon, or the acting assistant surgeon, or the acting house surgeon, or the administrator of anaesthetics, or any of them, were servants in the proper sense of the word; they are all professional men, employed by the defendant to exercise their profession to the best of their abilities according to their own discretion; but in exercising it they are in no way under the orders or bound to obey the directions of the defendant."

§ 434. The Schloendorff case. In Schloendorff v. Society of New York Hospital,[38] plaintiff went to defendant hospital to be treated for a stomach complaint. Defendant's "house physician" recommended an operation. Plaintiff took an anaesthetic, having, she testified, insisted that merely an examination and not an operation, be performed; however, the surgeon [39] performed an operation, removing a tumor, and causing, so plaintiff testified, intense suffering and the amputation of several fingers.

The hospital was held not liable. Cardozo, J., said: "It is the settled rule that such a [i. e., a charitable] hospital is not liable for the negligence of its physicians and nurses in the treatment of patients. . . . This exemption has been placed on two grounds. The first [is that a charity is not liable for torts to beneficiaries of the charity]. The second ground of the exemption is the relation subsisting between a hospital and the physicians who serve it. It is said that this relation is not one

[37] Mersey Docks Trustees v. Gibbs (1864) L. R. 1 H. L. 93.

[38] (1914) 211 N. Y. 125, 105 N. E. 92.

[39] The surgeon is described sim-ply as a "visiting surgeon"; how-ever, the court says: "There is no distinction . . . between the vis-iting and resident physicians. Whether the hospital undertakes to

of master and servant but that the physician occupies the position, so to speak, of an independent contractor, following a separate calling, liable, of course, for his own wrongs to the patient whom he undertakes to serve, but involving the hospital in no liability, if due care has been taken in his selection. On one or the other, and often on both, of these grounds, a hospital has been held immune from liability to patients for the malpractice of its physicians." [40]

§ 435. Comment. At first sight, Judge Cardozo's final suggestion is highly plausible. One finds difficulty in thinking of a high-powered (and high-priced) surgeon, performing a delicate operation on the brain, as a servant. One would as readily think of the high-priced barrister, arguing at the bar, as being a servant.[41]

A little reflection makes the matter more difficult. One is finally inclined to agree with Mr. Goodhart: [42] "If only un-

---

procure a physician from afar or to have one on the spot, its liability remains the same."

[40] These cases appear to suggest three different grounds for the hospital's immunity: (a) It is a charity and immune to any tort liability; (b) The hospital does not employ the surgeon, but simply picks him for the patient; (c) The nature of the surgeon's work is such that he is expected to exercise his own discretion and cannot be thought to be subject to the control which is a prime essential of the status of servant.

The first of these grounds involves considerations that cannot be gone into here; the student will have to look elsewhere for statement and discussion of the different rules that prevail as to the liability of a charity for the torts of its servants. The second ground

appears to involve questions of fact that are rather elusive; it is often difficult from the cases to tell precisely what is the status of a "consulting surgeon," a "house surgeon" and "member of the staff" and the like. This makes it seem likely that in making his famous observations, Farwell, L. J., was not particularly concerned with the contractual relations between the hospital and the surgeon, and that he doubted that a surgeon could be a servant, even if he was, from other standpoints, a full-time employee.

[41] Cf. Casselman v. Hartford Accident & Indemnity Co. (1940) 36 Cal.App.2d 700, 98 P.2d 539, with Clark v. Shea (1929) 130 Ore. 195, 279 Pac. 539.

[42] A. L. Goodhart, Hospitals & Trained Nurses, 54 L. Q. Rev. 553, 564.

skilled persons without responsibility are to be classed as servants, then the doctrine of master and servant will be limited to an astonishing degree." Ship captains and aeroplane pilots are undoubtedly servants; [43] neither the fact that their work involves very great skill and responsibility nor that their employers would usually not be competent to direct them is thought to prevent such a result.[44]

§ 436. **Current authorities.** The English courts still seem to follow the doctrine of the Hillyer case but with quite apparent reluctance,[45] and it seems only a question of time before it is abandoned. There is a sprinkling of modern American authority following it [46] but in general the American cases seem now quite willing to admit that a physician or surgeon

[43] See Restatement, § 223.

[44] The Restatement is cautious on the point, stressing the importance of "the custom of the community as to the amount of control ordinarily exercised in a particular occupation" (Sec. 220, e). Illustration 4, of Sec. 220 is: "P, a hospital, employs a house surgeon, putting him in charge of all operations within the hospital, except where patients require another surgeon. The inference is that the house surgeon is not the servant of the hospital in the conduct of surgical operations."

In Comment a of Sec. 223, it is said: "So . . . while the physician employed by a hospital to conduct operations is not, in the normal case, a servant of the hospital, yet it may be found that the house physicians or the internes, if subject to directions as to the manner in which their work is performed, are servants of the hospital while in the performance of their ordinary duties."

[45] In Gold v. Essex County Council [1942] 2 All. E. R. 237 a, patient in a public hospital was injured by the negligence of a radiologist, who was a full-time employee of the hospital. The hospital was held liable; it was intimated that the hospital would be liable for the negligence of nurses performing professional services as well as administrative; it was also intimated that the nonliability for the negligence of the surgeon in the Hillyer case was attributable to his position as a visiting surgeon and that a different result might follow in the case of a surgeon on the permanent staff of the hospital. See also Collins v. Hertfordshire County Council [1947] 1 All. E. L. R. 633.

[46] See Runyan v. Goodrum (1921) 147 Ark. 481, 228 S. W. 397, 13 A. L. R. 1403; Norwood Hospital v. Brown (1929) 219 Ala. 445, 122 So. 411; Iterman v. Baker (1938) 214 Ind. 308, 15 N.E.2d 365.

(at least in cases of private hospitals and clinics) [47] may be a servant.[48] In a recent Wisconsin case the court says: "However, the better and more generally adopted rule is that 'A hospital conducted for private gain is liable to its patient for injuries sustained by him in consequence of the incompetency or negligence of a physician treating him at its instance, under a contract binding it to furnish him proper treatment. A physician so employed is not an independent contractor.'" [49]

§ 437. Nurses. The Hillyer case implies that the hospital is not responsible for the negligence of a nurse, performing professional (rather than "administrative") functions. However, the language of later English cases implies that the hospital would be liable.[50] No doubt American cases, willing to hold a surgeon as servant, would have no difficulty in holding the same of a nurse, though acting in a professional capacity.[50a]

A more difficult and frequently litigated case has to do with liability for the negligence of nurses during the operation. In Hillyer's case, Farwell, L. J., said: ". . . as soon as the door of the theatre or operating room has closed on them for the purposes of an operation . . . they cease to be under the orders of the defendants, and are at the disposal and under the sole orders of the operating surgeon until the whole operation has

[47] As to the subsequent history of the Schloendorff case in New York, see Note, 25 N. Y. U. L. Rev. 612.

[48] Noren v. American School of Osteopathy (Mo. App., 1927) 298 S. W. 1061; Stuart Circle Hospital Corp. v. Curry (1939) 173 Va. 136, 3 S.E.2d 153, 124 A. L. R. 176; Woodburn v. Standard Forgings Corp. (1940) 112 F.2d 271, 129 A. L. R. 337; Giusti v. C. H. Weston Co. (1941) 165 Ore. 525, 108 P.2d 1010; Treptan v. Behrens Spa (1945) 247 Wis. 438, 20 N.W.2d 108; Knox v. Ingalls Shipbuilding Corp. (1947) 158 F.2d 973, noted in 33 Iowa L. Rev. 722.

[49] Treptan v. Behrens Spa, ante. In Knox v. Ingalls Shipbuilding Corp., ante, the court says: "There is no more reason to except employers of physicians from the doctrine of respondeat superior than there is to except employers of other highly skilled persons who perform technical services requiring discretion."

[50] See Gold v. Essex County Hospital [1942] 2 All. E. R. 237; Collins v. Hertfordshire County Council [1947] 1 All. E. R. 633.

[50a] See Hawkins v. Laughlin (Mo. App., 1951) 236 S.W.2d 375.

been completely finished; the surgeon is for the time being supreme and the defendants cannot interfere with or gainsay his orders." This proposition has been debated pro and con in the subsequent English cases but does not appear ever to have been decided. There are a number of clear American decisions on the point, however.

§ 438. —— A majority of these cases hold the nurse or interne to be the servant of the operating surgeon during the operation (though not in the post-operative period, at least in the absence of the surgeon). In a recent clear-cut decision by an important court, the defendant was performing a caesarian operation; when the child was delivered the surgeon turned it over to the assisting interne and directed the application of silver nitrate to the infant's eyes. (At this time the surgeon was still busy with the patient.) The interne carelessly administered too much of the silver nitrate and it was held that the surgeon was responsible for the interne's negligence.[51] The court said: "If, then, it be true that defendant had supervisory control and the right to give orders to the interne in regard to the very act in the performance of which the latter was negligent, it would follow according to the classical test of agency hereinbefore stated, that a jury would be justified in concluding that the temporary relationship between defendant and the interne was that of master and servant, and that consequently defendant was legally liable for the harm caused by any negligence on the part of the interne."

---

[51] McConnell v. Williams (1949) 361 Pa. 355, 65 A.2d 243, noted in 34 Minn. L. Rev. 266.

See also, holding the surgeon liable: Emerson v. Chapman (1929) 138 Okla. 270, 280 Pac. 820, noted in 15 Iowa L. Rev. 218 and 28 Mich. L. Rev. 464; Peterson v. Richards (1928) 73 Utah 59, 272 Pac. 229; Ales v. Ryan (1936) 8 Cal.2d 82, 64 P.2d 409; Meadows v. Patterson (1937) 21 Tenn. App. 283, 109 S.W.2d 417. Not liable: Guell v. Tenney (1928) 262 Mass. 54, 159 N. E. 451; Watson v. Fahey (1938) 135 Me. 376, 197 Atl. 402; Ingram v. Fitzgerald (1936) N. Z. L. Rev. 905, noted in 15 Can. B. Rev. 205. See also, Note, 19 Tenn. L. Rev. 368.

§ 439. Menial projects. In contrast to the surgeon, who might be classified as a contractor because of the dignity of his work and the skill it requires, is the case of the worker who is working under a contract, being paid by the job, and achieving a result, and yet doing a type of work ordinarily performed by servants, and so is treated as a servant.

The classic instance is Sadler v. Henlock,[52] where defendant employed one Pearson to clean out a drain for five shillings. Pearson was a common laborer and had originally made the drain. It was held that defendant was liable for his negligence; Wightman, J., remarked: "Pearson was not a person exercising an independent business, but an ordinary laborer, chosen by the defendant in preference to any other but not exercising an independent employment."

So when a road machinery company sold a new grader to a county and took in an old one in trade which they wished to have brought to their place of business, and arranged with an employee of the county to drive it over for them in his spare time, he to receive $25 and expenses for the trip, it was held that he was their servant and not an independent contractor in making the trip.[53] On the other hand, where a maker of trailers wished to have a trailer transported from its plant in Detroit to a customer in Buffalo, and hired a tractor owner who was in the business of hauling for manufacturing plants and who had often furnished a tractor and driver to haul trailers for defendant, charging a flat rate for the trip, it was held that the tractor operator was an independent contractor and that the owner of the trailer was not responsible for his negligent driving.[54]

[52] (1855) 4 El. & Bl. 570.

[53] La Bree v. Dakota Tractor & Equipment Co. (1939) 69 N. D. 561, 288 N. W. 476. And see Natwick v. Liston (1949) — W. Va. —, 52 S.E.2d 184. Cf. Dowsett v. Dowsett (1949) — Utah —, 207 P.2d 809.

[54] Fuller v. Palazzolo (1938) 329 Pa. 93, 197 Atl. 225. Cf. Joseph v.

United Workers Ass'n (1942) 343 Pa. 636, 23 A.2d 470.

See generally Brackett v. Lubke (1862) 4 Allen (Mass.) 138; Holmes v. Tennessee Coal, Iron & R. Co. (1897) 49 La. Ann. 1465, 22 So. 403; O'Neill v. Blase (1902) 94 Mo. App. 648, 68 S. W. 764; Smith v. Marshall Ice Co. (1928) 204 Iowa 1348, 217 N. W. 264; Aita v.

§ 440. Petroleum tank and filling stations. The methods adopted in recent times by large oil companies for the merchandising of their products have occasioned a very substantial amount of litigation. Two forms of distribution have been most conspicuous. In one the company sets up a wholesale outlet, commonly referred to as a tank station, from which the wholesaler distributes oil in tank wagons to customers, mostly retailers, in the vicinity. In such a case the company usually furnishes the building, tanks and other equipment, except for the trucks in which the oil is delivered, these being owned and supplied by the commission agent or consignee.

In the other form, the distributor usually operates a filling station of the familiar type; this is "leased" by the company to the distributor. In either form, the operator is under an elaborate contract, prepared by the company; the product remains the property of the company until sold, daily accounts are rendered, the operator has a bank account in which company funds are deposited, and from which they may not be withdrawn by the operator, credit sales are allowed only with the consent of the company, bills being rendered by and paid to the company, only the products of the company are to be sold, the buildings and trucks are to bear the advertising signs and name of the company. It is also provided that the operator is not to be the servant of the company, that he is to carry indemnity insurance, and that he is to indemnify the company for any liability resulting to it from the negligence of the operator or his servants. The contract is usually terminable by either party on a few days' notice.

§ 441. —— Under such contracts it is apparent that the company has sedulously sought to preclude any liability on its part as master. It is also apparent that the setup in fact is one which has all the other elements of a master-and-servant relation. The master's name is used and advertised, the goods

Bend (1928) 206 Iowa 1361, 222 N. W. 386, 61 A. L. R. 351; Chai v. Murata (1936) 34 Haw. 53; Kerr v. T. G Bright & Co. (1937) 2 D. L. R. 153, noted in 15 Can. B. Rev. 285; Waggaman v. General Finance Co. (1940) 116 F.2d 254.

sold are his and, when sold on credit, the bill is sent by the company and paid to the company. By its power to terminate the relation on short notice the company has a sanction for controlling the distributor, who can ill afford to risk the loss of his investment in trucks.[55]

It is also apparent that in many, perhaps most, instances the company in fact exercises an effective control. The extent to which this is true is hard to determine from the cases; it is likely that this element is stressed or slighted according to the court's predilection for or against allowing a recovery. No one, however, who patronizes filling stations will have missed the indicia of effective control. This is suggested by the uniformity of the equipment, the uniformity of the service routine, the company's "pledges" posted in large type as to the sanitary precautions taken in the rest rooms, and the like.[56]

These considerations have led a majority of courts to hold that the dealer, because of the control actually exercised over him, is in fact the servant of the company, which thus becomes liable for the negligent driving of the trucks, the common trick of letting a little gasoline get in the kerosene, and the like.[57]

§ 442. ——— Particularly in cases of the latter sort, where the injury arises from negligence in the sale of the company's products, it is surprising that the element of estoppel is not more relied on. One who has the family kerosene can filled from a big truck labelled "Gulf" and receives a receipt bearing the same name, might not unnaturally suppose that she was

[55] It has been suggested (see Latty, Introduction to Business Associations (1951) 179) that the fact that a realtor or attorney may be discharged at will does not make him a servant. True—but such persons do not normally 'have all their eggs in one basket.

[56] In Bieluczyk v. Crown Petroleum Corp. (1948) 134 Conn. 461, 58 A.2d 380, the operator was apparently discharged for failure to maintain the restroom properly.

[57] Gulf Refining Co. v. Brown (1938) 93 F.2d 870, 116 A. L. R. 449; Texas Co. v. Mills (1934) 171 Miss. 231, 156 So. 866; Darker v. Colby (1941) 375 Ill. 558, 31 N.E.2d 950; Washel v. Tankargas, Inc. (1942) 211 Minn. 403, 2 N.W.2d 43; Bieluczyk v. Crown Petroleum Corp. (1948) 134 Conn. 461, 58 A.2d 380; Sinclair Refining Co. v. Piles (1949) 215 Ark. 469, 221 S.W.2d 12.

dealing with the Gulf Company and that she could rely on them in case the transaction miscarried.[58] As pointed out above [59] liability has been imposed on such a basis in the case of an apparent ownership of stores, beauty parlors and the like. There seems to be no evidence, however, that this theory of liability has yet been applied to tank or service stations.

§ 443. —— A minority of cases has refused to impose liability on the oil company.[60] In such cases stress is usually laid on the terms of the contract (which it would seem can scarcely be binding on third parties who know nothing about it) [61] and on the claim that the company exercises no control in the small details of running the business. Of the latter it may be said that the evidence often suggests that the company does exercise control in small details where the matter is of importance to them, e. g., in the policing of rest rooms; further, it is the right to exercise control which is the decisive factor, and not the showing that control actually was exercised. It cannot be doubted that the position of the company gives them the right (or at least the power) to exercise any control they wish with respect to even the most trifling of details.

Many of the cases refusing to hold the company may turn on the point discussed in the following section, namely, the status of the employees of the operator.

§ 444. Status of operator's employees. In many, perhaps most, of the cases, the negligence is that of someone hired by the operator and it has been argued that he, at least, is not

[58] See Gulf Refining Co. v. Brown (1938) 93 F.2d 870, 116 A. L. R. 449.

[59] See §§ 424, 425, ante.

[60] Texas Co. v. Wheat (1943) 140 Tex. 468, 168 S.W.2d 632, noted in 3 Vand. L. Rev. 597; Cities Service Oil v. Kindt (1948) 200 Okla. 64, 190 P.2d 1007, noted in 1 Okla. L. Rev. 277; Helms v. Sinclair Refining Co. (1948) 170 F.2d 289.

[61] See Glielmi v. Netherland Dairy Co. (1930) 254 N. Y. 60, 171 N. E. 996, noted in 29 Mich. L. Rev. 519; Clark v. Lynch (1940) 139 S.W.2d 294; Bartle v. Travelers Ins. Co. (1948) 171 F.2d 469; Hahn v. Bucyrus-Erie Co. (1950) 178 F.2d 844. "By the terms of the contract it appears that appellant tried to make Wilkins an independent contractor and at the same

the servant of the company, even if the operator himself be so regarded. Some cases so hold.[62]

It is believed that this position is unsound. A possible way of phrasing an answer might be in terms of delegation. The company cannot fail to know that the job taken on by the distributor is too big to be handled by one man. They must contemplate, and so sanction, his employing personnel, paid by him, to help with the job.[63] With delegation thus impliedly authorized, the helpers become subagents or subservants.

Some difficulties suggest themselves, however. The Restatement, which goes into considerable detail in its treatment of subagents,[64] seems to make no mention of subservants.[65] Perhaps such a category really does not exist. A subservant would charge both the servant and the master; this may be difficult to conceive in view of the common assumption that some one particular person "controls" the servant.

§ **445.** —— A more realistic and fundamental answer would be to say that the helper, though hired and paid by the operator, is simply the company's servant. Since the company reserves the right to control the operation, it necessarily reserves the right of control over anyone who is performing under the contract. It would be absurd to say that the company may control the driving of Jones, the operator, but not that of Smith, hired by Jones to drive the truck.[66] If Smith were to

time retain complete control of the business. This cannot be done under the law." Gulf Refining Co. v. Nations (1933) 167 Miss. 315, 145 So. 327.

[62] Texas Co. v. Brice (1928) 26 F.2d 164; Gulf Refining Co. v. Shirley (Tex. Civ. App., 1936) 99 S.W.2d 613. And see Sams v. Arthur (1926) 135 S. C. 121, 133 S. E. 205.

[63] In fact they usually do just this by putting a provision in the contract purporting to free them

from any liability for torts committed by the operator's employees.

[64] See Restatement, § 5, for definition and reference to sections treating various problems raised by the subagent.

[65] There is no such heading in the index, nor has the writer encountered the term in a fairly careful study of the text.

[66] "What was the relation between the appellant [company] and [operator] Duncan's employees? If, when discharging the duties which

say to the company: "I am bound to obey Jones' orders, not yours," an appropriate answer would be: "Jones is bound to obey our orders; therefore our orders are his." In a number of cases in other contexts where there is prima facie a relationship of employer and independent contractor, but where it is held that enough control has been retained to make the putative contractor himself a servant, it seems to be taken for granted that those hired by him and working with him on the job, are likewise the employer's servants.[67] On this or some other theory a majority of the cases have held that the company is liable for the torts of the workers hired by the operator.[68]

Duncan owed the appellant, they were subject to the appellant's control as to the details of their work, they were, when discharging such duties, servants of the appellant . . . . Duncan's contract does not expressly provide for such control, but it is necessarily implied by the provision therein placing Duncan himself under the appellant's control." Texas Co. v. Mills (1934) 171 Miss. 231, 156 So. 866.

"Having concluded that Yarbrough was acting as an agent or servant of the Refining Company and that he was acting for the Refining Company in loading the tank, it further follows that his employees, Hicks and Roundtree, were also the servants of the Refining Company under the direction and control of Yarbrough, while the latter was acting as an agent or servant on the Company. *Qui facit per alium facit per se.* By virtue of the right of Yarbrough, while acting as an agent or servant of the Refining Company, to direct and control Hicks and Roundtree, it follows that the Refining Com-

pany, through its agent, Yarbrough, thereby also had the right to direct and control them, and by reason thereof Roundtree and Hicks might well be deemed to be special or borrowed servants of the Refining Company, for the actionable negligence of whom the Company would be liable to third parties, provided, of course, such negligence were committed in and about the business of the master and in the course of their employment." Helms v. Sinclair Refining Co. (1948) 170 F.2d 289.

And see Smith v. Howard Crumlay & Co. (La. App., 1936) 171 So. 188. Cf. Restatement, § 81.

[67] See First Presbyterian Congregation v. Smith & Minnahan (1894) 163 Pa. 561, 30 Atl. 279; Rait v. New England Furniture & Carpet Co. (1896) 66 Minn. 76, 68 N. W. 729; Atlantic Transport Co. v. Coneys (1897) 82 Fed. 177.

[68] See Magnolia Petroleum Co. v. Johnson (1921) 149 Ark. 553, 233 S. W. 680; Gulf Refining Co. v. Brown (1938) 93 F.2d 870, 116 A. L. R. 449; Monetti v. Standard Oil

§ 446. Salesmen. In recent years many cases have dealt
with the status of a salesman who travels about, in a territory
varying in size from part of a city to several states, peddling
his master's or principal's goods or services. Insurance salesmen have been conspicuous in the picture but by no means to
the exclusion of sewing machine salesmen, washing machine
salesmen, used car salesmen, and the like.

The disputed cases are commonly alike in one regard: the
salesman drives his own car in performing his function and
the injury results from his negligent driving. (Were the salesman driving his employer's car, the inference of control would
be strong, and he would likely be held a servant.) Where he
goes about on his feet, the cases are very scarce, no doubt
because of the small risk created by the pedestrian salesman.
A few cases deal with newspaper delivery boys, sometimes
held to be servants in spite of the very common practice whereby the delivery boy buys the papers from a distributor and
keeps what he collects from his customers.[69] Fuller brush and
vacuum cleaner salesmen, going on foot, appear to have been
held servants in most of the few cases involving them.[70]

§ 447. —— Salesmen of the type here discussed are usually
full-time employees, working on commission, and under considerable surveillance from their employers as manifested by
instructions, pep meetings and the like. Obviously, however,
they are under very little actual control in their driving. Less,
perhaps, than the average truckdriver, who may work in a
narrower and more observable zone and return to home base

Co. (La. App., 1940) 195 So. 89;
Helms v. Sinclair Refining Co.
(1948) 170 F.2d 289.

[69] See Gallaher v. Ricketts (La.
App., 1939) 187 So. 351, 191 So.
713; Greening v. Gazette Printing
Co. (1939) 108 Mont. 158, 88 P.2d
862; Scorpion v. American-Repub-
lican (1944) 131 Conn. 42, 37 A.2d
802; Moeller v. DeRose (1950) —
Cal.App.2d —, 222 P.2d 107.

[70] The cases found all involve
unemployment compensation. See
Electrolux Corp. v. Danaher (1941)
128 Conn. 342, 23 A.2d 135; In re
Electrolux Corp. (1942) 288 N. Y.
440, 43 N.E.2d 480; Murphy v.
Daumit (1944) 387 Ill. 406, 56
N.E.2d 800.

more often. However, it has to be admitted that actual control is largely irrelevant; as already suggested, the most that can be posited in regard to control in practically all situations is that the status is such that the tacit assumption exists that the propositus will drive according to the express or implied instructions of his employers and that, in a given situation, if he knew the employer's wishes, he would respect them. It is not to be doubted that if insurance companies learn that they are to be held liable for the negligent driving of their agents, they will promptly proceed to do all they can to control the driving. This, incidentally, illustrates how the "control" test is likely to lead one to reasoning in a circle.

§ 448. **Rationalization of the trend.** The classic approach was to hold the salesmen to be servants.[71] Currently, a considerable (and perhaps increasing) number of cases hold the salesmen not to be servants.[72] This is logically a little hard to understand. Here are full-time employees, most emphatically doing the business of their employer, in no sense carrying on businesses of their own [this discussion obviously has nothing to do with the insurance agent who does business in his office and represents a number of companies] and functioning under constant exhortation and direction as to the manner

[71] Perhaps the leading case is Singer Mfg. Co. v. Rahn (1889) 132 U. S. 518, 10 S. Ct. 175, 33 L. Ed. 440, a horse and wagon case. "[The company] might, if it saw fit, instruct him what route to take, or even at what speed to drive."

See also Auer v. Sinclair Refining Co. (1927) 103 N. J. L. 372, 137 Atl. 555, 54 A. L. R. 623; Vest v. Metropolitan Life Ins. Co. (1938) 342 Mo. 629, 117 S.W.2d 252, 116 A. L. R. 1381; Chatelain v. Thackeray (1940) 98 Utah 525, 100 P.2d 191; Modern Motors v. Elkins (1941) 189 Okla. 134, 113 P.2d 969; Cormin v. Port of Seattle

(1941) 10 Wash.2d 139, 116 P.2d 338; Peterson v. Brian & Jensen Co. (1938) 134 Neb. 909, 280 N. W. 17; Halverson v. Sonotone Corp. (1947) 71 S. D. 568, 27 N.W.2d 596.

[72] See Wesolowski v. John Hancock Mut. Life Ins. Co. (1932) 308 Pa. 117, 162 Atl. 166, 87 A. L. R. 783, noted in 37 Dick. L. Rev. 129; Stockwell v. Morris (1933) 46 Wyo. 1, 22 P.2d 189, noted in 32 Mich. L. Rev. 276; Henkelmann v. Metropolitan Life Ins. Co. (1942) 180 Md. 591, 26 A.2d 418; Atlas Life Ins. Co. of Tulsa v. Foraker (1946) 196 Okla. 389, 165 P.2d 323.

at least in which they negotiate. Indeed, when one reads in some of the cases of the daily routine of the insurance salesman, beginning with a pep meeting at eight a. m. and terminating with another one at six p. m., with statements of sales made, rewards for those who have been successful and reprimands for those who haven't, one gets the impression that it is not adequate to call these salesmen servants; they are more like slaves.[73]

However, the law of Master and Servant is not wholly controlled and delimited by logic. It is believed that there is a traditional "servant" concept and that judges are often reluctant to apply the status to a person who quite definitely does not fit the concept. Servants are not typically white-collar workers; insurance salesmen typically are. Probably no one enjoys being called a "servant" at the present time (unless it is the unorganized and generally downtrodden domestic worker); salesmen, however, would resent being called "employees." They are in a higher bracket, socially, educationally, and economically,[74] than the ordinary servant. They tend, in fact, to think of themselves as professional men. This is all inconsistent with the "servant" concept.[75]

§ 449. A further point, already suggested, and believed to be possibly one of the important inarticulate premises in the decision, is that traditionally servants have been persons whose activities are exceptionally dangerous because of equipment or facilities furnished them by their employers. We have seen that a simple rationalization of *respondeat superior*, currently widely accepted, is that the business should bear the risks of the business. Such a rationalization assumes that the

[73] Latty, Introduction to Business Associations (1951) 170, quotes figures showing that the earnings of the average agent selling industrial insurance varied from $14.86 in 1906 to $53.19 in 1929.

[74] But cf. n. 71, ante.

[75] If consistency is to be invoked, it may be recalled by way of argument that surgeons permanently attached to a hospital or clinic, though unquestionably professional men, and usually quite above salesmen socially, educationally, and economically, tend more and more to be classed as servants. True; however, surgeons work with their hands, are engaged in a specially

business has risks greater than, or at least different from, the risks of life in general. Otherwise there is no point in charging them to the employer.

This, as previously suggested,[76] could conceivably explain the reluctance of courts to hold that the servant of foot charges his master with the consequences of his errant pedestrianism, or that the salesman, *driving his own car*, is a business risk and not simply a community risk.[77]

The cases themselves, unfortunately, throw little light on the reasoning (or intuition, or hunch, or whatever) of the courts deciding them. Where the employer is held, his general control of the salesman's activities will be stressed; where the employer is not held, it will be pointed out that he can exercise no control over the employee's driving.

§ 450. **The Pennsylvania anomaly.** The Pennsylvania (and perhaps other)[78] courts have developed a curious doctrine on the point. The question was presented for the first time in 1932 in the Wesolowski case,[79] involving a life insurance salesman who was paid $15 a week plus commissions and whose territory was "less than a square mile in the city of Philadelphia." He had a car of his own which he occasionally used, with the knowledge and consent, but not the request, of the company. The court said: "If Adams had chosen to walk from person to person with whom he had his employer's business to transact and in walking he had negligently knocked over and

dangerous occupation and work on the premises of their constituents and are often chosen or recommended by those constituents. All these are factors tending towards the status of servant.

[76] See ante, § 354 et seq.

[77] Mr. Leidy, in a valuable and well-known article (28 Mich. L. Rev. 365) suggests a return to what he regards as the original view, namely that the prime attribute of the independent contractor is that he carries on an independent calling. By this test, if the writer understands it correctly, the salesman herein dealt with would be normally a servant since he is normally a regular member of the employer's organization. (See id., at 378.)

[78] See, e. g., Henkelmann v. Metropolitan Life Ins. Co. (1942) 180 Md. 591, 26 A.2d 418.

[79] Wesolowski v. John Hancock Mut. Life Ins. Co. (1932) 308 Pa. 117, 162 Atl. 166, 87 A. L. R. 783, noted in 37 Dick. L. Rev. 129.

injured another pedestrian, it could not reasonably be con-
tended that his employer should respond in damages for
Adams' negligent pedestrianism. So to hold would be to
construe the phrase 'respondeat superior' beyond its fundamental meaning and to carry its principle to absurd lengths
and to consequences forbidden by every sound consideration
of public policy."

§ **451.** Unfortunately the court does not say what these
considerations of public policy are. They further said, however, that to hold an employer liable for the negligence of
the employee in the use of an instrumentality "it must either
be proved that the master exercises actual or potential control
over that instrumentality, or the use of the instrumentality
at the time and place of the act complained of must be of
such vital importance in furthering the business of the master
that the latter's actual or potential control of it at that time
and place may reasonably be inferred." The employer was
accordingly held not liable.

This reasoning has been applied in later cases.[80] In none
of them does the exercise of "actual or potential control" over
the instrumentality appear to have been found, so they must
rest on the inference of such control from the vital importance
of the use of the instrumentality. In a number of cases the
test has been applied to persons not salesmen but servants by
any test; it is apparently thought applicable to any servant
not employed to operate an instrumentality, but using one
as a means of performing the services for which he is hired.

§ **452.** These cases are somewhat difficult to analyze. On
the one hand they do not take the position that the status of
a travelling salesman is inherently not that of servant. On the
other hand they assume that a servant, working full time for
a master at a job which assumes and requires some variety of

---

[80] See Cusick v. Hutchison (1935)
318 Pa. 316, 177 Atl. 479; Barr v.
Anchorage Inn, Inc. (1938) 328 Pa.
378, 196 Atl. 21; Holdsworth v.
Pennsylvania P. & L. Co. (1940)
337 Pa. 235, 10 A.2d 412; Feller
v. New Amsterdam Casualty Co.
(1950) 363 Pa. 483, 70 A.2d 299.

transportation, is not within the course of employment while walking (or bicycling or riding a horse, no doubt) about his job, or while driving about it in a car, unless the master is exercising actual or potential control over the car (which has never happened as far as the cases show) or unless the use of the car is of "vital importance"—and, it must be remembered, that means that it be vitally important to use a car rather than some other means of transportation, since *ex hypothesi* that job is one which requires some form of transportation.

Perhaps, at least remotely, they suggest the point of view sketched above, namely that an industry is not fairly to be charged with the risks of such industry unless it has risks greater than, or different from, the risks of ordinary living. This would explain the dictum that the insurance company would not be liable for the negligent walking of its salesman; it might throw some light on the court's reluctance to treat the salesman driving his own car as in the course of employment, at least except in cases where driving seems to be intimately associated with the job.

6. *The Borrowed Servant Problem*

§ 453. In general. One problem is of perhaps more frequent occurrence,[81] more importance and more difficulty than any other in this field, namely that arising where a servant is, at the time of the accident, acting in some sense as the servant of two masters. This may happen in innumerable ways. The owner may loan his car and chauffeur to a friend for the afternoon, telling the chauffeur to follow the instructions of the friend; an undertaker may loan or hire his car (or hack) and driver to another undertaker whose own equipment is inadequate to meet the demands of a particular funeral; the owner of a steamship, hiring

---

[81] In the writer's experience, based on many years' browsing through advance sheets, three groups of cases in the agency field are by all odds the most common, those dealing with "in and out of the employment" (workmen's compensation), those dealing with the commission claimed by the real estate broker, and those dealing with borrowed servant.

stevedores to unload it, may furnish his own winch and winchman, putting them at the disposition of the master stevedore. In
a famous early English case,[82] a country gentleman coming to
town, according to the current custom, with his own carriage,
but with no horses of his own, hired horses and driver from
a stablekeeper. The driver negligently drove the gentleman's
coach into another conveyance; the judges of the Court of
King's Bench divided, two to two, on the question of the
gentleman's liability.

§ 454. Joint masters. No difficulty arises where the several
masters are employing the servant jointly; it is a simple case
of joint liability. This may be the commonplace case of a
partnership having a servant; it may be a more special case
as where two railroads jointly operated a station and employed
a baggage agent who caused injury by negligent handling
of a revolver, which was found, by something of a stretch, to
be in the course of the joint employment.[83]

§ 455. Different jobs for different masters. It is conceivable that a servant could be, at the same moment, doing two
different jobs for two different employers. One could be simultaneously driving a truck for A and distributing handbills
for B. No necessary conflict of control would seem to be
involved and presumably A (and not B) would be liable for
negligent driving and B (but not A) would be liable for
negligence in distributing the handbills. Such cases would
seem to present no difficulties, but they are infrequent, if they
exist at all.

[82] Laugher v. Pointer (1826) 5
B. & C. 547.

[83] Moore v. Southern Ry. Co.
(1914) 165 N. C. 439, 81 S. E. 603.
And see Western Union Tel. Co. v.
Rust (1909) 55 Tex. Civ. App. 359,
120 S. W. 249; Rosander v. Market
St. Ry. Co. (1928) 89 Cal. App.
721, 265 Pac. 541; Seaboard Air
Line v. Ebert (1931) 102 Fla. 641,
138 So. 4, noted in 32 Col. L. Rev.
759; Hiner v. Olson (1937) 23
Cal.App.2d 227, 72 P.2d 890; Meri-
dian Taxicab Co. v. Ward (1939)
184 Miss. 499, 186 So. 636, 120
A. L. R. 1346; Stephanelli v. Yuhas
(1939) 135 Pa. Super. 573, 7 A.2d
124.

§ 456. **Different jobs involving the same act.** According to the Restatement,[84] one may be the servant of two masters, not joint employers, at one time as to one act. One instance given is of a messenger boy, M, hired by each A and B (unknown to each other) to deliver a package for each to the same destination. If M injures someone through negligent bicycle riding (the instrumentality authorized in the illustration) both A and B are liable.

This is doubtless true. For one thing, as a practical matter, it could readily happen, a decision would have to be made, and it is hard to think of any other. There are theoretical difficulties, however. Suppose that A told M to go by route X, B by route Y, the two routes being equally direct. M cannot go by both routes (although he could go by neither). Suppose he elects to go by route X, and while so doing, negligently runs into P ?

At least two possibilities suggest themselves. It could be said that by following route X, M temporarily renounced his allegiance to B and became pro tem exclusively A's servant. Or it could be said, and doubtless more plausibly, that as to B the use of route X was simply a detour, not relieving B of liability. Certainly if M elected to take route Z, a third route of equal directness, it is not to be doubted that both masters would be charged.

§ 457. **One job for two masters.** The common situation, however, is none of those just discussed; it is that typified by Laugher v. Pointer.[85] There, quite plainly the servant was doing one job: driving the carriage and team—and he was doing it in some sense for two masters, the stablekeeper and the country gentleman. In such a case, are both liable ? If not, which one ?

§ 458. **Should both be liable? The Pennsylvania cases.** It would seem simple and practical to hold both liable. Why not ?

---

[84] Restatement, § 226.
[85] Ante, n. 82.

Both are getting some kind of benefit from the work. Both are undoubtedly exercising control in some sense.

In Laugher v. Pointer at least one of the judges appears to have thought both employers could be liable. In a number of cases the Supreme Court of Pennsylvania has imposed liability on both, perhaps without awareness of any deviation from accepted canons. A typical instance is Gordon v. Byers.[86] There a seller of motor trucks trying to sell a tank truck to a wholesale gasoline dealer, turned over the truck and driver to the gasoline dealer for demonstration, the truck to be used for a week in the gasoline business, and then to be bought if satisfactory; otherwise, a daily rental to be paid. While the driver (in the general employment of the truck seller, and paid by him) was delivering gasoline he negligently injured the plaintiff.

§ 459. —— Both employers were held liable. The court put it on the ground that the driver was performing (generally) a different service for each: demonstrating the truck for one, and delivering gas for the other. At the time of the accident (caused by careless use of valves) the court said he was performing both services at once. Is it not apparent, however, that this was no more a case of different services than Laugher v. Pointer or any other of the innumerable similar cases? In Laughter v. Pointer, as in Gordon v. Byers, the benefit derived from the service was different; the driver was forwarding the stableman's business of renting horses, the gentleman's business of seeing the town, visiting his friends or what not—but the act or routine of acts by which he rendered those different benefits was one and the same; driving the horses and carriage. If in the suggested case of the messenger boy, he was employed by Western Union and was, as such, carrying a package for P, he would as above be rendering different benefits—P wants his package delivered and doesn't care whether Western Union makes money, Western

[86] 309 Pa. 453, 164 Atl. 334, noted in 37 Dick. L. Rev. 267 and 8 Temp. L. Q. 267.

Union wants business and profit and has no interest in P's package—but he would be doing only one act. This distinguishes from that of the boy carrying two packages for two masters.

The same observations seem to be applicable to other cases in which the Pennsylvania court has held both employers liable.[87] Whatever the theory the result seems to be a practical and sensible one. Since the liability is vicarious, there would be a right of contribution. Why not let each of the two employers pay half the damages?

§ 460. **The ordinary view holds only one.** In Laugher v. Pointer, Littledale, J., said: "The coachman or postilion cannot be the servant of both. He is the servant of one *or* the other, but not the servant of one *and* the other. . . ." It is true that further observations by His Lordship suggest that he based them on technical, procedural grounds and not on substantive ones. However, the cases for the most part, outside Pennsylvania, have seemed to assume that on substantive principles, only one may be held as *the* master.[88]

The logic of this is apparent enough: control is essential to the master-and-servant relationship and one person cannot very well be under the control of two different people (not acting jointly) at the same time. One or the other must, as a mere matter of definition, have the control.

It may be doubted if this is a place where logic and common sense agree. We have seen repeatedly that this much

---

[87] See Lang v. Hanlon (1930) 302 Pa. 173, 153 Atl. 143, (1931) 305 Pa. 378, 157 Atl. 788, noted in 44 Harv. L. Rev. 1136 and 79 U. of Pa. L. Rev. 973; Siidekum v. Animal Rescue League (1946) 353 Pa. 408, 45 A.2d 259; Kissell v. Motor Age Transit Lines (1947) 357 Pa. 204, 53 A.2d 593. The cases do not make it clear when this rule applies; perhaps when it is impossible to decide which is *the* master.

[88] "It is a doctrine as old as the Bible itself, and the common law of the land follows it, that a man cannot serve two masters at the same time; he will obey the one and betray the other. He cannot be subject to two controlling forces which may at the time be divergent." Phillips, D. J., in Atwood v. Chicago, R. I. & P. Ry. Co. (1896) 72 Fed. 447.

talked of "control" is ordinarily only a putative control. It should also be remembered that the law of Frolic and Detour can apply here. There seems no great likelihood that if the possibility of two masters were recognized there would often be a conflict of actual control. If there should, both could still be liable up to the point where submission to B's orders was such a violation of A's rights as to take S for the time being out of the course of employment as to A.

§ 461. The decision may often be made by the plaintiff.

Rightly or wrongly, most courts appear to take it for granted that only one employer is to be held liable. This forces on them the enormously difficult task (at least so it has proved) of deciding which one it shall be.

One point may be mentioned in passing. In most jurisdictions, judging from the reported cases, either tradition or procedural limitations (real or supposed) apparently preclude joining both employers and so getting a judicial determination, not only whether or not some master is liable, but which one, if any, it is. Thus the plaintiff is forced to choose and run the risk of having to start all over again if he makes the wrong choice. It is not unlikely that in consequence the determination as to which employer is to be liable is thus in fact made by plaintiff since, with the choice so even and so difficult, and with courts and juries so willing to have plaintiff recover, there may be a recovery, whichever employer plaintiff sues.

§ 462. Conflicting pulls.

As a matter of analysis the difficulty arises chiefly from the fact that there are primarily two plausible approaches which, unfortunately, lead to different results.

On the one hand, the ultimate control is in the general employer. It is to him that S owes allegiance. Insofar as S respects the wishes and directions of the special employer and attempts to please him, it is simply as an indirect way of pleasing the general employer. The latter hires and fires; but for him S would not be working (temporarily) for the special employer. Further, in such cases, S frequently, though of course not always, uses an instrumentality belonging to the general employer. Since it is the normal assumption that one using the instrument (particularly a valuable instrument) of another is using it under the instructions and control of that other, this tends to strengthen the inference that S is under the control ultimately of the general rather than the special employer.

§ 463. —— On the other hand it will normally be true that S is engaged in doing the business of the special employer. This may mean several things. It may mean that the special employer is engaged in a business enterprise in the ordinary sense and that S is doing work which is an integral part of that business. E. g., if the special employer is a road contractor, he will normally employ trucks in his business, and if he hires a truck and driver for a day or a week or a month to augment his own force of trucks, this will mean that the hired truck will temporarily be performing an integral part of the special employer's business. Or it may mean that the special employer is getting help which is either not a part of his regular business or not a part of his "business" at all in the ordinary sense of that term; he may be needing a truck and driver to cart leaves away from his estate in the fall, or to carry his employees to a spring outing. In the latter cases it can at least be said that some desire or need of the special employer is being attended to and that some "interest" of his is being forwarded.

§ 464. —— On either of these hypotheses, S is temporarily identifying himself with the special employer and his needs, and becoming a part of the enterprise which, at least for the moment, he is engaged in. It must not be forgotten that the lender is very seldom a donor; he is making the loan because it is directly or indirectly to his business advantage. Still, except in the case where he is in the business of supplying such service, it is externally the business of the borrower being done. If the X Milk Company loans a truck and driver to the Y Milk Company to deliver the latter's milk, we are

315

likely to think that it is primarily the Y Company's business that is being done.[89]

§ 465. Scope of the business.

Other analyses have been made. For example, as a variant of the "business of the special employer" approach, just suggested, it has been argued that to make the special employer liable, the work should be

---

[89] It is not difficult to turn this argument around. Cf. Schettino, J. S. C., concurring, in Devone v. Newark Tidewater Terminal, Inc. (1951) 14 N. J. Super. 401, 82 A.2d 425: "It is true that the right of control as to manner of doing work is an attribute of the master-servant relationship. This right of control, however, cannot be the basis of the doctrine of 'respondeat superior,' for if it were, it would excuse the master who was not present at the time of his servant's culpable conduct and therefore could not have controlled it. Indeed, no court, in holding the master responsible for the negligence of his servant, stops to consider whether the master, by the exercise of his right of control, could have avoided the injury. In the final analysis, the reason for the rule of 'respondeat superior' must be some public policy in favor of burdening one who acts through another in pursuit of his own ends with the injuries incidental to his servant's activities. The right of control is simply one of the tests whereby the courts determine whether the relation of master and servant exists; the liability attaching to that relation arises from considerations entirely foreign to the right of control. . . . In short, the independent contrac-tor is deemed to be furthering his own interests, whereas the employee is deemed to be furthering the interests of his employer, and on that basis the ultimate responsibility is distributed, in a rough way, among economic entrepreneurs.

"But here the question is not whether the engineer was an independent contractor. That he was an employee of someone is conceded. Rather the issue is whether a man, admittedly an employee, was transferred from one employment to another. Such being the issue, it is not clear why it should be resolved by the application of a test designed to aid in a different inquiry. If I am correct in saying that an employer's responsibility for his employee's actions does not depend upon the existence of a causal connection between the accident and the exercise or failure to exercise the right of control, but rather rests upon the stated public policy, then the sole inquiry here pertinent is this: Was the employee's negligence committed while he was acting in furtherance of his general employer's interests? If it was, then the basic public policy which underlies an employer's liability applies with unabated force. It is true that the employee also furthers the interests of the

316

within the "scope of his business." [90] Thus, it is without the scope of the business "where the buyer of a piece of machinery receives services from the factory's installation expert"; within it, where the case involves "a doctor's utilization in a surgical operation of a nurse borrowed from the general employment of another or a railroad's borrowing from a general employer an engine and crew for use in its system and for its purposes." [91]

It is undoubtedly true that a number of cases reach results consistent with this theory. Perhaps it is useful. It is not clear, however, precisely why this limitation should be set on the special employer's liability. If he wishes to make something his business pro tem, why should the law not humor him? Again, if this limitation is sought to be based on some general theory or liability, it raises awkward questions. If A has a car, which he uses for pleasure only, and a chauffeur to drive it, and he loans the car and chauffeur to B for the afternoon, B's objective also being exclusively pleasure, does it follow that the chauffeur is the servant of neither? Finally, the theory might not be so easy of application as its proponent apparently supposes. In the case put of the servicing of the machinery, if the machinery were an integral part of M's plant, it is hard to think that repairs on it made by M's own engineers would not be within the scope of the business. If so, some other theory must be advanced to exonerate M from liability when the repairs are made by the manufacturer's service man.

§ 466. The authorities.
It is not surprising that the cases dealing with this problem are confused and conflicting. At best, certain generalizations may be made. Apparently the

special employer when he performs the service which the general employer contracts to furnish, but that circumstance is common to all transactions whereby one business entity contracts for the services of another business entity, and does not militate against the continued responsibility of the general employer whose interests are likewise served."

[90] Talbot Smith, Scope of the Business: the Borrowed Servant Problem, 38 Mich. L. Rev. 1122.

[91] Id., at 1249, 1250.

considerations tending to impose liability on the general employer have by and large been more persuasive with courts. In a leading New York case,[92] the defendant, Adams Express Company, hired a van and driver from one S, who was "in the trucking business," for two dollars an hour. It does not appear what the term, if any, of this arrangement was, but it had clearly subsisted for some time. The van was used in "carrying express" for the defendant. In holding defendant not liable for the driver's negligence, Cardozo, J., said: "The rule now is that as long as the employee is furthering the business of his general employer by the service rendered to another, there will be no inference of a new relation unless command had been surrendered, and no inference of its surrender from the mere fact of its division."

Probably this represents the most common approach. The employee remains presumptively in the service of his general employer. The burden is on plaintiff to show that in fact allegiance has been transferred.[93]

A number of particular situations may be vaguely distinguished in which it is felt that a transfer may fairly be found.

[92] Charles v. Barrett (1922) 233 N. Y. 127, 135 N. E. 199.

[93] The later English decisions are very explicit in putting the burden on the general employer. Thus in McFarland v. Coggins & Griffiths (Liverpool) Ltd. [1945] 1 All. E. R. 605 (aff'd sub nom. Mersey Docks & Harbour Board v. Coggins & Griffiths (Liverpool) Ltd. [1946] 2 All. E. R. 345) it is said: "It is clearly established that if the regular employers of a workman wish to contend that they were not his employers at the time when his negligence in performing his duties caused an accident, the burden is on them to prove this. Prima facie, the persons who have engaged a man to serve them, who pay his wages, and who have the power to dismiss him if he misbehaves, are his employers during his hours of work, and it is by no means easy for them to prove that at the relevant time some other person had such complete control over the workman as to become his 'superior' for the purposes of the maxim 'respondeat superior.' . . . We would only observe that the burden of proof lying on the regular employers is particularly difficult to discharge in cases where the workman who caused the accident was driving a vehicle belonging to them, of which he was in sole charge, and which he alone was allowed to drive on the day of the accident. In such a case the vehicle has been placed under the control of the driver by his regular employers,

§ 467. **Situations in which the special employer may be liable.** Time may have a bearing here. If the use of the services is long continued and constant, the servant may become so affiliated de facto with the special employer as to put the general employer more or less in the position of an employment agent.[94] Or the special employer may in practice or by the terms of the agreement (or both) actually exercise such control over the servant as to make him seem the real master.[95] Or, perhaps most commonly, the work the servant is "borrowed" to do may be conspicuously the work in which the special employer is engaged (as distinguished from some service rendered to the special employer to enable him better to carry on his work) so as to make the servant seem clearly a part of the enterprise, for whose risks the enterpriser will be liable. This is especially true where the borrowed servant

who rely on him to use his own skill and exercise his own discretion in driving it."

Where the general employer is in the business of hiring out conveyances and drivers the presumption is specially strong that he remains the master: Baltimore Transp. Co. v. State (1945) 184 Md. 250, 40 A.2d 678; Pennsylvania Smelting & Refining Co. v. Duffin (1950) 363 Pa. 564, 70 A.2d 270.

Likewise where the equipment is furnished by the general employer and requires special exercise on the part of the servant, so that it is unlikely that the special employer will do more than ask for particular results, the presumption that the general employer is liable remains strong. Thus in the familiar case of Standard Oil Co. v. Anderson (1909) 212 U. S. 215, 29 S. Ct. 252, 53 L. Ed. 480, the special employer's stevedores were unloading a boat owned by the general employer, who furnished a winch and

winchman to do the lifting; the winchman lifted and lowered according to instructions given him by the special employer. The general employer was held liable, the court saying: ". . . the obedience to those signals showed cooperation rather than subordination and is not enough to show there has been a change of masters." And see Halliburton Cementing Co. v. Paulk (1950) 180 F.2d 79; Roberts v. Geo. M. Brewster & Son (1951) 13 N. J. Super. 462, 80 A.2d 638.

[94] See Atlantic Transport Co. v. Coneys (1897) 82 Fed. 177; Bobik v. Industrial Commission (1946) 146 Ohio St. 187, 64 N.E.2d 829.

[95] See New Orleans M. & C. Ry. Co. v. Hanning (1872) 15 Wall. 649, 21 L. Ed. 220; McGrath v. Edward G. Budd Mfg. Co. (1944) 348 Pa. 619, 36 A.2d 203; Larson v. LeMere (1945) 220 Minn. 25, 18 N.W.2d 696; Duff v. Corn (1947) 84 Ohio App. 403, 87 N.E.2d 731;

is working alongside unquestioned servants of the special
employer, doing the same work as they and apparently under
the same control.

§ **468.** —— Thus where Big Four locomotives and engineers pulled freight for the C. & O. over the C. & O. line for
a 12-mile stretch outside of Cincinnati, a job for which the
C. & O. was paid and which was done under the supervision
of their trainmaster, Taft, C. J., said for the supreme court:
"We do not think that the fact that the Big Four paid the
wages of Linstead and his crew or that they could only be
discharged or suspended by the Big Four, prevented their
being the servants of the Chesapeake & Ohio Company for the
performance of this particular job." [96]

Likewise where an undertaker, whose job included taking
the flowers from the funeral to the cemetery, had more flowers
than he could carry in his own truck and borrowed a truck and
driver from a florist, it was held that the undertaker was liable
for the [florist's] driver's negligence.[97]

It must not be assumed that these exceptions will always
operate. In many instances it will remain difficult to determine what were the factors impelling the court to their
decision.

American Stevedores Co. v. Industrial Commission (1951) 408 Ill.
445, 97 N.E.2d 329; Boyce v. Maine
Public Service Co. (1951) — Me.
—, 81 A.2d 670.

[96] Linstead v. Chesapeake & O.
Ry. Co. (1928) 276 U. S. 28, 48
S. Ct. 241, 72 L. Ed. 453, noted in
2 U. of Cin. L. Rev. 326 and 7 Tex.
L. Rev. 322.

[97] Moseman v. L. M. Penwell Undertaking Co. (1940) 151 Kan. 610,
100 P.2d 669. And see Gates v.
Pendleton (1921) 184 Cal. 797, 195

Pac. 664; Bowen v. Gradison Const.
Co. (1930) 236 Ky. 270, 32 S.W.2d
1014; B. & B. Building Material
Co. v. Winston Bros. Co. (1930)
158 Wash. 139, 290 Pac. 839; De-
vaney v. Lawler Corp. (1936) 101
Mont. 579, 56 P.2d 746; Wicklund
v. North Star Timber Co. (1939)
205 Minn. 595, 287 N. W. 7; Steele
v. Wells (Tex. Civ. App., 1939)
134 S.W.2d 377; McFarland v.
Dixie Machinery Co. (1941) 348 Mo.
341, 152 S.W.2d 67.

CHAPTER XV

DANGEROUS ACTIVITIES AND INSTRUMENTALITIES: EXTENSIONS OF VICARIOUS LIABILITY

§ 469. In general. In recent times there has not only on the whole been a tendency to extend the operation of *respondeat superior* by liberalizing the concept "course of the employment" but there has been a considerable increase in the incidence of vicarious liability in a group of situations on theories which are analogous to or extensions of *respondeat superior* but which can scarcely be regarded as proper instances of it. The common denominator has been danger.

Whether life looked any less dangerous to the citizen of a hundred years ago or whether he, in his time, rather complacently thought that life had grown more exciting and dangerous than that lived by his predecessors of a hundred years before, we cannot know. Certainly there is a current feeling that various developments, largely mechanical, have increased the danger of life and that the classic rules of *respondeat superior* have ceased to afford adequate protection. In this chapter a few of these recent developments will be examined.

1. *Dangerous Instrumentalities*

§ 470. History and obsolescence of the doctrine. One of the oldest of these special theories of liability—in fact one already so old as to be virtually obsolete—is the dangerous instrumentality doctrine. This is, in terms, a very broad doctrine. "It is that whenever the master, having under his control some specially dangerous agency or instrumentality, and which he is therefore under special obligation to keep with care, confides this duty to his servant or agent, he will be responsible if the duty be not performed, whether through the negligence or the wantonness or the malice of his servant or agent." [1]

---

[1] Mechem on Agency (2d Ed. 1914) p. 1512. See generally Hor- ack, "The Dangerous Instrumentality Doctrine," 26 Yale L. J. 224.

The mere reading of such a statement arouses suspicion. What is a "specially dangerous" instrumentality? A horse, an axe, an automobile, a garden hose? Why is the master liable for the servant's breach of duty, though not committed in the course of employment? What is the extent in manner, time and space of such a liability?

Examination of the cases discloses that they by no means substantiate the broad statement made. The doctrine is (or was) in large part confined to pranks done by railway employees with the locomotive whistle, signal torpedoes and the like.[2] In a leading case[3] a conductor, aspiring to frighten a lady friend riding on the train, put a torpedo on the track. It did not explode and was subsequently picked up by children, injuring them when it exploded in the course of their investigations. The railroad was held liable; otherwise, the court said, the master would be able to shift to the servant his duty in respect to the custody of such instruments.

§ 471. —— It is clear that the act was not done in the course of employment. It is also clear, in spite of what the court implies, that there is no rule requiring of the master "in respect to the custody" of torpedoes to do more than handle them with care himself and use reasonable care in selecting servants to handle them and in supervising such servants in their handling of the torpedoes.

It is believed that the courts were impressed, not unreasonably, with the number of injuries caused by such instrumentalities, and felt that the risk was one that might well be put on the railroads. In so doing they attempted as far as possible to keep within the traditional law of Agency. Indeed, it is

---

[2] See Toledo, W. & W. Ry. Co. v. Harmon (1868) 47 Ill. 298; Billman v. Indianapolis, C. & L. R. Co., (1881) 76 Ind. 166; Alsever v. Minneapolis & St. L. Ry. (1902) 115 Iowa 338 (with which cf. Johnson v. Chicago, R. I. & P. Ry. (1913) 157 Iowa 738, 141 N. W. 430); Stewart v. Cary Lumber Co. (1907) 146 N. C. 47, 59 S. E. 545; Euting v. Chicago & N. W. Ry. (1902) 116 Wis. 13, 92 N. W. 358.

[3] Pittsburgh, C. & St. L. Ry. v. Shields (1890) 47 Ohio St. 387, 24 N. E. 658 (with which cf. Galveston, H. & S. A. Ry. v. Currie (1906) 100 Tex. 136, 96 S. W. 1073).

quite possible that in many cases courts, persuaded by their own sophistries, supposed that they were really applying the traditional law of Agency.

Cases applying the dangerous instrumentality doctrine have become very rare.[4] This is doubtless not due to any gradual awareness of the fact that it was a heresy as much as to the fact that the urgency has disappeared. Horses are rarer, more sophisticated, and less susceptible to being frightened by the locomotive whistle; torpedoes are safer or superseded by different signaling devices. And, above all, the attention of courts has been shifted to newer and even more shocking dangers.

2. *Special Doctrines Applicable to Motor Cars*

§ 472. **In general.** Rather oddly, courts for the most part did not apply the dangerous instrumentality doctrine when a new and ultimately very dangerous instrumentality appeared in the field.[5] Perhaps it was because originally horseless vehicles were objects of ridicule rather than fear.

The dangers of the automobile are well enough understood now and a number of special doctrines have grown up, akin to or outgrowths of agency but not instances of it. Three of these will be mentioned briefly here: (a) the family-car doctrine; (b) bailors' liability statutes, and (c) presumptions arising from the ownership of a car driven by another.

§ 473. **(A) The family car.** This doctrine, like the dangerous instrumentality doctrine, is one nearly but not quite of ordinary agency. It says that when the head of the family

---

[4] The doctrine is rejected in Chesapeake & O. Ry. v. Ford (1914) 158 Ky. 800, 166 S. W. 605; Goupiel v. Grand Trunk Ry. (1902) 96 Vt. 191, 118 Atl. 586, 30 A. L. R. 690, noted in 21 Mich. L. Rev. 707 and 71 U. of Pa. L. Rev. 283; Vadyak v. Lehigh & N. E. Ry. (1935) 318 Pa. 580, 179 Atl. 435. Cf. Scrivner v. Boise Payette Lumber Co. (1928) 46 Idaho 334, 268 Pac. 19, noted in 42 Harv. L. Rev. 269.

[5] The Florida cases are, or were, an exception. See Southern Cotton Oil Co. v. Anderson (1920) 80 Fla. 441, 86 So. 629, 16 A. L. R. 255, noted in 5 Minn. L. Rev. 322; Herr v. Butler (1931) 101 Fla. 1125, 132

provides a car for the recreation and pleasure of the members of his family, he is responsible for the negligence of any one of the members of his family driving the car for his or her own purpose but with the permission of the head of the family.

This doctrine starts logically with the proposition that where a member of the family, e. g., a son or daughter, is driving another member of the family, e. g., the mother, to church or to market at the father's request, the son or daughter will normally become pro tem the father's servant in the ordinary sense.[6] The father, that is, may make it his enterprise to furnish transportation to the mother. Why, it is then asked, may the father not as well make it his enterprise to furnish transportation to the son, the son acting as servant for the occasion, just as much as if he were driving the mother?

§ 474. —— This question is a little difficult to answer. If the father were to tell the son that he was looking peaked and ask him to drive the father's car ten miles to get fresh air and build up his health, no doubt the father could be held a master in the ordinary sense.[7] The best answer probably is

So. 815, noted in 9 Tenn. L. Rev. 240; Crenshaw Bros. v. Harper (1940) 142 Fla. 27, 194 So. 353; Lynch v. Walker (1947) 159 Fla. 188, 31 So.2d 268, noted in 21 Fla. L. J. 273. And see Simon v. City Cab Co. (1935) 78 F.2d 506, cert. den. (1935) 296 U. S. 640, 56 S. Ct. 173, 80 L. Ed. 455, noted in 24 Geo. L. J. 178

[6] See Lashbrook v. Patten (1864) 1 Duv. (Ky.) 316; Denison v. M'Norton (1916) 228 Fed. 401; Mazi v. McAnlis (1950) 365 Pa. 114, 74 A.2d 108.

[7] See Fox v. Cahorowski (1917) 66 Pa. Super. 221. And see Murphey v. United States (1950) 179 F.2d 743, where the United States

was held liable under the Federal Tort Claims Act where a soldier, having taken men from camp to the movies in a government truck as authorized, went off on a private recreational venture with a friend and two women and the Government was held liable for his careless driving in the course of the venture on the theory that the soldier was authorized to use the truck in promoting the morale of soldiers. The dissenting judge suggested that the liability was based, by analogy, on the family-car doctrine. See also Meinhardt v. Vaughn (1928) 159 Tenn. 272, 17 S.W.2d 5, noted in 43 Harv. L. Rev. 133 and 8 Tenn. L. Rev. 44.

to point out that in the case of the son driving alone or with his friends, the father is not really making it his enterprise; such language is a palpable pretense to cover the fact that the son is driving for his own benefit and not his father's. Serving the master is an essential element of the relationship; its absence cannot be hidden by talking of the father making it his business to furnish entertainment for his family.

The real and sensible basis of the doctrine is not difficult to discover, namely that cars have come to constitute such an appalling hazard and to take such a shocking toll of life and property that conventional ideas of liability are inadequate; a conspicuous feature of the situation is the frequency with which the negligent driver is found to be judgment-proof; in one case at least this factor can be minimized by insisting that if the head of the family allows his wife and children to use his car for their own pleasure he may do so only at the price of being liable for any negligent harm they may do.[8]

A very interesting case clearly showing the policy basis of the rule is Felcyn v. Gamble,[9] in which a majority of the Supreme Court of Minnesota held the doctrine not applicable to a motorboat. "It is evident that in practically all the decisions the doctrine was applied to automobiles in the interest of justice and as a necessity. The situation as regards motorboats is in no way comparable to that of automobiles."

---

[8] "The doctrine undoubtedly involves a somewhat novel application of the rule of respondeat superior. However, it is supported by definite and logical considerations: principally the financial responsibility of the owner is thus always associated with a motor car while it is being used by another member of the family—who is likely to be irresponsible—in the pursuit and furtherance of the purpose for which the car is kept; also this doctrine relieves the injured person of the difficult, and, at times, impossible task of meeting the owner; claim that upon the occasion in question the vehicle was not being used for his pleasure or business." Dimon, Dist. J., in Burns v. Main (1950) 87 F. Supp. 705.

[9] (1932) 185 Minn. 357, 241 N. W. 37, 79 A. L. R. 1159, noted in 12 B. U. L. Rev. 497, 31 Mich. L. Rev. 132, 16 Minn. L. Rev. 870 and 6 So. Cal. L. Rev. 340.

§ 475. **Limits of the doctrine.** The family-car doctrine is probably in force in nearly half of the states of the Union,[10] although if any trend is perceptible it is perhaps away from rather than in favor of the doctrine.[11] The limits of the doctrine are broad and simple and in many ways the liability of the head of the family is like that of a master. It is sometimes said that it is not enough that the head owns the car but that it must be kept for family use;[12] however it is hard to find authority enforcing this limitation or defining exactly what constitutes family use. The defendant must be the economic and de facto head of the family; usually this is the father but it may be a mother or a grandparent. The driver must be a regular member of the family.[13] Finally the use must be with the head's actual or implied authority and the use must be within the permission. It is on this point that the cases are numerous and largely resemble master and servant cases, with "scope of the permission" substituted for "scope of the employment." [14]

[10] Cases are collected in 132 A. L. R. 981 and earlier annotations therein cited. Much has been written on the topic; in particular see Lattin, "Vicarious Liability and the Family Automobile," 26 Mich. L. Rev. 846; McCall, "The Family Automobile," 8 N. C. L. Rev. 256. The doctrine is rejected by the Restatement; see § 238, Comment c.

The leading case for the doctrine is probably Birch v. Abercrombie (1913) 74 Wash. 486, 133 Pac. 1020; opposed, Van Blaricom v. Dodgson (1917) 220 N. Y. 111, 115 N. E. 443.

[11] See Sare v. Stetz (1950) 67 Wyo. 55, 214 P.2d 486, where in an acute decision, based on an exhaustive collection of authorities, the doctrine was rejected. See also Redding v. Barker (1950) 33 Tenn. App. 132, 230 S.W.2d 202; cf. Burns v. Main (1950) 87 F. Supp. 705, where the doctrine was adopted for Alaska.

[12] See O'Keefe v. Fitzgerald (1927) 106 Conn. 294, 137 Atl. 858; Redding v. Barker (1950) 33 Tenn. App. 132, 230 S.W.2d 202.

[13] See McGinn v. Kimmel (1950) 36 Wash.2d 786, 221 P.2d 467.

[14] See Kennedy v. Wolf (1927) 221 Ky. 111, 298 S. W. 188, noted in 16 Ky. L. J. 273; Scates v. Sandefer (1931) 163 Tenn. 558, 44 S.W.2d 310; McDowell v. Hurner (1933) 142 Ore. 611, 20 P.2d 395, noted in 46 Harv. L. Rev. 149 and 12 Ore. L. Rev. 72; Forman v. Shields (1935) 183 Wash. 333, 48 P.2d 599; Vaughan v. Booker (1940) 217 N. C. 479, 8 S.E.2d 603, 132 A. L. R. 977; Cohen v. Whiteman (1947) 75 Ga. App. 286, 43 S.E.2d 184; Dibble v. Wolff (1949) 135 Conn. 428, 65 A.2d 479.

§ 476. (B) Bailors' liability statutes. In at least half a dozen [15] jurisdictions the policy behind the family-car doctrine has been extended to cover the case of any car owner who allows another to drive it. Thus the New York statute provides that every owner of a motor vehicle or motorcycle shall be liable for injuries resulting from negligence in the operation of such vehicle "by any person legally using or operating the same with the permission, express or implied, of such owner."

Under such statutes, as under the family-car doctrine, familiar problems arise. The bailee, in violation of the permission, allows another to drive or takes aboard an unauthorized guest, or, leaving the authorized route he takes what may be a detour or a frolic. For the most part such cases have been treated as governed by master and servant analogies.[16]

§ 477. Is the owner barred by the negligence of the bailee? One very interesting problem, which has now arisen in a majority of the states having such statutes, and which has resulted in about an even split of the authorities, is this: if the bailor's car is injured by the concurring negligence of the bailee and a third party, may the bailor recover from the third party or is he barred by the negligence of his bailee?

Plainly the bailee is liable to the bailor, just as the servant would be to the master. Plainly the master would be barred by the servant's negligence.[17] Whether the head of the family

[15] At least California, District of Columbia, Iowa, Michigan, Minnesota and New York. On the statutes generally see notes, 45 Harv. L. Rev. 171, 48 Harv. L. Rev. 498 and 21 Minn. L. Rev. 823.

[16] See Grant v. Knepper (1927) 245 N. Y. 158, 156 N. E. 650, 54 A. L. R. 845; Psota v. Long Island Ry. (1927) 246 N. Y. 388, 159 N. E. 180, 62 A. L. R. 1163; Heavilin v. Wendell (1932) 214 Iowa 844, 241 N. W. 654, 83 A. L. R. 872; Kieskowski v. Odlewany (1937) 280 Mich. 388, 273 N. W. 741, noted in

24 Minn. L. Rev. 271; Abbey v. Northern States Power Co. (1937) 199 Minn. 41, 271 N. W. 122; Sonza v. Corti (1943) 22 Cal.2d 454, 139 P.2d 645, 147 A. L. R. 861, noted in 31 Calif. L. Rev. 572; Foster v. Bock (1949) 229 Minn. 428, 39 N.W.2d 862; Clemens v. U. S. (1950) 88 F. Supp. 971.

[17] Mannix v. Lamberton (1950) 167 Pa. Super. 393, 74 A.2d 515; Restatement, § 317.

would be barred by the negligence of a family member under the family-car doctrine is not clear.[18]

On the precise problem one group of cases has simply assumed that the statute sets up a system, not of master and servant but analogous thereto and with similar consequences. Hence the bailor is barred because the master would be.[19]

Another group of cases, and, it is believed, one that is to be preferred, treats the matter in the light of the policy of the statute. This, it is said, is simply to protect the public. Under the statute the injured party who gets a judgment will have a better chance to collect it; owners of cars will be more cautious in lending them. There is, however, nothing to suggest that policy requires or even favors penalizing bailors as against third parties who have negligently injured their property. Full operation is given both to the language and the policy of the statute by applying it no further than to hold bailors liable for injury negligently done to third parties by the bailee. Hence the bailor is not barred.[20]

This incidentally suggests a question, seldom discussed in the cases, namely whether under current rationalizations of *respondeat superior* it is inevitable that the negligence of the servant be imputed to the master so as to bar a recovery against a third person.

§ 478. (C) Presumptions arising from the operation of cars. A plaintiff seeking to recover on a master and servant basis is, in most jurisdictions, helped by various presumptions; perhaps it is more accurate to say different versions of the

[18] It would seem that cases involving this problem must have arisen; the writer, however, has not been able to locate them. Presumably the plaintiff is barred, since courts have struggled so to demonstrate that the family-car doctrine is a genuine manifestation of master and servant law.

[19] Secured Finance Co. v. Chicago, R. I. & P. Ry. (1929) 207 Iowa 1105, 224 N. W. 88, 61 A. L. R. 855, noted in 29 Col. L. Rev. 840; National Trucking & Storage Co. v. Driscoll (1949) 64 A.2d 304, noted in 34 Minn. L. Rev. 57 and 1 Syr. L. Rev. 328.

[20] Mills v. Gabriel (1940) 259 App. Div. 60, 18 N.Y.S.2d 78, noted in 40 Col. L. Rev. 928 and 53 Harv. L. Rev. 1386; Christensen v. Hennepin Transp. Co. (1943) 215 Minn. 394, 10 N.W.2d 406, 147 A. L. R. 945.

same basic presumption. As most commonly stated, the rule is that establishment of the defendant's ownership of the car which caused the injury raises a prima facie case against him; that is, a presumption arises that the car was being driven by defendant's servant and that the servant was in the course of employment.[21] According to some cases, the presumption does not arise until it is shown that the driver was in the defendant's employ.[22] According to others the presumption operates only in the case of commercial vehicles.[23] The presumption is one of fact, not of law, and is rebuttable; it is often rationalized in terms like those used in rationalizing res ipsa loquitur.

If defendant puts in no evidence the presumption will of course permit a verdict for plaintiff.[24] The chief disagreement is as to the effect of uncontradicted evidence by the defendant tending to show that the driver was not his servant or was not in the course of employment. Some cases say that with the introduction of rebutting testimony the presumption disappears and there must be a directed verdict for defendant unless plaintiff introduces sufficient affirmative evidence to support a verdict. Other cases hold that the truth of the rebutting testimony is always for the jury and hence there is always a jury question.[25]

---

[21] Gasque v. Saidman (1945) 44 A.2d 537; Taylor v. Freeman (1946) 186 Md. 474, 47 A.2d 500; Florida Motor Lines v. Millian (1946) 157 Fla. 21, 24 S.2d 710; Arrigo v. Lindquist (1949) 324 Mass. 278, 85 N.E.2d 782 (statute); Capello v. Aero Mayflower Transit Co. (1949) 116 Vt. 64, 68 A.2d 913; McGinn v. Kimmel (1950) 36 Wash.2d 786, 221 P.2d 467. See annotations, 96 A. L. R. 634; 5 A.L.R.2d 196.

[22] Middletown Trust Co. v. Bregman (1934) 118 Conn. 651, 174 Atl. 67; Bell v. Washam (1950) 82 Ga. App. 63, 60 S.E.2d 408; General Foods Corp. v. Coney (1950) 35 Ala. App. 492, 48 So.2d 781.

[23] See Kunkel v. Vogt (1946) 354 Pa. 279, 47 A.2d 195.

[24] Florida Motor Lines v. Millian, ante, n. 21.

[25] Frew v. Barto (1942) 345 Pa. 217, 26 A.2d 905; Bushnell v. Yoshika Tashiro (1931) 115 Cal. App. 563, 2 P.2d 550; Ashland Coca Cola Bottling Co. v. Ellison (1933) 352 Ky. 172, 66 S.W.2d 52; Nicosia v. Marangi (1951) 13 N. J. Super., 550, 81 A.2d 20.

§ 479. **Abuse of the presumption.** In the great majority
of cases this presumption is a useful and fair procedural device, forcing the defendant, who normally has the best or
even the only access to the pertinent facts, to tell what he
knows and preventing injustice to a plaintiff who has been
injured by defendant's vehicle under circumstances normally
indicating it was being driven by defendant's servant in the
course of employment but who is unable to introduce evidence to prove it. In some instances, however, the suspicion
arises that the court, in allowing the jury to find for the plaintiff in spite of defendant's plausible and uncontradicted evidence, is virtually using the presumption as a way of imposing
absolute liability on automobile owners for the negligence of
those who happen to be driving their cars.[26] This possibility
(which is thought to justify treating the presumption at this
point rather than in connection with the master's liability
proper) is a serious one and its effects would go far beyond
those of the family-car doctrine or the bailor's liability statutes since it would involve liability where the car was not
even being used with the owner's consent. Thus in Steiner
v. Royal Blue Cab Co.[27] defendant was held liable for an injury
caused by its cab although the uncontradicted testimony of its
witnesses was that the cab had been stolen.

3. *Disappearing Immunity of the Employer of an Independent Contractor*

§ 480. **In general.** A conspicuous development of recent
years has been the increase in the extent to which the employer
of an independent contractor is liable for the negligence of the
contractor or his employees. By the classical doctrine [see § 427,
ante] once it is determined from the nature of the work, the
identity and relationship of the parties, and so on, that the in-

---

[26] See Steiner v. Royal Blue Cab
Co. (1933) 172 Wash. 396, 20 P.2d
39; Bushnell v. Yoshika Tashiro
(1931) 115 Cal. App. 563, 2 P.2d
550; Miller v. Service & Sales, Inc.
(1934) 149 Ore. 11, 38 P.2d 995, 96
A. L. R. 628; Arrigo v. Lindquist
(1949) 324 Mass. 278, 85 N.E.2d
782; General Foods Corp. v. Coney
(1950) 35 Ala. App. 492, 48 So.2d
781.

[27] Ante, n. 26.

dependent contractor is such, his employer is automatically insulated from any responsibility for his misconduct.

At the present time it must be said either that the classic doctrine has been fundamentally modified or that it has become subject to an extraordinary number of exceptions.

§ 481. —— The first statement may contain a substantial amount of truth. There is no doubt that the inevitability of the classic rule has ceased to be apparent and that some thinkers would start with the assumption that one who has work being done for his benefit (and particularly if it is on his own premises) should be at least prima facie liable for negligent incidental injuries done to third parties, regardless of the extent of "control" he was theoretically exercising over the work or any similar technical test for determining the precise status of the worker.

Thus Mr. Harper, in his treatise on torts, after commenting on the increased probability of collection by the injured party if the employer is liable, the employer's normal ability to spread the cost, and the facility with which any liability can be avoided by the use of straw men or the creation of dummy corporations, remarks: [28] "These considerations, in fact, constitute such a powerful argument for the liability of the employer of an independent contractor that it would seem highly desirable for the courts to adopt the rule of liability and confine nonliability to a few exceptional cases. This, the American courts, at least, have not yet done, but there is every reason to believe that sound social policy will induce the courts to make further inroads upon the rule of nonliability in this class of cases."

Nevertheless, as Mr. Harper himself points out, the American courts have not yet expressly made liability the rule and nonliability the exception. It is still necessary to put the rule of liability in terms of exceptions. The exceptions are vaguely defined and tend to blend into one another. It nevertheless seems possible to put most of the instances of liability into two or three general groups.

[28] P. 646.

§ 482. The employer's own fault. In the cases in this category the employer's liability is clearly not vicarious but based on pure tort theory; in others, the liability would appear to be somewhere between primary and vicarious. Nevertheless, since in all these cases the pressure to treat the cases *as if they were* instances of vicarious liability is so apparent as to justify treating them together and dealing with them here.

In the first place the employer may be liable for his negligence in the selection or direction of the contractor. Thus in Mullich v. Brocker [29] it was held that a jury might find the defendant negligent in employing a sixteen-year-old boy to break a horse, when it was not shown that the boy was qualified for the job or that defendant made any particular efforts to ascertain his qualifications. A number of cases assert such a rule,[30] and its logical soundness is not subject to question; it is to be observed, however, that in the cases where it is employed it often seems to be in the nature of a makeweight, and that the facts supporting a finding of negligence are not extremely convincing.

Akin to this is the situation where the so-called "independent" contractor is in fact a dummy corporation organized by the employer primarily to avoid possible liability.[31]

§ 483. —— Liability also may be imposed where the plans or directions of the employer necessarily or probably involve injury to plaintiff [32] or where the employer, entitled to check the progress of the work, does so negligently [33] or where the employer affirmatively takes charge, as in Weldon v. Steiner [34]

---

[29] (1905) 119 Mo. App. 332, 97 S. W. 549.

[30] Board of Commissioners of Wabash County v. Pearson (1889) 120 Ind. 426, 22 N. E. 134; Norwalk Gaslight Co. v. Norwalk (1893) 63 Conn. 495, 28 Atl. 32; Joslin v. Idaho Times (1939) 60 Idaho 235, 91 P.2d 386; Richton Tie & Timber Co. v. Smith (1950) 210 Miss. 148, 48 So.2d 618. Cf. Berg v. Parsons (1898) 156 N. Y. 109, 50 N. E. 957.

[31] See Holbrook v. Perkins (1906) 147 Fed. 166.

[32] See Marbury v. Louisiana Highway Commission (La. App., 1934) 153 So. 590; Pannella v. Reilly (1939) 304 Mass. 172, 23 N.E.2d 87.

[33] See Hanley v. Central Savings Bank (1938) 255 App. Div. 642, 8 N.Y.S.2d 371.

[34] (1939) 138 Pa. Super. 66, 10 A.2d 19.

where the employer of a contractor erecting a street sign insisted that the latter continue with the work in spite of his protests that the high wind made the work dangerous. And where the work is illegal the employer is liable for its negligent performance although there is little causal connection between the illegality and the negligence. Thus in the leading English case of Ellis v. Sheffield Gas Company [35] defendant, without a license and so illegally, employed a contractor to dig a trench in a public street to lay pipes in. In so doing, the contractor left a pile of stones in the street, over which the plaintiff tripped, injuring herself. Defendant was held liable, Wightman, J., saying:

"It seems to me, as it did at the trial, that the fact of the defendants having employed the contractors to do a thing illegal in itself made a distinction between this and the cases which have been cited. But for the direction to break up the streets, the accident could not have happened; and though it may be that if the workmen employed had been careful in the way in which they heaped up the earth and stones the plaintiff would have avoided them, still I think the nuisance which the defendant employed the contractors to commit was the primary cause of the accident."

§ 484. **Nondelegable duty.** Perhaps logically not to be distinguished from the cases just dealt with is a group of cases in which the liability of the employer is rationalized on the theory that he was under a nondelegable duty. (Normally a breach of duty resulting in injury is treated as a tort; if such a concept of duty is involved here, the employer becomes a tortfeasor as in the cases, ante.) This includes the duties of carriers and innkeepers, a subject, however, too extensive and independent to be treated here. It includes duties imposed by statute, as those of a railroad to install cattleguards or to keep highway crossings in safe condition.[36] It includes the

---

[35] (1853) 2 El. & Bl. 767. See also Dinger v. Burnham (1950) 360 Mo. 465, 228 S.W.2d 696.

[36] Chicago, K. & W. R. Co. v. Hutchinson (1891) 45 Kan. 186, 25 Pac. 576; Choctaw, O. & W. Ry. Co. v. Wilker (1906) 16 Okla. 384, 84 Pac. 1086.

duty of a municipality to keep its streets in safe condition [37] and of a landlord who has assumed the duty of making a repair to see that it is done safely, as in Bailey v. Zlotnick,[38] where a landlord who had undertaken to install a hot water system in the demised premises was held liable for the negligence of the contractor who installed it so negligently that it leaked and ruined the walls. And the owner of an apartment building cannot delegate to a contractor the delegation to keep the building's elevator safe for tenants.[39]

§ 485. —— Likewise is included the duty of a storekeeper to keep the premises safe for business visitors, as in Lineaweaver v. Wanamaker,[40] where defendant's department store had a large court in the center which was covered by a skylight. A contractor employed to make improvements in the skylight took inadequate safety precautions and a customer was injured by a falling piece of glass. The court held that defendant had failed to fulfill its duty to exercise reasonable care to protect its customers from harm.[41]

Another situation which perhaps can be rationalized in terms of nondelegable duty is that where a license or some other form of permission is required, usually because the dangerous character of the work is thought to make it imperative that it be done only by those who have met stipulated standards of competency. In such case where the employer and not the contractor holds the license, the employer is normally regarded as responsible for the negligence of the contractor. In such cases, it has been suggested [42] that the privilege is regarded as personal to the holder of the license, and

[37] See Baltimore v. Leonard (1917) 129 Md. 621, 99 Atl. 891; Hirsch v. Schwartz & Cohn, Inc. (1931) 256 N. Y. 7, 175 N. E. 353.

[38] (1945) 149 F.2d 505.

[39] Brown v. Pepperdine Foundation (1943) 23 Cal.2d 256, 143 P.2d 929, noted in 32 Calif. L. Rev. 196. See also Suttar v. Texas Co. (1950) 90 F. Supp. 7.

[40] (1930) 299 Pa. 45, 149 Atl. 91.

[41] And see Wilson v. Thayer County Agricultural Society (1927) 115 Neb. 579, 213 N. W. 966, noted in 6 Neb. L. Bull. 179 and 37 Yale L. J. 113, where an invitee at a county fair was injured by the negligence of a contractor putting on an exhibition of fireworks. See also Paleockrasas v. Garcia (1950) 183 F.2d 244.

[42] Restatement of Torts, § 417.

as only granted on condition that he assume personal responsibility. Another possible rationalization of the rule might be that plainly the license is to be held by the person doing the work; to make the situation consistent with this assumption we must treat the contractor as the employer's servant; on no other interpretation would the license holder be "doing" the work.

§ 486. ——— A common current instance of this is furnished by the trucking company which operates as a carrier under a required state or federal license and which does its business wholly or in part by trucks which it does not own but which are owned and driven by individuals or corporations who furnish them under contract to the trucking company. The trucking company is normally held liable for the negligence of the driver. In such a case the Supreme Court of Indiana said: "Appellant [defendant] furnished the permit to transport interstate shipments as a common carrier, and furnished the freight to be transported. . . . Glade [owner-driver] could not engage in that business except as the agent or employee of appellant. The appellant does not deny that it authorized Glade to transport the freight contained in the truck on the evening of the accident, nor does it dispute that Glade transported that freight without any permit issued to him by the Public Service Commission of Indiana, nor does it dispute that it held a permit issued by that commission over the designated route from Chicago to Louisville. The appellant was the one party concerned which held such permit and such right under the law of the state of Indiana. It cannot escape liability upon the theory of its affirmative paragraph of answer, that Glade was an independent contractor." [43]

[43] Bates Motor Transport Lines, Inc. v. Mayer (1938) 213 Ind. 664, 14 N.E.2d 91. See also Sanford v. Goodridge (1944) 234 Iowa 1036, 13 N.W.2d 40; Venuto v. Robinson (1914) 118 F.2d 679; Kissell v. Motor Age Transit (1947) 357 Pa. 204, 53 A.2d 593; Kemp v. Creston Transfer Co. (1947) 70 F. Supp. 521; Costello v. Smith (1950) 179 F.2d 715; Simon v. McCullough Transfer Co. (1951) 155 Ohio St. 104, 98 N.E.2d 19.

§ 487. **Inherently dangerous work.** The most common and logically most troublesome of the exceptions to the normal non-liability of the employer of an independent contractor is that involved where the work to be done is "dangerous in the absence of special precautions," "inherently dangerous" [44] or "intrinsically dangerous."

The phrases quoted indicate clearly the basic concept which underlies this exception; they also show the difficulty, if not the impossibility, of taking any distinctions other than general ones of degree. Nearly any work may cause harm if proper precautions are not taken; whatever danger may lie in doing a job is necessarily intrinsic or inherent in it; the point is not that the danger is intrinsic but that the intrinsic danger is greater than the intrinsic danger in some other activities. It should be noted further that this exception does not require, or even involve, activities which for one reason or another the general tort law requires to be done at peril, such as blasting or keeping a tiger for a pet. In such cases, while the work could readily be categorized as intrinsically dangerous [45] it seems that the employer's liability could be put on a simpler ground, namely that one who causes work of this type to be done, is liable for possible harmful consequences. [46]

§ 488. —— Probably all that can be done by way of classification is to use the most descriptive adjectives possible and speak of the work as conspicuously, exceptionally, unusually dangerous and the like, to signify that its salient characteristic is that the mention or sight of such work immediately causes the reaction "DANGER!" in the mind of the listener or witness in a way that other work, perhaps in fact equally dangerous, does not. Thus one observing a tree being cut

---

[44] See Restatement of Torts, §§ 416 and 427. The treatment of this subject generally in the Restatement of Torts, §§ 409–429, is so subtle and subdivided into various sections based on propositions resting on distinctions im-perceptible to the naked eye, as to make it of little use.

[45] See Asheville Const. Co. v. Southern Ry. (1927) 19 F.2d 32.

[46] See Baier v. Glen Alden Coal Co. (1939) 332 Pa. 561, 3 A.2d 349.

down in a populous area or a heavy electric sign being put in place above a much-travelled street is instinctively impressed with the danger and the need for special precautions as he is not where he sees a neighbor's porch being painted, although he may be drenched the next moment with paint from a fallen bucket.

Two factors that in fact usually limit the doctrine may be mentioned: (a) the work is normally work done on the employer's premises, and (b) the plaintiff is normally a member of the public properly going about his business in the danger zone. This is not surprising. It is hard to think of common instances of work sent to the contractor's shop to be done which would be dangerous; if such instances arose the same psychology that suggests throwing the risk on the employer where the danger exists on his premises would probably put it on the contractor who was making a dangerous use of his premises. And, if the plaintiff were not a member of the public outside the defendant's premises the question of liability to him would doubtless turn on his status on the defendant's property and what care was owed to him because of that status.

§ 489. **Inherently dangerous work: Instances.** Instances of this type of liability are legion. Typical is Stubblefield v. Federal Reserve Bank [47] where a contractor was making repairs and alterations on defendant's roof and plaintiff, a pedestrian, was hit by a falling wooden wedge, eight inches long and weighing about three and one half ounces. The court thus sets forth the scene and the law: ". . . the independent contractor . . . was removing and resetting the cornice stones, each stone weighed from 300 to 500 pounds, one hundred feet above one of the downtown streets of St. Louis. The superintendent testified that the wooden wedges would fall when the stones were moved unless the workmen held on to them. The sidewalk was unprotected. The mere recital of the nature of the work demonstrates its inherent danger and there was a primary, non-

---

[47] (1947) 356 Mo. 1018, 204 S.W.2d 718.

delegable duty on the owner and the general contractor to take
measures commensurate with the danger.''

Typical also is a question the case raises. Suppose the defendant had employed a painter to paint his portrait on the
roof and the painter had carelessly dropped over the edge a
small brush, a tube of paint, or any other bit of equipment
not more than eight inches long or weighing more than three
and one half ounces. Would defendant have been liable?
Plainly in the actual case plaintiff's position would have been
better (however much worse his condition might have been)
had he been hit by one of the stones weighing from 300 to 500
pounds. Aspects of this kind of question are dealt with in
§ 491, post.

§ 490. —— In Luthringer v. Moore,[48] the owner of a city
building employed a contractor to rid the basement of cock-
roaches. To do so the contractor used cyanide gas, some of
which leaked out and injured the plaintiff, employed as a
clerk in a store in the same building. It was held that the
defendant would be liable but for the fact that he had not
known, or had reason to know, that the contractor would use
so deadly a type of gas.[49]

Other typical situations where liability has been imposed
are where a contractor located a high tension wire so that it
sagged against a guy wire and caused the electrocution of the
plaintiff,[50] where a contractor erecting an electric sign negligently dropped a bucket on the plaintiff,[51] where a contractor
delivering coal left the coal hole in the sidewalk open,[52] where
a window cleaner, working without safety belt, fell on the
plaintiff [53] and where a contractor furnishing the steelwork

[48] (Cal. App., 1947) 181 P.2d 89,
affirmed without opinion on this
point, (1948) 31 Cal.2d 489, 190
P.2d 1.

[49] And see Ferguson v. Ashken-
azy (1940) 307 Mass. 197, 29
N.E.2d 828.

[50] Person v. Cauldwell-Wingate
Co. (1949) 176 F.2d 237.

[51] Richman Bros. Co. v. Miller

(1936) 131 Ohio St. 424, 3 N.E.2d
360.

[52] Cole v. Durham (1918) 176 N.
C. 289, 97 S. E. 33, 11 A. L. R. 560.
And see Globe Indemnity Co. v.
Schmitt (1944) 142 Ohio St. 595,
53 N.E.2d 790.

[53] Doll v. Ribetti (1913) 203
Fed. 593.

in the building of a subway left beams so carelessly piled that one of them fell on a child.[54]

It should be noted that the predictability in this type of situation is not high. In a considerable number of cases, many not differing markedly from those mentioned above, recovery has been refused because of lack of sympathy for the doctrine, a holding that the work was not dangerous enough to come within it, or a finding that the contractor's negligence was collateral.[55]

§ 491. **Collateral negligence.** The term "collateral negligence"[56] appears to have originated in the English case of Hole v. Sittingbourne & Sheerness Ry.,[57] where the defendants were authorized by Parliament to build a drawbridge across a certain navigable stream. The contractor employed to do this did it so negligently that the bridge refused to open and plaintiff's ship could not pass through. For the ensuing delay and damages resulting therefrom, plaintiff sought and recovered damages. Two of the judges who wrote opinions spoke of collateral negligence, holding the negligence of the contractor not to be in that category. Neither made the matter very clear; perhaps the most suggestive of the two statements is that of Wilde, B.:

"The distinction appears to me to be that, when work is being done under a contract, if an accident happens and an injury is caused by negligence in a matter entirely collateral to the contract, the liability turns on the question whether the relation of master and servant exists. But when the thing

---

[54] Boylhart v. DiMarco & Reiman (1936) 270 N. Y. 217, 200 N. E. 793.

[55] See Mercer v. Ohio Fuel Gas Co. (Ohio, 1947) 80 N.E.2d 635; Barlow v. Krieghoff Co. (1944) 310 Mich. 195, 16 N.W.2d 715; Smith v. Bank of Commerce (1916) 135 Tenn. 398, 186 S. W. 465, 18 A. L. R. 788; Swearsky v. Stanley Dry Goods Co. (1936) 122 Conn. 7, 186 Atl. 566; Silveus v. Grossman

(1932) 307 Pa. 272, 161 Atl. 362, noted in 81 U. of Pa. L. Rev. 232; Davis v. Whiting & Son Co. (1909) 201 Mass. 91, 87 N. E. 199, 18 A. L. R. 782.

[56] See Smith, "Collateral Negligence," 25 Minn. L. Rev. 399; Chapman, "Liability for the Negligence of Independent Contractors," 50 L. Q. Rev. 71.

[57] (1861) 6 H. & N. 488.

contracted to be done causes the mischief, and the injury can only be said to arise from the authority of the employer because the thing contracted to be done is imperfectly performed, there the employer must be taken to have authorized the act and is responsible for it. The present defendants were authorized . . . to build a bridge over the Swale. Instead of erecting the bridge themselves, they employed another person to do it. What was done was done under their authority. In the course of executing their order, the contractor by doing the work imperfectly, obstructed the navigation. It is the same as if they had done it themselves."

§ 492. —— Precisely what does this mean? It is hard to say. No doubt it means that if the contractor while bringing up material in a barge negligently collides with a vessel on the stream, defendant would not be liable (although he plainly would have had the contractor been a servant). This was collateral; the injury resulted from no failure of the defendant's obligation to build a proper bridge. But suppose a workman, at work on the bridge, drops a wrench on a person passing in a boat below. Is this collateral? Perhaps so, though one can scarcely say that the opinions afford any answer. But, in any event, this would be what most commonly appears to be involved in modern decisions speaking of collateral negligence.

§ 493. Thus in Bailey v. Zlotnick [58] where the landlord was held liable for injuries resulting from leaking pipes installed by a contractor, the court remarks that the landlord would not have been liable had the contractor dropped a pipe on the tenant. In Rosenquist v. Brookdale Homes [59] the employer was held not liable for the negligence of the contractor's employees in allowing water from a hose to accumulate and freeze, whereby the plaintiff slipped on it and was injured. This negligence, it was said, was collateral to the work the contractor was employed to perform. In Jourdenais v. Hay-

[58] Ante, n. 38.
[59] (1945) 133 N. J. L. 305, 44 A.2d 33.

den [60] the employer was held not liable where the servants of a contractor, employed to install an electric sign, stretched rope across the sidewalk in such a way that plaintiff tripped. The court remarked that the injuries "resulted, not from the hazards inhering in the work, but from one created by the careless act of the men who were doing it."

By Sec. 427 of the Restatement of Torts the employer's liability for work "inherently dangerous" is limited to "harm resulting from the dangerous character of the work." In the Comment it is said: "The liability stated in this Section extends only to harm which is caused by the failure so to act as to minimize to the utmost the danger inherent in the work or in the instrumentalities used. It does not extend to harm caused by negligence in a particular detail of the work which in itself is not inherently dangerous."

§ 494. ——— It is believed that the idea of "collateral negligence" is best explained in terms of legal causation as that phrase is used (or misused) in tort law. The question is one of risk: for what risks, and to whom, has the employer assumed responsibility? When the guard in the famous Palsgraf case shoved the ascending passenger, he created an unreasonable risk of injuring the passenger or, at least, of injuring his package, but not of injuring Mrs. Palsgraf, 25 feet away, by causing the scales by which she was standing to fall on her. That being so, there was no liability although the scales were in fact thereby caused to fall on Mrs. Palsgraf.

So, if the employer's liability is based on his negligence in employing a particular contractor the resulting injury must be within the particular risk created. For example, if the contractor was unsuitable because his equipment was inadequate or because he was prone to be drunk on the job, the employer is not responsible for the carelessness of the contractor's servant in dropping a brick, though he would be for an injury attributable to the inadequacy of the equipment or to the contractor's drunkenness. Similarly, if the employer's

[60] (1932) 104 Vt. 215, 158 Atl. 664.

liability is based on his negligence in supervision, it plainly
has to be shown that what happened was within the risk
created by the faulty supervision.

§ 495. —— Again, if the liability is to be based on nondelegable duty the precise nature and extent of the duty must
be examined. The storekeeper is obliged to use reasonable
care in keeping the premises in a safe condition. If he fails
in that obligation, personally, vicariously, or through a contractor, he is liable. He is not responsible for the misconduct
of persons lawfully on the premises, at least unless he has special reason to anticipate such misconduct. Hence he is no more
responsible for the careless handling of a wrench by a contractor than he would be for the careless handling of an um-
brella by a customer. The same considerations apply to the
landlord who has assumed the obligation of putting in a heating system. He must have a proper one installed but he is
not responsible for the plumber's mishandling of a wrench.

§ 496. —— In the "inherently dangerous" cases the same
analysis can be used. The employer is not strictly at fault,
since such a doctrine assumes the work to be lawful. Because
of the inherent danger, however, he is treated somewhat as
if he were at fault: he is responsible for consequences within
the inherent danger zone. A man driving a dynamite-laden
truck down a bumpy street at 25 miles per hour might be
thought not to be driving negligently, qua driving, so as to
be responsible if he ran into a pedestrian, and yet still be
thought negligent qua the risk of explosions so as to be liable
if the bumps set off the dynamite. In the same way the employer who contracts to have inherently dangerous work done
becomes liable for the special risks involved but not for the
others. Thus if the work involved is tearing down a rickety
old building the obvious special dangers are that the building
or part of it will fall on a passer. If this happens through the
contractor's negligence, the employer is liable. But if the
contractor (or his servant) carrying a ladder to the job,
negligently strikes a pedestrian, the employer will not be

liable; from the standpoint of ladder risk to pedestrians there was nothing inherently dangerous about the enterprise.

From this standpoint the facts of the Stubblefield case [61] can profitably be reconsidered. Was the inherent danger there associated specially with the moving of heavy stones high above a street, or simply with working high above a street, with its incidental risk that *some* object might be dropped? If only the former, the contractor's negligence in dropping a block of wood weighing only three and one half ounces would seem to be merely collateral.

It is believed that most (though certainly not all) of the cases in this field are susceptible of analysis in the manner suggested.[62]

§ 497. **Incidence of liability among employer, contractor and subcontractor.** Obviously the fact that the employer is liable does not exonerate the contractor from liability. He has (at least where no subcontractor is involved) either been personally at fault or is liable for the tort of his servant; there is no reason why ordinary principles of torts and agency should not operate. And, in spite of the fact that the employer's liability is often put in terms of breach of duty, he is treated as so far free from active fault as to be entitled to indemnity against the contractor.[63]

If the immediate cause of the injury is the misconduct of a subcontractor, is the incidence of liability altered? The liability of the employer would appear to be the same, at least where it is based on inherent danger or nondelegable duty.[64]

---

[61] Ante, § 228.

[62] For a full citation of authorities on "collateral negligence" see Smith, article cited, ante, n. 56; Prosser, Torts, pp. 488–490.

The most exhaustive collection of cases on "inherent danger" "nondelegable duty" and the like will be found in three notes, 23 A. L. R. 984, 23 A. L. R. 1016 and 23 A. L. R. 1084. See also the excellent analysis in a note in 39 Yale L. J. 861.

[63] See Tipaldi v. Riverside Memorial Chapel (1948) 273 App. Div. 414, 78 N.Y.S.2d 12, aff'd memorandum decision (1948) 298 N. Y. 686, 82 N. E. 585; Globe Indemnity Co. v. Schmitt (1944) 142 Ohio St. 595, 53 N.E.2d 790.

[64] See Schwartz v. Merola Bros. (1943) 290 N. Y. 145, 48 N.E.2d 299.

The facts of the particular case would seem to govern in other situations.

§ 498. —— It is less obvious that the contractor should be liable, where the case is one of inherent danger or nondelegable duty. He is not under the nondelegable duty, nor was it his choice to do the dangerous work. In the latter case the employer's liability seems to be associated with his ownership of the premises and to be thought of in some sense as based on a duty to keep one's property from being harmful to the public. Such a consideration has no applicability to the contractor.

However, it seems commonly to be held that the contractor is liable. "The exception [to the general rule of nonliability] arises when the contract directly requires the performance of a work intrinsically dangerous, however skilfully it may be performed. [In this instance blasting.] This is true because the original contractor is the author of the mischief resulting from it, whether he does the work himself, or lets it to another." [65]

---

[65] Loyd v. Herrington (Tex. Civ. App., 1944) 178 S.W.2d 694, rev'd (1944) 143 Tex. 135, 182 S.W.2d 1003, on the ground that the subcontractor's negligence was "collateral." See also Gulf Refining Co. v. Walker (1942) 124 F.2d 420; Blair v. Durham (1943) 134 F.2d 729; Person v. Cauldwell-Wingate Co. (1949) 176 F.2d 237.

CHAPTER XVI

THE DUTIES AND LIABILITIES OF THE AGENT TO THE PRINCIPAL

§ 499. In general. It is not possible to consider here every possible duty which the representative may owe to his constituent, but the most important duties may be briefly dealt with, and the principles given will suggest the rules which will govern other cases. The cases largely concern agents rather than servants, but some obligations peculiar to servants are included. It is also true that the principles involved are equally valid as to servants, where they are applicable.

§ 500. Agent's duty of loyalty: In general. It is the duty of the agent to conduct himself with the utmost loyalty and fidelity to the interests of his principal, and not to place himself or voluntarily permit himself to be placed in a position where his own interests or those of any other person whom he has undertaken to represent may conflict with the interests of his principal.

When the principal employs an agent, the law presumes that he does so in order to secure to himself the benefits of the agent's skill, experience or discretion, and to reap the fruits of the performance of the undertaking. The law presumes that he expects—and it gives him the right to expect—that the agent so employed will endeavor to further the principal's interests, and will use his powers for the principal's benefit. If, then, instead of serving the principal, the agent is seeking to serve himself, or some other person—if, instead of promoting his principal's interests, the agent is endeavoring to promote his own or some other person's interest at the expense of the principal's—the fundamental considerations underlying the existence of the relation will be defeated. This the law constantly aims to prevent.[1]

[1] See, in general, People v. 222; Tisdale v. Tisdale (1855) 2 Township Board (1863) 11 Mich. Sneed (Tenn.) 596; Porter v.

The rule, however, is one based upon the presumed intention of the principal and is designed to protect his interests. The principal may therefore waive the benefit of the rule so far as he is concerned, if he does so with full knowledge of the facts. In the absence of such a waiver, the rule is absolute.

§ 501. Incapacity resulting: May not be agent of both parties.

In order to secure the performance of this duty of the agent and to remove as far as possible all temptation and opportunity to violate it (and also to prevent extended and unprofitable litigation as to the agent's good faith) the law positively forbids the agent's doing many acts which might otherwise seem harmless. Proof of actual injury to the principal is not ordinarily required. The law judges these cases rather by the tendency of similar acts, and will often strike down a transaction even though it could be shown that nothing improper was done in that case or intended to be done, if its general character brings it within the forbidden class. Consequently, the law does not ordinarily permit a person to assume to become an agent where he already has in the same transaction such an interest, either of his own or as agent for some other person, as may prevent his acting fairly toward his principal. The law recognizes that "no man can serve two masters" and give to each of them his undivided allegiance and support.

§ 502. ——
Where, however, the principal is fully advised of the adverse interest, and is given an opportunity to protect himself and to refuse to be represented by an agent who cannot give him undivided attention, and he still is willing

Woodruff (1882) 36 N. J. Eq. 174; Levy v. Spencer (1893) 18 Colo. 532, 33 Pac. 415; Hofflin v. Moss (1895) 67 Fed. 440; Ramspeck v. Pattillo (1898) 104 Ga. 772, 30 S. E. 962; Wildberger v. Hartford Fire Ins. Co. (1894) 72 Miss. 338, 17 So. 282; Lum v. McEwen (1894) 56 Minn. 278, 57 N. W. 279; Everhart v. Searle (1872) 71 Pa. 256; Economy Baler Co. v. Cohen (1924) 296 Fed. 904; Fast v. Judy (1925) 83 Ind. App. 85, 147 N. E. 728; Doyen v. Bauer (1941) 211 Minn. 140, 300 N. W. 451; Faultersalk v. Clintonville Sales Corp. (1949) 253 Wis. 432, 34 N.W.2d 56.

to employ the agent, he may do so; and if he does, the law holds that he has waived the benefit of the rule, so far as he is concerned.

If, however, there was already a principal on the other side represented by the agent in question, the willingness of the second principal to accept him would not be conclusive of all the questions which might arise. If I knowingly induce or permit the agent of the other party to the transaction to enter into my service, I would ordinarily be doing that other party an injury. Although I might not complain, he might. Transactions entered into through the common agent, while the other principal was ignorant of and not consenting to such double agency, could ordinarily be set aside by him, and I could claim no benefit through them. The guilty agent also would be implicated, and could ordinarily recover no compensation from either principal: Not from the first principal, because he had betrayed him; nor could he ordinarily recover from me, because both he and I were parties to an illegal contract. Even if I were innocent he would be guilty.[2]

Except with the full knowledge and consent of both principals, therefore, a person who is already agent of one party may not ordinarily undertake to act as agent of the other also in any case wherein, by reason of the confidence reposed or the judgment, discretion, or protective devotion required to be exercised, there may be a conflict in the performance of the duties which he has undertaken to each.

§ 503. **Exceptions: Middlemen, etc.** While however the above rule is abundantly established, there may be cases wherein, by reason of differences in the circumstances, it does not apply. If his duties to each do not conflict, the same person may be the agent of two principals even though those principals are having dealings with each other.[3] Thus he

---

[2] See Rice v. Wood (1873) 113 Mass. 133; Everhart v. Searle (1872) 71 Pa. 256; Andrews v. Ramsay (1903) 2 K. B. 635.

The privilege of repudiation is personal to the principal and can-

not be exercised by a third party. Newton v. Mann (1943) 111 Colo. 76, 137 P.2d 776, ann. 147 A. L. R. 772.

[3] See Northrup v. Germania Fire Ins. Co. (1879) 48 Wis. 420, 4 N.

might properly be the agent of one to make payment, and of the other to receive payment, of an agreed or ascertained sum.[4]

So where he is not relied upon to bargain for either party but is merely an introducer or middleman, whose function is merely to bring parties together who may then bargain for themselves—as is often the case with the real estate broker— it is frequently held that there is no legal objection to his serving in this double capacity, and that he may properly recover commissions from both principals.[5] The exceptional character of this employment, however, should clearly appear.[6]

Of course, if the double agency might otherwise be held to be objectionable, the fact that both principals with full knowledge assented to it would cure the objection.

§ 504. **May not deal with himself.** The same general considerations apply where the agent at the time he undertakes to act is also secretly acting in the same transaction on his own account. Except with the full knowledge and consent of his principal, an agent authorized to buy for his principal may not buy of himself;[7] an agent authorized to sell, may

W. 350; Nolte v. Hulbert (1882) 37 Ohio St. 445; Adams Mining Co. v. Senter (1872) 26 Mich. 73; Wassell v. Reardon (1851) 11 Ark. 705.

In case of a conflict in interest, the agent, it is said, may decline to act for both, but act for one. Shepherd v. Lanfear (1833) 5 La. 336.

Some agents, like the auctioneer, regularly and openly act for both parties, as in making the memorandum of sale, and as this is done with the implied consent of both parties it is unobjectionable. See Scott v. Mann (1871) 36 Tex. 157.

[4] See Nolte v. Hulbert, ante.

[5] See Rupp v. Sampson (1860) 82 Mass. (16 Gray) 398; McClure v. Luke (1907) 154 Fed. 647; Ranney

v. Donovan (1889) 78 Mich. 318, 44 N. W. 276; Friar v. Smith (1899) 120 Mich. 411, 79 N. W. 633; Knauss v. Brewing Co. (1894) 142 N. Y. 70, 36 N. E. 867.

[6] See Walker v. Osgood (1867) 98 Mass. 348; Scribner v. Collar (1879) 40 Mich. 375; Raisin v. Clark (1874) 41 Md. 158; Rossi v. Fireman's Ins. Co. of Newark (1933) 310 Pa. 342, 165 Atl. 16.

[7] See Conkey v. Bond (1867) 36 N. Y. 427; Taussig v. Hart (1874) 58 N. Y. 425; Disbrow v. Secor (1889) 58 Conn. 35, 18 Atl. 981; Haines v. Biddle (1937) 325 Pa. 441, 188 Atl. 843.

An agent alone cannot effect a contract between himself and his principal. Notice of an attempted

not sell to himself;[8] an agent authorized to buy or sell for his principal may not buy or sell for himself;[9] nor may an agent take advantage of the knowledge of his principal's business, acquired while acting in a confidential capacity, to make profit for himself at his principal's expense.[10]

§ 505. —— And what the agent may not do directly, he will not be permitted to do indirectly, as by buying, selling,

contract works as an offer to the principal. Fulkerson v. National Union Fire Ins. Co. (1923) 291 Fed. 784.

[8] See Rich v. Black (1896) 173 Pa. 92, 33 Atl. 380; Greenfield Bank v. Simons (1882) 133 Mass. 415; Shannon v. Marmaduke (1855) 14 Tex. 217; People v. Township Board (1863) 11 Mich. 222; Dwight v. Blackmar (1852) 2 Mich. 330; Jansen v. Williams (1893) 36 Neb. 869, 55 N. W. 279; Meek v. Hurst (1909) 223 Mo. 688, 122 S. W. 1022; Robertson v. Chapman (1893) 152 U. S. 673, 14 S. Ct. 741, 38 L. Ed. 592; Blank v. Aronson (1911) 187 Fed. 241. But see Hutton v. Sherrard (1914) 183 Mich. 356, 150 N. W. 135; Doyen v. Bauer (1941) 211 Minn. 140, 300 N. W. 451; Eagle Indemnity Co. v. Cherry (1950) 182 F.2d 298.

In Spalding v. Mattingly (1887) 89 Ky. 83, 1 S. W. 488, it is said that this rule applies only to agents who owe some discretionary or fiduciary duty, and not to mere servants.

[9] See Rose v. Hayden (1886) 35 Kan. 106, 10 Pac. 554; Snyder v. Wolford (1885) 33 Minn. 175, 22 N. W. 254; Wood v. Rabe (1884) 96 N. Y. 414; Wolford v. Herrington (1873) 74 Pa. 311; Gladiator

Consolidated Gold Mines & Milling Co. v. Steele (1906) 132 Iowa 446, 106 N. W. 737.

[10] See Davis v. Hamlin (1883) 108 Ill. 39; Gower v. Andrew (1881) 59 Cal. 119; Essex Trust Co. v. Enwright (1913) 214 Mass. 507, 102 N. E. 441; McKinley v. Williams (1896) 74 Fed. 94; Trice v. Comstock (1903) 121 Fed. 620; Horn Pond Ice Co. v. Pearson (1929) 267 Mass. 256, 166 N. E. 640, 9 B. U. L. Rev. 259, 28 Mich. L. Rev. 95, 14 Minn. L. Rev. 546 (cases in which the agent attempted to acquire and hold leases, etc., of property of which, while acting in a confidential capacity, the agent had learned the value and of the principal's desire and intention to acquire for himself). See also Forlaw v. Augusta Naval Stores Co. (1905) 124 Ga. 261, 52 S. E. 898. Byrne v. Barrett (1935) 268 N. Y. 199, 197 N. E. 217; ann. 100 A. L. R. 684; Fairchild Engine & Airplane Corp. v. Cox (1943) 50 N.Y.S.2d 643; Junker v. Plummer (1946) 320 Mass. 76, 67 N.E.2d 667; ann. 165 A. L. R. 1453; Colonial Laundries, Inc. v. Henry (1927) 48 R. I. 332, 138 Atl. 47. Cf. Fulton Laundry Co. v. Johnson (1922) 140 Md. 359, 117 Atl. 753.

or dealing in the name of another, but really for himself.[11] A fortiori does the rule apply to his clerks and agents.[12]

Of course, in all these cases the transaction may be upheld if done with the full knowledge and consent of the principal, but the agent must show that fact, and he certainly cannot succeed if it appears that he withheld important information, or did not make a full and frank disclosure of the facts.[13]

§ 506. **May not give his time or efforts to competing interests.** It may also be a violation of the duty of fidelity and loyalty for the agent to give his time or efforts to competing enterprises or interests. As is said in one case, "Manifestly, when a servant becomes engaged in a business which necessarily renders him a competitor and rival of his master, no matter how much or how little time and attention he devotes to it, he has an interest against his duty." [14]

§ 507. **Remedies of principal.** In all of these cases wherein the principal finds that, without his knowledge or consent, he has been dealing with his agent, the transaction is voidable at the election of the principal. It makes no difference that the

---

[11] See Shannon v. Marmaduke (1855) 14 Tex. 217; In re Boschulte's Estate (1936) 130 Neb. 284, 264 N. W. 881; Shepard & Co. v. Kaufman (1926) 88 Pa. Super. 57.

[12] See Gardner v. Ogden (1860) 22 N. Y. 327; Bedford Coal Co. v. Parke County Coal Co. (1909) 44 Ind. App. 390, 89 N. E. 412.

[13] See Van Dusen v. Bigelow (1904) 13 N. Dak. 277, 100 N. W. 723; Norris v. Tayloe (1868) 49 Ill. 17; Cook v. Berlin Mills (1877) 43 Wis. 433; Pittsburgh Equitable Meter Co. v. Paul C. Loeber & Co. (1947) 160 F.2d 721.

[14] Dieringer v. Meyer (1877) 42 Wis. 311. See also Thompson v. Havelock (1808) 1 Camp. 527; Puritas Laundry Co. v. Green

(1911) 15 Cal. App. 654, 115 Pac. 660; Michigan Crown Fender v. Welch (1920) 211 Mich. 148, 178 N. W. 684, 13 A. L. R. 896; Connelly v. Special Road & Bridge Dist. No. 5 (1930) 99 Fla. 456, 126 So. 794; ann. 71 A. L. R. 933; Singletary v. Mann (1946) 157 Fla. 37, 24 So.2d 718.

Compare Lindsay v. Swift (1918) 230 Mass. 407, 119 N. E. 787.

An agent who has agreed to give his entire time to his principal may not deal in the business of the agency for his own benefit. Michigan Crown Fender Co. v. Welch, ante; cf. Mayberry v. Newell (1925) 200 Iowa 458, 204 N. W. 413.

principal has not been injured, or that the agent has given him as good terms as anybody would, or even perhaps better terms, or that the sale or purchase has been at the price fixed by the principal; or that there was no bad faith or intention to defraud; it is still voidable at the option of the principal.

On the other hand, the principal is not obliged to disaffirm: if he is satisfied with the transaction he may permit it to stand. The agent may not set up his own default to escape. Nor, ordinarily, may third persons raise the question if the principal does not.

§ 508. —— If what the agent has done is to acquire for himself what it was his duty to acquire for the principal, the principal may charge him as a trustee,[15] and, upon reimbursing him for his proper expenses, may compel a transfer to himself. And even though the agent owed no duty, because it was not within the scope of his agency, to acquire the thing in question for the principal, still if his acquisition of it was a breach of loyalty to the principal, as where its acquisition was the result of taking advantage of information acquired in a confidential capacity, the principal may charge him as a trustee. This duty of the agent not to compete with his principal does not necessarily terminate with the agency.[16]

---

[15] Statute of Frauds: Where what the agent does is not merely a breach of an oral contract, but a breach of trust—a violation of a fiduciary obligation,—a fraud,— the statute of frauds requiring a written contract or memorandum does not, by the weight of authority, prevent charging him as a trustee. The law creates the trust. See Rose v. Hayden, ante; Boswell v. Cunningham (1893) 32 Fla. 277, 13 So. 354; Brookings Land Co. v. Bertness (1903) 17 S. Dak. 293, 96 N. W. 97; Havner Land Co. v. MacGregor (1915) 169 Iowa 5, 149 N. W. 617; Wakeman v. Dodd

(1876) 27 N. J. Eq. 564; Johnson v. Hayward (1905) 74 Neb. 157, 107 N. W. 384; Quinn v. Phipps (1927) 93 Fla. 805, 113 So. 419; Stephenson v. Golden (1937) 279 Mich. 493, 272 N. W. 881; Whitten v. Wright (1939) 206 Minn. 423, 289 N. W. 509; cf. Carkonen v. Alberts (1938) 196 Wash. 575, 83 P.2d 899; ann. 42 A. L. R. 28; 135 A. L. R. 232.

See also Schmidt v. Beiseker (1905) 14 N. Dak. 587, 105 N. W. 1102, 1123 (action at law).

[16] He cannot free himself from the disability merely by resigning his agency. See Dennison v.

If the agent buys or acquires for himself in violation of his duty, and then sells at a profit, the principal, instead of disaffirming, may require him to account for the profit.[17]

§ 509. —— If the agent has caused a loss to his principal as by selling at a less price than he could have obtained, or by permitting the principal to deal in ignorance of material information which the agent had, and the like, the principal may ordinarily recover damages from the agent.[18]

The agent also, as will be seen, usually forfeits his right to compensation.[19] And the principal may lawfully discharge an agent guilty of disloyal conduct.

§ 510. **Further illustrations.** For like reasons, an agent authorized to settle or compromise a claim against his principal cannot buy it and enforce it himself;[20] an agent charged, for example, with the duty of paying taxes, removing incumbrances, and the like, will not be permitted, by neglecting his duty, to allow liens or claims against his principal to accumulate, and then buy or acquire the liens or claims, or through them the property, for himself;[21] and an agent employed to

Aldrich (1905) 114 Mo. App. 700, 91 S. W. 1024; Trice v. Comstock (1903) 121 Fed. 620; New Era Co. v. Shannon (1892) 44 Ill. App. 477; Eoff v. Irvine (1891) 108 Mo. 378, 18 S. W. 907; Byrne v. Barrett (1935) 268 N. Y. 199, 197 N. E. 217. Compare Pittsburgh Equitable Meter Co. v. Paul C. Loeber & Co. (1947) 160 F.2d 721, where the fact that an exclusive agent to sell obtained an option himself from the principal was held not to terminate the agency or alter the duty of full disclosure.

[17] See McNutt v. Dix (1890) 83 Mich. 328, 47 N. W. 212; Kramer v. Winslow (1890) 130 Pa. 484, 18 Atl. 923; Jensen v. Sidney Stevens Implement Co. (1922) 36 Idaho 348, 210 Pac. 1003.

[18] See Hegenmyer v. Marks (1887) 37 Minn. 6, 32 N. W. 785; Holmes v. Cathcart (1903) 88 Minn. 213, 92 N. W. 956; Mickleson v. Helm (1923) 89 Okla. 90, 214 Pac. 117; Rattray v. Scudder (1946) 28 Cal.2d 214, 169 P.2d 371; Doyen v. Bauer (1941) 211 Minn. 140, 300 N. W. 451.

[19] See post, Chapter XVII.

[20] See Albertson v. Fellows (1889) 45 N. J. Eq. 306, 17 Atl. 816; Noyes v. Landon (1887) 59 Vt. 569, 10 Atl. 342.

[21] See Bowman v. Officer & Pusey (1880) 53 Iowa 640, 6 N. W. 28; Hudson v. Herman (1910) 81 Kan. 627, 107 Pac. 35; Backus v. Cowley (1910) 162 Mich. 585, 127 N. W. 775; Page v. Webb (Ky., 1888) 7 S. W. 308, 9 Ky. L. Rep. 868; As-

investigate the state of his principal's title and report it to him, will not be permitted upon discovering an outstanding lien, or interest, to purchase it and claim under it himself.[22] The agent in such a case will be deemed to hold in trust for the principal.

§ 511. —— If the agent in discharging his duty gets a good bargain or makes profits which are the fruits of the agency, the gain or profit belongs to the principal, who can compel a transfer to himself. The same rule applies to rebates, discounts or other savings which the agent effects in the execution of the agency.[23]

sunto v. Coleman (1925) 158 La. 537, 104 So. 318.

[22] See Ringo v. Binns (1836) 35 U. S. (10 Peters) 269, 9 L. Ed. 420; Vallette v. Tedens (1887) 122 Ill. 607, 14 N. E. 52.

There are many other cases which fall within the operation of the same principle. Thus an agent employed to sell, and in the meantime to more or less care for and protect his principal's interest in, certain real estate was held incompetent to buy it at a foreclosure sale and hold it against his principal, even though he did not make that sale. Kimball v. Ranney (1899) 122 Mich. 160, 80 N. W. 992. See also Adams v. Sayre (1881) 70 Ala. 318.

[23] If the agent sells for more, or buys for less, or gets more for the same price, than was expected, the principal is entitled to the benefit. If the agent exacts extra bonuses, commissions or rewards for performing his duty, the principal may demand them. If he conceals important facts, as for example that the property can be sold for more, inducing his principal to convey to him at the lesser price, and he then sells for the greater price, the profit belongs to the principal.

See Rochester v. Levering (1885) 104 Ind. 562, 4 N. E. 203; Leach v. Hannibal & St. J. R. Co. (1885) 86 Mo. 27; Andrews v. Ramsay [1903] 2 K. B. 635; Turnbull v. Garden (1869) 38 L. J. Ch. 331; Hegenmyer v. Marks (1887) 37 Minn. 6, 32 N. W. 785; Kramer v. Winslow (1890) 130 Pa. 484, 18 Atl. 923; Simons v. Vulcan Oil Co. (1869) 61 Pa. 202; Michigan Crown Fender Co. v. Welch (1919) 211 Mich. 148, 178 N. W. 684, 13 A. L. R. 896; Pittsburgh Equitable Meter Co. v. Paul C. Loeber & Co. (1947) 160 F.2d 721; American Life Ins. Co. v. Florida Anglers Ass'n (1950) 185 F.2d 460.

This rule would not apply to gratuities or "tips" which the agent was expected to keep as part of or in addition to his wages or salary, like the tips of the Pullman car porter, or of the waiter in a restaurant. So of the tips given to the employee at a shoe polishing stand. See Polites v. Barlin (1912) 149 Ky. 376, 149 S. W. 828; Zappas v.

It is immaterial whether the profit or advantage is the result of the performance or of the violation of the agent's duty, if it be the fruit of the agency.

§ 512. Usage does not alter rule. The rule which forbids the agent's dealing with himself or taking advantage of his position to make profit for himself at the expense of his principal, or having compensation from both parties, cannot be defeated by any local or temporary usage,[24] nor does it make any difference that the agent was acting without pay.[25]

§ 513. Liability of agent for exceeding his authority. Where the agent, through a culpable failure to observe the limits of his authority, has caused a natural and proximate loss to his principal, he will be liable to the latter for the loss so sustained.[26]

§ 514. Liability of mere intermeddler. A fortiori where a person who has not been appointed agent for any purpose wrongfully pretends to be the agent of another, and without any authority does an act which causes him loss or expense,

Roumeliote (1912) 156 Iowa 709, 137 N. W. 935.

Nor to purely personal and unusual gifts or presents if they were not covertly bribes or bonuses. Compare Aetna Ins. Co. v. Church (1871) 21 Ohio St. 492; Mitchell v. Sparling (1910) 3 Sask. L. Rev. 213.

As to things found by the agent, see Burns v. Clark (1901) 133 Cal. 634, 66 Pac. 12, and cases cited.

As to agent's earnings in principal's time, see Jackson v. Seevers (1902) 115 Iowa 370, 88 N. W. 931; Clarke v. Kelsey (1894) 41 Neb. 766, 60 N. W. 138.

As to the right to discharge for taking gifts from customers, see

Wade v. Dry Goods Co. (1911) 155 Mo. App. 405, 134 S. W. 1084.

[24] See Robinson v. Mollett (1874) L. R. 7 H. L. 802; Merchants Ins. Co. v. Prince (1892) 50 Minn. 53, 52 N. W. 131; Raisin v. Clark (1874) 41 Md. 158; Farnsworth v. Hemmer (1861) 83 Mass. (1 Allen) 494.

[25] See Hunsaker v. Sturgis (1865) 29 Cal. 142.

[26] See Pape v. Westacott [1894] 1 Q. B. 272; Rush v. Rush (1897) 170 Ill. 623, 48 N. E. 990; Persons v. Smith (1903) 12 N. Dak. 403, 97 N. W. 551; Cooper v. Cooper (1911) 90 Neb. 209, 133 N. W. 243; Holmes v. Langston (1900) 110 Ga. 861, 36 S. E. 251.

as, for example, when he assumes to make a contract for the sale of his land and causes that contract to be put upon the public records, so that the alleged principal is put to trouble and expense in clearing his title, the wrongdoer will be liable for the loss so caused.[27]

§ 515. **Agent must obey instructions.** It is the duty of the agent to obey the lawful instructions of his principal; and if he disobeys them without sufficient excuse, he is liable to the principal for any loss which the principal may thereby sustain.

Illustrations of the operation of this rule are very numerous. Thus, if the principal instructs his agent to insure property, and it is lost, without insurance, such failure of insurance being attributable to the agent's disobedience, the agent must answer for it;[28] if the agent of an insurance company is directed to cancel a certain policy, and he fails to do so, during which failure the property is destroyed and the company has to pay for the loss, the agent will be liable to the company;[29] if an agent is instructed to sell or buy goods at a certain time, and he neglects until a change in price causes the principal loss, or a change in circumstances destroys the market, the agent will be liable;[30] if he is instructed to sell for cash only, and gives credit to irresponsible persons or takes checks which prove to be worthless, and the like, the agent will be

[27] See Philpot v. Taylor (1874) 75 Ill. 309.

[28] See Thorne v. Deas (1809) 4 Johns. (N. Y.) 84; Schoenfeld v. Fleisher (1874) 73 Ill. 404; Sawyer v. Mayhew (1863) 51 Me. 398; Backus v. Ames (1900) 79 Minn. 145, 81 N. W. 766.

[29] See Phoenix Ins. Co. v. Frissell (1886) 142 Mass. 513, 8 N. E. 348; Kraber v. Union Ins. Co. (1889) 129 Pa. 8, 18 Atl. 491; Queen City Fire Ins. Co. v. First Nat. Bank (1909) 18 N. Dak. 603, 120 N. W. 545; British-American Ins. Co. v. Wilson (1905) 77 Conn. 559, 60 Atl.

293; Continental Ins. Co. v. Clark (1904) 126 Iowa 274, 100 N. W. 524; Washington v. Mechanics & Traders Ins. Co. (1935) 174 Okla. 478, 50 P.2d 621.

[30] See Galigher v. Jones (1888) 129 U. S. 193, 9 S. Ct. 335, 32 L. Ed. 658; Zimmerman v. Heil (1895) 86 Hun 114, 33 N. Y. S. 391, aff'd 156 N. Y. 703, 51 N. E. 1094; Fuller v. Ellis (1867) 39 Vt. 345.

See also Henry v. Buckner (1889) 13 Colo. 18, 21 Pac. 916; Levison v. Balfour (1888) 34 Fed. 382; Union Hardware Co. v. Plume & Atwood (1889) 58 Conn. 219, 20

liable; [31] if an agent who undertakes to collect a debt is instructed to take certain steps, or to act at once or at a given time, and disobeys or disregards the instructions with the result that a collectible debt is lost to the principal, the agent must answer for it; [32] if an agent for the sale of goods or other property is instructed not to let it go without obtaining security, and does part with it without security, to the principal's loss, the agent must answer for it.[33]

§ 516.   Good faith, etc., no excuse.   The fact that the agent in disobeying the instructions, acted in good faith, or intended to benefit the principal, is no defense if his disobedience caused the loss.[34] Neither is the fact that he was not to be paid for his services, if he has actually entered upon the performance of his undertaking; if he has not so entered upon its performance, then a want of consideration would be a good defense for not undertaking the performance.[35]

If the agent could show that, notwithstanding his disobedience, the same loss would have followed from other causes for which he was not responsible, that might be a defense, but such a showing would usually be very difficult to make. Thus where an agent who had collected money for his principal was directed to send it in bills of large denomination, and, instead, he sent it in a necessarily bulkier package of bills of small denomination, and this package was lost, the court said:

Atl. 455; Oppenheimer Bros. v. J. L. Price Brokerage Co. (Mo. App., 1923) 248 S. W. 310.

[31] See Pape v. Westacott [1894] 1 Q. B. 272; Hall v. Storrs (1858) 7 Wis. 253; Robinson Machine Works v. Vorse (1879) 52 Iowa 207, 2 N. W. 1108; Harlan v. Ely (1886) 68 Cal. 522; Sheffield v. Linn (1886) 62 Mich. 151, 28 N. W. 761.

[32] See Whitney v. Express Co. (1870) 104 Mass. 152; Butts v. Phelps (1883) 79 Mo. 302.

[33] See Leven v. Lolcama (1922) 72 Colo. 427, 211 Pac. 870.

Other cases: Same rule where agent to deliver a deed on certain conditions delivered it in violation of them. Triggs v. Jones (1891) 46 Minn. 277, 48 N. W. 1113; Farmers Life Ins. Co. v. Ignacio (1928) 85 Colo. 46, 272 Pac. 1116; Shrewsbury v. Dupont Nat. Bk. (1926) 10 F.2d 632.

[34] See Switzer v. Connett (1847) 11 Mo. 88; Rechtsherd v. Bank of St. Louis (1870) 47 Mo. 181.

[35] See Passano v. Acosta (1832) 4 La. 26; Nixon v. Bogin (1886) 26 S. C. 611, 2 S. E. 302; Thorne v. Deas (1809) 4 Johns. (N. Y.) 84; Williams v. Higgins (1868) 30 Md.

"It is not sufficient that the deviation was not material, if it appears that the party giving the instructions regarded them as material, unless it be shown affirmatively that the deviation in no manner contributed to the loss. This may be a difficult task in a case like the present; but the defendant [the agent] voluntarily assumed it when he substituted his own plan for that prescribed by the plaintiff." [36]

§ 517. **In what form of action liable.** If the agent's breach of instructions relates merely to the manner of doing the act authorized, that is, if he does that act but does not do it as he was directed to do it, then the principal's action against him will be an action on the case for damages; but if the agent's default has consisted in the doing of some other act, e. g., in the disposition of property in an entirely different way, that is, in a way or for a purpose not authorized at all, he will be liable to the principal in an action of trover for a conversion.[37]

§ 518. **Sudden emergency as excuse.** A departure from instructions may be justified by a sudden emergency not caused by the agent's fault, where there is no time to communicate with the principal, but something must be done and a strict compliance with the instructions becomes impossible or would be detrimental to the interests of the principal.[38]

Primarily, of course, it is for the principal, rather than for the agent, to decide what shall be done in an emergency; and it is only where the principal cannot be consulted, and where

404; Marshall v. Ferguson (1902) 94 Mo. App. 175, 67 S. W. 935; Jones v. Central Nat. Bank & Trust Co. (1933) 110 Fla. 262, 148 So. 765; Guggisberg v. Otsego County Co-op. Ass'n (1932) 258 Mich. 553, 242 N. W. 749.

[36] See Wilson -- Wilson (1856) 26 Pa. 393.

[37] See Laverty v. Snethin (1877) 68 N. Y. 522; Minneapolis Trust Co. v. Mather (1905) 181 N. Y. 205, 73 N. E. 987; Baer v. Slater (1927) 261 Mass. 153, 158 N. E. 328. In re Mohr's Estate (1933) 212 Wis. 198, 248 N. W. 143, held that a bequest could be offset by loss caused by a legatee in his capacity as agent of the estate.

[38] See Greenleaf v. Moody (1866) 13 Allen (95 Mass.) 363; Bartlett v. Sparkman (1888) 95 Mo. 136, 8 S. W. 406; Harter v. Blanchard (1873) 64 Barb. (N. Y.) 617; Williams v. Shackleford (1849) 16 Ala. 318.

the circumstances will not admit of delay that the agent may decide.[39]

And even where an emergency justifies a departure from instructions, the agent must go no further than the emergency reasonably demands; he may not loosely assume any and all powers.[40]

§ 519. **Ambiguous instructions.** If the instructions are ambiguous, and the agent in good faith adopts one reasonable construction, he will not be liable because the principal may have intended another.[41] Usage may aid in the interpretation of doubtful instructions, though, as will be seen in the following section, it will not justify a breach of positive instructions to the contrary.

And, because the instructions are ambiguous, the agent will not be justified in disregarding them altogether, and following ideas of his own not within any interpretation of the instructions.[42]

§ 520. **Effect of custom.** It is ordinarily not only the right but the duty of the agent to observe and comply with such valid and established customs and usages as apply to the subject matter or the performance of his agency.[43] Such customs and usages, however, cannot, as between the principal and the agent, overrule positive instructions to the contrary.[44]

[39] See Gwilliam v. Twist [1895] 2 Q. B. 84; Hawtayne v. Bourne (1841) 7 Mees. & W. 595.

[40] See Foster v. Smith (1865) 42 Tenn. (2 Cold.) 474 (where an agent was employed to transport grain by river boat, and the boat sank in shallow water, it was said that the emergency would have justified measures to save the cargo, but did not justify selling it to the carrier in consideration of the freight).

[41] See Minnesota Linseed Oil Co. v. Montague (1884) 65 Iowa 67, 21 N. W. 184; Hopwood v. Corbin (1884) 63 Iowa 218, 18 N. W. 911;

Berry v. Haldeman (1897) 111 Mich. 667, 70 N. W. 325; Falsken v. Falls City Bank (1904) 71 Neb. 29, 98 N. W. 425; Bevis v. Big Bend Abstract Co. (1911) 62 Wash. 513, 114 Pac. 191; Smith v. Union Savings & Loan Ass'n (1935) 97 Colo. 440, 50 P.2d 538.

[42] See Oxford Lake Line v. First Nat. Bank (1898) 40 Fla. 349, 24 So. 480; Canada S. S. Lines v. Inland Waterways Corp. (1948) 166 F.2d 57.

[43] See Leroy v. Beard (1850) 49 U. S. (8 How.) 451, 12 L. Ed. 1151.

[44] See Wanless v. McCandless (1873) 38 Iowa 20; Robinson Ma-

§ 521. **Illegality of act required.** No general undertaking to act as agent would be construed to include the obligation to perform illegal or immoral acts. If there were an express agreement to perform such an act, it would not be enforced.[45]

§ 522. **Acts which would imperil agent's security.** An agent who has advanced money to his principal or incurred obligations for him, upon the security of the principal's goods or property in the agent's possession, would not be obliged to obey subsequent instructions to sell or otherwise dispose of the property in such a way as to imperil his security, unless the principal should either reimburse him or give him other security.[46]

§ 523. **Ratification of disobedience.** Even though the agent may have disobeyed the principal's instructions, the doing of the act as it was done may be ratified and approved by the principal, and if it is, the agent's liability to the principal will be released.[47]

Such ratification, as in other cases, must be with knowledge of the facts; but in these cases between principal and agent, courts have often shown a tendency to interpret the facts liberally in favor of ratification, and a failure to dissent after knowledge has frequently been held to be enough, especially where the agent has himself reported his action to the princi-

chine Works v. Vorse (1879) 52 Iowa 207, 2 N. W. 1108; Osborne v. Rider (1885) 62 Wis. 235, 22 N. W. 394; Hall v. Storrs (1858) 7 Wis. 253; Cohen v. Kittell (1889) 22 Q. B. Div. 680.

[45] Compare Sykes v. Beadon (1879) 11 Ch. Div. 170, 193; Brown v. Howard (1817) 14 Johns. (N. Y.) 119; Davis v. Barger (1877) 57 Ind. 54; Elmore v. Brooks (1871) 53 Tenn. (6 Heisk.) 45.

[46] See Davis v. Kobe (1886) 36 Minn. 214, 30 N. W. 662; Feild v. Farrington (1869) 77 U. S. (10 Wall.) 141, 19 L. Ed. 923; Brown v. McGran (1840) 39 U. S. (14 Peters) 479, 10 L. Ed. 550; Heffner v. Cotton Co. (1908) 160 Fed. 635. As to agent's disregard of instructions where power coupled with an interest, see McHaney v. McHaney (1945) 209 Ark. 337, 190 S.W.2d 450, ann. 162 A. L. R. 1182.

[47] See Lunn v. Guthrie (1902) 115 Iowa 501, 88 N. W. 1060; Wann v. Scullin (1911) 235 Mo. 629, 139 S. W. 425; Osborne v. Durham (1911) 157 N. C. 262, 72 S. E. 849.

pal.[48] But the facts of a given case may rebut any inference of approval.[49]

§ 524. **Duty to exercise reasonable care.** By accepting an employment whose requirements he knows, without stipulating otherwise, the agent impliedly undertakes that he possesses a degree of skill reasonably or ordinarily competent for the performance of the service, and that in performing his undertaking he will exercise reasonable care, skill and diligence. He does not agree that he will make no mistakes whatever, or that he will exercise the highest skill or diligence, but he does agree that he will exercise reasonable skill, and that he will take the usual precautions.[50]

§ 525. **Special skill required in some cases.** There are many cases, however, wherein more than the skill possessed by the ordinary man may reasonably be required. Thus, where the agent is employed and undertakes to serve in a capacity which implies the possession and exercise of special skill, as, for example, when an attorney at law, a physician, a broker, etc., undertakes to do some act in the line of his special calling,

[48] See Bray v. Gunn (1874) 53 Ga. 144; Austin v. Ricker (1881) 61 N. H. 97; Meyer v. Morgan (1875) 51 Miss. 21; Halloway v. Arkansas City Milling Co. (1908) 77 Kan. 76, 93 Pac. 577; Allen v. McAllister (1905) 39 Wash. 440, 81 Pac. 927.

[49] See Triggs v. Jones (1891) 46 Minn. 277, 48 N. W. 1113.

[50] See Page v. Wells (1877) 37 Mich. 415; Johnson v. Martin (1856) 11 La. Ann. 27; Bowerman v. Rogers (1887) 125 U. S. 585, 8 S. Ct. 986, 31 L. Ed. 815; Paul v. Grimm (1895) 165 Pa. 139, 30 Atl. 721; Richardson v. Taylor (1883) 136 Mass. 143; Lake City Flouring Mill Co. v. McVean (1884) 32 Minn. 301, 20 N. W. 233; Adams v. Robinson (1880) 65 Ala. 586; Morrison v. Orr (1832) 3 Stew. & P. (Ala.) 49; Walker v. Smith (1804) 4 Dall. 387, 1 L. Ed. 878; Briere v. Taylor (1905) 126 Wis. 347, 105 N. W. 817; Georgia Casualty Co. v. Mann (1932) 242 Ky. 447, 46 S.W.2d 777; In re Mohr's Estate (1933) 212 Wis. 198, 248 N. W. 143; Reily v. Fleece (1935) 259 Ky. 330, 82 S.W.2d 341; O'Connor v. Burns Potter & Co. (1949) 151 Neb. 9, 36 N.W.2d 507; Rianda v. San Benito Title Guarantee Co. (1950) 35 Cal.2d 170, 217 P.2d 25; Holey v. Nickels (Tex. Civ. App., 1950) 235 S.W.2d 683.

then the skill ordinarily possessed and exercised by persons pursuing that calling may reasonably be required.[51]

More than the ordinary skill may also be reasonably required where the agent, though perhaps not belonging to any of the specially skilled classes, has in the particular case specially undertaken to exercise or has held himself out as possessing extraordinary skill.[52]

§ 526. **How when services gratuitous.** When an agent professing or exercising a calling which implies the possession of special skill is employed in the line of his calling, the fact that he was not to be paid for his services is no excuse for not exercising such skill; but one serving gratuitously in other cases would not be expected to possess special skill, and unless he had it in fact or specially undertook to exercise it, he would not be liable in the absence of what is often termed gross negligence or bad faith.[53]

§ 527. **Negligence in loaning money.** An agent employed to make loans does not impliedly warrant the safety of his loans or the solvency of the borrower, but he does undertake to use reasonable and proper care, and he will be liable for losses occurring from his negligence, as, e. g., in loaning to irresponsible parties, or from a neglect to obtain suitable security, or to secure and perfect the proper evidences of the loan.[54]

[51] See Craig v. Chambers (1876) 17 Ohio St. 253; Howard v. Grover (1848) 28 Me. 97; McNevins v. Lowe (1866) 40 Ill. 209.

[52] See Isham v. Post (1894) 141 N. Y. 100, 35 N. E. 1084.

[53] See Foster v. Essex Bank (1821) 17 Mass. 479; Shiells v. Blackburne (1789) 1 H. Bl. 158; Williams v. McKay (1885) 40 N. J. Eq. 189; First Nat. Bank v. Ocean Nat. Bank (1875) 60 N. Y. 278; Isham v. Post (1894) 141 N. Y. 100, 35 N. E. 1084; Allen v.

Adams (1928) 16 Del. Ch. 77, 140 Atl. 694; Barile v. Wright (1935) 256 N. Y. 1, 175 N. E. 351; cf. Guggisberg v. Otsego Cty. Co-op. Ass'n (1932) 258 Mich. 553, 242 N. W. 749.

An agent who in fact possessed special skill would be expected to exercise it, though serving gratuitously, unless the circumstances or the terms of the employment excluded it. Wilson v. Brett (1843) 11 Mees. & Wels. 113.

[54] See Bank of Owensboro v.

§ 528. **Negligence in effecting insurance.** In the same way, an agent employed to effect insurance does not impliedly guarantee the soundness of the company or the collection of the insurance money, but he would be liable for a loss proximately resulting from his negligence, as, for example, in insuring in a company not in good standing, or in taking defective policies, or in procuring insufficient amounts, or in ignoring the instructions of his principal.[55] A fortiori would he be liable if he neither insured at all, nor advised his principal so that he could protect himself.

§ 529. **Negligence in collecting.** So an agent employed to make collections does not impliedly guarantee that he will collect the money, or (unless charged with the duty of special diligence) that he will drop all other business and attend solely to that; but he is liable for a loss of the debt which results from his failure to exercise reasonable care, skill and diligence in collecting the money, as by unreasonable delay until the debtor had become insolvent, granting unwarranted extensions, failing to institute the proper proceedings, neglecting proper demands, or presentments for payment, omitting required notices, accepting worthless funds, and the like; or, having once collected the money, for a loss of the proceeds caused by negligence or disregard of instructions in remitting it.[56]

Western Bank (1877) 13 Bush (Ky.) 526; Harlow v. Bartlett (1898) 170 Mass. 584, 49 N. E. 1014; DeHart v. DeHart (1906) 70 N. J. Eq. 774, 67 Atl. 1074; Momsen v. Atkins (1900) 105 Wis. 557, 81 N. W. 647; Hitchcock v. Cosper (1904) 164 Ind. 633, 73 N. E. 264; Wagner v. Phillips (1900) 12 S. Dak. 335, 81 N. W. 632.

[55] See Storer v. Eaton (1861) 50 Me. 219; Strong v. High (1842) 2 Rob. (La.) 103; Schoenfeld v. Fleisher (1874) 73 Ill. 404; Sawyer v. Mayhew (1863) 51 Me. 398;

Brant v. Gallup (1885) 111 Ill. 487; Milburn Wagon Co. v. Evans (1882) 30 Minn. 89, 14 N. W. 271; Thorne v. Deas (1809) 4 Johns. (N. Y.) 84; Elam v. Smithdeal Realty & Insurance Co. (1921) 182 N. C. 599, 109 S. E. 632; Barile v. Wright (1935) 256 N. Y. 1, 175 N. E. 351.

[56] See Butts v. Phelpa (1883) 79 Mo. 302; Walker v. Walker (1871) 5 Heisk. (Tenn.) 425; Wilson v. Wilson (1856) 26 Pa. St. 393; Foster v. Preston (1828) 8 Cowen (N. Y.) 198; Kerr v. Cotton (1859) 23

§ 530. **Liability of collection agent for defaults of his correspondents.** An attorney who takes a claim "for collection" without qualification as to his liability is liable for the defaults of his own clerks and agents, and if he sends the claim to another attorney for collection, he is generally held liable for the latter's defaults.[57] Whether a bank which undertakes to collect is liable for the default of its correspondent banks, is disputed. Many distinguished courts hold that it is so liable where it has not limited its liability at the time of accepting the service. A large number, perhaps a majority, of the state courts hold that the liability of the bank normally extends no further than to exercise due care in the selection of its correspondent, giving it proper instructions, and the like. Banks and other collecting agencies now quite generally attempt to limit their liability by notices to or agreements with their patrons. The great extent and complexity of this subject preclude any attempt to analyze it thoroughly here; the reader must be referred to treatises on Banking Law.[58]

Tex. 411; Buell v. Chapin (1868) 99 Mass. 594; Richards v. New Hampshire Ins. Co. (1861) 43 N. H. 263; First Nat. Bank v. Fourth Nat. Bank (1879) 77 N. Y. 320; Omaha Nat. Bank v. Kiper (1908) 60 Neb. 33, 82 N. W. 102; Dern v. Kellogg (1898) 54 Neb. 560, 74 N. W. 844; Sahlien v. Bank of Lonoke (1891) 90 Tenn. 221, 16 S. W. 373; Kirkeys v. Crandall (1891) 90 Tenn. 532, 18 S. W. 246; Morris v. Eufaula Nat. Bank (1898) 122 Ala. 580, 25 So. 499; Luckehe v. First Nat. Bank (1924) 193 Cal. 184, 223 Pac. 547; Federal Reserve Bank v. Malloy (1924) 264 U. S. 160, 44 S. Ct. 296, 68 L. Ed. 617; W. L. Douglas Shoe Co. v. Rollwage (1933) 187 Ark. 1084, 63 S.W.2d 841; McNeal v. Steinberger (1943) 192 Okla. 283, 135 P.2d 490. Compare Hartzell v. Bank of Mur-ray (1926) 211 Ky. 263, 277 S. W. 270.

[57] See Cummins v. Heald (1880) 24 Kan. 600; Walker v. Stevens (1875) 79 Ill. 193; Abbott v. Smith (1853) 4 Ind. 452; Rhines v. Evans (1870) 66 Pa. 192.

For commercial or collection agencies, see Bradstreet v. Everson (1872) 72 Pa. 124; Weyerhauser v. Dun (1885) 100 N. Y. 150, 2 N. E. 274; Sanger v. Dun (1879) 47 Wis. 615, 3 N. W. 388.

Express companies: American Express Co. v. Haire (1863) 21 Ind. 4.

[58] See generally Federal Reserve Bank v. Malloy (1924) 264 U. S. 160, 44 S. Ct. 296, 68 L. Ed. 617, ann. 31 A. L. R. 1261; Steffen, The Check Collection Muddle (1936) 10 Tulane L. Rev. 537; 8 Zollman, Banks & Banking, § 5304 et seq.

§ 531. **Negligence in making sales.** An agent who under-takes to sell real or personal property would not ipso facto agree that he would certainly make a sale, or that he would do it within any particular time or at any particular price, though he might agree to any or all of these things by special contract. In the absence of that, his obligation would be to exercise reasonable care, skill and diligence in the matter. Frequently there will be special stipulations with or instruc-tions to him as to the terms, conditions, prices, and the like, which he shall endeavor to secure, and these he should observe. If there were no such instructions, he should proceed in the usual and ordinary manner. He should sell, and not mortgage, pledge, exchange, or give away. If he were entrusted with goods to sell it would be his duty, in the absence of a usage or authority to the contrary, to sell for cash only,[59] and even if authorized to sell upon credit, he must exercise reasonable care and prudence in selling only to responsible purchasers.[60] If the terms of his employment required that he should exact notes, mortgages, endorsers, or other forms of security, he would ordinarily be liable if he let the goods go without ob-taining them.[61]

§ 532. **Liability for loss to principal resulting from agent's negligence as to third person.** Thus far the person injured directly by the agent's negligence has been assumed to be

[59] See Payne v. Potter (1859) 9 Iowa 549; Norton v. Nevills (1899) 174 Mass. 243, 54 N. E. 537; Kops v. Smith (1904) 137 Mich. 28, 100 N. W. 169; Bowles v. Rice (1907) 107 Va. 51, 57 S. E. 575; Ott v. Schneiter (1936) 56 Ohio App. 359, 10 N.E.2d 947. Contra: Benton-ville Ice & Cold Storage Co. v. An-derson (1932) 186 Ark. 473, 53 S.W.2d 933. See also Bareco Oil Co. v. Alexander (1940) 33 F. Supp. 32.

[60] See Tate v. Marco (1887) 27 S. C. 493, 4 S. E. 71; Frick v. Larned (1893) 50 Kan. 776, 32 Pac. 383; Morris v. Bradley (1910) 20 N. Dak. 646, 128 N. W. 118.

[61] See Clark v. Roberts (1873) 26 Mich. 506; Robinson Machine Works v. Vorse (1879) 52 Iowa 207, 2 N. W. 1108; Harlow v. Bart-lett (1896) 170 Mass. 584, 49 N. E. 1014; Osborne v. Rider (1885) 62 Wis. 235, 22 N. W. 394; Avery Planter Co. v. Murphy (1897) 6 Kan. App. 29, 49 Pac. 626; Wages v. Garmon (1924) 75 Colo. 507, 226 Pac. 667.

the principal; but it is also the duty of the agent to his principal not to cause loss to his principal by his negligent injury of a third person. Thus if a servant acting in the course of his employment negligently injured a third person, for which injury the master was made to respond in damages, the master would be entitled to recover from his servant who caused the injury the amount of the loss the master had thereby sustained.[62]

§ 533. **Duty to account.** It is the duty of the agent to account to his principal for all money or property which comes to his hands belonging to the principal.[63]

This includes not only all property and money received by the agent directly from his principal, or from third persons for the principal, but also all that which by law enures to the benefit of the principal, like profits, rebates or similar advantages which come to the agent's hands as a fruit of the agency.[64]

The fact that the receipt or acquisition of the property or money was not originally authorized would not be material, if the agent acted as such and the principal has ratified the act. Money or property put into the agent's hands for a purpose which was subsequently abandoned, countermanded or found impossible of attainment, before the agent had acted or bound himself to others to act, would be within the rule.

§ 534. **Agent may not deny his principal's title.** It is not ordinarily competent for an agent who has received money or property from or for his principal, and who is called upon

[62] See Grand Trunk Ry. Co. v. Latham (1874) 63 Me. 177; Smith v. Foran (1875) 43 Conn. 244.

[63] See Dodge v. Hatchett (1903) 118 Ga. 883, 45 S. E. 667; Jett v. Hempstead (1869) 25 Ark. 462; Salem Traction Co. v. Anson (1902) 41 Ore. 562, 67 Pac. 1015, 69 Pac. 675; Coffin v. Craig (1903) 89 Minn. 226, 94 N. W. 680; Taul v. Edmondson (1872) 37 Tex. 556;

Bills v. Hyde (1925) 49 S. D. 18, 205 N. W. 708; Camp v. Roanoke Guano Co. (1937) 235 Ala. 61, 177 So. 343; Justin v. Delta Motor Lines (La. App., 1949) 43 So.2d 53.

[64] See Forlaw v. Naval Stores Co. (1905) 124 Ga. 261, 52 S. E. 898; Hair v. Dailey (1896) 161 Ill. 379, 43 N. E. 1096; Salsbury v. Ware (1900) 183 Ill. 505, 56 N. E. 149; Schick v. Suttle (1905) 94

to account for it, to undertake to show that it did not then belong to his principal. Even if that were so, it would not therefore become the property of the agent. His act in receiving it as the principal's is, in a sense, an acknowledgment of the principal's title, and the agent may not officiously make himself the protector or defender of the rights of some other alleged owner who is making no claim for himself.[65] If the agent has already been divested by or has yielded to the paramount title he may show that fact in his defense.[66]

§ 535. **May not set up the illegality of the origin of the money.** So an agent who has received money or property for his principal, and who is called upon to account for it, may not show that the property or money was the proceeds of some illegal transaction in which the principal was or had been engaged, but which was independent of and separate from the undertaking of the agent to receive and account for it.[67] But where compelling the agent to account would require the court to enforce the illegal act or contract itself, the illegality would be a bar.[68]

Minn. 135, 102 N. W. 217; Graham v. Cummings (1904) 208 Pa. 516, 57 Atl. 943; Connelly v. Special Road & Bridge Dist. No. 5, 99 Fla. 456, 126 So. 794; Singletary v. Mann (1946) 157 Fla. 37, 24 So.2d 718; East & West Coast Service Corp. v. Papahagis (1942) 344 Pa. 183, 35 A.2d 339.

[65] See Monongahela Nat. Bank v. First Nat. Bank (1910) 226 Pa. 270, 75 Atl. 359; Collins v. Tillou (1857) 26 Conn. 368; Hancock v. Gomez (1871) 58 Barb. (N. Y.) 490; Witman v. Felston (1859) 28 Mo. 601; Dixon v. Hamond (1809) 2 B. & Ald. 310; Pittsburg Mining Co. v. Spooner (1889) 74 Wis. 307, 42 N. W. 259; Floyd v. Patterson (1888) 72 Tex. 202, 10 S. W. 526;

Courts v. Jones (1940) 61 Ga. App. 874, 8 S.E.2d 178.

[66] See Moss Mercantile Co. v. First Nat. Bank (1905) 47 Ore. 361, 82 Pac. 8.

[67] See Peters v. Grim (1892) 149 Pa. 163, 24 Atl. 192 (unlawful transaction wholly ended, and money in question not the proceeds of it); Repplier v. Jacobs (1892) 149 Pa. 167, 24 Atl. 194 (same); Baldwin v. Potter (1874) 46 Vt. 402; Gilbert v. American Surety Co. (1902) 121 Fed. 499; Cuffman v. Blunkall (1939) 22 Tenn. App. 513, 124 S.W.2d 289.

[68] See Leonard v. Poole (1889) 114 N. Y. 371, 21 N. E. 707; McMullen v. Hoffman (1899) 174 U. S. 639, 19 S. Ct. 839, 43 L. Ed. 1117;

Where the principal has put property or money into the hands of an agent to be thereafter devoted to an unlawful purpose, the principal may repent and recover the property or money, if he does so while the transaction still remains unexecuted.[69]

§ 536. **Agent's duty to keep accounts.** It is not the duty of every agent to keep his principal's accounts, but where an agent is entrusted with money to be used, or is engaged in a transaction which requires expenditures or involves collections or receipts, and the like, it is his duty to keep and be prepared to render true and correct accounts of his transactions.[70] Where it is conceded or shown that money or property came into his hands, the burden is on him to show what he did with it, and he cannot expect to satisfy his duty merely by general assertions that it was properly expended or disposed of: he must be prepared to account for it, and to produce the usual vouchers or other evidence.[71] Where he

Kennedy v. Lonabaugh (1911) 19 Wyo. 352, 117 Pac. 1079; Citizens Bank v. Mitchell (1909) 24 Okla. 488, 103 Pac. 720; Central Trust Co. v. Respass (1902) 112 Ky. 606, 66 S. W. 421.

Compare Mitchell v. Fish (1911) 97 Ark. 444, 134 S. W. 940.

[69] See Bernard v. Taylor (1893) 23 Ore. 416, 31 Pac. 968; Kiewert v. Rindskopf (1879) 46 Wis. 481, 1 N. W. 163; Ware v. Spinney (1907) 76 Kan. 289, 91 Pac. 787; Wasserman v. Sloss (1897) 117 Cal. 425, 49 Pac. 566; Clarke v. Brown (1886) 77 Ga. 606; Munns v. Donovan Commission Co. (1902) 117 Iowa 516, 91 N. W. 789; Smith v. Blachley (1898) 188 Pa. 550, 41 Atl. 619.

[70] See Dodge v. Hatchett (1903) 118 Ga. 883, 45 S. E. 667; Chicago Title & Trust Co. v. Ward (1904)

113 Ill. App. 327; Brigham v. Newton (1901) 106 La. 280, 30 So. 849; Boyce v. Boyce (1900) 124 Mich. 696, 83 N. W. 1013; Riley v. Bank of Allendale (1899) 57 S. C. 98, 35 S. E. 535; Pennsylvania Trust Co. v. Billman (1932) 61 F.2d 382. The agent need make only one accounting to satisfy the duty. Spitzleberger v. Johns (1942) 291 Ky. 87, 163 S.W.2d 286. Of course, this would presuppose that the accounting was satisfactory.

[71] See Webb v. Fordyce (1880) 55 Iowa 11, 7 N. W. 385; Gay v. Householder (1912) 71 W. Va. 277, 76 S. E. 450. Initially the burden is on the principal to show that the agent in fact received money or property. Hartzell v. Bank of Murray (1926) 211 Ky. 263, 277 S. W. 270.

claims to be reimbursed for expenditures, he must be able
to show what they were, and that they were proper in purpose
and amount.[72]

The principal may, of course, waive the requirement, or
show by his words or conduct that he does not expect it, but
unless he does so, the rule is as stated.[73]

Doubts caused by the agent's failure to keep proper accounts
will be resolved against him.[74]

§ 537. **Duty to give notice of collection.** Upon collecting
money for his principal, the agent—unless he already has
instructions from the principal, or there is an established
course of business, as to remitting or disposing of it, with which
he may and should comply without waiting for any further
instructions [75]—should give the principal notice of the collection within a reasonable time, and if he has done so, the
agent cannot ordinarily be sued for the money until the
principal has made a demand for it with which the agent
has refused or neglected to comply.[76] If the principal has
learned, through some other source, of the collection, he may,
of course, demand the money without waiting to be informed
by the agent, though he seems not to be obliged to do so where
the agent is already in default. No demand is ordinarily neces-

---

[72] See Moyses v. Rosenbaum
(1900) 98 Ill. App. 7; East & West
Coast Service Corp. v. Papahagis
(1942) 344 Pa. 183, 25 A.2d 339.

[73] See Rich v. Austin (1867) 40
Vt. 416. As to whether and under
what circumstances the defense of
accord and satisfaction is available
to the agent, see Topas v. John
MacGregor Grant (1927) 18 F.2d
724; Hudson v. Yonkers·Fruit Co.
(1932) 258 N. Y. 168, 179 N. E.
373; City of Indianapolis v. Dom-
hoff & Joyce Co. (1941) 69 Ohio
App. 109, 36 N.E.2d 153, ann. 80
A. L. R. 1056

[74] See Illinois Linen Co. v. Hough
(1878) 91 Ill. 63.

[75] It would, of course, in many
cases be the duty of the agent,
either because of his instructions
or of the established methods of
procedure in such business, to at
once remit the money without waiting for any further instructions.
See Clark v. Moody (1821) 17
Mass. 145; Brown v. Arrott (1843)
6 Watts & Serg. (Pa.) 402.

[76] See Jett v. Hempstead (1869)
25 Ark. 462; Bedell v. Janney
(1847) 9 Ill. 193; Jetter v. Little Falls Dairy Co. (1951) 101
N.Y.S.2d 980.

sary where it appears that the agent denies or has repudiated the agency.[77]

§ 538. —— The agent will be liable for interest if he fails to give notice of the collection, or if he uses or applies the money contrary to instructions, or if he fails to pay it over upon demand.[78]

The statute of limitations will usually not begin to run in the agent's favor until he has given notice of the collection, or until a demand has been made upon him, or at least until the principal who has learned of the collection could have made a demand,[79] though the cases upon this point seem to be in some confusion.[80]

§ 539. **Agent must not mix principal's funds with his own.** The agent should not mix his principal's funds with his own; if he does so and they are lost, he will be liable for their loss.[81] Neither should the agent mingle his principal's property with his own; if he so commingles the two that they cannot be

[77] See Hammett v. Brown (1877) 60 Ala. 498; Judith Transp. Co. v. Williams (1907) 36 Mont. 25, 91 Pac. 1061; Waddell v. Swann (1884) 9 N. C. 108.

[78] See Thorp v. Thorp (1902) 75 Vt. 34, 52 Atl. 1051; Courts v. Jones (1940) 61 Ga. App. 874, 8 S.E.2d 178.

[79] See Jett v. Hempstead, ante; Teasley v. Bradley (1900) 110 Ga. 497, 35 S. E. 782; Whitehead v. Wells (1874) 29 Ark. 99; Wolcott & Lincoln v. Butler (1942) 155 Kan. 105, 122 P.2d 720.

[80] See Campbell v. Roe (1891) 32 Neb. 345, 49 N. W. 452; Mast v. Easton (1885) 33 Minn. 161, 22 N. W. 253; Campbell v. Boggs (1865) 48 Pa. 524; Goodyear Rubber Co. v. Baker (1908) 81 Vt. 39, 69 Atl. 160; Guarantee Trust Co. v. Farmers' Bank (1902) 202 Pa.

94, 51 Atl. 765, ann. 141 A. L. R. 361.

[81] Where lawyers who had collected money for clients deposited it in their own names in a bank, pending a distribution to their respective clients, and before this was effected the bank failed, it was held that the loss must fall upon the lawyers. Naltner v. Dolan (1886) 108 Ind. 500, 8 N. E. 289. The court said: "In case it becomes the duty of an agent or trustee to deposit money belonging to his principal, he can escape the risk only by making the deposit in his principal's name, or by so distinguishing it on the books of the bank, as to indicate in some way that it is the principal's money. If he deposit in his own name, he will not, in case of loss, be permitted to throw such loss on his prin-

separated, or his own cannot be identified, the principal may claim the whole mass.[82]

The principal may follow and recover his money or property, so long as he can identify it, and until it comes into the hands of a bona fide holder for value and without notice.[83] As to money, which ordinarily has no "ear-mark," such a holder would usually prevail.[84] As to property of the nonnegotiable class, even such a holder could not ordinarily defeat the principal's claim.[85]

cipal. In such a case the good faith or intention of the trustee is in no way involved."

See also Massachusetts Life Ins. Co. v. Carpenter (1870) 32 N. Y. Super. 734, (aff'd 49 N. Y. 668); Cartmell v. Allard (1871) 70 Ky. (7 Bush) 482; Hibberd v. Furlong (1934) 269 Mich. 514, 257 N. W. 737; Pine Bluff Iron Works v. Arkansas Foundry Co. (1932) 186 Ark. 532, 54 S.W.2d 299; New England Acceptance Corp. v. Nichols (1939) 110 Vt. 478, 8 A.2d 665; Wangsness v. Berdahl (1944) 69 S. D. 586, 13 N.W.2d 293.

[82] See First Nat. Bank v. Schween (1889) 127 Ill. 573, 20 N. E. 681; Lance v. Butler (1904) 135 N. C. 419, 47 S. E. 488; Otero v. Banco de Sonora (1924) 26 Ariz. 356, 225 Pac. 1112.

[83] Riehl v. Evansville Foundry Ass'n (1885) 104 Ind. 70, 3 N. E. 633; Pearce v. Dill (1897) 149 Ind. 136, 48 N. E. 788; Farmers' Bank v. King (1868) 57 Pa. 202; Baker v. New York Nat. Bank (1885) 100 N. Y. 31, 2 N. E. 452; Englar v. Offutt (1888) 70 Md. 78, 16 Atl. 497; Central National Bank of Baltimore v. Connecticut Mutual Life Insurance Co. (1881) 104 U. S. 54, 26 L. Ed. 693; Roca v. Byrne (1895) 145 N. Y. 182, 39 N. E. 812.

[84] Thus in Mobile & M. Ry. Co. v. Felrath (1880) 67 Ala. 189, the court said: "The general proposition that a principal may pursue his property or his money which his agent may have misapplied, is not doubted. From the necessity of the case an exception obtains as to money or that which is a circulating medium used and employed as money. Having no 'ear-marks,' —not capable of being identified and distinguished,—if the agent misuses or misapplies it, and it passes to the possession of one, upon a valuable consideration, and without notice, it may not be reclaimed." See also Lime Rock Bank v. Plimpton (1835) 17 Pick. (Mass.) 159; Burnham v. Holt (1843) 14 N. H. 367; Porter v. Roseman (1905) 165 Ind. 255, 74 N. E. 1105.

But a bank in which an agent deposits his principal's money in his own name is merely a debtor, not a purchaser for value. Roca v. Byrne, ante; and where the bank has notice that the deposit belongs to the principal, it may not, with the agent's consent, apply it in payment of the agent's debt to the bank. Baker v. New York Nat. Bank, ante.

[85] See Barker v. Dinsmore (1872)

§ 540.   Form of action.   The form of action in which the agent's duty to account may be enforced will usually depend upon the circumstances. In many cases an action for the breach of an express or implied contract to pay or deliver would be appropriate.[86] If the agent has received money which it is his duty to pay or account for to the principal, an action for money had and received may be maintained.[87] As has been seen, if an agent applies his principal's money or property to an end or purpose not authorized, he may often be held liable for a conversion.[88] Specific goods may often be recovered by an action of replevin.[89]

Law and not equity is usually the forum, but where the agent's duties are fiduciary in character and involve a dealing with trust funds, an action in equity for an accounting may be

72 Pa. 427; Saltus v. Everett (1838) 20 Wend. (N. Y.) 267; Edwards v. Dooley (1890) 120 N. Y. 540, 24 N. E. 827; Anderson v. Patten (1912) 157 Iowa 23, 137 N. W. 1050; Stevenson v. Kyle (1896) 42 W. Va. 229, 24 S. E. 886.

[86] See Greentree v. Rosenstock (1875) 61 N. Y. 583; Conaughtey v. Nichols (1870) 42 N. Y. 83; Philips v. U. S. (1932) 59 F.2d 881.

[87] See Guernsey v. Davis (1903) 67 Kan. 378, 73 Pac. 101; Gordon v. Hostetter (1867) 37 N. Y. 99, 4 Abb. Prac. (N. S.) 263; Dodge v. Harbor Boat Bldg. Co. (1950) 99 Cal.App.2d 782, 222 P.2d 697.

[88] See Laverty v. Snethen (1877) 68 N. Y. 522, 53 How. Prac. 152; Bartels v. Kinninger (1889) 144 Mo. 370, 46 S. W. 163; Wells v. Collins (1889) 74 Wis. 341, 43 N. W. 160; Salem Traction Co. v. Anson (1902) 41 Ore. 562, 67 Pac. 1015, 69 Pac. 675; Chase v. Baskerville (1904) 93 Minn. 402, 101 N. W. 950; Bridgeport Organ Co. v. Snyder (1908) 147 N. C. 271, 61 S. E. 51; Comley v. Dazian (1889)

114 N. Y. 161, 21 N. E. 135; Britton v. Ferrin (1902) 171 N. Y. 235, 63 N. E. 954.

Failure to turn over the identical money or thing received will or will not be a conversion, depending upon the duty. It may be the duty of a mere servant or special agent to turn over the very thing he received; or, as in the case of a general sales or collection agent, to pay over the amount collected but not in the identical money received. Compare Hazelton v. Locke (1908) 104 Me. 164, 71 Atl. 661; Farrelly v. Hubbard (1896) 148 N. Y. 592, 43 N. E. 65; Vandelle v. Rohan (1901) 36 Misc. 239, 73 N. Y. S. 285.

In Walter v. Bennett (1857) 16 N. Y. 250, it is said: "The duty of an agent for sale is to account for the proceeds of his principal's property, but he is not guilty of a conversion if he does not deliver the specific proceeds to his principal."

[89] See Terwilliger v. Beals (1872) 6 Lans. (N. Y.) 403.

maintained.[90] So also may it where the accounting would be so complicated and involved that it could not be settled at law without great difficulty,[91] and, ordinarily, where third persons also were sought to be held liable as trustees of the principal's property or money.

§ 541. **Duty to give notice of material facts coming to his knowledge.** It is the duty of the agent to give the principal timely notice of all facts coming to the agent's knowledge, relating to the subject matter of the agency, which it is material for the principal to know for the protection of his interests, and which the agent can and may communicate to him.[92]

This duty may present itself under a great variety of circumstances. Thus the duty of loyalty, as has been seen, may require the agent to disclose to his principal any interests or engagements which the agent may have, either on his own account or for other persons, which may disqualify him for loyal devotion to the principal's interests.

If he has undertaken to care for, protect or represent the principal's property or interests, and such property or interests are attacked or threatened or imperiled by hostile forces or impending dangers or wrongful acts, it would ordinarily be the agent's duty to inform the principal, so that he may take such steps as he desires to protect his interests. If the agent finds himself unable or unwilling to carry out undertakings for which the principal depends upon him, he should

90 See Moxon v. Bright (1869) L. R. 4 Ch. App. 292; Marvin v. Brooks (1883) 94 N. Y. 71; Dillman v. Hastings (1891) 144 U. S. 136, 12 S. Ct. 662, 36 L. Ed. 378; Warren v. Holbrook (1893) 95 Mich. 185, 54 N. W. 712; Williams v. Finlaw, Muller & Co. (1928) 292 Pa. 244, 141 Atl. 47.

91 See Taylor v. Tompkins (1876) 49 Tenn. (2 Heisk.) 89.

92 See Devall v. Burbridge (1842) 4 Watts & Serg. (Pa.) 305; Clark v. Bank of Wheeling (1851) 17 Pa. 322; Brown v. Arratt (1843) 6 Watts & Serg. (Pa.) 402; Emerson v. Turner (1910) 95 Ark. 597, 130 S. W. 538; Dorr v. Camden (1904) 55 W. Va. 226, 46 S. E. 1014; Hegenmyer v. Marks (1887) 37 Minn. 6, 32 N. W. 785; McLennan v. Cole (1923) 224 Mich. 225, 195 N. W. 63; Render & Hammett v. Hartford Fire Ins. Co. (1925) 127 S. E. 902, 33 Ga. App. 716.

give the principal timely notice, that he may make other arrangements. If debts which were to be paid to him are not paid, if deliveries which were to be made to him are not made, if notices, demands, waivers, permissions, and the like which should come to him do not come or if those which should not come do come,—in these and a great variety of similar cases, he should give the principal timely notice.

CHAPTER XVII

THE DUTIES AND LIABILITIES OF
THE PRINCIPAL TO THE AGENT

§ 542. **In general.** The chief duties of the principal to the agent—using that term in its broadest sense so as to include both those technically agents and those more commonly characterized as servants—are (1) to pay him his compensation for services rendered; (2) to reimburse him for expenses, and indemnify him against losses and liabilities, properly incurred in the execution of the agency; and (3) to compensate him for such physical injuries received in the principal's service as were the result of the principal's negligence, or, under modern statutes, are compensable by the principal, irrespective of the negligence of either party.

I. The Payment of Compensation

§ 543. **Preliminary considerations.** The agent's right to compensation may be determined by the contract of the parties, or be implied by law. In most instances the parties have come to an understanding, and where they have expressly agreed that the agent shall or shall not be entitled to compensation, their agreement is usually conclusive.[1]

It is thus apparent that the agent's right to compensation will rest on either express or implied contract and that a thorough analysis of it would involve an investigation and a summary of virtually the whole law of Contract. Such a

[1] See Resso v. Lehan (1895) 96 Iowa 45, 64 N. W. 689 (compare Magarrell v. Magarrell (1888) 74 Iowa 378, 37 N. W. 961); Faloon v. McIntyre (1886) 118 Ill. 292, 8 N. E. 315; Collar v. Patterson (1891) 137 Ill. 403, 27 N. E. 604; Allen v. Allen (1886) 60 Mich. 635, 27 N. W. 702; Disbrow v. Durand (1892) 54 N. J. L. 343, 24 Atl. 545; Hall v. Finch (1871) 29 Wis. 278; Lockwood v. Robbins (1890) 125 Ind. 398, 25 N. E. 455.

project is plainly impossible here, not only because of considerations of space but because of the stated scope and purpose of this text. The reader must be referred to standard treatises on the subject of contract.[2] Here it is proposed only to state a few general rules in the briefest form and then to deal, in slightly more detail with several particular problems that are both highly characteristic of the principal and agent relation and of great practical importance because of the amount of litigation engendered thereby.

1. *Interpretation of the Contract and Rights on Termination*

§ 544. **Necessity of express agreement.** An express agreement to pay is not usually necessary. As a rule, wherever services have been rendered by one at the express request of another, and especially when rendered in the line of the business or profession of the one rendering them, it will be presumed, until the contrary is shown, that they were to be paid for.[3] If the person who requested them contends that they were to be gratuitous, he will have the burden of proving it.

A request may be at times implied, as where one knowingly receives without protest services of a sort usually paid for, which, as he had reason to believe, were being rendered upon the basis that they had in fact been requested by the recipient and were to be paid for by him.[4]

But no promise to pay will be implied, even for requested services, where the parties are near relatives or others who are

[2] Neither the Restatement of Contracts nor the standard treatises of Corbin and Williston contain unified treatments of employment contracts; recourse must be had to the index for particular topics. A compact summary of the subject will be found in Restatement, §§ 432–457.

[3] See Gilbert v. Judson (1890) 85 Cal. 105, 24 Pac. 643; Morehouse v. Remson (1890) 59 Conn. 392, 22

Atl. 427; Zerrahn v. Ditson (1895) 117 Mass. 553; Beatty v. Russell (1894) 41 Neb. 321, 59 N. W. 919; Ames v. Lamont (1900) 107 Wis. 531, 83 N. W. 780.

[4] See Bradford v. Kimberly (1818) 3 Johns. Ch. (N. Y.) 431; Succession of Kreheler (1892) 44 La. Ann. 726, 11 So. 35; Dougherty v. Whitehead (1860) 31 Mo. 255; Linn v. Linderoth (1891) 40 Ill. App. 320; Prince v. McRae (1881)

members of the same family and are therefore presumptively acting from other motives than pecuniary ones.[5] In such a case, the promise to pay must be express.

So no promise to pay will be implied where the circumstances rebut such an inference, as where the services were rendered as a mere act of kindness,[6] or upon the hope or expectation, merely, that they would be paid for.[7] *A fortiori* not for services officiously and obtrusively thrust upon another without shadow of request.[8]

§ 545. **The amount of compensation.** If it be found that the agent is entitled to compensation, the next question will be as to the *amount*. Where the parties have agreed upon the amount of compensation to be paid, the agreement will usually be conclusive, both as to the maximum and the minimum recovery.[9] In such a case, evidence of the customary rate or the reasonable value is irrelevant.

Where no amount is agreed upon, the law will imply a promise to pay the market or customary rate if the parties are dealing with reference to such a rate;[10] if not, to pay

84 N. C. 674; Harrel v. Zimpleman (1886) 66 Tex. 292, 17 S. W. 478.

[5] See Wood v. Brewer (1880) 66 Ala. 570; McCrary v. Ruddick (1871) 33 Iowa 521; Shelton v. Johnson (1874) 40 Iowa 84; Muscott v. Stubbs (1880) 24 Kan. 520; Coe v. Wager (1879) 42 Mich. 49, 3 N. W. 248; Kinder v. Pope (1905) 106 Mo. App. 536, 80 S. W. 315; Garrey v. Stadler (1886) 67 Wis. 512, 30 N. W. 787; Harrison v. Gotlieb (1888) 2 O. C. D. 109, 3 Ohio Cir. Ct. 191.

[6] See Chadwick v. Knox (1855) 31 N. H. 226.

[7] See Scott v. Maier (1885) 56 Mich. 554, 23 N. W. 218; St. Jude's Church v. Van Denberg (1875) 31 Mich. 287; Allen v. Bryson (1885) 67 Iowa 591, 25 N. W. 820.

[8] See Welch v. Collenbaugh (1911) 150 Iowa 692, 130 N. W. 792; Samuels v. Luchenbach (1903) 205 Pa. 428, 54 Atl. 1091.

[9] See Wallace v. Floyd (1857) 29 Pa. St. 184; Hamilton v. Frothingham (1886) 59 Mich. 253, 26 N. W. 486; Jefferson v. Burhans (1898) 85 Fed. 949; Prouty v. Perry (1909) 142 Iowa 294, 120 N. W. 722; Ames v. Lamont (1900) 107 Wis. 531, 83 N. W. 780; Ullmann v. May (1947) 147 Ohio St. 468, 72 N.E.2d 63.

[10] See Hollis v. Weston (1892) 156 Mass. 357, 31 N. E. 483; Potts v. Aechternacht (1880) 93 Pa. 138; Vilas v. Downer (1849) 21 Vt. 419.

the usual sum, if there be a usage, and if not, then to pay what the services are reasonably worth.[11]

For the purpose of determining what they are reasonably worth, the opinions of witnesses who are familiar with the subject may be received.[12]

The agent *may* agree that the amount of his compensation shall be fixed by the principal, as where he agrees to work for what the latter "thinks he is worth," [13] but such an unusual agreement must be clearly shown.[14]

§ 546. Where employment terminated by principal.

Where the employment was merely at will, and not for a definite time, the principal may terminate it at any time; in which case the agent will only be entitled to compensation for such services as he has already performed, and which the principal has accepted.

Where the employment was for a definite time, different considerations arise. Even here the employer may terminate it rightfully, although the prescribed time has not expired, if he has reserved the right to do so by the contract. He may also do so rightfully where the employee is guilty of conduct which will justify his discharge, such as wilful disobedience or misconduct, disloyalty, and the like.

Even though the employer may have no legal justification for terminating the employment, he usually has the *power* to do so, because, though he may thereby break the contract, such contracts are not usually specifically enforced, and the employee must resort to an action at law for damages. What his remedy is, in such a case, is considered in the following section.

[11] See Tucker v. Preston (1887) 60 Vt. 473, 11 Atl. 726; Slater v. Cook (1896) 93 Wis. 104, 67 N. W. 15; Stockbridge v. Crooker (1852) 34 Me. 349; Jorgenson v. Midland Nat. Life Ins. Co. (1945) 71 S. D. 43, 21 N.W.2d 54; Meyers v. Wells (1948) 252 Wis. 352, 31 N.W.2d 512.

[12] See Eggleston v. Boardman (1877) 37 Mich. 14; Bowen v. Bowen (1881) 74 Ind. 470; Johnson v. Thompson (1880) 72 Ind. 167.

[13] See Butler v. Winona Mill Co. (1881) 28 Minn. 205, 9 N. W. 697.

[14] See Millar v. Cuddy (1880) 43 Mich. 273, 5 N. W. 316.

§ 547. **Where employment wrongfully terminated.** Where the agent has been employed for a definite time, and his employment is wrongfully terminated before that time has expired, he has usually his choice of three remedies (though the second and third differ only as to the time when the action is brought):

1. He may treat the contract as *rescinded,* and bring an action at once to recover, without reference to the contract, the reasonable value of the services already rendered, less any amount already paid him.[15]

2. He may treat the contract as in force but *broken,* and bring an action at once to recover damages for the *probable* loss which he has sustained by its violation—i. e., the damages based upon the reasonable expectation of his finding other employment.[16]

3. He may treat the contract as in force but broken and wait until the expiration of the term (if the statute of limitations does not prevent), and then recover damages for the *actual* loss which he has sustained by its violation.[17]

---

[15] The justification for this right to treat the contract as "rescinded," is commonly said to be found in the conduct of the employer; he has shown that he regards the contract as not existing, and the employee, it is said, "may take him at his word," and may also treat the contract as ended.

[16] It is held in some cases that, if the action is tried before the expiration of the term, there can be no recovery for damages beyond the time of the trial, as they would be too speculative. See Gordon v. Brewster (1858) 7 Wis. 355; Van Winkle v. Satterfield (1894) 58 Ark. 617, 25 S. W. 1113; Mt. Hope Cemetery Ass'n v. Weidenmann (1891) 139 Ill. 67, 28 N. E. 834.

But the weight of authority permits reasonably probable future damages to be recovered. See Cutter v. Gillette (1895) 163 Mass. 95, 39 N. E. 1010; Webb v. Depew (1908) 152 Mich. 698, 116 N. W. 560; Heffelrich v. Sherman (1912) 28 S. Dak. 627, 134 N. W. 815; Hamilton v. Love (1899) 152 Ind. 641, 53 N. E. 181.

See also Pierce v. Tennessee Coal Co. (1898) 173 U. S. 1, 19 S. Ct. 335, 43 L. Ed. 591.

[17] See Howard v. Daly (1875) 61 N. Y. 362; Sutherland v. Wyer (1877) 67 Me. 64; Olmstead v. Bach (1893) 78 Md. 132, 27 Atl. 501; Boland v. Glendale Quarry Co. (1895) 127 Mo. 520, 30 S. W. 151; Hamilton v. Love (1899) 152 Ind. 641, 53 N. E. 181, 54 N. E. 437; James v. Allen Co. (1887) 44 Ohio St. 226, 6 N. E. 246; Baltimore Base Ball Club v. Pickett (1894)

He cannot pursue all of these remedies, and a recovery upon one will bar a recovery upon another.[18]

The second and third are in addition to his right to recover wages already earned, but not paid, at the time of the discharge.

§ 548. Agent's duty to mitigate his damage.

It is in general the duty of an agent wrongfully discharged before the expiration of his term, to use reasonable diligence to obtain other employment of a like kind, and thus reduce his damage as far as possible; but he is generally held not obliged to take employment of an entirely different kind, or to move away to a different place to find it.[19] Some of the cases state this exception much more strongly than others.[20]

Re-employment by the original employer himself is not to be declined upon that ground alone, though there may be other circumstances, such as his objectionable character or his former treatment, which would justify declining it.[21]

78 Md. 375, 28 Atl. 279; Doherty v. Schipper (1911) 250 Ill. 128, 95 N. E. 74; Harrington v. Empire Cream Separator Co. (1921) 120 Me. 388, 115 Atl. 89.

[18] Thus there are many cases in which a recovery of even a small sum "quantum meruit," has been held to bar any later recovery for breach of contract. See James v. Parsons (1904) 70 Kan. 156, 78 Pac. 438; Keedy v. Long (1889) 71 Md. 385, 18 Atl. 704; Olmstead v. Bach, ante; Doherty v. Schipper, ante.

[19] See Wilkinson v. Black (1885) 80 Ala. 329; Elbert v. Los Angeles Gas Co. (1893) 97 Cal. 244, 32 Pac. 9; Hinchcliffe v. Koontz (1889) 121 Ind. 422, 23 N. E. 271; Farrell v. School Dist. (1893) 98 Mich. 43, 56 N. W. 1053; Fuchs v. Koerner (1889) 107 N. Y. 529, 14 N. E. 445.

What he earns, or could have earned, in such other employment is, of course, to be deducted from his damages. Hunt v. Lehrack (Mo. App., 1922) 245 S. W. 52; Stoffed v. Metcalfe Const. Co. (1945) 145 Neb. 450, 17 N.W.2d 3.

Voluntarily to surrender employment found has the same effect as not seeking for it: Sutherland v. Wyer (1877) 67 Me. 64.

[20] Some cases hold that if he is unable to find other employment of the same kind, he should then, rather than remain idle, accept some other employment for which he is fitted. See Simon v. Allen (1890) 76 Tex. 398, 13 S. W. 296; Perry v. Simpson Co. (1871) 37 Conn. 520; Maynard v. Royal Worcester Corset Co. (1908) 200 Mass. 1, 85 N. E. 877.

[21] See Strauss v. Meertief (1879) 64 Ala. 299; Birdsong v. Ellis

The burden of proof is usually held to be upon the employer to show that the agent, with proper diligence, might have found other employment and failed to do so.[22]

§ 549. Where employment rightfully terminated. Where, though employed for a definite term, the agent's employment has been rightfully terminated before the expiration of that term, as because of his misconduct or breach of duty, it is held, in many cases, that he cannot recover anything.[23] Where his misconduct was treacherous, fraudulent, disloyal, wilful or malicious, this holding is doubtless right,[24] but the true rule in other cases, such as negligent misconduct, seems to be that if, notwithstanding his misconduct, his services have been of some substantial value to the principal over and above the damage sustained by the principal from his misconduct, the agent may recover such excess.[25]

§ 550. Where employment terminated by operation of law. Where the employment is terminated by operation by law— as by reason of the death or insanity of one of the parties—no damages for the termination can ordinarily be recovered;

(1884) 62 Miss. 418; Beymer v. McBride (1873) 37 Iowa 114.

[22] See Van Winkle v. Satterfield (1894) 58 Ark. 617, 25 S. W. 1113; Farrell v. School Dist., ante; Odeneal v. Henry (1892) 70 Miss. 172, 12 So. 154. *Contra:* Lewis Co. v. Scott (1894) 95 Ky. 484, 16 Ky. L. Rep. 49, 26 S. W. 192.

[23] This is sometimes put upon the ground that by his misconduct he forfeits his compensation; in other cases upon the ground that, where the contract was an entire one to pay for a certain period, his failure to perform for that period, because of his justifiable discharge, defeats his right to recover,—full performance being a condition precedent. See Beach v. Mullin (1870)

34 N. J. L. 343; Peterson v. Mayer (1891) 46 Minn. 468, 49 N. W. 245.

[24] See Wadsworth v. Adams (1890) 138 U. S. 380, 11 S. Ct. 303, 34 L. Ed. 984; Sea v. Carpenter (1847) 16 Ohio 412; Vennum v. Gregory (1866) 21 Iowa 326; Brannan v. Strauss (1874) 75 Ill. 234; Sumner v. Reicheniker (1872) 9 Kan. 320. But see Massey v. Taylor, 5 Coldw. (Tenn.) 477.

[25] See Hildebrand v. American Fine Arts Co. (1901) 109 Wis. 171, 85 N. W. 268; Lawrence v. Gullifer (1854) 38 Me. 532; Kessee v. Mayfield (1859) 14 La. Ann. 90 (under the Code). Cotton v. Rand (1899) 93 Tex. 7, 51 S. W. 838, (a more liberal case).

but there may be recovery for services already rendered and accepted.[26]

Unforeseen illness usually has the same effect; but not such a disqualifying fact as bankruptcy.

§ 551. **Where agent abandons his undertaking.** Where the agent abandons his undertaking, and the employment was at will, merely, he may recover for the services already rendered. If, however, having agreed, under an entire rather than a severable contract, to serve for a definite time, the agent abandons his undertaking without cause, before the expiration of that time, it is held, in many cases, that he can recover nothing.[27] But a more liberal rule prevails in a number of states, which enables the agent, in such cases, to recover the reasonable value of the services rendered, not exceeding the contract price, after deducting damages for whatever loss the principal may have sustained by reason of the abandonment.[28]

Brief absences do not necessarily constitute an abandonment: it would depend upon the circumstances. Absence caused by an epidemic or a *vis major*, would not be a volun-

[26] See Yerrington v. Greene (1863) 7 R. I. 589; Clark v. Gilbert (1863) 26 N. Y. 279.

See Griggs v. Swift (1889) 82 Ga. 392, 9 S. E. 1062; but cf. Hughes v. Gross (1896) 166 Mass. 61, 43 N. E. 1031

[27] See Stark v. Parker (1824) 2 Pick. 267; Diefenback v. Stark (1883) 56 Wis. 462, 14 N. W. 621; Timberlake v. Thayer (1893) 71 Miss. 279, 14 So. 446; Steeples v. Newton (1879) 7 Ore. 110; cf. Todd v. Huntington (1884) 13 Ore. 9, 4 Pac. 295; Angle v. Hanna (1859) 22 Ill. 429; Miller v. Goddard (1852) 34 Me. 102; Lantry v. Parks (1827) 8 Cow. (N. Y.) 63; Natalizzio v. Valentino (1904) 71 N. J. L. 500, 59 Atl. 8; Hutchinson v. Wet-

more (1852) 2 Cal. 310; Cody v. Raynaud (1871) 1 Colo. 272.

[28] See Britton v. Turner (1834) 6 N. H. 481; Allen v. McKibbin (1858) 5 Mich. 449; McClay v. Hedge (1864) 18 Iowa 66; Parcell v. McComber (1889) 11 Neb. 209, 7 N. W. 529; Duncan v. Baker (1878) 21 Kan. 99; Carroll v. Welch (1864) 26 Tex. 147; Coe v. Smith (1853) 4 Ind. 79; Downey v. Burke (1856) 23 Mo. 228. See generally Laube, "The Defaulting Employee—Britton v. Turner Reviewed," 83 U. of Pa. L. Rev. 825 (with comment by Williston, 84 id. 68, and answer by Laube, 84 id. 69); McGowan, "The Divisibility of Employment Contracts," 21 Iowa L. Rev. 50; Woodward, Quasi-Con-

tary abandonment; neither would an absence caused by sickness, though if continued long enough it might justify the principal in terminating the contract. The agent is usually not entitled to wages during absence because of sickness, even though it is not deemed an abandonment.

2. *Special Problems:* (a) *Contracts for "Permanent" or "Life" Employment*

§ 552. Nature of the problem. It is not infrequent for an agent or servant to be employed under terms which provide that the employment shall be "permanent" or "for life." Such contracts, followed by an allegedly premature termination (nearly always on the part of the employer) [29] are very likely to lead to litigation. The cases are in general unsatisfactory; sometimes an arbitrary rule is stated, with no attempt to justify it; sometimes dubious propositions as to consideration or mutuality are urged; sometimes justifications are made that don't hold water.

§ 553. "Permanent" employment. Postponing discussion of "life" employment (and the interesting question whether there is any difference between permanent and life employment) it is apparent that the real difficulty in dealing with cases of "permanent" employment arises from the fact that the term, in this context, really means nothing. Courts assume—and no doubt with reason—that it is doubtful either if the employer supposes he has bound himself to employ the employee indefinitely or if the employee supposes he has signed himself up to work for the employer the rest of his life. On the other hand the employee certainly supposes he has achieved some sort of tenure and is not to be discharged at the whim of the employer. Assuming this to be a correct appraisal of the assumptions involved, what kind of employment has been

tracts, §§ 167–174; Williston, Contracts, § 1477; notes, 24 Col. L. Rev. 885; 43 Harv. L. Rev. 647.

[29] In the very extensive annotation, 135 A. L. R. 646, there seems to be no case in which the employer is complaining of the employee's alleged breach in quitting his job.

created? Obviously one neither really permanent, nor one at will. But—this is the difficulty—there is no such thing.

§ 554.   ——Courts have struggled manfully to create and define some intermediate variety of tenure. Thus in Heideman v. Tall's Travel Shops,[30] the court says that plaintiff was to have "a steady job, as that term is commonly understood; an employment terminable at the will of either party." And in Arentz v. Morse Dry Dock and Repair Company,[31] the court defines a permanent employment very simply: it is one that is not temporary, as to build a ship or paint a house. However, it is scarcely to be supposed that one offered a permanent position as general manager needed to have it emphasized that it was not seasonal or differed from the job of painting a house.

Factually, the cases can be divided into three groups.

§ 555. (A) Where the employer neither suffers a special detriment nor gives a special consideration for the permanence of tenure. In many instances the nature of the contract can be simply and briefly stated: S promises—often orally [32]—to work permanently for M in consideration of M's promise to employ him permanently. Nothing more. S suffers no special detriment and gives no special consideration which can be particularly attributed to M's promise to employ him permanently. In such cases the virtually universal view is that the contract is one at will and that the employer can discharge the employee as soon as he likes, with or without cause. Courts are apt to say that this is the well-settled rule, and let it go

---

[30] (1937) 192 Wash. 513, 73 P.2d 1323.

[31] (1928) 249 N. Y. 439, 164 N. E. 342, 62 A. L. R. 231.

[32] This is usually treated as causing no statute of frauds difficulty, since the employee might die and the contract be terminated, within a year. See Carnig v. Carr (1897) 167 Mass. 544, 46 N. E. 117; Roxana Petroleum Co. v. Rice (1925) 109 Okla. 161, 235 Pac. 502. The factor may nevertheless be of significance, because of the facility with which the employee can remember that he was assured that the employment would be permanent or for life.

at that.[33] Perhaps the real reason is the feeling of courts that, absent the special equities mentioned in the following sections, this is the least objectionable of the two possible interpretations, neither of which is satisfactory. And it is further to be noted that in a number of the cases there is a real lack of mutuality since it affirmatively appears that the employee did not regard himself as bound to work indefinitely.[34]

§ 556. **(B) Where the employee suffers a special detriment in consideration of permanence of tenure.** In a considerable number of cases the employee makes a considerable change of position in order to take the job; e. g., he relinquishes a good job he already has, moves himself and family to a new home, or the like. It is true, as has been suggested,[35] that something like this is apt to be involved every time a

[33] See Weiner v. Pictorial Paper Package Corp. (1939) 303 Mass. 123, 20 N.E.2d 458 (implying that the discharge must be "in good faith"); Gensman v. West Coast Power Co. (1940) 3 Wash.2d 404, 101 P.2d 316; Littell v. Evening Star Newspaper Co. (1941) 120 F.2d 36; Lewis v. Minnesota Mut. Life Ins. Co. (1949) 240 Iowa 1249, 37 N.W.2d 316, noted in 28 Tex. L. Rev. 585.

In Faulkner v. Des Moines Drug Co. (1902) 117 Iowa 120, 90 N. W. 585, where the writing provided: "This contract in effect until mutually agreed void," the court said: "It is not conceivable that in entering into the contract in suit plaintiff supposed he was entering a service from which nothing but death or the consent of the defendant could relieve him. It is equally incredible that defendant supposed or understood that it was thereby taking into its employment a person whom it was bound to retain

in its service until such time as that person should consent to his own discharge. . . . Who can place any reasonable estimate upon the period which would probably elapse before the parties 'mutually agree' that the contract between them shall be considered 'void'? To say nothing of other quite manifest objections to the validity of a contract of this kind, it seems clear that it is entirely too indefinite to afford any reasonably certain basis for the assessment of damages, and is therefore void."

[34] See, e. g., Heideman v. Tall's Travel Shops, ante, n. 30.

[35] In Minter v. Tootle Campbell Dry Goods Co. (1915) 187 Mo. App. 16, 173 S. W. 4, it is said: "The effort of plaintiff to show an additional consideration passing from him to defendant was abortive since it shows that he merely abandoned other activities and interests to enter into the service of defendant—a thing almost every de-

person takes a new job; however, in the cases in question the change of position is usually both substantial in extent, and a known and discussed factor in the bargaining which leads to the new position.

Such a change of position, it should be noted, adds nothing technically to the employee's case, if the promises are mutual.[36] Otherwise, if treated as consideration, it might support what is sometimes spoken of as an "option" in the employee to work if he sees fit; put in different terms, it could be consideration for the employer's conditional promise to pay the employee—the condition, of course, being the employee's election to work.[37] However, it is believed that this change of position is of greatest importance from two standpoints: (a) it emphasizes to the employer (and the court) that the employee could scarcely have expected only the "steady job" [38] described in the Heideman case but must have felt he was contracting for something that could realistically

sirable servant does upon entering a new service, but which, of course, cannot be regarded as constituting any additional consideration to the master."

[36] In Littell v. Evening Star Newspaper Co., ante, n. 33, the court says: "Some of the courts have reasoned . . . that to prove a contract of permanent employment, *two* considerations *must* be shown; that is, a consideration in addition to the services to be performed; and that in the absence of two considerations there can be no contract. This misconception results from mistaking the form for the substance. If it is their purpose, the parties may enter into a contract for permanent employment—not terminable except pursuant to its express terms—by stating clearly their intention to do so, even though no other consideration

than services to be performed is expected by the employer or promised by the employee." It is to be noted that such a contract was not found in the instant case by the court, nor does it seem that in any case the intent to make such a contract has been "clearly" enough stated.

[37] See Rague v. New York Evening Journal Publishing Co. (1914) 164 App. Div. 126, 149 N. Y. S. 668.

[38] It is not meant to imply that the term "steady" employment means nothing. Doubtless it means a relationship which has subsisted for some time and gives promise of subsisting for an indefinite time to come. However, in none of the cases dealt with could the employee have expected less, so that making the characterization explicit is of little significance.

be described as permanent; (b) since the change of position has been made in reliance on the promise of the employer, there is to some extent an estoppel created against the latter.

§ 557. —— Perhaps for these reasons a considerable number of cases of this type have given relief to the employee. The reasoning and the extent of the tenure given in such cases is well illustrated by an excerpt from the leading case of Riefkin v. E. I. du Pont de Nemours & Company: [39]

"The circumstances surrounding the making of this contract largely control the interpretation to be given the words 'permanent employment' as used therein, for it must be assumed that the parties, knowing those circumstances, contracted with reference to them. The plaintiff held a position with the United States government, and the defendant agreed that, if he would resign from that position and take charge of the purchase of coal for the defendant, he would be given 'permanent employment in that capacity so long as he rendered satisfactory services and was loyal to its interests.' Relying upon this agreement, plaintiff did resign and perform his part of the contract. May it be said that it was within the contemplation of either party that 'permanent employment,' as used in the contract, meant that the plaintiff, the day following his resignation from his position with the government and the assumption of his new duties, could have been summarily discharged without any liability on the part of the defendant? Such a result could not have been contemplated by either party. The more reasonable view is that the parties contemplated that, so long as the defendant continued in a business requiring the purchase of coal and the plaintiff

---

[39] (1923) 290 Fed. 286. See also Roxana Petroleum Co. v. Rice (1925) 109 Okla. 161, 235 Pac. 502; Alabama Mills v. Smith (1939) 237 Ala. 296, 186 So. 699; Lucacher v. Kerson (1946) 159 Pa. Super. 437, 45 A.2d 245; Phelps v. Shawprint, Inc. (1951) — Mass. —, 103 N.E.2d 687. But cf. Skagerberg v. Blandin Paper Co. (1936) 197 Minn. 291, 266 N. W. 872; Edwards v. Kentucky Utilities Co. (1941) 286 Ky. 341, 150 S.W.2d 916, 135 A. L. R. 642; Savage v. Spur Distributing Co. (1949) 33 Tenn. App. 27, 228 S.W.2d 122; Chesapeake & Potomac Tel. Co. v. Murray (1951) — Md. —, 84 A.2d 870.

performed loyal and satisfactory service, he would continue
to be employed in the capacity specified in the contract. The
defendant, having introduced no evidence, is not in a position
to contend that plaintiff's discharge was for any other reason
than stated in its affidavit of defense, namely, 'because of the
fact that his services were no longer required.' In other words,
the defendant simply concluded that it could get along without plaintiff's services, and therefore, exercising a right it
assumed it possessed, discharged him. This, in the circumstances, it had no right to do."

§ 558. (C) Where the employee gives a special consideration for permanence of tenure. The common instance in this
category is that of the servant (often a railroad worker) who
releases a tort claim against the master in consideration of
the latter's promise to give him employment for life. The
question, postponed above, may be given brief notice here:
does a promise of employment "for life" differ from one of
"permanent" employment? It can be argued that "permanent," from the standpoint of the employee, would literally
mean "for the balance of his working life," which is just what
"life" means. However, the use of the latter term makes the
matter more explicit; it is hard to argue that one employed
for life is subject to discharge the next day.[40]

Whichever form the agreement takes, the equity of the one
who has released a presumably valid claim is very compelling.
He is to be paid for services at some stipulated (and presumably usual) rate; the release can only have been given to buy
permanence of tenure. As pointed out in a well-known case,[41]
if plaintiff had given five hundred dollars for a promise of
life employment, it is impossible to suppose that defendant
could keep the money and refuse the opportunity to work

[40] This is perhaps corroborated
by the fact that a number of cases
have enforced contracts for life
employment although there was no
special consideration for the tenure.
See Eggers v. Armour & Co. of Delaware (1942) 129 F.2d 729; Abbott
v. Arkansas Utilities Co. (1948)
165 F.2d 339; Eilen v. Tappin's,
Inc. (1951) 16 N. J. Super. 53, 88
A.2d 817.

[41] The Pennsylvania Co. v. Dolan
(1892) 6 Ind. App. 109, 32 N. E.
802.

promised therefor; the case is not different where a release is given rather than money.

§ 559. —— In addition to the equity mentioned, the plaintiff is likely to have in his favor the fact that the work promised is manual and humble and the defendant a large corporation not likely either to go out of business or to cease needing workers like the plaintiff. Whatever hardship there might be on an employer in forcing him to retain a general manager or an insurance agent in charge of a large territory, after relations between the parties had become strained, there is likely to be none in the case of a brakeman who asks only to be employed as such for the rest of his able working life. It is not surprising that in such cases the plaintiff ordinarily prevails.[42]

(b) Brokers' Commissions

§ 560. In general. The aspect of the agent's right to compensation which causes the most constant and extensive litigation deals with the real estate broker's right to a commission. Because of the importance of this subject it is given a brief separate treatment here. In modern practice the client is usually given a standard listing contract to sign and this, if well drafted, should eliminate many of the uncertainties that lead to litigation. Unfortunately not all clients sign contracts, not all contracts are well drafted, and there are certain difficult questions of fact that cannot be eliminated by any amount of drafting.

It will be remembered that the real estate broker barely qualifies as being technically an agent at all; his real position is more that of one to whom an offer is made which the broker tries to accept. The offer is to pay a commission (usually of specified amount) on the performance of a certain service, viz., finding for the offeror (client) a person who is ready, able

[42] See Pierce v. Tennessee Coal, Iron & Ry. Co. (1899) 173 U. S. 1, 19 S. Ct. 335, 43 L. Ed. 591; Fisher v. Roper Lumber Co. (1922) 183 N. C. 485, 111 S. E 857, 35 A. L. R. 1417; Duff v. Ford Motor Co. (1936) 91 S.W.2d 871; annotations, 35 A. L. R. 1432 and 135 A. L. R. 646.

and willing to buy the offeror's property on the terms which he has named to the broker. The difficult questions are likely to be: (a) has the broker produced a buyer meeting the qualifications specified, before the offer was effectively revoked by the lapse of time, express revocation by the owner, or implied revocation resulting from the sale of the property, by the owner, in person or through the offices of another broker; (b) to what extent, and how, may the owner by contract preclude himself from revoking the offer, and what are the broker's remedies for breach of such a contract?

§ 561. **Statutory requirements.** As a preliminary consideration it should be noted that the broker's right to commission is in many states limited by one or both of two types of statutes. The first, in the nature of a statute of frauds, requires that contracts to pay a broker's commission shall not be valid unless in writing. Such statutes, often rather strictly construed,[43] not only preclude a suit on the express contract but are almost universally held to bar the quasi-contractual recovery possible under some other statutes of frauds, since such a recovery would give the plaintiff precisely what the statute forbids, namely compensation for services rendered as broker.[44]

The second type of statute provides for the qualification and licensing of brokers and prohibits unlicensed brokers from carrying on business. Such statutes, unless construed as for the purpose of raising revenue only,[45] are usually held to prevent the recovery of commission by an unlicensed broker;[46]

---

[43] See Brest v. Meanat Realty Co. (1944) 245 Wis. 631, 15 N.W.2d 798; Breen v. Debron (1950) 10 N. J. Super. 167, 76 A.2d 837; Ward v. Potts (1950) 228 Ind. 228, 91 N.E.2d 643.

[44] See Hale v. Kreisel (1927) 194 Wis. 271, 215 N. W. 227, 56 A. L. R. 780; Baugh v. Darley (1947) 112 Utah 1, 184 P.2d 335; Featherman v. Kennedy (1948) 122 Mont. 256, 200 P.2d 243.

[45] See Baskett v. Jones (1920) 189 Ky. 391, 225 S. W. 158; Garvin v. Gordon (1932) 36 N. M. 304, 14 P.2d 264; Note, 31 Col. L. Rev. 157.

[46] See Phelan v. Hilda Gravel Mining Co. (1928) 203 Cal. 264, 263 Pac. 520, 56 A. L. R. 476; Massie v. Dudley (1939) 173 Va. 42, 3 S.E.2d 176.

often the statute contains an express provision to this effect. More problems of interpretation arise under these than under statutes of frauds, since there is often difficulty in determining just what persons are within the prohibition.[47]

§ 562. **Broker must not be mere volunteer.** Another preliminary consideration is to be noted: it must be clear that there has been an offer by the owner. Plainly a mere volunteer cannot find a buyer for one whom he knows or suspects to be interested in selling property, and then claim compensation for the unasked service. Further, while courts are liberal in finding an offer, it is not enough that the owner has expressed to the broker his willingness to sell; he must also in some way have expressed or implied a willingness to pay for the production of a buyer.[48]

§ 563. **Nonexclusive listings: In general.** In the simplest case the client does not agree not to revoke the offer nor to give the broker any exclusive rights. The commission will be earned if, and only if, the broker produces a buyer ready, able and willing [49] to buy on the owner's terms before the offer is

[47] The statute does not apply to the employee of a firm engaged in selling its own property, Strumpf v. State (1944) 31 Ala. App. 409, 18 So.2d 104, nor to one not professionally a broker and engaging in an isolated transaction: Downing v. Marks (1935) 318 Pa. 289, 178 Atl. 676; cf. Corson v. Keane (1950) 4 N. J. 221, 72 A.2d 314, wherein it appears that the New Jersey legislature, after such a decision, amended the statute to cover single transactions. One who has voluntarily paid the commission, though not compellable to do so under the statute, cannot recover it back: Buschbaum v. Barron (1948) 1 N. J. Super. 4, 61 A.2d 512.

[48] See Dunn v. Price (1894) 87

Tex. 318, 28 S. W. 681; Monill v. Farr (1931) 130 Me. 384, 156 Atl. 383; McCoy v. Wachovia Bank & Trust Co. (1933) 204 N. C. 721, 169 S. E. 644; Whiston v. David Meyer Bldg. Corp. (1949) 337 Ill. App. 67, 84 N.E.2d 858. As to the amount of compensation, see Watson v. Durepo (1950) 76 R. I. 375, 71 A.2d 103; Coldicott v. Miller Development Co. (1946) 47 A.2d 518; Weinreb v. Strauss (1951) 80 A.2d 47; Driscoll v. Bunar (1952) — Mass. —, 103 N.E.2d 809.

[49] As to the prospective buyer's financial ability, see Hare v. Bauer (1947) 223 Minn. 285, 26 N.W.2d 359; Mangano v. Rooney (1950) — R. I. —, 74 A.2d 867; Schanerman v. Everett & Carbin, Inc.

revoked or the land is sold by the owner or another broker. In practice "produce" normally means to present to the owner an offer signed by the prospective buyer to buy on the stipulated terms; it is doubtless also sufficient if the broker notifies the owner that he has found a proper buyer, and is presently able to bring him or his signed contract to the owner.[50] The broker, it will be remembered, has ordinarily no power to contract on behalf of the owner. The latter is not bound to the prospective buyer and may refuse to contract with him, or it may be that he is unable to enforce a contract, because his title is not marketable. In either case, however, he is bound to pay the commission, since the broker has tendered proper performance, and his rights cannot be defeated by the owner's default.[51]

§ 564. **Must the asking price be obtained?** However, the generality of the proposition stated in the previous section needs some qualification. It is true that the owner, if he wishes and the broker is willing to comply, may provide that no commission shall be owing unless there is a complete and literal compliance with the terms he names; the broker, having

(1952) 18 N. J. Super. 552, 87 A.2d 28; Driscoll v. Bunar (1952) — Mass. —, 103 N.E.2d 809.

[50] See Johnson Bros. v. Wright (1904) 124 Iowa 61, 99 N. W. 103; Schamberg v. Kahn (1924) 279 Pa. 477, 124 Atl. 138.

[51] See Kaercher v. Schee (1933) 189 Minn. 272, 249 N. W. 180, 88 A. L. R. 294; Schimpf v. Schmidt (1937) 146 Kan. 917, 73 P.2d 1052; O'Hara v. Bronx Consumers Ice Co. (1930) 254 N. Y. 210, 172 N. E. 472; Blitzer v. Burns (1937) 15 N. J. Misc. 736, 165 Atl. 628; Knowles v. Henderson (1945) 156 Fla. 31, 22 So.2d 384, 169 A. L. R. 600; Paul v. Markle (1947) 250 Wis. 81, 26 N.W.2d 276; Broomfield v. Abass (1848) 320 Mich. 291, 30

N.W.2d 874; Dillon v. Barnard (1951) — Mass. —, 101 N.E.2d 345; Hummel v. Thomas (1951) 345 Ill. App. 275, 102 N.E.2d 683.

Nor can the owner defeat the broker's right to commission by selling to another after he knows that the broker has found a buyer: Gumo v. Lind (1945) 219 Minn. 438, 18 N.W.2d 125.

The broker may be the effective cause of the sale and so entitled to commission although the sale is made not to the prospect but to someone associated with him: White v. Grovier (1946) 237 Iowa 377, 21 N.W.2d 769; Thornton v. Forbes (1950) 326 Mass. 308, 93 N.E.2d 742.

It is generally not a bar to the

agreed, is bound.[52] This interpretation, however, is not one which courts are prone to make, and it will not be made unless the facts leave no doubt that such was the intent. Normally courts will construe terms, particularly as to price, as preliminary and nominal; the price named is simply an asking price, which the owner would like to get, but which he scarcely expects to get and certainly does not mean to insist on. Thus where the owner, as a result of dickering with the prospective buyer, finally sells to him for less or on different terms than those originally specified, the broker's right to a commission is not affected (save, as under the listing contract, the amount of his commission may be affected by the price actually paid).[53]

§ 565. **The owner may not revoke in bad faith.** A further and analogous qualification needs to be made. In general, there seems to be no rule which prohibits the owner from revoking the listing or from locating, negotiating with, and ultimately selling to, a buyer of his own—even one found by a different broker—in spite of his knowledge that the original broker is dealing with a possible buyer and expects presently to produce him. It is enough that he sells before the original broker's buyer is technically produced. The owner's power to revoke, however, is affected by one very important (and obviously very necessary) limitation: he may not "in bad faith"

broker's recovery that the owner did not know that the buyer had been located and sent to deal with him by the broker: Jordan v. Hilbert (1932) 131 Me. 56, 158 Atl. 853; Libby v. Ivers & Pond Piano Co. (1945) 317 Mass. 478, 58 N.E.2d 834; Ranney v. Rock (1949) 135 Conn. 479, 66 A.2d 111; Bowie v. Martin (1952) — Md. —, 85 A.2d 786. Cf. Mecklenborg v. Niehaus (1948) 85 Ohio App. 271, 84 N.E.2d 763.

[52] See Patton, Temple & Williamson v. Garnett (1926) 147 Va.

1009, 133 S. E. 495; Murphy v. Bradley (1940) 200 Ark. 208, 138 S.W.2d 791, 128 A. L. R. 427.

[53] See Eldridge v. Usry and Zollner (1925) 273 S. W. 624; Colvin v. Post Manufacturing & Land Co. (1919) 225 N. Y. 510, 122 N. E. 454; Wilson v. Schmidt & Wilson, Inc. (1945) 184 Va. 642, 35 S.E.2d 737; Morton v. Drichel (1946) 237 Iowa 1209, 24 N.W.2d 812; Palmtag v. Danielson (1947) 30 Cal.2d 517, 183 P.2d 265; Restatement, § 447, Comment b.

revoke the broker's authority and then proceed to sell to a buyer discovered by the broker and with whom the broker is negotiating.

§ 566. —— The "bad faith" spoken of here appears to mean no more than that the owner is deliberately trying to get the broker's services for nothing, either to avoid payment of the promised commission, or to give the benefit thereof to a favored buyer or another broker.[54] Where such a scheme is charged, it will be a question of fact—and often a very difficult one— whether the owner is trying to cheat the broker, or whether either the broker had given up trying to convince the buyer, or the owner, genuinely feeling that the prospects did not justify further negotiation, had notified the broker that his authority was terminated. In either of the latter contingencies mentioned, the broker has had his opportunity and failed. If the owner thereafter reopens negotiations with the buyer and finally sells to him, no commission has been earned.[55]

§ 567. **Commission to be paid "upon consummation of sale."** As already stated, it is naturally within the power of the parties to make any agreement they wish as to the conditions upon which commission is due. A number of cases deal with a contract providing for the payment of commission "upon consummation of sale" or some similar language. This presents a troublesome problem of construction. The literal import of the language is clear: commission is to be paid when, and only when, title passes. This interpretation, however, would permit the owner to defeat the broker's right to commission by his own deliberate default, a result not readily to be accepted.

[54] See Baskett v. Jones (1920) 189 Ky. 391, 225 S. W. 158; Goodman v. Marcol, Inc. (1933) 261 N. Y. 188, 184 N. E. 755, noted in 33 Col. L. Rev. 914; Houston v. H. G. Wolff & Son Investment Co. (1933) 94 Colo. 73, 28 P.2d 255; Chicago Title & Trust Co. v. Guild (1946) 329 Ill. App. 374, 68 N.E.2d 615; Restatement, § 454.

[55] Rosenfield v. Wall (1920) 94 Conn. 418, 109 Atl. 409, 9 A. L. R. 1189; Owens v. Mountain States Telephone & Telegraph Co. (1936) 50 Wyo. 331, 63 P.2d 1006; Robert A. Cline, Inc. v. Union Thread Co.

The cases indicate that under such a listing contract the owner need not affirmatively proceed to attempt enforcement. If the buyer refuses to perform, the owner may let the matter drop, without liability to the broker. He may even retain a down payment. If he sues for damages, however, and recovers, this is a notional consummation and he owes commission. The same is true if specific performance is sought but cannot be had because of the owner's defective title.[56]

§ 568. Contracts for "exclusive agency" or "exclusive sale." Increasingly, litigation involves listing contracts promising the broker an exclusive agency or an exclusive right of sale. It has been doubted on high authority that there is a difference between the two [57] and this is doubtless true in the sense that both types raise the same basic problem. However, it is ordinarily said that where there is an exclusive agency the owner retains the right to sell himself, though not by another agent, whereas when there is an exclusive right of sale the owner relinquishes for the duration of the listing the right to sell even without the intervention of another agent.[58] Under modern exclusive sale contracts there is often an express provision entitling the broker to the commission where the property is sold by anyone within a specified time.

(1943) 73 Ohio App. 393, 56 N.E.2d 517; Glaserud v. Hoff (1947) 75 N. D. 311, 27 N.W.2d 305; Snedker v. Baltimore Brick Co. (1951) — Md. —, 84 A.2d 868.

56 See Peak v. Jurgens (1935) 5 Cal.App.2d 573, 43 P.2d 569; Feist & Feist, Inc. v. Spitzer (1930) 107 N. J. L. 138, 150 Atl. 406; Amies v. Wesnofske (1931) 255 N. Y. 156, 174 N. E. 436, 73 A. L. R. 918, noted in 31 Col. L. Rev. 701; Stern v. Gepo Realty Corp. (1942) 289 N. Y. 274, 45 N.E.2d 440, noted in 43 Col. L. Rev. 108; Goldstein v. Rosenberg (1947) 331 Ill. App. 374, 73 N.E.2d 171; Keifhaber v. Yannelli (1950) 9 N. J. Super. 139, 75

A.2d 478. As to other typical conditions, see Cooper v. Liberty Nat. Bank of Chicago (1947) 332 Ill. App. 459, 75 N.E.2d 769; MacNeill Real Estate, Inc. v. Rines (1949) — Me. —, 64 A.2d 179; Finch v. Donella (1950) 136 Conn. 621, 73 A.2d 336; Borowski v. Meyers (1950) — Md. —, 72 A.2d 701; Richard v. Falleti (1951) 13 N. J. Super. 534, 81 A.2d 17.

57 See Williston, Contracts (Rev. Ed. 1936) § 60A, n. 2.

58 See Des Rivieres v. Sullivan (1924) 247 Mass. 443, 142 N. E. 111; Hood v. Gillespie (1950) 190 Tenn. 548, 230 S.W.2d 997; Restatement, § 449, Comment b.

§ 569. ——— If the broker produces a buyer within the specified time, the case does not differ from one where a nonexclusive listing is involved. Likewise, if no buyer is found, and no sale made. The difficult question arises when the broker produces no buyer but the owner sells in violation of the contract. Is there any consideration to support the owner's express or implied promise not to make the sale? [59] If so, what is the broker's measure of relief? The older view finds a lack of mutuality, pointing out that the agent has not promised to do anything, and that no action would lie against him by the owner if he never made any effort to find a buyer.[60] Probably a majority of the more modern cases hold the owner liable.[61] As said in a recent Ohio decision: [62] "Although the reasoning is not always the same, most of the cases dealing with the subject hold that where a real estate agent, under the type of instrument involved in the instant case, has expended time, effort [63] or money in attempting to secure a purchaser for the property, the consideration is supplied to make a binding and enforceable contract."

Most commonly the broker is held entitled to the agreed commission, whether or not the contract specifically provides for this.[64] In a Kansas case [65] it was held that the broker

[59] See Chamberlain v. Grisham (1950) 360 Mo. 655, 230 S.W.2d 721, where the contract provided expressly that the listing by the broker and his efforts to find a buyer should be deemed consideration.

[60] See Kolb v. Bennett Land Co. (1896) 74 Miss. 567, 21 So. 233; Des Rivieres v. Sullivan (1924) 247 Mass. 443, 142 N. E. 111, and extension thereof in Bartless v. Keith (1950) 325 Mass. 265, 90 N.E.2d 308. Cf. Coan v. Holbrook (1951) — Mass. —, 97 N.E.2d 649.

[61] See Harris v. McPherson (1921) 97 Conn. 164, 115 Atl. 723, 24 A. L. R. 1530, noted in 31 Yale L. J. 674; Harry H. Rosin Co. v. Eksterowicz (1950) — Del. —, 73 A.2d 648; Chamberlain v. Grisham (1950) 360 Mo. 655, 230 S.W.2d 721; Geyler v. Dailey (1950) 70 Ariz. 135, 217 P.2d 583; Prager v. Winn (1952) 170 Pa. Super. 224, 85 A.2d 628.

[62] Bell v. Dimmerling (1948) 149 Ohio St. 165, 78 N.E.2d 49.

[63] In Fischer v. Patterson (1952) — N. H. —, 86 A.2d 851, it is held that the broker's failure to make reasonable efforts to sell the property may justify the owner in rescinding the contract and selling through another broker.

[64] See cases in note 61, ante.

[65] Isern v. Gordon (1929) 127 Kan. 296, 273 Pac. 435, 64 A. L. R.

was entitled to reimbursement for expenses incurred and "such prospective profits as he can reasonably establish would have been his but for the wrongful revocation of his authority."

II. REIMBURSEMENT AND INDEMNITY OF AGENT

§ 570. Agent's right to reimbursement. An agent, who, at the actual request of his principal, expends or advances his own money for the principal's benefit, is entitled to be reimbursed by the principal. Equally so is the agent who advances money or incurs for the principal's benefit, upon an implied request, inferred from the fact that he was asked or directed by the principal to perform a service, in the proper execution of which, or as a proper incident to which, the disbursement or advance became suitable or necessary.[66]

Thus if the agent were requested to buy goods for the principal for cash, but was not given the cash; or was requested to go upon a journey for the principal which involved the payment of railroad fares or hotel bills, but was not supplied with funds, or was directed to secure services or labor which must be paid for when rendered, but was not provided with the necessary funds; and the agent should fairly and reasonably advance his own money for the purpose, a claim for reimbursement would properly arise.

Clearly, on the other hand, he could not recover for officious or obtrusive payments, or for sums expended to cure or remove the results of his own misconduct or breach of duty, or for sums expended in promoting an enterprise which he knows to be illegal.[67]

391. And see Louis Schlesinger Co. v. Rice (1950) 4 N. J. 169, 72 A.2d 197.

[66] See Clifton v. Ross (1894) 60 Ark. 97, 28 S. W. 1085; Arnold v. Arnold (1910) 83 Kan. 539, 112 Pac. 163; Blazo v. Gill (1894) 143 N. Y. 232, 38 N. E. 101; Monnet v. Notz (1891) 127 N. Y. 151, 27 N. E. 827; Lyon v. Sweeney (1892) 91 Mich. 478, 51 N. W. 1006; Perin v. Parker (1888) 126 Ill. 201, 18 N. E. 747; Ward v. Tucker (1893) 7 Wash. 399, 35 Pac. 126, 1086; Bibb v. Allen (1892) 149 U. S. 481, 13 S. Ct. 950, 37 L. Ed. 819.

[67] See Child v. Morley (1800) 8 T. R. 610; Hurst v. Holding (1810)

§ 571. Agent's right to indemnity. The agent is entitled to assume that if the principal requests or directs him to do an act for the principal which involves the pledging of the agent's own credit, as, for example, to buy goods, borrow money, or secure services upon the agent's own responsibility, the principal intends to indemnify the agent against any loss thereby. He is also entitled to assume that acts which the principal directs him to perform and which the agent does not know to be and are not obviously unjustified or illegal, may be performed without incurring loss or legal liability to third persons, or, at least, that if such loss or liability is incurred in carrying out the principal's directions, the principal intends to assume the responsibility. The agent is therefore entitled to be indemnified by the principal for any liability so incurred at the principal's request, and to be indemnified by the principal for any loss which the agent may sustain by reason of performing and as the proximate result of his performing, at the direction of the principal, any act which is not manifestly illegal and which the agent did not know to be wrong. In such cases the law implies a promise by the principal to indemnify the agent.[68]

§ 572. —— Within the same principle must doubtless be included cases in which the principal permits an agent to go on acting, after a revocation of the authority, known to the principal, but of which, as he knows, the agent is ignorant.

This does not, of course, extend to liabilities or losses caused solely by the agent's own misconduct or default,[69] nor to those

---

3 Taunt. 32; Samuels v. Oliver (1889) 130 Ill. 73, 22 N. E. 499; Mohr v. Miesen (1891) 47 Minn. 228, 49 N. W. 862.

[68] See D'Arcy v. Lyle (1813) 5 Binn. (Pa.) 441; Powell v. Newburgh (1822) 19 Johns. (N. Y.) 284; Beach v. Branch (1876) 57 Ga. 362; Searing v. Butler (1873) 69 Ill. 575; Henderson v. Eckern (1911) 115 Minn. 410, 132 N. W. 715; Hoggan v. Cahoon (1903) 26 Utah 444, 73 Pac. 512; Evans, Coleman & Evans, Ltd. v. Pistorino (1923) 245 Mass. 94, 139 N. E. 848; Abrams v. Harry A. Roth & Co. (1941) 310 Ill. App. 490, 34 N.E.2d 725; Lauderdale v. Peace Baptist Church of Birmingham (1944) 246 Ala. 178, 19 So.2d 538; Differential Steel Car Co. v. Macdonald (1950) 180 F.2d 260.

[69] See Duncan v. Hill (1873) L. R. 8 Exch. 242.

which are in no way the result of the execution of the agency, or which are caused by the independent and unexpected wrongful acts of third persons for which the principal is in no wise responsible.

§ 573. **None where act illegal.** But no promise to indemnify will be implied, and even an express promise will not be enforced, if the act directed to be done was one which the agent knew or must be presumed to have known was illegal.[70]

III. PROTECTION FROM PHYSICAL INJURY

1. *Common-law Rules*

§ 574. **In general.** This topic, naturally, has to do with the relation of master and servant. No doubt a principal might tortiously injure his agent but, if so, the liability would be based on ordinary tort rules, unaffected by any special consideration stemming from the law of Principal and Agent.

In a certain sense, the same might be said of master and servant. However, the control exercised by the master over the servant, and the fact that the servant is subject to a constant danger of being injured by the master's machinery or by the negligence of the master's other servants, has resulted in a body of law, characteristic of the relation.

§ 575. —— At the same time, it is well to remember that the law applicable is basically tort law. The idea that policy requires that the injured servant be looked after, wholly irrespective of his or his master's fault, is a modern one, quite uncharacteristic of the tough and individualistic common law of a hundred years ago. No doubt the idea is a good one, and few wish the "good" old days back. Nevertheless, in fairness to the often-criticized law of the past, it should be noted that much of it is not only unreasonable but unsuitable, so long as the basic premise is that the servant has no claim against the master unless he can make out a case in tort.

[70] See Coventry v. Barton (1819)   Hanke (1894) 155 Ill. 617, 40 N. E. 17 Johns. (N. Y.) 142; Pope v.   839.

§ 576. **Risks incident to the business — Master generally not liable.** Every undertaking for the rendition of services is attended with more or less of risk incident to the business itself, even when carried on with ordinary and reasonable care. These risks are usually as well known to the servant as to the master. Often the servant knows them better than the master. By the hypothesis they result from no fault or neglect of the master; but from the very nature of the thing to be done, or the circumstances under which it must be done. By the very act of accepting the employment, without stipulating to the contrary, it is held that the servant assumes the risk of injury from such dangers, and if he is injured by them, the master, otherwise free from fault, will not be liable.[71]

§ 577. **Master responsible for his own negligence.** On the other hand, if the servant is injured by the personal negligence of the master, occurring, e. g., where servant and master work side by side, as they often do upon the farm and in smaller enterprises, the master will be personally liable to the servant. Such injuries do not arise from the inherent nature of the work, but from the negligence of the one who caused the injury; and the servant, by merely accepting the employment, has not assumed that risk.[72]

The question of the master's responsibility for his own negligence may arise in a variety of cases with reference to injuries from places, agencies and instrumentalities contributed to the situation by the master and controlled by him. As to these,

[71] See Sweeney v. Central Pac. R. Co. (1880) 57 Cal. 15; Orman v. Mannix (1892) 17 Colo. 564, 30 Pac. 1037; Hayden v. Smithville Mfg. Co. (1861) 29 Conn. 548; Sweeney v. Berlin & Jones Envelope Co. (1886) 101 N. Y. 520, 5 N. E. 358; Lewis v. Seifert (1887) 116 Pa. 628, 11 Atl. 514.

Thus where an elderly lady was employed to exercise a dog, she could not recover from her employer when the dog ran away and the lady fell on the ice in trying to recapture him: Woodring v. Pastoret (1945) 221 Minn. 50, 21 N.W.2d 97. Cf. Cotoia v. Seale (1940) 306 Mass. 101, 27 N.E.2d 706.

As to the master's duty to give aid to a sick or injured servant, see Burns v. Bakelite Corp. (1952) — N. J. Super. —; 86 A.2d 289.

[72] See Rhoades v. Varney (1898) 91 Me. 222, 39 Atl. 552; Ashworth v. Stanwix (1861) 3 E. & E. 701.

certain duties are said to attach to the master, which will now
be considered.

§ 578. Master's duty as to place of work.

The master does
not always furnish the place to work. When he does undertake to furnish it, as he so commonly does in the case of shop,
mine, farm, yards, quarry, and other similar places, and no
other agreement respecting it is made, the law entitles the
servant to expect, and deems the master to assure him, that
the master will exercise reasonable care to furnish and maintain, so far as such care can secure it, reasonably safe conditions as to the place in which to work.[73] The law does not
demand perfection, or make the master a guarantor of safety.
If the master has performed the duty as thus stated, and the
servant nevertheless is injured, the master is not liable. The
servant assumes such a risk. If the master has not performed
this duty, and the servant, by reason thereof, and without
contributory negligence on his own part, is injured, the master
will be liable to an action for damages.[74]

If, in the place provided, there are unexpected dangers
existing or impending, known to the master but not to the
servant, and not obvious to ordinary observation, the master
owes a duty to give the servant warning.[75] This duty of warn-

[73] See Louisville & N. R. Co. v.
Stutts (1894) 105 Ala. 368, 17 So.
29; Kennedy v. Chase (1898) 119
Cal. 367, 52 Pac. 33; Williams v.
Sleepy Hollow Mining Co. (1906)
37 Colo. 62, 86 Pac. 337; McElligott
v. Randolph (1891) 61 Conn. 157,
22 Atl. 1094; Bowden v. Derby
(1903) 97 Me. 536, 55 Atl. 417;
Downey v. Gemini Mining Co.
(1902) 24 Utah 431, 68 Pac. 414;
Western Stone Co. v. Muscial
(1902) 196 Ill. 382, 63 N. E. 664;
Voet v. Lampert Lumber Co. (1944)
70 S. D. 142, 15 N.W.2d 579; Cool
v. Curtis-Wright, Inc. (1949) 362
Pa. 60, 66 A.2d 287.

[74] The duty of the master is not

absolute. It extends no further
than to exercise reasonable and
ordinary care to furnish a reasonably safe place. See Gaither v.
Clement (1922) 183 N. C. 450, 111
S. E. 782; Nelson v. Smeltzer
(1936) 221 Iowa 972, 265 N. W.
924; Canonico v. Celanese Corp. of
America (1951) 11 N. J. Super.
445, 78 A.2d 411.

[75] See Louisville & N. R. Co. v.
Hall (1888) 87 Ala. 708, 6 So. 277;
Burnside v. Peterson (1908) 43
Colo. 382, 96 Pac. 256; Louisville,
N. A. & C. Ry. Co. v. Wright
(1888) 115 Ind. 378, 16 N. E. 145,
17 N. E. 584; Ribich v. Lake
Superior Smelting Co. (1900) 123

400

ing will be enhanced in case of the youth of the servant, or his known ignorance or inexperience.[76]

§ 579. **Qualifications.** The duty as to the safe place does not extend to places into which the servant had no duty or invitation to go, and into which the master had no reasonable ground to anticipate that he would go, whether the servant went there merely out of curiosity, a desire to do something for his own interests, or even to perform a service which was not a part of h.s undertaking and as to which he was an uncalled for and unexpected volunteer.[77]

For obvious reasons, the duty as to the safe place will be much modified in the cases in which, as part of their work and as it progresses, the servants are to construct the place to work,[78] or the facilities or appliances for the work, as is often

Mich. 401, 82 N. W. 279; Brennan v. Gordon (1890) 118 N. Y. 489, 23 N. E. 810; Hewett v. Women's Hospital Aid Ass'n (1906) 73 N. H. 556, 64 Atl. 190; Blaisdell v. Davis Paper Co. (1910) 75 N. H. 497, 77 Atl. 485; Kress v. City of Newark (1952) — N. J. —, 86 A.2d 185.

The master's decision to start some other enterprise or to set free some force which he controls, which will render the place unsafe, may impose a duty of warning. See Cook v. Camp Mfg. Co. (1922) 183 N. C. 48, 110 S. E. 608.

[76] See Tedford v. Los Angeles Electric Co. (1901) 134 Cal. 76, 66 Pac. 76; Ingerman v. Moore (1891) 90 Cal. 410, 27 Pac. 306; May v. Smith (1893) 92 Ga. 95, 18 S. E. 360; Norton v. Volzke (1895) 158 Ill. 402, 41 N. E. 1085; Meier v. Way (1907) 136 Iowa 302, 111 N. W. 420; Ciriack v. Merchants Woolen Co. (1890) 151 Mass. 152, 23 N. E. 829; Greenberg v. Whitcomb Lumber Co. (1895) 90 Wis. 225, 63 N. W. 93.

Duty to warn nondelegable: Brice-Nash v. Barton Salt Co. (1908) 79 Kan. 110, 98 Pac. 768; Anderson v. Pittsburg Coal Co. (1909) 108 Minn. 455, 122 N. W. 794; Lawson v. Royal Riding Stables (1940) 305 Mass. 494, 26 N.E.2d 348; Jenkins v. Jenkins (1945) 220 Minn. 216, 19 N.W.2d 389.

[77] See Severy v. Nickerson (1876) 120 Mass. 306; Pioneer Mining & Manufacturing Co. v. Tallay (1907) 152 Ala. 162, 43 So. 800; Kennedy v. Chase (1898) 119 Cal. 637, 52 Pac. 33; O'Brien v. Western Steel Co. (1889) 100 Mo. 182, 13 S. W. 402; McCue v. National Starch Mfg. Co. (1894) 142 N. Y. 106, 36 N. E. 809; Buel v. Hines (1922) 218 Mich. 353, 188 N. W. 422.

[78] Where the workmen are to make their own place to work as they go along, as often in the case of mines, quarries, clearings, and the like, the liability of the master as to furnishing a safe place is obviously limited by the inherent

true of scaffolds, staging, platforms, and the like. Here if the master supplies suitable materials and labor, he is usually deemed to have performed his full duty; and the men who build these structures and the men who use them are likely to be fellow-servants, and one can not recover from the master if he is injured by the negligence of another.[79]

Much the same sort of cases is presented where the danger is not so much in the place as in the very nature of the work being done, as in the case of excavating, erecting buildings, tearing down buildings, and the like,[80] and also in the

risks of making the place. See Consolidated Coal Co. v. Clay (1894) 51 Ohio 542, 38 N. E. 610; Mielke v. Chicago & N. W. Ry. Co. (1899) 103 Wis. 1, 79 N. W. 22.

[79] If the master undertakes to supply scaffolds, for example, the master's duty will attach to these; so where they are constructed under his direction, or he adopts for his own uses one erected for another purpose. See McBeath v. Rawle (1901) 192 Ill. 626, 61 N. E. 847; Blomquist v. Chicago, M. & St. P. Ry. Co. (1895) 60 Minn. 426, 62 N. W. 818; Cheatham v. Hogan (1908) 50 Wash. 465, 97 Pac. 499.

If he merely undertakes to supply materials, his duty will not ordinarily extend beyond supplying reasonably suitable ones. He would be liable for not doing that: Farrell v. Eastern Machinery Co. (1904) 77 Conn. 484, 59 Atl. 611; Donahue v. Buck (1908) 197 Mass. 550, 83 N. E. 1090.

But if the workmen are to build their own scaffolds, etc., as the work progresses and as part of it, those using them will usually be fellow-servants of those building them. See Beesley v. Wheeler (1894) 103 Mich. 196, 61 N. W.

658; Lambert v. Missisquoi Pulp Co. (1900) 72 Vt. 278, 47 Atl. 1085; Gombert v. McKay (1911) 201 N. Y. 27, 94 N. E. 186; Ross v. Walker (1891) 139 Pa. 42, 21 Atl. 157, 159; Buck v. New Jersey Zinc Co. (1902) 204 Pa. 132, 53 Atl. 740; Haakensen v. Burgess Sulphite Fibre Co. (1912) 76 N. H. 443, 83 Atl. 804; Leishman v. Union Iron Works (1905) 148 Cal. 274, 83 Pac. 30; Metzler v. McKenzie (1904) 34 Wash. 470, 76 Pac. 114; Swanson v. Sound Construction & Engineering Co. (1912) 67 Wash. 128, 120 Pac. 880.

[80] See Maloney v. Florence & C. C. Ry. Co. (1907) 39 Colo. 384, 89 Pac. 649; Citrone v. O'Rourke Engineering Const. Co. (1907) 188 N. Y. 339, 80 N. E. 1092; Russell v. Lehigh Valley Ry. Co. (1907) 188 N. Y. 344, 81 N. E. 122; Petaja v. Aurora Iron Mining Co. (1895) 106 Mich. 463, 64 N. W. 335, 66 N. W. 951; Miller v. Moran (1905) 39 Wash. 631, 81 Pac. 1089; Moore v. Pennsylvania Ry. Co. (1895) 167 Pa. 495, 31 Atl. 734; Oleson v. Maple Grove Coal & Mining Co. (1901) 115 Iowa 74, 87 N. W. 736.

.case of repairing or restoring safe conditions after accidents, wrecks, floods, fires, and the like.[81] It would be unreasonable to expect the same degree of safety in a place which the servant is then laboring to make safe, as in a place in which no disturbance has occurred.

§ 580. **Duty as to tools, machinery, appliances, and the like.** Sometimes the servant furnishes his own tools and equipment. When the master undertakes to supply them, and no other agreement is made respecting the matter, the law entitles the servant to expect, and deems the master to assure him, that the master will exercise reasonable care to supply, maintain, and keep in repair, tools, machinery, implements, appliances, and the like, which, so far as such care will secure it, shall be reasonably safe.[82] This rule does not demand the very latest or the most improved, or make the master a guarantor of safety.[83] If the master performs his duty in this

[81] See Arkansas Land Co. v. Cooper (1922) 156 Ark. 58, 245 S. W. 192; Dartmouth Spinning Co. v. Achard (1889) 84 Ga. 14, 10 S. E. 449; Kletschka v. Minneapolis & St. L. R. Co. (1900) 80 Minn. 238, 83 N. W. 133; Negle v. Syracuse, B. & N. Y. R. Co. (1906) 185 N. Y. 270, 77 N. E. 1064; Vaughn v. California Cent. Ry. Co. (1890) 83 Cal. 18, 23 Pac. 215.

[82] See Louisville & N. R. Co. v. Stutts (1894) 105 Ala. 368, 17 So. 29; Last Chance Mining Co. v. Ames (1896) 23 Colo. 167, 47 Pac. 382; Brazil Coal Co. v. Gibson (1902) 160 Ind. 319, 66 N. E. 882; Hannibal & St. J. R. Co. v. Kanaley (1888) 39 Kan. 1, 17 Pac. 324; Griffin v. Boston & A. R. Co. (1889) 148 Mass. 143, 19 N. E. 166; Johnson v. Spear (1889) 76 Mich. 139, 42 N. W. 1092; Service v. Shoneman (1900) 196 Pa. 63, 46 Atl. 292; Purdy v. Westinghouse Co. (1900)

197 Pa. 257, 47 Atl. 237; International & G. N. R. Co. v. Keenan (1890) 78 Tex. 294, 14 S. W. 668; Richmond & D. R. Co. v. Williams (1889) 86 Va. 165, 9 S. E. 990.

If the master was negligent, the fact that the negligence of a fellow-servant also contributed to cause the plaintiff's injury, does not release the master: Griffin v. Boston & A. R. Co., ante; Norfolk & W. R. Co. v. Nuckols (1895) 91 Va. 193, 21 S. E. 342; Harrison Engineering & Construction Corp. v. Rollison (1940) 109 F.2d 602.

[83] See Davis v. Augusta Factory (1893) 92 Ga. 712, 18 S. E. 974; Chicago & E. I. R. Co. v. Driscoll (1898) 176 Ill. 330, 52 N. E. 921; Burns v. Chicago, M. & St. P. R. Co. (1886) 69 Iowa 150, 30 N. W. 25; Wormell v. Maine Cent. R. Co. (1887) 79 Me. 397, 10 Atl. 49; Ross v. Pearson Cordage Co. (1895) 164 Mass. 257, 41 N. E. 284; Anderson

regard, and the servant is nevertheless injured, the master is not responsible. The servant assumes that risk. If the master does not perform his duty, and the servant is injured thereby, without contributory negligence on his own part, the master will be liable to him for damages.

§ 581. —— If there are concealed dangers, known to the master but not to the servant, and not obvious upon ordinary observation, a duty of warning arises, as in the case of the place to work.[84]

The duty to repair and maintain obviously includes inspection where that is necessary, and replacement or renewal where that is required.

As in the case of the place to work, this duty as to tools, etc., does not extend to those which the servant injured was not required, invited or expected to use. So if a reasonably safe tool, etc., is furnished, the fact that the servant so carelessly or unreasonably or unexpectedly uses it as to sustain injury, does not make the master liable.[85]

§ 582. **Duty as to employing other servants.** When the master invites a servant to serve in an employment in which other servants are also known to be employed, and no other agreement is made respecting the matter, the servant has the right to expect, and the master is deemed in law to assure him, that in employing and retaining such other servants to serve with him in the same employment, the master will exercise reasonable care to employ and retain only such as are reasonably competent and suitable, so far as that may affect the safety of the servant in question.[86] If the master does that,

v. Sherman (1942) 232 Iowa 705, 6 N.W.2d 703.

[84] Dowling v. Allen (1881) 74 Mo. 13; Fleming v. Northern Tissue Paper Mill (1908) 135 Wis. 157, 114 N. W. 841; Symons v. Great Northern Ry. Co. (1940) 208 Minn. 240, 293 N. W. 303; Harvey v.

Welch (1932) 86 N. H. 72, 163 Atl. 417.

[85] McDonald v. Fryberger (1951) 233 Minn. 156, 46 N.W.2d 260.

[86] See First Nat. Bank v. Chandler (1905) 144 Ala. 286, 39 So. 882; Still v. San Francisco & N. W. Ry. Co. (1908) 154 Cal. 559, 98 Pac.

and nevertheless the servant is injured by the negligence of such other servant, the master is not liable. The risk of such an injury by a fellow-servant is one of those which the servant assumes. If the master does not perform his duty in this regard and the servant is injured thereby without contributory negligence on his own part, the servant so injured may recover damages from the master.[87] The so called "fellow-servant" rule, hereafter considered, does not exempt the master from liability for his own negligence in employing or retaining such fellow-servants.

§ 583. —— So far as the number of the other servants is concerned, where the reasonable safety of one servant at his task depends upon there being an adequate number of other servants of the master at their respective places, the servant who undertakes that task, without any other agreement, is entitled to assume that the master will exercise reasonable care to supply a reasonably adequate number of others, so that his task may be performed with reasonable safety.[88]

Here, again, the master is not a guarantor of safety. His duty is to use reasonable care, and a failure in fact may exist without the master's fault, measured by that duty. He is then not liable.

§ 584. **Duty as to rules, regulations and superintendence.** Where the business to be carried on is a complex one, and dangerous unless regulated and superintended, as in the case of most railroads, mines, and the like, it is the duty of the master to exercise reasonable care to make and promulgate such time tables, schedules, rules, and regulations as are neces-

672; Western Stone Co. v. Whalen (1894) 151 Ill. 472, 38 N. E. 241; Conover v. Neher-Ross Co. (1905) 38 Wash. 172, 80 Pac. 281; Williams v. Kimmberly (1907) 131 Wis. 303, 111 N. W. 481.

[87] See cases ante.

[88] See Flike v. Boston & Albany R. Co. (1873) 53 N. Y. 549;

Cheeney v. Ocean S. S. Co. (1893) 92 Ga. 726, 19 S. E. 33; Supple v. Agnew (1901) 191 Ill. 439, 61 N. E. 392; Jones v. Old Dominion Cotton Mills (1886) 82 Va. 140; Johnson v. Ashland Water Co. (1888) 71 Wis. 553, 37 N. W. 823.

sary and suitable to enable the business to be carried on with reasonable safety, and then to exercise like care to see that such rules, regulations, etc., are enforced and obeyed.[89] If, from time to time, they are altered, there will be a fresh duty of promulgation. Even though the whole business may not require special regulation, some portions of it may, or even particular operations.[90] Skilled superintendence of the work as it progresses may also be necessary in order to make the work reasonably safe; and it is the master's function to supply this.[91]

§ 585. **These duties nondelegable—Vice-principal.** These duties of the master are often said to be nondelegable, meaning by this that if the master, instead of performing his duties in person, confides their performance to a superintendent, manager, or other agent (hence often called a vice-principal), and this agent, however carefully he may have been selected, does not perform the master's duties so confided to him, the

[89] See Sprague v. New York & N. E. R. Co. (1896) 68 Conn. 345, 36 Atl. 791; Fitzgerald v. Worcester & S. S. Ry. Co. (1908) 200 Mass. 105, 85 N. E. 911; Reagan v. St. Louis, K. & N. W. Ry. Co. (1887) 93 Mo. 348, 6 S. W. 371; Abel v. President, etc., Delaware & H. Canal Co. (1891) 128 N. Y. 662, 28 N. E. 663; Pool v. Southern Pac. R. Co. (1899) 20 Utah 210, 58 Pac. 326; Merrill v. Oregon Short Line R. Co. (1905) 29 Utah 264, 81 Pac. 85; Richlands Iron Co. v. Elkins (1897) 90 Va. 349, 17 S. E. 890; Little Miami R. Co. v. Stevens (1851) 20 Ohio 415; Southern Package Corp. v. Mitchell (1940) 109 F.2d 609.

[90] "In a business conducted by many employees performing work independently of each other and in which the work of one becomes periodically dangerous to another, it is the duty of the master to provide reasonable regulations against such danger, and amongst these is promulgating rules and regulations for the giving of warning, to the persons likely to be endangered, when such dangerous acts are about to be performed." Polaski v. Pittsburgh Coal Dock Co. (1908) 134 Wis. 259, 114 N. W. 437.

There is ordinarily no duty to warn of occasional dangers which the servant knows fully as well as the master: Ahern v. Amoskeag Mfg. Co. (1908) 75 N. H. 99, 71 Atl. 213.

[91] See McElligott v. Randolph (1891) 61 Conn. 157, 22 Atl. 1094; Philadelphia & P. R. Co. v. Trainor (1890) 137 Pa. 148, 20 Atl. 632; Engelking v. Spokane (1910) 59 Wash. 446, 110 Pac. 25.

master will be liable for an injury to his servant caused by such nonperformance.[92]

Such an agent, in his undertaking to perform these duties of the master, is not a fellow-servant with the servants for whose protection the duties were imposed, and hence his neglect to perform them is not negligence within the operation of the fellow-servant rule.

§ 586. —— The same doctrine is usually applied where the master, instead of performing in person, entrusts performance of his duties to an independent contractor. If the latter does not perform, the master, by the weight of authority, will be liable to a servant injured because of such nonperformance.[93] A few cases are *contra*.[94]

According to the prevailing view, the master would not perform his whole duty merely by confiding performance even to a reputable contractor: he must still exercise reasonable care to see that the latter has performed.

[92] See Wilson v. Williamantic Linen Co. (1883) 50 Conn. 433; Baier v. Selke (1904) 211 Ill. 512, 71 N. E. 1074; Brice-Nash v. Barton Salt Co. (1908) 79 Kan. 110, 98 Pac. 768; Shanny v. Mills (1876) 66 Me. 420; Brown v. Gilchrist (1890) 80 Mich. 56, 45 N. W. 82; Grant v. Nihill (1922) 64 Mont. 420, 210 Pac. 914; Bushby v. New York, L. E. & W. R. Co. (1887) 107 N. Y. 374, 14 N. E. 407; Clavin v. Tinkham Co. (1909) 29 R. I. 599, 73 Atl. 342; Sullivan v. Wood (1906) 43 Wash. 259, 86 Pac. 629; Massy v. Milwaukee Electric Railway & Light Co. (1910) 143 Wis. 220, 126 N. W. 544; Ryan v. Gray (1944) 316 Mass. 259, 55 N.E.2d 700; Myers v. Little Church by the Side of the Road (1951) 37 Wash.2d 897, 227 P.2d 165.

[93] See Pullman Car Co. v. Laack (1892) 143 Ill. 242, 32 N. E. 285; Bernheimer v. Bager (1908) 108 Md. 551, 70 Atl. 91; Sweat v. Boston & A. R. Co. (1892) 156 Mass. 284, 31 N. E. 296; Burnes v. Kansas City, Ft. S. & M. Ry. Co. (1895) 129 Mo. 41, 31 S. W. 347; Story v. Concord & M. R. R. Co. (1900) 70 N. H. 364, 48 Atl. 288; Ortlip v. Philadelphia & W. C. Traction Co. (1901) 198 Pa. 586, 48 Atl. 497; Moran v. Corliss Steam-Engine Co. (1899) 21 R. I. 386, 43 Atl. 874; Walton, Witten & Graham v. Miller (1909) 109 Va. 210, 63 S. E. 458; Vickers v. Kanawha & W. V. R. Co. (1908) 64 W. Va. 474, 63 S. E. 367.

[94] See Devlin v. Smith (1882) 89 N. Y. 470, 11 Abb. N. C. 322; Norfolk & W. Ry. Co. v. Stevens (1899) 97 Va. 631, 34 S. E. 525, distinguished in Walton, Witten & Graham v. Miller, ante.

§ 587. Negligence of a fellow-servant. Although the master is liable to a servant for an injury caused by the master's personal negligence, and although he is liable to a third person for an injury caused by the negligence of his servant within the course of his employment, it is the settled doctrine of English and American law (where not changed by statute as hereinafter pointed out), that a master, who has exercised due care in the selection and retention of his servants, is not liable to one of his servants for an injury caused by another of his servants in the same employment, although the latter servant was at the time acting within the course of that employment.[95] For such an injury, the servant injured must look for redress to the servant who injured him. This is the so-called "fellow-servant rule."

§ 588. Who are fellow-servants. By the rule generally prevailing, all of the servants employed by the same master, and engaged in furthering the same general enterprise, are to be deemed fellow-servants. If they are employed upon the same enterprise but by different masters,—as in the case of the servants of different contractors engaged in erecting the same building,—while all the servants of each contractor will be fellow-servants as to each other, the servants employed by one contractor will not be fellow-servants with the servants em-

---

[95] See Priestley v. Fowler (1837) 3 Mees. & Wels. 1; Murray v. South Carolina R. Co. (1841) 1 McMul. (S. C.) 385; Farwell v. Boston & W. R. Corp. (1842) 4 Metc. (Mass.) 49 (this is the leading American case); Tennessee R. Co. v. Bridges (1905) 144 Ala. 229, 39 So. 902; Peterson v. New York, N. H. & H. R. Co. (1904) 77 Conn. 351, 59 Atl. 502; Parrish v. Pensacola & A. R. Co. (1891) 28 Fla. 251, 9 So. 696; Larsen v. LeDoux (1905) 11 Idaho 49, 81 Pac. 600; Indianapolis Transit Co. v. Foreman (1904) 162 Ind. 85, 69 N. E. 669; Colling- wood v. Illinois & I. Fuel Co. (1904) 125 Iowa 537, 101 N. W. 283; Atchison Bridge Co. v. Miller (1905) 71 Kan. 13, 80 Pac. 18; Blake v. Maine Cent. R. Co. (1879) 70 Me. 60; Smith v. Potter (1881) 46 Mich. 258, 9 N. W. 273; McMaster v. Illinois Cent. Ry. Co. (1887) 65 Miss. 264, 4 So. 59; Hastings v. Montana Union Ry. Co. (1896) 18 Mont. 493, 46 Pac. 264; Enright v. Oliver (1903) 69 N. J. L. 357, 55 Atl. 277; Cowles v. Richmond & D. R. Co. (1881) 84 N. C. 309; Metzler v. McKenzie (1904) 34 Wash. 470, 76 Pac. 114; Novotny v.

ployed by another contractor.[96] If they are all employed by
the same master but are engaged upon entirely distinct enterprises, as where the common master is carrying on several
unconnected and distinct lines of business, those employed in
one of such distinct occupations will not be fellow-servants
with those employed in another.[97]

§ 589.　Superior servant rule.　It has sometimes been held
that where one servant, who might otherwise be regarded as
a fellow-servant, was given by the master a power of direction
or control over the other servants while engaged in the performance of the work—even though he did not rise to the rank
of what is usually called a vice-principal—he was, merely by
reason of such power of control, and as to all injuries resulting
from the manner in which he exercised it, not to be regarded
as a fellow-servant with those working with and under him.
Such a servant has been sometimes designated as a "superior
servant," not a fellow-servant.[98]

It has, however, come pretty generally to be recognized that
the giving of a certain class of directions or orders, i. e., those

Bonley (1947) 223 Minn. 592, 27
N.W.2d 813; Ryan v. Unsworth
(1931) 52 R. I. 86, 157 Atl. 869;
Bell v. Sawyer (1943) 313 Mass.
250, 47 N.E.2d 1; Brown v. Root
(1950) 92 F. Supp. 257.

The rule applies to infant servants: Houston & G. N. R. Co. v.
Miller (1879) 51 Tex. 270; Fisk v.
Central Pac. R. Co. (1887) 72 Cal.
38, 13 Pac. 144; Ohio & M. R. Co.
v. Hammersley (1867) 28 Ind. 371.

[96] Swainson v. Railway Co.
(1878) L. R. 3 Exc. Div. 341; Morgan v. Smith (1893) 159 Mass. 570,
35 N. E. 101; Kelly v. Tyra (1908)
103 Minn. 176, 114 N. W. 750, 115
N. W. 636; Coates v. Chapman
(1900) 195 Pa. 109, 45 Atl. 676.

If, however, the general servant
of one contractor has become for
the time being the special servant
of another (see § 453 et seq.), he
would, during that time for the
work involved, become a fellow-
servant with the other servants of
that contractor. See Murray v.
Dwight (1900) 161 N. Y. 301, 55
N. E. 901.

[97] See McTaggart v. Eastman
(1899) 27 Misc. 184, 57 N. Y. S.
222, 28 id. 127, 58 N. Y. Supp. 1118;
Bain v. Athens Foundry & Machine Works (1885) 75 Ga. 718.

[98] It is, for example, a master's
duty to furnish the place to work;
to supply tools, machinery and appliances; to employ and discharge
servants; to make the necessary
general rules, schedules, time-
tables, etc.; and to generally super-
intend and regulate the enter-

required as the work proceeds as a condition of its orderly conduct, and as a necessity of its various exigencies—as distinguished from that more general planning and direction which belongs to those who shape the policies but do not do the work—is just as much a part of the work as the merely physical or muscular effort, and that the person who gives them may be just as much a worker as those whose present movements he directs. It is a question, not merely of rank or authority, but of the nature of the thing done.[99] It is also

prise. One to whom these duties or any of them may be delegated would usually be a vice-principal. Thus, the general manager of a railroad, for example.

But what about the conductor of a freight train, who may signal the engineer when to start or stop; who may send a brakeman back with a flag or torpedo to guard against an approaching train; who may direct cars to be set out at sidings; who may direct a brakeman to make a coupling or apply brakes; and the like? Is he a manager or a worker? Or a section boss who goes out with a gang of men to work, under his direction, upon the roadbed or tracks?

The most potent influence in establishing (though not the originator of) the rule that such a person was either a vice-principal or at least a superior servant, was doubtless the case of Chicago, M. & St. P. Ry. Co. v. Ross (1884) 112 U. S. 377, 5 S. Ct. 184, 28 L. Ed. 787 (often referred to as "the Ross case") which held (four justices dissenting) that the conductor "represented" the company, which was therefore responsible for his negligence. This case was later overruled, in fact, in Balti-

more & O. R. Co. v. Baugh (1893) 149 U. S. 368, 13 S. Ct. 914, 37 L. Ed. 772, and formally in New England R. Co. v. Conroy (1899) 175 U. S. 323, 20 S. Ct. 85, 44 L. Ed. 181; but before it had been repudiated it was followed by a number of state courts, some of which later overruled their own decisions, but some of which refused to follow the supreme court in its later views.

See Bloyd v. St. Louis & S. F. Ry. Co. (1893) 58 Ark. 66, 22 S. W. 1089; Walker v. Gillet (1898) 59 Kan. 214, 52 Pac. 442; Williams v. W. R. Pickering Lumber Co. (1910) 125 La. 1087, 52 So. 167; Bell v. Rocheford (1907) 78 Neb. 304, 110 N. W. 646; Purcell v. Southern Ry. Co. (1896) 119 N. C. 728, 26 S. E. 161; Berea Stone Co. v. Kraft (1877) 31 Ohio St. 287; Louisville R. Co. v. Dillard (1904) 114 Tenn. 240, 86 S. W. 313; Sweeney v. Gulf C. & S. F. Ry. Co. (1892) 84 Tex. 433, 19 S. W. 555; Johnson v. Union Pacific Coal Co. (1904) 28 Utah 46, 76 Pac. 1089; Olson v. Erickson (1909) 53 Wash. 458, 102 Pac. 400.

[99] See Baltimore & O. R. Co. v. Baugh, ante; New England R. Co. v. Conroy, ante; Schroeder v. Flint

recognized that the same person may at one moment be even a vice-principal as to one aspect of the work, and at the next moment be merely a worker and hence a fellow-servant.

The cases which adopt a superior servant doctrine are difficult to reconcile; even those in the same state are often in great conflict. The weight of authority is opposed to that doctrine.

§ 590. **What risks included in fellow-servant rule.** The risks which are included in the fellow-servant rule, as has been stated, are those arising to the servant while in the service from fellow-servants within the same service. The servant injured must at the time have been in the service. If he had temporarily withdrawn, as by taking a day off, or if the service begins only when he gets to a certain place or premises and he had not yet arrived there, or if it ends when he has left a certain place or premises, and he had left that place,[1] an

---

& P. M. R. Co. (1894) 103 Mich. 213, 61 N. W. 663; Pasco v. Minneapolis Steel & Machinery Co. (1908) 105 Minn. 132, 117 N. W. 479; LeSneur v. Ayres (1950) 191 Va. 119, 60 S.E.2d 26.

[1] See Northwestern Union Packet Co. v. McCue (1873) 84 U. S. (17 Wall.) 508, 21 L. Ed. 705: Held, competent for jury to find that a man employed on shore to carry goods onto a boat, and who was paid off on the boat, ended his services on the boat, so as not to be in the service in going ashore the last time.

See also Baird v. Pettit (1872) 70 Pa. 477 (where the court said: "As soon as he left the building he was his own master. He was then no more in the defendant's service than any other citizen passing along the street, and he was entitled to the same rights and immunities"); Baltimore & O. R. Co. v. State (1870) 33 Md. 542 (going home from work); Cincinnati, N. O. & T. P. Ry. Co. v. Conley (1892) 14 Ky. L. Rep. 568, 20 S. W. 816 (not working on the day of the injury); Savannah, etc., R. Co. v. Flanagan (1889) 82 Ga. 579, 9 S. E. 471.

But otherwise if he were on the premises for purposes of the service though not at work at the moment, as where he was going to the place of starting work: Olsen v. Andrews (1897) 168 Mass. 261, 47 N. E. 90; Ewald v. Chicago & N. W. Ry. Co. (1888) 70 Wis. 420, 36 N. W. 12; Boldt v. New York Cent. R. Co. (1858) 18 N. Y. 432; or going to another place on the premises to eat his lunch: Boyle v. Columbian Co. (1902) 182 Mass. 93, 64 N. E. 726; or to change his clothes before leaving for the day:

injury from one who at other times might be his fellow-servant would not then ordinarily come within the rule.[2]

Whether, under the circumstances, the service had begun or ended, would, where different inferences might reasonably be drawn, be a question for the jury.[3]

§ 591. **Contributory negligence of servant.** Notwithstanding the negligence of the master or of those for whom he is responsible, the servant's right of recovery may be defeated by his own contributory negligence. In general, the same rules which apply to contributory negligence in other cases operate

Willmark v. Cardoza (1910) 176 Fed. 1; or waiting a call for work: St. Louis, A. & T. Ry. Co. v. Welch (1888) 72 Tex. 298, 10 S. W. 529.

[2] An employee who has gone to the place where he enters the service and rides from there to the spot where the work for the day is to be done, upon his employer's gravel-train, hand-car, elevator, etc., or who returns in the same way, is in the service while so riding, and the fellow-servant rule applies: Gillshannon v. Stony Brook R. Corp. (1852) 10 Cush. (Mass.) 228. See also, Tunney v. Railway Co. (1866) L. R. 1 C. P. 291; Goldrick v. Partridge (1910) App. Cas. 77; Vick v. New York Cent. & H. R. R. Co. (1884) 95 N. Y. 267. See also Indianapolis Transit Co. v. Foreman (1903) 162 Ind. 85, 69 N. E. 669; Shannon v. Union R. Co. (1906) 27 R. I. 475, 63 Atl. 488 (here he rode on an "employee's ticket"); Martin v. Atcheson, T. & S. F. R. Co. (1896) 166 U. S. 399, 17 S. Ct. 603, 41 L. Ed. 1051; Abend v. Terre Haute & I. R. Co. (1884) 111 Ill. 202. So held, also, where a laundress was being taken home in her employer's

wagon in pursuance of an arrangement to that effect: McGuirck v. Shattuck (1893) 160 Mass. 45, 35 N. E. 110.

So while riding down on the elevator at the noon hour to the basement where he was to eat his lunch: Boyle v. Columbian Co. (1902) 182 Mass. 93, 64 N. E. 726. But cf. Williams v. Union Switch & Signal Co. (1916) 37 S. Dak. 423, 158 N. W. 901.

But a streetcar employee who has finished his run for the day, left his car, and is riding home free on another car of the company in accordance with a regulation that employees may do so, is not in the service: Dickinson v. West End St. Ry. Co. (1901) 177 Mass. 365, 59 N. E. 60; nor is he, where he rides on a ticket given to him as part of his compensation: Enos v. Rhode Island Suburban Ry. Co. (1907) 28 R. I. 291, 67 Atl. 5; or where he is entitled to free transportation in addition to his wages: McNulty v. Pennsylvania R. Co. (1897) 182 Pa. 479, 38 Atl. 524.

[3] See Packet Co. v. McCue (1873) 84 U. S. (17 Wall.) 508, 21 L. Ed. 705.

here. The servant cannot recover if his own negligence directly contributed to cause the injury.[4] It is not, at common law, a matter of comparative negligence or of attempting to apportion damages according to the degrees of negligence. Statutes, however, sometimes provide for such an apportionment.

The law, nevertheless, attributes such influence to the directions of the master, and to the natural inference that he will not direct an act to be done unless it can be done with reasonable safety, that where the act, which is charged to the servant as contributory negligence, was one which he undertook by the express command of the master or his agent, his doing it will not be deemed to be negligent unless the danger was so inevitable or so obviously imminent that a man of ordinary prudence would not, under the circumstances, have undertaken it.[5]

So the fact that the servant was young or inexperienced may also be taken into account, since he may have had neither

[4] See Warden v. Louisville & N. R. Co. (1891) 94 Ala. 277, 10 So. 276; St. Louis Ry. Co. v. Dupree (1907) 84 Ark. 377, 105 S. W. 878; Novelty Theater Co. v. Whitcomb (1909) 47 Colo. 110, 106 Pac. 1012; New York, C. & St. L. R. Co. v. Hamlin (1907) 170 Ind. 20, 79 N. E. 1040; Vicksburg R. Co. v. Wilkins (1872) 47 Miss. 404; O'Hare v. Cocheco Mfg. Co. (1901) 71 N. H. 104, 51 Atl. 257; Johnston v. Syracuse Lighting Co. (1908) 193 N. Y. 592, 86 N. E. 539; Houston, E. & W. T. Ry. Co. v. DeWalt (1902) 96 Tex. 121, 70 S. W. 531; Darracutts v. Chesapeake & O. R. Co. (1887) 83 Va. 288, 2 S. E. 511; Stratton v. C. H. Nichols Lumber Co. (1905) 39 Wash. 323, 81 Pac. 831; Groat v. Clansen (1941) 139 Neb. 689, 298 N. W. 563.

See, as to disobedience of express rules prescribed by the master to insure safety, as constituting contributory negligence, Smith v. Centennial Eureka Mining Co. (1904) 27 Utah 307, 75 Pac. 749.

[5] See Southern Ry. Co. v. Shields (1898) 121 Ala. 460, 25 So. 811; Choctaw, O. & G. R. Co. v. Jones (1906) 77 Ark. 367, 92 S. W. 244; Fox v. Chicago, St. P. & K. C. R. Co. (1892) 86 Iowa 368, 53 N. W. 259; St. Louis & S. F. R. Co. v. Morris (1907) 76 Kan. 836, 93 Pac. 153; Noble v. John L. Roper Lumber Co. (1909) 151 N. C. 76, 65 S. E. 622; Schiglizzo v. Dunn (1905) 211 Pa. 253, 60 Atl. 724; Tuckett v. American Steam & Hand Laundry (1906) 30 Utah 273, 84 Pac. 500.

the judgment to realize the danger, nor the strength of will to resist an unwarranted command.[6]

§ 592. **Assumption of risk by servant.** A servant injured by the negligence of the master may sometimes lose his right to recover because he is held to have assumed the risk. The term "assumption of risk" is often used in two senses. The first is that already referred to, namely, the servant by the mere acceptance of the service is usually deemed to have assumed the ordinary, inherent risks which are attendant upon such an enterprise even when conducted with the standard degree of care. These are not attributable to the fault or negligence of the master, but are naturally inherent in the enterprise.

But if after the servant has entered upon the service he finds that, owing to defects in place or equipment, the retaining of incompetent servants, and the like, due to the negligent manner in which the master conducts the business, these ordinary and inherent risks are increased or aggravated, a different situation is presented. The servant may lawfully quit the service. Even if he had agreed to remain for a definite time, this unexpected breach by the master of the implied condition upon which the service was accepted would justify the servant in repudiating his agreement.[7] If, however, instead of quitting as he might, the servant stays on, in face of obvious dangers, without making any new arrangement, he is ordinarily held, by so remaining, to have assumed the risk of the enhanced danger, and if he is later injured by it, he may not recover.[8] *Volenti non fit injuria* has often been said to be a maxim applicable here.[9]

---

[6] See Foley v. California Horseshoe Co. (1896) 115 Cal. 184, 47 Pac. 42; Dougherty v. Dobson (1906) 214 Pa. 252, 63 Atl. 748.

[7] If he were, in fact, physically constrained, the result would be different: See Eldridge v. Atlas S. S. Co. (1892) 134 N. Y. 187, 32 N. E. 66, where there was evidence that if a seaman had refused to obey an order he would have been put in irons and fined.

[8] See Birmingham Railway & Electric Co. v. Allen (1892) 99 Ala. 359, 13 So. 8; Choctaw R. Co. v. Jones (1906) 77 Ark. 367, 92 S. W. 244; Limberg v. Glenwood Lumber Co. (1900) 127 Cal. 598, 60 Pac.

§ 593. **Where the master promises to repair defect.** If however, instead of merely staying on, without protest or any new arrangement,. the servant complains to the master or his authorized representative, and secures from him a promise that the defect will be remedied or the danger removed, and stays on in reliance upon such promise, where the danger is not so imminent that no reasonable man would run the risk, he does not assume the risk as long as the promise is operative.[10]

If, indeed, after a fair time for performance, it becomes apparent that the master does not intend to perform his promise to repair or remove the difficulty, and yet the servant still stays on without exacting a fresh assurance, he will, in accordance with this theory, be deemed to have henceforth assumed the risk.[11]

176; Ill. Cent. R. Co. v. Fitzpatrick (1907) 227 Ill. 478, 51 N. E. 529; Martin v. Chicago, R. I. & P. R. Co. (1902) 118 Iowa 148, 91 N. W. 1034; Lamson v. American Ax & Tool Co. (1900) 177 Mass. 144, 58 N. E. 585; Lynch v. Saginaw Valley Traction Co. (1908) 153 Mich. 174, 116 N. W. 983; Reberk v. Horne (1902) 85 Minn. 326, 88 N. W. 1003; Chicago, B. & Q. R. Co. v. Curtis (1897) 51 Neb. 442, 71 N. W. 42; Sanderson v. Panther Lumber Co. (1901) 50 W. Va. 42, 40 S. E. 368; Sjostedt v. Webster (1940) 306 Mass. 344, 28 N.E.2d 237; Lang v. United States Reduction Co. (1940) 110 F.2d 441.

Contra: Jewell v. Kansas City Bolt & Nut Co. (1910) 231 Mo. 176, 132 S. W. 703; Russ v. Harper (1911) 156 N. C. 444, 72 S. E. 570; Richmond & D. R. Co. v. Norment (1887) 84 Va. 167, 4 S. E. 211.

9 Cf. Lord Bramwell, in Memberry v. Railway Co. (1889) 14 App. Cas. 179, 187.

10 See Clarke v. Holmes (1862)

7 H. & N. 937; Eureka Co. v. Bass (1886) 81 Ala. 200, 8 So. 216; Cheeney v. Ocean S. S. Co. (1893) 92 Ga. 726, 19 S. E. 33; Morden Works v. Fries (1907) 228 Ill. 246, 81 N. E. 862; Southern Kansas Ry. Co. v. Crocker (1889) 41 Kan. 747, 21 Pac. 785; Breckenridge v. Hicks (1893) 94 Ky. 362, 15 Ky. L. Rep. 143, 22 S. W. 554; Dempsey v. Sawyer (1901) 95 Me. 295, 45 Atl. 1035; Rice v. Eureka Paper Co. (1903) 174 N. Y. 385, 66 N. E. 979; Brownfield v. Hughes (1889) 128 Pa. 194, 18 Atl. 340; Gulf, C. & S. F. Ry. Co. v. Donnelly (1888) 70 Tex. 371, 8 S. W. 52; Yerkes v. Northern Pac. Ry. Co. (1901) 112 Wis. 184, 88 N. W. 33; Price v. McNeill (1946) 237 Iowa 1120, 24 N.W.2d 464.

11 See Eureka Co. v. Bass, ante; Union Mfg. Co. v. Morrissey, ante; Illinois Steel Co. v. Mann (1897) 170 Ill. 200, 48 N. E. 417; Albrecht v. Chicago & N. W. Ry. Co. (1901) 103 Wis. 530, 84 N. W. 882; Crutchfield v. Richmond & D. R. Co.

§ 594. **Knowledge of defect and of risk necessary.** In order to bring a case within the operation of this rule, the servant must actually have known of the situation or it must have been so open and obvious that an ordinary prudent person exercising reasonable care for his own safety could not be ignorant of it. And not only must the *defect* be known or obvious, but so also must be the *risk.*[12]

Where, therefore, the servant was young or inexperienced or ignorant, the inference of assumption of risk is reluctantly drawn and it becomes usually a question for the jury whether, under all the circumstances, there was an intelligent appreciation of the risk and a voluntary assumption of it.[13]

§ 595. **Effect of economic pressure—Of master's command.** The fact that the servant stays on because of fear of losing his job is ordinarily held not to affect the case.[14] Neither, ordinarily, does the fact that he is expressly commanded by the master to do the act; he did not have to stay or he did not have to obey the command.[15] But however sound that may be

(1877) 78 N. C. 300; Boucher v. Namasket Co. (1940) 91 N. H. 215, 17 A.2d 98; Stahl v. Dow (1947) 332 Ill. App. 233, 74 N.E.2d 907.

[12] See Texas & P. Ry. Co. v. Swearingen (1904) 196 U. S. 51, 25 S. Ct. 164, 49 L. Ed. 382; Choctaw, O. & G. R. Co. v. McDade (1903) 191 U. S. 64, 24 S. Ct. 24, 48 L. Ed. 96; St. Louis, I. M. & S. Ry. Co. v. Birch (1909) 89 Ark. 424, 117 S. W. 243; Rase v. Minneapolis St. P. & S. S. M. Ry. Co. (1909) 107 Minn. 260, 120 N. W. 360; McDuffee v Boston & M. R. (1908) 81 Vt. 52, 69 Atl. 124.

[13] See Bare v. Crane Creek Coal & Coke Co. (1906) 61 W. Va. 28, 55 S. E. 907; Lane v. Manchester Mills (1908) 75 N. H. 102, 71 Atl. 629; Dallemand v. Saalfeldt (1898) 175 Ill. 310, 51 N. E. 645; DiBari

v. Bishop (1908) 199 Mass. 254, 85 N. E. 89.

Held, not to apply where the danger complained of is the possibility of injury by the unexpected negligence of a fellow servant: Vogt v. Honstain (1900) 81 Minn. 174, 83 N. W. 533.

[14] See Wescott v. New York & N. E. R. Co. (1891) 153 Mass. 460, 27 N. E. 10; Lamson v. American Ax & Tool Co. (1900) 177 Mass. 144, 58 N. E. 585; Burke v. Davis (1906) 191 Mass. 20, 76 N. E. 1039.

[15] See Briggs v. Tennessee Coal, Iron & R. Co. (1909) 163 Ala. 237, 50 So. 1025; Showalter v. Fairbanks (1894) 88 Wis. 376, 60 N. W. 257; Hencke v. Ellis (1901) 110 Wis. 532, 86 N. W. 171; Maltbie v. Belden (1901) 167 N. Y. 307, 60 N. E. 645; Bier v. Hosford (1904)

where there has been time for observation and consideration, it is recognized that when the whole question of defect or risk arises suddenly, perhaps in an emergency, and there is a command or occasion to act under such circumstances that there may not be time or opportunity to consider, or the servant's attention may be so absorbed in the act that he cannot consider the circumstances, it becomes a question of fact whether there was an assumption of the risk, which must be left to the jury to decide rather than to be disposed of as an inference of law.[16]

§ 596. **Dissents from general doctrine.** A few courts in this country do not accept this doctrine of assumption of risks by remaining in the employment,[17] and the English courts have attached more importance to the actual voluntariness of the case than most of the American courts have done.[18]

§ 597. **Assumption of risks existing in violation of statutes.** The question of the assumption of risks where the defect or risk was one resulting from the nonperformance of some statutory duty designed to promote safety, instead of the nonperformance of what may be termed the common-law duties of the master, has given rise to several distinctions. The statute may expressly provide that there shall be no assumption. If it does not, some courts hold that the imposition of the statutory duty creates a public policy which forbids assumption.[19] Other courts hold that there is no distinction in this respect between statutory and nonstatutory duties.[20]

35 Wash. 544, 77 Pac. 867; Hanson v. Hammell (1899) 107 Iowa 171, 77 N. W. 839.

[16] See Perrier v. Dunn Worsted Mills (1909) 29 R. I. 396, 71 Atl. 796.

[17] See Richmond & D. R. Co. v. Norment (1887) 84 Va. 167, 4 S. E. 211.

An express contract in advance to assume risks of master's negli-

gence not enforceable: Johnston v. Fargo (1906) 184 N. Y. 379, 77 N. E. 388.

[18] See, for example, the changed forms of expression in such cases as Smith v. Baker (1891) App. Cas. 325; Williams v. Birmingham Battery Co. (1899) 2 Q. B. 338. Cf. 15 L. Q. Rev. 336.

[19] See Narramore v. Cleveland, C., & St. L. Ry. Co. (1899) 96 Fed.

2.　*Statutory Modification of Common-law Rules*

§ 598.　Employers' liability acts. Whatever may be thought of the logic of the common-law rules applicable to injuries suffered by workers in the course of employment, there is no doubt that in practice they gave the worker, or his family, little help. Aside from the trinity of common-law defenses, applicable in the great majority of cases, the worker who had a case free of such defenses found that the cost of litigation as well as the long delays incident thereto, both because of the persistence with which employers fought claims and of the crowded courts, made a profitable outcome most unlikely.

In the latter part of the last century, agitation for reform, both in England and this country, finally began to produce legislation designed to relieve the situation. The first statutes in this country were of the type known as Employers' Liability Acts, and their chief effect was to abolish some or all of the common-law defenses. Thus, many abolished the defense of fellow-servant and provided that contributory negligence should not bar the employee's recovery, but only limit his recovery in proportion to his negligence. The statutes usually applied only to specified industries, most commonly to railroads, mines, or both.[21]

§ 599.　F. E. L. A. Of statutes of this type, the only one of substantial importance today is the Federal Employers' Liability Act.[22] This provides that "every common carrier by

298; Johnson v. Mammoth Vein Coal Co. (1908) 88 Ark. 243, 114 S. W. 722, 123 S. W. 1180; Streeter v. Western Wheeled Scraper Co. (1912) 254 Ill. 244, 98 N. E. 541.

[20] See St. Louis Cordage Co. v. Miller (1903) 126 Fed. 495; Denver & R. G. R. Co. v. Norgate (1905) 141 Fed. 247 (cert. den. 202 U. S. 616, 26 S. Ct. 764, 50 L. Ed. 1172); Birmingham Railway & Electric Co. v. Allen (1892) 99 Ala. 359, 13 So. 8; Denver & R. G. R. Co. v.

Gannon (1907) 40 Colo. 195, 90 Pac. 853.

[21] The classic study of the common-law system and of the need for, and the ultimate passage of, modern legislation, in Dodd, Administration of Workmen's Compensation, 1936, especially pp. 3–16.

[22] U. S. C. Tit. 45, §§ 51–60.

ra lroad while engaging in commerce between any of the several states or territories shall be liable in damages to any person [23] suffering injury while he is employed by such carriei in such commerce . . . resulting in whole or in part from the negligence of any of the officers, agents or employees of such carrier. . . ." It is apparent from the language quoted that the defense of fellow-servant is automatically abolished. By section 53, "the fact that the employee may have been guilty of contributory negligence shall not bar a recovery, but the damages shall be diminished by the jury in proportion to the amount of negligence attributable to such employee." The original act was construed as not abolishing assumption of risk but this was changed by amendment in 1939.[24]

A tremendous body of litigation has arisen under the F. E. L. A. and very large recoveries have been sustained. That it has ameliorated the position of the railway employee is not to be doubted. On the other hand it is clear that it has by no means achieved its presumed purpose. It is not to be expected that the injured employee will find quick and inexpensive relief so long as he carries the burden of establishing such troublesome issues as that the injury occurred in interstate commerce and that the defendant was negligent. The very volume of the litigation that has arisen tells the story. Proposals have been made that the act be superseded by a genuine federal compensation act,[25] and it seems likely that these proposals will sooner or later bear fruit.

3. Workmen's Compensation

§ 600. History. The first workmen's compensation law was enacted in England in 1897 and agitation for similar legislation in this country resulted in the passage of compensation acts in various states in the first decades of the new century. There was bitter opposition to them and in some instances

[23] An omitted portion of § 51 provides for compensation to the representatives of the employer in case of his death.

[24] See Tiller v. Atlantic Coast Line (1943) 318 U. S. 54, 63 S. Ct. 444, 87 L. Ed. 610, 143 A. L. R. 967.

[25] See Justice Frankfurter's opinion in Wilkerson v. McCarthy

early acts were held unconstitutional.[26] But their constitutionality was ultimately established beyond doubt and such legislation, now taken as a matter of course, is believed to be in effect in every state.

§ 601. Policy. The policy of workmen's compensation is wholly different from that of common-law liability. The right to compensation is not based on the employer's fault nor barred by the employee's fault; it is paid on the assumption that a certain amount of injury to flesh and blood is an inevitable incident of business and should be paid for by business like any other cost of operation. Payments are made by a fixed scale, usually based on the employee's wage; administration is in the first instance in the hands of some administrative body established for the purpose, so that litigation is normally unnecessary and the compensation, though modest in amount, can be had promptly, and usually without dispute. Provision for judicial review is everywhere provided, and litigation is by no means uncommon, but the number of cases going to court is trifling compared to those settled by voluntary payment by the company or on informal proceedings before a referee or commissioner. Different forms of securing payment are provided by different statutes; most commonly an employer operating under the act is required to take out compensation insurance.

§ 602. Effect on common-law remedies. Where the parties are operating under the act, the remedy is exclusive and no common-law suit may be brought against the employer, even though grounds exist and more could be recovered than the compensation payable under the act.[27] Some statutes are

(1949) 336 U. S. 53, 69 S. Ct. 413, 93 L. Ed. 497; editorial, 35 A. B. A. J. 318.

[26] The best-known instance is Ives v. South Buffalo Ry. Co. (1911) 201 N. Y. 271, 94 N. E. 431.

[27] Where the workman is injured by the negligence of a third party, he may still sue him. In such a case the common provision of the statutes is that the employer is entitled to so much of the recovery as will compensate him for compensation already paid the employee for the same injury. For analysis of the statutes and cases, see Note, 40 Col. L. Rev. 1452.

optional and the employer (or, sometimes, employee) may elect not to operate thereunder; in such a case, the employee is left to his common-law remedy.[28] More commonly, the case may not be within the act because the employment or the type of injury is one not covered. Thus, at least in the past, occupational diseases were commonly not compensable; statutes in most jurisdictions still do not apply to domestic or agricultural workers. Hence the large proportion of common-law cases today dealing with domestic or farm accidents.

§ 603. **What injuries are compensable.** The statutes have usually been phrased or construed to apply only to "accidental injuries" arising "out of and in the course of the employment." The bulk of the litigation involving the substantive law of the statutes has dealt with these phrases. The subject is too extensive and detailed to permit of treatment here; only a few very broad generalizations may be made.

§ 604. **Accidental.** The question whether an injury is "accidental" or "an accident" arises most often in connection with illness. Thus, one who is hospitalized for a common cold or dies of typhoid fever is not, in common parlance, the subject of an accident.[29] On the other hand, where some sudden and identifiable act brings on or aggravates some illness, as where the exertion of lifting a heavy package causes a rupture or a heart attack, it may be classified as an accident.[30] By this

[28] Although the statutes often penalize an employer who elects not to operate under the act, by depriving him of some or all of his common-law defenses.

[29] Cf. MacRae v. Unemployment Compensation Commission of North Carolina (1940) 217 N. C. 769, 9 S.E.2d 595, noted in 20 B. U. L. Rev. 770, with Smith's Case (1940) 307 Mass. 516, 30 N.E.2d 536. And see Groom v. Cardillo (App. D. C. 1941) 119 F.2d 697; Dyviniek v. Buffalo Courier Express Co. (1947)

296 N. Y. 361, 73 N.E.2d 552; Harman v. Republic Aviation Corp. (1948) 298 N. Y. 285, 82 N.E.2d 785; Perron's Case (1949) 325 Mass. 6, 88 N.E.2d 637.

[30] Cf. Crispin v. Leedom & Worrall Co. (1940) 142 Pa. Super. 1, 15 A.2d 549, with McCormick Lumber Co. v. Department of Labor (1941) 7 Wash.2d 40, 108 P.2d 807. And see American Maize Products Co. v. Nichiporchik (1940) 108 Ind. App. 502, 29 N.E.2d 801; Gmeiner & Grearson v. Industrial

interpretation, as suggested above, occupational diseases are normally noncompensable. This defect has been remedied in many states by legislation specially providing for compensation for occupational diseases. Unfortunately, the legislation has often been insufficiently thought out and may result in an arbitrary and inadequate list of diseases included.

§ 605. **Out of and in the course of.** This language, perhaps difficult to improve on, has raised a troublesome problem. "In the course of" would cover everything happening to the worker while at work; it is not to be supposed that the legislature meant to insure the worker against all possible calamities that might befall him while at work, and the other phrase "out of" plainly suggests some kind of causal limitation. But just *what* limitation? It has been suggested that the idea was to compensate for injuries peculiar to the trade as distinguished from those all the world is subject to. This overlooks the fact that dangers characteristic of some occupations are by no means limited to that occupation. No doubt, having one's toes stepped on or being knocked down by a car is a conspicuous hazard of the messenger boy's trade—but so is it of the daily life of everyone who uses the streets.

§ 606. —— In practice, courts have been very liberal, falling not very far short of covering all the hazards of the worker's life. Analysis and classification are very difficult. Perhaps it may be suggested, very broadly, that compensable injuries fall usually into one of three categories:

§ 607. **Plant risks.** In a leading English case [31] S was in M's shed packing kippered herrings when the wall of adjoining premises fell on the shed, crushing it and injuring S. The injury

Commission (1945) 248 Wis. 1, 20 N.W.2d 543; Hagopian v. City of Highland Park (1946) 313 Mich. 608, 22 N.W.2d 115; McNees v. Cincinnati St. Ry. Co. (1949) 152 Ohio St. 269, 89 N.E.2d 138; Kelly-Springfield Tire Co. v. Daniels (1952) — Md. —, 85 A.2d 795;

Neylon v. Ford Motor Co. (1952) 8 N. J. 586, 86 A.2d 577.

[31] Thom v. Sinclair [1917] A. C. 127. See also Brooker's Case [1933] A. C. 669; Caswell's Case (1940) 305 Mass. 500, 26 N.E.2d 328, noted in 20 B. U. L. Rev. 586 and 26 Iowa L. Rev. 433; E. I. Du Pont de

was held compensable. S had to work in the shed. If it collapsed for any reason, S would be injured. This was one of the risks of the occupation. Likewise where S had a sudden attack of dizziness and fell, striking his head on an iron motor box that was part of the M's equipment.[32] Where S's work is carried on in the open so that a part of the outdoors is incorporated into M's premises, the cases differ somewhat as to the legal consequences of S's unhappy contacts with the elements. Rather surprisingly, an Illinois case [33] held that when a golf caddy at work was struck by lightning the injury was not compensable. Other authorities have been more willing, where, e. g., extreme heat or cold are part of the working conditions, to hold that an injury resulting from them is compensable.[34]

§ 608. **Personnel risks.** If one of the risks to which S's employment subjects him is that of coming into painful contact with the hard, physical aspects of his environment, plainly another is that of injury resulting from the behaviour of those persons with whom his work naturally brings him into contact. If he is injured by the negligent performance of the job by a fellow workman, it is not to be doubted that he is entitled to compensation; to give the injured party recompense in such case was one of the primary and avowed purposes of Workmen's Compensation. Even if the injury does not strictly arise in the course of employment, it may be a natural hazard of the business. Thus there are many cases awarding compensation where a workman is injured as the result of disputes with fellow workmen naturally arising while at work;[35] the same is true even

Nemours Co. v. Lilly (1948) 226 Ind. 267, 79 N.E.2d 387; Chouinard's Case (1949) 325 Mass. 152, 89 N.E.2d 347; O'Leary v. Brown-Pacific-Maxon, Inc., (1951) 340 U. S. 504, 71 S. Ct. 470, 95 L. Ed. 483.

[32] Varoa's Case (1944) 316 Mass. 363, 55 N.E.2d 451.

[33] Illinois Country Club, Inc. v. Industrial Commission (1944) 387 Ill. 484, 56 N.E.2d 786.

[34] See Thompson v. Masonic Cemetery Ass'n (1926) 103 Ind. App. 74, 5 N.E.2d 145, noted in 13 Ind. L. J. 164; Ciocca v. National Sugar Refining Co. (1939) 124 N. J. L. 329, 12 A.2d 130, noted in 25 Corn. L. Q. 645; Consumers' Co. v. Industrial Commission (1926) 324 Ill. 152, 154 N. E. 423; Gates v. Central City Opera House Ass'n (1940) 107 Colo. 93, 108 P.2d 880.

[35] See Industrial Commission v.

where the injury results from habitual horseplay or pranking on the part of fellow employees.[36] Likewise an injury done by a third party may be compensable if a natural incident of the job. So night watchmen have often been compensated when injured by intruders and employees obliged to carry funds in dangerous localities may be compensable if attacked by a hold-up man.[37] It has been held, however, that a night watchman may not claim compensation when shot by his wife's sweetheart.[38]

§ 609. **Street risks.** Frequently S's job involves getting from place to place, in cars, trams, trains or even on foot. In such cases the ordinary hazards of such forms of transportation become hazards of the job. So when an executive assistant walking to a business engagement, stumbled and fell, the resulting injury was held compensable.[39] So where a filling station operator was obliged to cross the street on an errand, personal in nature but naturally incident to his job, and was killed by a passing car, it was held that his employment was the cause of his accident.[40] But where an employee is on his way to work, an injury is normally held not to arise from the employment;[41] aliter, if the employer furnishes the transportation.[42]

Strome (1940) 107 Colo. 54, 108 P.2d 865; Penker Const. Co. v. Cardillo (App. D. C. 1941) 118 F.2d 14; Container Corp. of America v. Industrial Commission (1948) 401 Ill. 129, 81 N.E.2d 571; Dillon's Case (1949) 324 Mass. 102, 85 N.E.2d 69.

[36] See Cassell v. United States Fidelity & Guaranty Co. (1926) 115 Tex. 371, 283 S. W. 127, 46 A. L. R. 1137; West Penn Sand & Gravel Co. v. Norton (1938) 95 F.2d 498; Industrial Commissioner v. McCarthy (1946) 295 N. Y. 443, 68 N.E.2d 434.

[37] See Appleford v. Kimmel (1941) 297 Mich. 8, 296 N. W. 861; Cole v. I. Lewis Cigar Co. (1949) 3 N. J. 9, 68 A.2d 737.

[38] See January-Wood Co. v. Schumacher (1929) 231 Ky. 705, 22 S.W.2d 117, noted in 14 Minn. L. Rev. 827.

[39] Oram v. Byron G. Moon Co. (1941) 285 N. Y. 42, 32 N.E.2d 785.

[40] Whitham v. Gellis (1940) 91 N. H. 226, 16 A.2d 703. See also Moak v. Industrial Commission (1947) 398 Ill. 361, 75 N.E.2d 859; Kennedy v. Thompson Lumber Co. (1947) 223 Minn. 227, 26 N.W.2d 459; Lauer v. Citizens Lumber & Supply Co. (1952) — Pa. —, 85 A.2d 609.

[41] Popovitch v. Atlantic Products Corp. (1941) 125 N. J. L. 533, 17 A.2d 492. Cf. Simpson v. Lee &

§ 610. **Conclusion.** These categories obviously do not purport to include all possible cases. They may, however, perhaps serve as a rudimentary map to the territory covered by the multitudinous and conflicting decisions.[43]

Cady (1940) 294 Mich. 460, 293 N. W. 718.

[42] Denver & R. G. W. R. Co. v. Industrial Commission (1928) 72 Utah 199, 269 Pac. 512, 62 A. L. R. 1436; Taylor v. M. A. Gammino Const. Co. (1941) 127 Conn. 528, 18 A.2d 400.

[43] The classic discussion of this subject is Brown, Arising out of and in the Course of the Employment, 7 Wis. L. Rev. 15, 8 Wis. L. Rev. 134, 217.

INDEX

References are to sections. Where a topic is treated in several consecutive sections, only the number of the first will be given.

A

ACCOUNT—
  duty of agent to, 535.

ACQUIESCENCE—
  authority by, 54.
  ratification by, 218.

ACTUAL AUTHORITY—
  see REAL AUTHORITY.

ADMISSIONS—
  of agent will not establish agency, 95.
  authority to make, 95.

ADVERSE INTEREST—
  agent may not assume, 500.

AGENCY—
  as part of the law of Business Organizations, 3.
  different uses of the word, 1.
  formalities essential to creation of, 23.
  necessity of contract to establish relation, 23.
  principal and agent, master and servant, and employer and independent
    contractor contrasted, 12.
  treated as not including
    labor law, 8.
    unemployment compensation, 9.

AGENCY POWER—
  in general, 105.
  rationale, 111.
  automobile dealers, 119.
  distinguished from apparent authority, 107.
  bill of lading cases, 105.
  created by indicia of title, 115.

431

I

441

TERMINATION OF AGENT'S POWER TO BIND PRINCIPAL—Cont.

notice of
    in general, 282.
    where revocation by act of parties
        special agents, 283.
        general agents, 284.
        where principal undisclosed, 285.
    where revocation by operation of law
        in general, 286.
        death, 287.
        insanity, 290.
        bankruptcy, 290.
        war, 290.
        destruction of subject matter, 291.

TITLE, INDICIA OF—
    see AGENCY POWER.

TORTS—
    see AGENT'S LIABILITY TO THIRD PARTIES; DUTIES AND LIABILITIES OF THE AGENT TO THE PRINCIPAL; DUTIES AND LIABILITIES OF THE PRINCIPAL TO THE AGENT; MASTER'S LIABILITY FOR THE TORTS OF HIS SERVANTS.

U

UNDISCLOSED PRINCIPAL—

rationale, 145.
liability of, 151.
merger, as affecting liability, 154, 162.
election, as affecting liability of, 155.
liability of, as based on agent's right of exoneration, 161.
joinder of, with agent, 163.
rights in general, 150.
exceptions to right to enforce contracts, 164.
personal contracts, 166.
misrepresentations as to existence of principal, 167.
specific performance against, 171.
apparent authority of agent of, 174.
setoff against, 177.
liability of, as affected by payment to agent, 184.
ratification by, 204.

UNEMPLOYMENT COMPENSATION—

not treated as part of agency, 9.

UNIFORM CONDITIONAL SALES ACT, 123, 125.

UNIFORM SALES ACT, 123.

UNIFORM TRUST RECEIPTS ACT, 123, 126.

W

WIFE—
    as husband's agent, 47.

WORKMEN'S COMPENSATION—
    why treated as part of agency, 10.
    history, 600.
    constitutionality, 600.
    policy, 601.
    effect on common-law remedies, 602.
    what injuries compensable, 603.
    accidents, 604.
    occupational diseases, 602.
    out of and in the course of, 605.
    plant risks, 607.
    personnel risks, 608.
    street risks, 609.

WRITTEN INSTRUMENTS CREATING AUTHORITY—
    construction of, 41.
    parol evidence to explain, 42.